Concepts of
Chemical Dependency

HAROLD E. DOWEIKO

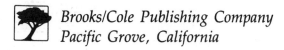
Brooks/Cole Publishing Company
Pacific Grove, California

Brooks/Cole Publishing Company
A Division of Wadsworth, Inc.

© 1990 by Wadsworth, Inc., Belmont, California 94002. All rights reserved. No part of this book may be reproduced, by any means—electronic, mechanical, photocopying, recording, or otherwise—without the prior written permission of the publisher, Brooks/Cole Publishing Company, Pacific Grove, California 93950, a division of Wadsworth, Inc.

Printed in the United States of America

10   9   8   7   6   5   4   3   2

Library of Congress Cataloging-in-Publication Data

Doweiko, Harold, [date]
  Concepts of chemical dependency / by Harold Doweiko.
    p.   cm.
  Includes bibliographical references.
  ISBN 0-534-12834-3
  1. Substance abuse.   I. Title.
RC564.D68   1990
362.29—dc20
                                                        89-38181
                                                        CIP

Sponsoring Editor: *Claire Verduin*
Senior Editorial Assistant: *Gay C. Bond*
Production Editor: *Ben Greensfelder*
Manuscript Editor: *Robert E. Baker*
Permissions Editor: *Carline Haga*
Interior Design: *Vernon T. Boes*
Cover Design and Illustration: *E. Kelly Shoemaker*
Art Coordinator: *Cloyce J. Wall*
Typesetting: *Kachina Typesetting, Inc.*
Cover Printing: *Southeastern Color Graphics*
Printing and Binding: *The Maple-Vail Book Manufacturing Group*

To Jan, for everything

Preface

This book has emerged over the course of many years. I first became involved in drug rehabilitation while an undergraduate in the early 1970s, doing volunteer work at a telephone crisis-counseling center. Many of the calls that I received concerned drug abuse. Some of the telephone calls were from concerned parents who wanted information about specific pills that they had found, the effects of certain drugs, or how they might recognize if their son or daughter was addicted.

To answer these questions, I started to gather information about the various drugs of abuse and compiled an information file. Over the years, as drug abuse trends changed, new drugs were added to the file. I continued with the project during graduate school, where I again worked as a volunteer for a call-in crisis center.

Later, while preparing my doctoral dissertation, I worked as a clinical psychologist in a maximum security penitentiary for men. This was a rather depressing and violent experience. Many inmates turned to drugs for relief, and violence was a way of life. While working in the prison, I was struck by the amount of *mis*information that the prison staff and the inmates possessed. Staff members were often unprepared for the realities of dealing with addicted persons.

Following graduation, I elected not to continue my association with the penitentiary and went to work for a state hospital chemical dependency unit. Work on the drug information file languished for a while, although I continued to gather journal articles about the effects of various drugs of abuse. This material formed the basis for a series of introductory undergraduate classes on drug addiction and the pharmacology of the various chemicals of abuse.

In the years since then, I have worked as a staff psychologist at a private hospital chemical dependency unit, and in private practice as a clinical psychologist. In this time, I have come to understand something of the elusive nature of chemical dependency and the many disguises behind which drug addiction will hide, and I have continued to work on my drug information file, which has now grown into a series of lecture notes for college classes.

I have been impressed by the fact that, while drug use is epidemic in this country, accurate information about the effects of the drugs of abuse is limited. Physicians, in my experience, are rarely trained to work with addicts. On occasion, physicians have argued that a particular patient "was once addicted to drugs, but isn't an addict anymore" because she or he had not used chemicals in several years. Unfortunately, the physicians have not understood that the addict might be *recovering* but has never fully *recovered*.

Attorneys, teachers, supervisors, co-workers, spouses, and many parents have approached me over the years, asking for information about various chemicals of abuse, their effects, and the treatment of addiction. As a teacher, I have attempted to share my knowledge and experience; however, I have been frustrated by the fact that many people who are involved with an addicted person in one way or another lack a basic understanding of chemical dependency or its treatment. Often, when I mention in class a Twelve Step program, or the need for a comprehensive treatment plan, I am greeted by a sea of blank faces.

Some of the students in my various college classes have been alcoholics or narcotics addicts who were taking the first steps toward recovery. While these students were well versed about alcoholism or narcotic use they often knew virtually nothing about chemicals other than their drug of choice. Other students were nursing students who were taking classes on drug addiction as electives. These nursing students knew the *medical* applications of various drugs but knew next to nothing of the abuse potential of various medications currently in use. Some even expressed shock to learn that addicts would share needles, and one individual went so far as to deny that such a thing could ever happen!

Many of the students who had a basic understanding of the drugs of abuse knew little about the theory behind drug rehabilitation. These students were able, often on the basis of personal experience, to discuss what *their* specific treatment program was like. But when asked to devise an individual treatment plan for another person, these students were surprised to learn that such a document even existed! These students had no understanding of common treatment terms such as *outpatient day treatment* or *family intervention session*.

In searching for a suitable text to work with while teaching, I was surprised to find that there did not appear to be a single textbook available that might be used for the introductory level class. There were some very good textbooks to be sure, but each covered only a portion of what I thought was needed for the introductory text. I failed to find a book that I felt was suitable for the newcomer to the field of drug dependency.

In discussions with other professionals who were training drug rehabilitation professionals, it became clear that others in the field also felt a need for a basic introductory text to the field of chemical addiction. Such a text would serve as a reference guide for professionals who might on occasion need a working knowledge of the basics of chemical dependency rehabilitation but have no desire to become full-time addictions counselors. At the same time, such a text would serve as an introductory text for chemical-dependency professionals who were just starting to explore the field of addiction.

The earliest stages of this book were guided by the questions most often asked by my students and by the drug information file that I had started in the late 1960s. If, as was often the case, a number of students were to ask for more information about one topic, I would write a note to myself to keep in mind the need for a chapter that addressed those questions. If I received a number of telephone calls about a specific topic, I would again write a note to myself about the need for information on that topic. Over the years, the outline for this text began to emerge.

Unfortunately, I have been trained to think in terms of *chemical dependency,* a term common to the upper Midwest, especially Minnesota. I have found, however, that professionals in other parts of the country speak of *drug addiction.* By habit, I have used the term chemical dependency throughout much of this book, although from time to time I have also used the terms *chemical addiction* or *drug dependency.* These terms are used interchangeably throughout this text, and I would hope that this does not cause too much confusion to the reader.

ACKNOWLEDGMENTS

It would not be possible to mention each and every person who has helped to make this book a reality. However, I would like to thank Jim Plantikow for everything that he has shared with me. His knowledge and insights are reflected in this book. I have found him a valuable resource in my struggle to work with, and understand, the person addicted to chemicals.

Most certainly, I would like to acknowledge my debt to C. Kent Olson, M.D., for his encouragement and support during the early stages of this book. Ken's gentle strength, his wisdom, and his warmth are all reflected in these pages. I certainly will miss working with him!

I would also like to thank Ruth Anderson, Ruth Sherwood, and Shar Roeder for their support. Ruth Anderson was most helpful in finding obscure references for this text. Ruth Sherwood shared many of the lessons that she learned during the course of a long career working with addicted persons. Shar's friendship, energy, and dedication to the field of nursing are the equal of any professional that I have known. Her desire to learn more about drug addiction so that she might be of better service to her patients is most commendable.

Finally, I would like to thank my editor-in-chief, best friend, and wife, Jan. She has read each chapter many times over. She has corrected my spelling (again, many times over) and encouraged me when I was up against the brick wall of writer's block. Her feedback was received with the same openness with which any author receives "constructive criticism." But in spite of that fact she persisted, and more often than not she was right. She is indeed my editor-in-chief. Thanks, Jan!

Several reviewers provided valuable input on the content and structure of this book, and I thank them all. They are Marvin D. Feit, of Norfolk State University, Virginia; Father James E. Royce, of Seattle University,

Washington; Milton Trapold, of Memphis State University; Elaine F. Tyrie, of Eastern Washington University; and Lewis Zachary, of Minneapolis Community College.

DISCLAIMER

This text was written in an attempt to share the knowledge and experience of the author with others interested in the field of chemical dependency. While every effort has been made to ensure that the information reviewed in this text is accurate, the reader is cautioned that this text is *not* designed to function as a guide for patient care. It is necessary to consult many sources of information in order to completely understand the impact that drug abuse or dependency might have on the individual, the family, and society—and to plan for patient care.

This text provides a great deal of information about the current drugs of abuse, their dosage levels, and their effects. This information is provided to inform the reader of current trends in the field of drug addiction. This text is not intended as a guide to self-medication, and the author assumes no responsibility for individuals who attempt to use this text as a guide for the administration of drugs to themselves or others, or as a guide to treatment.

I hope that you find this text helpful and useful in your work or studies. A pre-addressed, postage-paid mailer is provided at the back of the book. Your comments, and suggestions for future editions, are most welcome.

Harold E. Doweiko

Contents

CHAPTER 14

Addiction as a Disease of the Spirit   163

CHAPTER 15

Hidden Victims of Chemical Dependency   179

CHAPTER 16

Codependency and Enabling   197

CHAPTER 1

The Scope of the Problem of Chemical Dependency

There once was a time, before the introduction of antibiotic drugs, when syphilis was called "the Great Imposter." Shortly after the spirochete *treponema pallidum* gained admission, the bacteria would invade any of the various body systems. Depending on the particular part of the body most heavily involved with the infectious process, the current stage of the infection, the age, the sex, and the race of the individual, the symptoms of syphilis varied.

Diagnosis of syphilis was difficult and often required an element of detective work on the part of the physician. During the initial stages, syphilis would frequently leave little or no outward sign of infection. In many cases syphilis mimicked the symptoms of other diseases, making diagnosis difficult. When left undetected and untreated, between 5% and 10% of those persons infected went on to develop an organic brain syndrome known as *general paresis* (Coleman, Butcher, and Carson, 1984; Penna and Addis, 1980).

Although modern antibiotics have brought syphilis under control, there is a lesson that syphilis might still teach us. This is the lesson that one must look beneath the surface to understand the actual cause of the observed symptoms. In many cases, syphilis was able to masquerade as another, possibly unrelated, condition. Unless the physician were to rule out syphilis, valuable time might be spent treating the patient for the wrong condition.

Chemical dependency, in all of its forms, is very much like syphilis in this sense. Depending on the specific drug involved; the duration of the addiction; the addict's overall health; and the addict's financial, social, and personality resources, chemical dependency might also express itself in different ways. The amphetamine addict who is independently wealthy will not demonstrate the same pattern of addiction as would the unemployed amphetamine addict. But each person is equally addicted to chemicals.

When confronted with a new case, many professionals are unlikely to probe beneath the surface problem of depression, suicidal tendencies, spouse abuse, or the sudden onset of hallucinations, to inquire whether the person is using chemicals. Professionals who have worked in the field of chemical dependency for any length of time may relate similar stories of how addicts successfully kept their addiction hidden for months, if not years, while in therapy for other "problems."

The addictions hide behind a wall of various problems that are, in reality, complications caused by the addiction itself. In this sense, the addictive disorders are "imposters," and all too many mental health professionals have adopted a head-in-the-sand philosophy that overlooks various signs that addiction might exist in troubled families, that addiction is involved in cases of depression, or that addiction is involved in a range of other human problems.

In recent years, however, there has been a growing awareness that many of the problems encountered by human service and health care professionals are either caused by, or at least complicated by, drug addiction in one form or another. In the past generation, as the drug abuse crisis has grown, a new appreciation of the many faces of addiction has been gained by professionals in a variety of fields. There is still much to be discovered about chemical dependency, but at last many professionals are starting to accept the possibility that drug addiction is perhaps the greatest problem faced by society today.

THE UNITY OF ADDICTIVE DISORDERS

Unfortunately, over the years there has continued to be a dichotomy in the minds of many between alcoholism and drug addiction. Happily, this is changing. Miller (1980) notes that where professionals would once speak of "alcoholism" or "drug addiction," there is a growing trend for professionals to speak of "the addictive behaviors" (p. 3), a term that includes alcoholism, drug addiction, obesity, smoking, and compulsive gambling.[1]

Miller observed that one common element of the addictive disorders is that they all "involve some form of indulgence for short-term pleasure or satisfaction at the expense of longer-term adverse effects" (p. 4). Robertson (1988), in addressing this point, noted that *all* compulsive behaviors, including drug addiction, have a neurochemical foundation. Thus, Robertson views compulsive use of *any* chemical as being a reflection of the same core addictive process.

Mental health professionals have long been aware of the fact that the "pure alcoholic or pure drug addict is rapidly becoming extinct" (Washton, 1988, p. 76). Increasingly, one sees not alcoholism *or* drug addiction but poly-drug use in the same person. The implication is that if addicts find it so easy to switch addictions, perhaps these are not different diseases but different manifestations of a single condition: addiction.

Franklin (1987) also concluded that addiction is a disease that might express itself through the compulsive use of any of a number of different chemicals. Indeed, it was Franklin's contention that, among the various

---

[1] The problems of obesity and compulsive gambling lie outside of the scope of this text; however, the reader should be aware of the fact that these are also forms of addictive behavior.

drugs of abuse, there is almost a social stratification process at work. Alcoholism is barely tolerated, but it is more socially acceptable to be hospitalized for an alcohol problem than for a narcotic dependency problem. Although the underlying process of addiction might be the same, the seriousness of a diagnosis of "addiction" is judged on the basis of how socially acceptable the use of that particular drug might be.

Franklin further observed that different social groups tended to gravitate toward different chemicals: ". . . to many inner-city blacks . . . heroin was their history, their balm . . . and their master" (p. 58), while white heroin addicts were a minority. In contrast to this, barbiturates were widely used as sleeping pills by middle-class America, until replaced by the ". . . opiate of the suburbs" (p. 57): Valium.

These were not isolated problems but different manifestations of the hidden addiction found in America. Indeed, Franklin found that when

> alcoholism statistics were combined with those on illegal drugs, and these figures were added to those on addiction to prescription drugs like Valium, it appeared that perhaps one in every five Americans was hopelessly addicted to something—and another one or two were steady users. (p. 59)

Gazzaniga (1988) postulated that perhaps 10% of the population "falls into addictive patterns with drugs" (p. 143). Phelps and Nourse (1986) advanced an even higher figure, stating that approximately 40% of the population suffered from a biological predisposition toward addiction. The authors included sugar addiction as part of the spectrum of addictive disorders. It is interesting to note, however, that Phelps and Nourse's (1986) estimate that 40% of the population had a biological predisposition toward addiction is quite similar to Franklin's (1987) observation that one in five Americans (20%) is addicted to chemicals, while another one in five (another 20%) was a steady user.

Weil (1986) advanced the theory that "The use of drugs to alter consciousness is nothing new" (p. 17). He went on to support his argument on the grounds that people traditionally have attempted to find ways to alter the normal state of consciousness by such means as the use of naturally occuring hallucinogenics, oxygen deprivation, and the use of alcohol.

Alcohol is, pharmacologically, as much a drug as any other chemical substance. However, as Weil pointed out, alcohol has been used by so many people for such a long period of time that they have stopped thinking of it as a drug. Even if a person is willing to admit that alcohol is a drug, ". . . at least it is not one of those bad drugs that the hippies use" (p. 18).

The outcome of this misperception is that:

> We are spending much time, money, and intellectual energy trying to find out why people are taking drugs, but, in fact, what we are doing is trying to find out why some people are taking some drugs that we disapprove of. (Weil, 1986, p. 18)

Thus, as more and more is discovered about addiction, it is becoming increasingly apparent that there are fewer and fewer differences between the habitual use of drugs and socially approved chemicals such as tobacco and alcohol. Evidence is rapidly accumulating that suggests a common foundation to *all* addictions, though the final expression of this addiction might be molded by many different forces (Donovan, 1988).

Dole (1988) postulated that ultimately all disorders of behavior, including addictions, might be reduced to biochemical interactions that are only now starting to be understood by science. Furthermore, Dole advanced the theory that one form of compulsive drug use, that of narcotic addiction, reflected a dysfunction of a specific subsystem in the brain. The implication is that other forms of addiction also reflect dysfunction of certain biochemical systems within the brain that are yet to be discovered.

Khantzian (1986) explored the psychodynamic foundation for addiction and discovered that all addictions seemed to come about as a result of similar evolutionary forces. He hypothesized that addicts turn to drugs in order to regulate their "internal life" (p. 214), which is to say their emotional state. In an earlier paper, Khantzian (1985) suggested that the specific drug that an individual came to obsessively use was selected "on the basis of personality organization and ego impairments" (p. 1260). Forrest (1985) agreed with this hypothesis, stating that, "The addict learns to use mood-altering substances in order to feel in control of himself or herself" (p. 316).

Thus, a psychodynamic viewpoint holds that the addict turns to the chemical in order to control internal feeling states. The only significant difference between the various addictions is *which drug will offer the greatest subjective relief to the individual?*

Further evidence of the unitary nature of addictive disorders might be found in the observation that addicts, as a general rule, use the same psychological defense mechanisms. Addicts, no matter what the exact nature of their specific addiction, all struggle to defend, as well as to control, their individual addiction. They engage in many of the same behaviors while addicted, and often use many of the same drugs.

The alcoholic, for example, might use amphetamines to help fight off the sedating effects of alcohol, so that she or he might drink more. At the same time, the amphetamine or cocaine addict might use alcohol to fight the overstimulation often found from amphetamine or cocaine abuse.

Another reflection of the similarities between addictions is the observation that there are very few major differences between the self-help programs of Alcoholics Anonymous (AA), Narcotics Anonymous (NA), and Cocaine Anonymous (CA). With few exceptions, all three programs use the same language and the same concepts to help addicts come to terms with their addiction.

The very fact that it was possible to adapt the AA philosophy for NA and CA demonstrates the common nature of addiction. Unfortunately, much of the research conducted into addiction to date has addressed only the isolated addiction to alcohol. Washton (1988) did observe that the cocaine epidemic of the 1980s has been a catalyst for research into this area; however, the results of these research efforts are still years in the future.

This is because, until quite recently, the common basis for addictive behaviors has not been recognized. Thus, the central issue is not one of alcoholism versus heroin addiction versus cocaine addiction. Rather, the problem is one of drug dependency, which may express itself through many different specific addictive behaviors, *depending on the individual.*

CHEMICAL DEPENDENCY: UNDERRECOGNIZED, UNDERREPORTED

It is a little recognized fact that chemical dependency is perhaps *the* most common "disease" encountered by modern medicine. It is also only rarely diagnosed. For example, the orthopedic surgeon might work with a patient whose leg was shattered in an automobile accident, while the general surgeon might remove a portion of the stomach of a patient with a history of perforated ulcers, both of which were directly caused by the patients' alcoholism. The patient's anesthesia, in each example, is supervised by an anesthesiologist.

All three physicians will possibly carry out a technically correct treatment of the patients' presenting problems, without ever addressing the patients' central problem, that of addiction. Indeed, Colquitt, Fielding, and Cronan (1987) reviewed the medical and legal consequences of some 252 motor vehicle accidents admitted to a major New England hospital and found that in slightly less than half of the cases *no* attempt was made to determine the patient's blood-alcohol level. Of the remainder, 84 individuals were legally intoxicated at the time of their accidents. Only three of these individuals were ultimately arraigned for driving under the influence of alcohol, and there were no convictions.

This study is important for two reasons. First, the study by Colquitt, et al. (1987), demonstrates that physicians are hesitant to look for alcoholism, even in cases where there is strong evidence that alcoholism exists (an alcohol-related automobile accident). Secondly, Colquitt, et al. found that even when charges of drunk driving were filed, it was still difficult to get a conviction for this charge in court.

Depending on the community, between a quarter and a half of those patients seen in the emergency room are there either directly or indirectly because of alcoholism (Schuckit, 1984). These cases are often treated as isolated medical problems by the emergency room physician, and the patient might accumulate a rather extensive medical history over the years without the patient's addictive disorder being addressed. Zimberg (1978a) postulated that, when alcoholism is one of a number of problems found in a patient already in psychiatric treatment, the alcoholism is rarely diagnosed, and drinking behavior will be ignored by the professional.

Beasley (1987) provides an example of a male alcoholic who, before his first hospitalization for the treatment for alcoholism, had accomplished a record of multiple medical hospitalizations for such alcohol-related problems as pneumonia, accidents, and bleeding ulcers, all without his alcoholism being addressed.

Indeed, it is the contention of Beasley that, either directly or indirectly, alcoholism is perhaps *the* condition most frequently encountered by a physician in practice today. It was observed that the medical treatment of alcoholism and drug addiction, combined with the various psychiatric consequences of these disorders, accounts for some 40% of hospital usage in this country (Beasley, 1987).

In spite of these statistics, however, Peyser (1989) was able to conclude that

> . . . we do not adequately teach about alcohol and drug abuse in our schools of medicine, social work, and psychology. Where it is taught, it is minimized as a second-class disorder. . . . The mental health profession in general ignores this major underrecognized and untreated mental health problem. (p. 221)

Peyser's assertion is one supported by Galanter (1986), who concluded that "Relatively few therapists are experienced in offering proper care to addicted persons" (p. 769). Johnson (1980) reported that most physicians have no formal training in the treatment of alcoholism. Zimberg (1978a), in his discussion of the outpatient treatment of alcoholism, observed that most of the 25,000-plus psychiatrists in the United States were uninterested in treating alcoholism and went on to claim that most psychiatrists actually believed that alcoholism could not be treated by psychiatry.

Along these same lines, Brown (1985) noted that no psychologist is required to take a class whose only subject matter is the recognition and treatment of alcoholism, which is perhaps the most common form of chemical addiction. Admittedly, some class work might touch on the subject of addiction in passing. For example, the text *Abnormal Psychology and Modern Life* (Coleman, et al., 1984) devotes several pages out of a total of 700 pages to the subject of chemical addiction.

OUT OF THE SHADOWS INTO THE MAINSTREAM: RESEARCH INTO THE CAUSES OF ADDICTION

Franklin (1987) noted that there was, during the pre-Viet Nam era, almost a class stratification in terms of the drugs of abuse. Heroin was found mainly in the ghetto, far from middle-class America, while many middle-class drug addicts used alcohol, barbiturates, and Valium. Little money was appropriated for research into the causes or treatment of addiction, at least until the sons and daughters of middle-class America began to use "hard" drugs.

In the time since the American involvement in Viet Nam, the social stratification of drugs has broken down. Since the mid 1960s, increasing numbers of Americans have been using and becoming addicted to chemicals. Since that time, chemical dependency and its treatment have become a growth industry; however, much of the research into drug addiction has centered on that most common of chemical agents: alcohol. Indeed, it was not until recently that the common nature of addictive disorders was recognized (Miller, 1980).

Prior to this, alcohol addiction was thought to be different from benzodiazepine addiction, and both were thought to be different from narcotic addiction. Much of the available literature centered only on the most common (and least objectionable to middle-class America) form of addiction: alcoholism.

The limited money that was available thus tended to drift in the direction of alcoholism research. It was not until the post-Viet Nam era saw larger and larger numbers of middle-class addicts to heroin, benzodiazepines, cocaine, amphetamines, marijuana, and alcohol that attention shifted away from research into alcoholism as a unitary disorder to alcoholism as one of the addictive disorders. However, even today, the greater proportion of the available literature still addresses alcoholism, rather than the other forms of drug addiction.

To further complicate matters, much of the limited research on addiction has centered only on *male* addicts (Peluso and Peluso, 1988). Griffin, Weiss, Mirin, and Lang (1989) in exploring differences between male and female cocaine abusers, concluded that "The drug abuse literature has paid relatively little attention to women" (p. 122). According to Griffin, Weiss, Mirin, and Lang, much of the research conducted has failed to differentiate between male and female drug abusers. Also, much of what is known about the drugs of abuse is based on research involving adults. As Mikkelsen (1985) observed, there is a "relative paucity of investigations" (p. 6) concerning addiction in the young. Newcomb and Bentler (1989) concluded that there is virtually no information on chemical use in the first decade of life, and that research into adolescent chemical use "is almost as rare" (p. 243).

Gazzaniga (1988) observed that much of the research conducted into the subject of addiction is based on a distorted sample. He suggested that many patients who abuse chemicals will, at some point in their lives, simply stop the use of those chemicals without professional help. Gazzaniga based this conclusion on the fact that, of the 1,400 American soldiers who tested positive for drugs upon their return from Viet Nam in 1971, only one-third, or 495 men, still were using chemicals eight months later. The rest apparently stopped the use of chemicals without professional intervention. The patients who end up in drug rehabilitation programs thus

> . . . are not a random sampling of the population with an addiction. They are a subculture that cannot easily give up their addictions. Yet it is the patients from these centers who make up most of the studies about addiction and about how hard it is to kick the drug habit. (p. 143)

There is thus a great deal to be discovered about drug abuse and addiction. Of the available literature on the subject of drug addiction, only a small portion addresses forms of addiction other than alcoholism. An even smaller proportion addresses the impact of chemicals on women. Virtually no research has been done on the subject of drug abuse/addiction in children or adolescents (Mikkelsen, 1985).

The reader should keep these facts in mind as he or she reads this text. There is still much to learn, and any doctoral student in search of a thesis theme should explore the wilderness of drug addiction in search of a possible dissertation topic. The contribution to the understanding of addiction would be welcome indeed.

THE SCOPE OF CHEMICAL DEPENDENCY

The American Psychiatric Association (1985) estimated that approximately *10 million adults* and another *3 million children and adolescents* are addicted to alcohol. Beasley (1987) presented a higher figure, reporting that between 10 to 15 million Americans are currently alcoholic, with an additional 10 million being "on the cusp of alcoholism" (p. 21). L. Siegel (1989) reported that approximately 100 *million* Americans use alcohol, and estimated that 10 to 12 million Americans were addicted to the drug. According to the American Psychiatric Association (1985), another 30 to 40 million people were indirectly affected by alcoholism through family ties to either the alcoholic or a victim of the alcoholic.

In addition to alcoholism, however, the American Psychiatric Association (1985) estimated that there were 500,000 known heroin addicts, and *at least* 7 million people who were using prescription drugs, usually psychoactive agents, without medical supervision. L. Siegel (1989) agreed that about 500,000 Americans are addicted to heroin. Peluso and Peluso (1988) estimated that, of the 500,000 known heroin addicts, perhaps as many as 100,000 were women. Furthermore, it was estimated that another 1 *million* women experimented with heroin but were not addicted to the drug (Peluso and Peluso, 1988).

It has been estimated that there are anywhere from between 4 and 5 million regular cocaine users (Miller, 1985), to upwards of 24 *million* regular users of cocaine (Peluso and Peluso, 1988). Siegel (1989) reported that there were between 500,000 to 750,000 *daily* users of cocaine in this country. O'Malley, Johnston, and Bachman (1985) reported that 1 high school senior in 6 had admitted to using cocaine at least once. Peluso and Peluso (1988) reported that perhaps 2 million Americans are dependent on cocaine.

Sbriglio and Millman (1987) reported that the number of people in the United States who had tried cocaine at least once increased from 5.4 million in 1974 to 22.2 million in 1985, while the number of current users of cocaine had increased from 1.6 million in 1977 to 5.8 million in 1985. Chasnoff (1988) estimated that 20 million people have tried cocaine at least once, while 5 million Americans use it on a regular basis. Obviously, a significant proportion of Americans have at least experimented with cocaine, and a smaller (but still significant) percentage of Americans use it on a regular basis.

L. Siegel (1989) estimated that 20 million Americans use marijuana on a regular basis, while three times that number of people smoke cigarettes on a regular basis. It was further noted that tobacco use results in 320,000 deaths each year, while to date there has been no death attributed to marijuana use alone.

It was reported (American Psychiatric Association, 1985) that alcohol was implicated in 28,000 motor vehicle deaths each year. Beasley (1987) estimated that, when one combines the alcohol-related traffic accidents with the alcohol-related household accidents, and those deaths from such alcohol-related complications as cirrhosis of the liver and heart disease, approximately 98,000 Americans die each year as a result of alcoholism.

L. Siegel (1989) gave an even higher figure, estimating that 100,000 Americans die each year from alcohol-related diseases. Nace (1987) reported that in 1983, alcoholism *alone* cost the United States in excess of $116 *billion* dollars in direct medical costs, and indirect losses such as lost work productivity.

There is a known relationship between chemical dependency in one form or another and various forms of psychopathology. Fossum and Mason (1986) reported that some adolescent-chemical-dependency-treatment centers have found that *three-quarters* of their female clients reported having been sexually abused. Black (1981) noted that over 50% of incest victims come from homes where alcohol abuse is also present.

Approximately one-quarter of the successful suicides in any given year are alcoholics (Hyman, 1984). Sixty percent of suicide attempts might either directly or indirectly be traced to alcoholism (Beasley, 1987). There is no way to determine the role of drug abuse/addiction in suicide, but certain classes of drugs, specifically the amphetamines and cocaine, can cause suicidal depression following prolonged use.

Walker, Bonner, and Kaufman (1988) observed that both alcohol and drug addiction are "frequently associated with physical abuse" (p. 45). Alcohol alone is estimated to be involved in approximately 50% of the cases of spouse abuse, and 38% of the cases of child abuse (Beasley, 1987).

Black (1981) reported that her clinical experience suggested that some 66% of the children raised in alcoholic families were either themselves abused or witnessed the abuse of another family member. Chasnoff (1988) arrived at a similar figure, noting that alcohol and/or drug abuse was involved in 64% of all child abuse cases in New York City.

Gold (1988) reported that chemical abuse might result in various forms of sexual dysfunction, including changes in the individual's ability to achieve a stage of sexual excitement, orgasm, and resolution following sexuality activity. Furthermore, drug abuse could result in various forms of performance dysfunction, as well as interfere with the individual's ability to enjoy sexual relations. The use of alcohol, benzodiazepines, or similar agents could result in impotence in the male, and decreased vaginal secretions in the female.

Beasley (1987) noted that alcohol-induced brain damage is second only to Alzheimer's disease as a known cause of mental deterioration in adults. Schuckit (1984) reported that one-third of the beds in American nursing homes are occupied by individuals whose alcohol-induced brain damage has become permanent. Finally, it has been reported that 65 of every 100 persons in the United States will be involved in an alcohol-related auto accident at some point in their lives (Beasley, 1987).

There is no estimate possible as to the economic or social impact that these various forms of chemical addiction have on society. When one considers the possible economic impact of medical costs incurred, lost productivity, or other indirect costs from such "hidden" addiction, one can begin to appreciate the impact that chemical addiction has on society.

DEFINITIONS: "DRUG OF CHOICE," "SOCIAL CHEMICAL USE," "CHEMICAL ABUSE," AND "ADDICTION"

Chemical dependency has a terminology that is often confusing to the newcomer to the field. Occasionally, addicts themselves will use the ambiguity of this terminology as a defense. For example, there was the woman who hotly denied being alcoholic, although the opinion of numerous human service professionals, and the judge, was somewhat different. This woman defined herself as simply a "problem drinker."

When asked to define the difference, between a problem drinker and the alcoholic, she was unable to do so. In this case one finds an example of a rationalization, which was in the form of this woman's belief that she was not alcoholic, only a problem drinker. In this way, this woman demonstrated the addict's tendency to try and avoid the admission of his or her addiction.

The concept of the *drug of choice* is often difficult to explain, especially in this era of poly-addiction. The person's drug of choice is just that: of all the possible drugs that a person might use, of all the drugs that this person may have used over the years, *what specific drugs would **this** person use if they had the choice?*

Many cocaine addicts will drink alcohol or use minor tranquilizers to supplement their cocaine or amphetamine use. They do this in order to take the edge off of the "coke jitters," which is to say that the side effects of the cocaine or amphetamines are so uncomfortable that addicts must use a tranquilizing drug. But, they do so only to supplement their cocaine use.

The individual's primary drug of choice in this case is the cocaine family of drugs, which he or she will seek out whenever having a chance to do so. Such an individual will also use other chemicals from time to time, but this is only in addition to, or in place of, their primary drug of choice: cocaine.

Finally, there is the concept of *addiction*. In order to more clearly define addiction, it will be necessary to first of all focus on a single drug, in order to avoid possible confusion about different drugs. In this case, we will use alcohol as the prototype drug of addiction.

Greenblatt and Shader (1975) noted that there were three elements necessary to the diagnosis of alcoholism. These were the elements of: (1) a deterioration in the person's work performance, family relationships, and social behavior, which they termed *a pathological psychosocial behavior pattern*, (2) *a classic drug addiction process*, which included withdrawal symptoms following abstinence from alcohol (these were withdrawal symptoms severe enough for the person to try and avoid them by continued use of alcohol), and (3) a *medical disease*, which is to say one of many complications of alcoholism, such as cirrhosis of the liver, certain nutritional disorders, and certain forms of neurological damage.

Greenblatt and Shader go on to point out that alcoholism is easy to recognize when all three elements outlined above are present; however, the authors also point out that many skid row alcoholics who have been hospitalized many times for alcohol withdrawal symptoms such as the *DTs* may never develop diseases associated with chronic alcoholism (conditions 1 and 2, but not 3) . The authors also present the example of the heavy-drinking business executive whose drinking pattern never interferes with family or occupational performance, but who goes on to develop withdrawal symptoms when hospitalized for elective surgery (condition 2, but not 1 or 3).

Greenblatt and Shader also pointed out that many binge drinkers may never become addicted to alcohol and may never develop any of the physical complications of alcoholism. However, many of these individuals will ultimately suffer broken families and loss of jobs as a result of their drinking, in spite of the fact that they are only binge drinkers (conditions 1 and 3, but not 2) . Thus, as Greenblatt and Shader (1975) point out, even the diagnosis of alcoholism is not always clear-cut.

The key element to Jellinek (1960) was that of a *loss of control* over one's drinking, a concept that continues to be central to definitions of chemical addiction. The best definition of addiction is that the person's chemical use has reached the point where the body has adapted itself to the continued presence of the drug in the body to the point where the drug is now necessary to carry out normal biological activity.

The concept of loss of control means that *the person is no longer able to consistently predict in advance how much they will use.* In many cases, the person will require the drug in order to live on a day-to-day basis and will experience *withdrawal symptoms* if they do not continue to use the drug. But, the key element is the loss of control over the ability to predict in advance how much of a drug the individual will use.

ADDICTION AS A PROCESS

One of the most difficult myths for the clinician to work with is the myth that chemical addiction is an either/or condition. Which is to say that many people, both professionals and nonprofessionals alike, think that chemical dependency is either present, or it is not. Unfortunately, there are few clear-cut lines between the "social" use of a chemical, the abuse of that same chemical, and chemical addiction, even in the case of alcohol.

Addiction is a process that evolves over a period of time, the length of which varies from individual to individual. As such, the individual might be thought of as not being addicted, *in the process of becoming addicted to chemicals,* or actually addicted to a drug or drugs. Chemical use might thus be thought of as falling on a continuum ranging from no use of chemicals whatsoever to clear-cut addiction, with various points in between. This continuum is illustrated in Figure 1-1.

As with any continuum, movement back and forth from one stage to another is possible. For example, the rare social drinker might go through a period of frequent abusive drinking following the break up of an engagement, after which she or he might return to the occasional social use of alcohol.

The advantage of this continuum is that it allows for the classification of chemical use of various intensities and patterns. The clinician is thus able to think not in terms of whether this person is or is not addicted to chemicals, but rather in terms of where on the continuum of drug use this particular individual might fall. The different stages of chemical use on this continuum are:

Level 0: Total abstinence: The individual abstains from any and all recreational chemical use.

Level 1: Rare social use: The individual will rarely use chemicals for recreational purposes, but is able to use without social, financial, interpersonal, or legal problems.

Level 2: Heavy social use/problem drug use: At this point, the individual might be seen as an *abusive* drinker, or as a person whose chemical use is clearly above the norm for his or her social group. At this point in the continuum one begins to see the onset of various combinations of legal, social, financial, occupational, and personal problems associated with chemical use. These might be hidden or denied by the individual, and in some cases it might not be clear that the person has passed through this stage until after they have entered the stage of early addiction.

Level 3: Early addiction: At this point on the continuum, the person has become addicted to chemicals, although they may argue that they are not "really" addicted to drugs or alcohol. For some of the drugs of abuse,

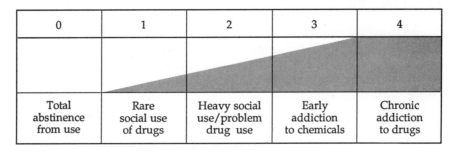

0	1	2	3	4
Total abstinence from use	Rare social use of drugs	Heavy social use/problem drug use	Early addiction to chemicals	Chronic addiction to drugs

FIGURE 1-1 Chemical dependency continuum.

one begins to see medical complications associated with addiction. Also, at this phase, the individual will demonstrate classic withdrawal symptoms when they are unable to continue the use of drugs or alcohol.

One will also find various combinations of ongoing legal, financial, social, occupational, and personal problems associated with the chemical use starting to clearly emerge during this phase.

Level 4: Late addiction: At this point on the continuum, the individual demonstrates the classic addiction syndrome, in combination with multiple social, legal, financial, occupational, and personal problems found in chemical addiction. The person also will demonstrate various medical complications associated with chemical abuse and may be near death as a result of chronic addiction. However, a surprising number of chronic addicts are in relatively good health. Thus, the person's state of health is but one of many indicators that suggest the possibility that this person is in the stage of late addiction.

Admittedly, this classification system, like all others, is imperfect. The criteria used to determine what level an individual might fall are arbitrary and subject to discussion. As Vaillant (1983) observed, it is often "the variety of alcohol-related problems, not any unique criterion, that captures what clinicians really mean when they label a person alcoholic" (Vaillant, 1983, p. 42). Which is to say that it is *a constellation of various symptoms, rather than the existence of any single symptom, that identifies the existence of alcoholism,* or any other drug dependency.

THE STATE OF THE ART: UNANSWERED QUESTIONS, UNCERTAIN ANSWERS

As the reader has discovered by now, there is much confusion in the professional community. Even in the case of alcoholism, which is perhaps the most common of the drug addictions, this uncertainty is expressed by the fact that there is disagreement over what the essential elements of alcoholism are (Helzer, 1987), or even if alcholism is really a *disease* (Dreger, 1986).

Vaillant (1983) observed that "often it is not who is drinking but who is watching that defines a symptom" (p. 22) of alcoholism. The same observation may be made in the identification of other forms of drug addiction. To a middle-class adult, the use of heroin might be a sure sign of addiction. However, to a lower-class man who is trapped by economics and a limited education into a lifetime of underemployment, the same drug might seem to be an escape from a social prison.

The diagnosis of chemical dependency is often difficult (Lewis, Dana, and Blevens, 1988) and in the final analysis may be called a value judgment. This professional opinion might be made easier by lists of agreed-on criteria such as the American Psychiatric Association's *Diagnostic and Statistical Manual of Mental Disorders*, third edition, revised *(DSM-III-R)*. However, the diagnosis of chemical dependency is still, in the final analysis, a value judgment that is made by a professional about another person's chemical use. There is still much to be learned, and many questions that must be answered, before a final solution is found to the problem of the addictions.

CHAPTER 2

Alcohol: A Brief Summary of the Acute Effects

Alcohol has been a part of civilization thousands of years before the dawn of written history. Nobody *really* knows how it all began; however, Siegel (1986) hypothesized that thousands of years ago early man learned to ingest alcohol by watching animals eat fermented fruits from the forest floor. Once the discovery was made, man kept on enjoying alcohol, making it man's oldest psychoactive chemical.

Alcohol has become such an integral part of human culture that it has become one of the yardsticks by which social development is measured. Beasley (1987) notes that

> . . . virtually all cultures in time and place—whether hunter-gatherers or farmers; whether technologically advanced or primitive—share two universals: the development of a noodle and the discovery and use of the natural fermentation process. (p. 17)

Thus alcohol, which is also known as *ethanol*, or *ethyl alcohol*, is found in virtually every human culture, past or present. Other forms of alcohol also exist, but these are not normally used for human consumption and will not be discussed further here.

A BRIEF HISTORY OF ALCOHOL

Ray (1983) notes that *mead*, a form of beer made from fermented honey, was in common use around the year 8000 B.C., more than 10,000 years ago. Youcha (1978) relates a 4000-year-old Persian legend about the discovery of wine. According to this legend, a mythical Persian king, Jamshid, had vats of grapes stored in the basement of the palace. Jamshid loved grapes and apparently wanted to store some away to enjoy during the cold winter months when grapes were out of season. However, as time passed, he discovered that some of the vats developed a sour liquid at the bottom and, thinking that this liquid was poison, set the sour fluid aside for future use in palace politics.

According to the legend, a lady of his court was subject to severe headaches and, consequently, had decided to end her life. She opened the jar marked "poison" and, expecting death, drank some of the fluid. Instead of death, she found relief from her headaches and began to sneak into the storeroom from time to time to drink some of the mystical fluid. Over time, the supply of the fluid was exhausted. Our nameless heroine then confessed her discovery to the king, who ordered that grapes be fermented and that the secret of wine be made known to his countrymen. The rest is history, or at least the subject of much historical speculation.

This is, admittedly, only a legend. As noted above, man has known how to make mead for some 10,000 years, or since around the year 8000 B.C. Ray (1983) notes that historical evidence suggests that both beer and wine were being made from berries by about the year 6400 B.C. Wine made from grapes is actually a relative newcomer, dating back only to around 400 B.C.

In Homer's *Iliad* and *Odyssey* people often drank wine with meals. Even today, in many parts of the world, people drink wine with meals on a regular basis. In part, this seems to be because one can not trust the local water supply, which may or may not be fit to drink. In ancient times, and for much of history, wine was considered a natural part of any meal.

The importance of alcohol might be measured by the fact that both the Egyptian and Roman empires had a god, or goddess, of wine. Both beer and wine are also mentioned several times in Homer's *Iliad* and *Odyssey*, legends that date back thousands of years. It was not by accident that Ulysses helped the Cyclops become drunk before attempting his escape. Knowledge of alcohol's depressive effects on the central nervous system was discovered (perhaps by experimentation?) a long time before Ulysses set sail for Troy.

The process of distillation was developed in Arabia, but within two centuries had spread to Europe. It is reported that by the year 1000 A.D. Italian wine growers were distilling wine to produce various drinks with higher concentrations of alcohol, mixing the obtained distilled "spirits" with various herbs and spices. This mixture was then used for medicinal purposes. Indeed, distilled spirits were viewed as the ultimate in medicines in Europe, where they were called the *aqua vitae*, or the "water of life" (Ray, 1983).

The history of alcohol in western society is marked by increasing use over time. Over the years, there have been a number of efforts at control or regulation of alcohol use. These attempts at alcohol regulation have been almost uniformly unsuccessful. If you are interested in this aspect of the history of alcohol, Ray's (1983) text is an excellent place to learn more about the various attempts at the regulation of alcohol use throughout history.

HOW ALCOHOL IS PRODUCED

By whatever means, somehow man discovered that if you crush certain forms of fruit and allow them to stand for a period of time in containers, alcohol is produced. We now know that unseen microorganisms called *yeast*, which float in the air, settle on the crushed fruit and digest the sugars in the fruit in a chemical process called *fermentation*. Yeast breaks down the carbon, hydrogen, and oxygen atoms in sugar for food, and in the process recombines these atoms into ethyl alcohol and carbon dioxide.

The alcohol is actually a waste product of the process of fermentation. When the concentration of alcohol rises above about 15%, it becomes toxic to the yeast, causing the yeast to die. Fermentation thus stops when the concentration in the container of crushed fruit rises above about 15%. Thus, man has been able since prehistory to produce alcoholic beverages whose highest concentration of alcohol was about 15%.

It took several thousand more years to obtain alcohol concentrations above the 15% limit imposed by the nature of yeast. This is the process of *distillation*, which did not appear until around the year 800 A.D. Distillation is the process where the wine obtained from fermentation is heated, causing some of the alcohol content to boil off as a vapor, or steam. Alcohol boils at a much lower temperature than does water, so the steam that forms when wine is boiled contains more alcohol vapor than water vapor. When the steam is collected and cooled down, it forms a liquid that contains a higher concentration of alcohol, and a lower concentration of water, than did the original mixture. The vapor is collected in a special coil, which allows the vapor to cool into a liquid. The liquid, with its higher alcohol content, then drips from the end of the coil, into a container of some kind. This is the famous still.

Unfortunately, in the process of distillation, many of the vitamins and minerals that were in the original wine are lost. Where the original wine might have contributed *something* to the nutritional requirements of the individual, even this modest contribution is lost when one uses distilled spirits. Further, when the body breaks down alcohol, it finds "empty calories," which is to say the body obtains carbohydrates from the alcohol without the protein, vitamins, calcium, and other minerals needed by the body. This may contribute to a state of vitamin depletion called *avitaminosis*, which will be discussed in the next chapter.

ALCOHOL TODAY

Over the last 900 years, since the development of the distillation process, various forms of fermented wines using various ingredients, different forms of beer, and distilled spirits combined with various flavorings have emerged. With the march of civilization, some degree of standardization has resulted in uniform definitions of various classes of alcohol. Today, most American beer has an alcohol content of about 4 or 5%. As a class, wine continues to be made by allowing fermentation to take place in vats containing various grapes or other fruits. Occasionally, fermentation involves products other than grapes, such as the famous "rice wine" from Japan called *sake*. Wine tends to have an alcohol content of approximately 9 to 12%, and there are only minor variations in how different wines are made.

In addition to wine, there are the "fortified" wines. These are produced by a process in which distilled wine is added to fermented wine to raise the total alcohol content to about 20%. This class contains the various brands of sherry and port (Ray, 1983). Finally, there are the "hard liquors," the distilled spirits, whose alcohol content may range from 20% to 95% (in the case of Everclear and similar distilled spirits).

THE PHARMACOLOGY OF ALCOHOL

Alcohol itself is a small molecule and is usually introduced into the body in liquid form. (Actually, alcohol may also be introduced into the body intravenously, or even as a vapor; however, these methods of introducing alcohol into the body are *very* dangerous and are used by physicians only in extremely rare cases. We will not discuss these methods of introducing alcohol into the body further, but will discuss orally administered alcohol in great detail, since in the majority of cases the individual *drinks* the alcohol that eventually enters their body.) Julien (1981) reported that about 20% of the alcohol one drinks is immediately absorbed through the stomach lining, while the other 80% is absorbed into the body through the small intestine. Rose (1988) suggested however that, when a person drinks on an empty stomach, all of the alcohol will pass into the bloodstream through the stomach lining. Indeed, Rose suggested that, when a person drinks on an empty stomach, alcohol will appear in the bloodstream in as little as one minute.

When alcohol is mixed with food, only about 20% of the alcohol is absorbed immediately. The speed at which the remaining 80% of the alcohol enters the bloodstream is determined by how quickly the stomach empties into the small intestine (Julien, 1981). But, sooner or later, *all* of the alcohol ingested will be absorbed. The only exception to this rule is when the ingested alcohol is removed from the body before it passes from the stomach into the bloodstream. This may be accomplished by either "pumping" a person's stomach (a medical procedure whereby a tube is passed into a person's stomach and its contents pumped out) or vomiting. Vomiting, however, can be fatal if the person is unconscious, or can result in a form of pneumonia if the person happens to inhale any of the material being regurgitated.

Once in the body, alcohol tends to rapidly pass into all body tissues, including those of the brain. Since alcohol may diffuse into muscle tissue and fat tissue, an obese or muscular person would normally have a slightly lower blood alcohol level than would a leaner person after a given dose (Julien, 1981).

About 95% of the alcohol is metabolized by the liver before it is excreted at the rate of about one-third of an ounce of pure alcohol per hour in the normal, healthy individual. The other 5% of the alcohol is excreted unchanged through the lungs and skin, as well as through the urine (Schuckit, 1984).

The rate of metabolism for alcohol is equal to about one mixed drink or one can of beer per hour. Julien (1981) observed that the rate at which alcohol is metabolized by the liver is "relatively slow, constant, and independent of the amount ingested" (p. 61). Thus, if a person drinks at the rate of about one ounce of whiskey per hour, or one can of beer per hour, the blood alcohol level (BAL) will stay relatively constant until the alcohol is detoxified by the liver.

If, as is often the case, the person consumes *more* than one ounce of whiskey, or one can of beer, per hour the amount of alcohol in his or her bloodstream will increase. The effects of alcohol place it in the class of drugs having a depressant effect on the central nervous system: the *CNS depressants*. This class of drugs includes the barbiturates, the benzodiazepines, and the so-called minor tranquilizers. Indeed, Lingeman (1974) described alcohol's effects as being "analogous to a general anesthetic" (p. 4).

The effects of other CNS depressants are *potentiated* when combined with alcohol. Potentiation is a process where one drug will enhance or exaggerate the action of another, similar, drug. In many cases, the potentiation effect between alcohol and other CNS depressants has been fatal, resulting in many accidental—and occasionally intentional—deaths by drug overdose.

THE SUBJECTIVE EFFECTS OF ALCOHOL

At Normal Doses for the Average Drinker

After a couple of drinks in the normal individual, respiration may initially be stimulated, and the blood vessels in the surface of the skin will dilate. This causes the person to feel warm. But, while the person might *feel* warmer, the alcohol actually allows the body to lose heat more rapidly as the warm blood rushes to the skin from the deeper parts of the body. It has also been found that respiration and heart rate are initially increased when the person begins to drink. Years ago, people used to interpret this effect as evidence that alcohol was a stimulant. Lingeman (1974) terms this a "pseudo-stimulant" effect, for alcohol acts as a CNS depressant, *not* a stimulant, as was once thought.

A team of researchers (Brown, Goldman, Inn, and Anderson, 1980) has found that the individual's *expectations* play a role in how a person interprets the effects of alcohol at low to moderate dosage levels. Brown, et al. (1980), concluded that, ". . . less exposure to alcohol and limited consumption were associated with more general, positive expectancies . . . whereas longer exposure and heavier consumption were paired with expectancies of sexual enhancement and arousal and aggressive behavior" (p. 424).

In other words, it was found that, "expectancies vary with drinking patterns" (p. 425), with less experienced drinkers having their alcohol experience shaped not by the actual pharmacological effects of alcohol so much as by their *expectations* for the alcohol. Males were found to be more likely to expect the alcohol to make them more aggressive, while females were more likely to anticipate more pleasurable changes from moderate drinking (Brown, et al. 1980). Critchlow (1986) found that expectations for the effects of alcohol are common and suggested that these beliefs helped to reinforce the tendency to use alcohol.

A recent study by Brown, Creamer, and Stetson (1987) found similar results when the expectations for alcohol by adolescents who did and did not abuse it were compared. It was found that adolescents who abused alcohol were more likely to anticipate a positive experience when they drank, while those adolescents who did not abuse alcohol were less likely to anticipate positive drinking experiences. This finding was attributed to the home environment of the adolescent, with adolescents who abused alcohol being more likely to come from homes where their parents reported positive experiences with alcohol.

Thus, one factor that influences the effect of alcohol on the individual is the expectations that the person has for the alcohol, at least at low to moderate dosage levels. It is also known that alcohol has a *disinhibition effect* on the individual. The disinhibition effect comes about as alcohol starts to interfere with the normal function of nerve cells in the cortex. This is the part of the brain most responsible for man's "higher" functions, such as abstract thinking, speech, and so on.

The cortex is also the part of the brain where much of our voluntary behavior is planned. As alcohol interferes with normal nerve functions, one tends to temporarily "forget" social inhibitions. Julien (1981) estimated that this disinhibition effect could be achieved after the person had ingested as little as one to three ounces of whiskey. This would lead to an inability on the part of individuals to judge the effects of their actions, such as their ability to drive a car, contributing to alcohol-related accidents at home and on the road.

In the normal individual, the effects of one or two drinks are interpreted as pleasant and relaxing. The individual might feel more confident, more sure of themselves, or less tense. There seems to be a tendency for people to attribute *any* pleasant change to the drink itself, in spite of the alcohol's actual effects on the body (Critchlow, 1986). This again seems to reflect the individual's expectations for the alcohol more than the actual effects of the alcohol itself, at least to some degree.

At Above-Normal Doses for the Average Drinker

As noted above, alcohol is a CNS depressant, which at high dosage levels is an anesthetic (Schuckit, 1984; Julien, 1981). Although many people do not understand that it is possible to die from an alcohol overdose, occasionally this does indeed happen.

Julien (1981) noted that CNS depressants might function as *sedatives*, *tranquilizers*, *hypnotic* (sleep inducing) agent, or *anesthetics, depending on the dose*. At extremely high blood levels, death may result from an overdose of any of the CNS depressants. Indeed, for *all* drugs classified as CNS depressants, there is a progression from mild sedation to heavy sedation, coma, and ultimately to death as the blood levels increase.

For alcohol, Ray (1983) reported that a BAL of 0.05% would result in lowered alertness, feelings of euphoria, a loss of inhibitions, and impairment of judgment. A person with a BAL of 0.10% would be expected to have slowed reaction times and an impaired ability to coordinate muscle actions (a condition called *ataxia*). This person would also be legally intoxicated in most states.

A person with a BAL of 0.15% could be expected to have serious difficulty reacting in time to avoid an accident while driving (Lingeman, 1974). A person with a BAL of 0.20% is most definitely intoxicated, with a marked ataxia (Matuschka, 1985). A person with a BAL of 0.25% would stagger around and have difficulty comprehending sensory data (Ray, 1983). A person with a BAL of 0.30 would be stuporous and, although conscious, would likely be unable to remember later what happened to him or her while intoxicated (Matuschka, 1985).

With a BAL of 0.35% the stage of surgical anesthesia is achieved (Matuschka, 1985), and about 1% of the people whose BAL is this high will die, in the absence of medical supervision and support (Ray, 1983). A BAL of 0.40% will result in about a 50% death rate from alcohol overdose without medical intervention (Ray, 1983), although Schuckit (1984) has noted that a person who is tolerant to the effects of alcohol *might* still be conscious and able to talk with a BAL as high as 0.78%.

Segal and Sisson (1985) reported that the *approximate* lethal BAL in human beings is 0.5%, while Lingeman (1974) notes that the fatal concentration of alcohol in the blood lies somewhere between 0.5 and 0.8%. However, since a BAL of 0.35% or above may result in death, it is suggested that *all* cases of known or suspected alcohol overdose be immediately treated by a physician.

The Hangover

Alcohol is a toxic chemical, and both the stomach and the brain react to its effects. If a person has ingested enough alcohol, she or he will experience a hangover the next day, which may include malaise, headache, tremor, and nausea (Kissin, 1985). While the hangover may, according to some, cause an individual to wish that he or she could die, in general the alcoholic hangover is self-limiting and will respond to self-treatment that may include antacids and aspirin (Kissin, 1985).

For the majority, the hangover following a night's drinking is viewed as the price to be paid for a night's indulgence. Few people view seriously the alcoholic hangover. The hangover might be an early withdrawal syndrome from alcohol (Kissin, 1985). Alcoholic hangovers might be found in the earlier stages of addiction, where the individual's body has started to adapt to the continued use of alcohol. The individual who is suffering from a hangover, be it after a single night of drinking or a more protracted period of drinking, is thus going through a mild alcohol withdrawal process.

THE EFFECTS OF ALCOHOL ON SLEEP

Alcohol interferes with the normal sleep cycle. While it may, like the other CNS depressants, bring about sleep, it does not allow for a normal dream cycle. This usually will not matter very much in the person who drinks only on a social basis. However, in the chronic alcoholic, the cumulative effects might be quite disruptive. The impact of chronic alcohol use on the normal sleep cycle will be discussed in the next chapter.

Even the occasional drinker should be aware, however, of the impact of alcohol on the individual's ability to breathe during sleep. For alcohol, like other CNS depressants, has the ability to contribute to *sleep apnea,* a potentially fatal disorder in which the individual's ability to breathe is disrupted during sleep. Persons with *any* breathing disorder thus should not drink, especially during the hours prior to sleep.

SUMMARY

In this chapter we have explored how alcohol affects the body, and some of the more common complications of short-term alcohol use. The short-term effects of alcohol include a mild disinhibition effect, a mild sedative effect, a vasodilation effect on the blood vessels on the surface of the body, and, depending on the dose, possible death from alcohol overdose. Research has demonstrated that, especially at lower dosage levels, the individual's expectations for the drug influence how the chemical's effects are interpreted.

In order to understand the effects of alcohol, however, one must consider both the short-term effects and the impact of long-term use of alcohol on the individual. In the next chapter, the effects of the chronic use of alcohol will be explored.

CHAPTER 3

The Chronic Use of Alcohol

So far, we have spoken for the most part of the acute effects of alcohol on the "average" person. When working with alcohol, however, one needs to evaluate both the *immediate* effects of alcohol, and the *long-term* effects of alcohol use over time. In the last chapter, we examined the immediate, or *acute*, effects of alcohol on the infrequent social drinker. The immediate effects of alcohol were found to often reflect the individual's expectations for the chemical, which are culturally learned.

In this chapter, we will examine the long-term effects of alcohol use on the individual's body. Research has demonstrated that these effects are often quite debilitating. The long-term effects of alcohol are usually irreversible. These long-term consequences are found not in the occasional, social drinker, but in the individual who engages in abusive drinking for extended periods of time.

ALCOHOL TOLERANCE AND DEPENDENCE

In the last chapter, it was noted that a person who was *tolerant* to the effects of alcohol *might* still be conscious and able to talk with a BAL of 0.78% (Schuckit, 1984). Alcohol, like the other CNS depressants, brings about a state of *tolerance* when used over an extended period of time at high-dosage levels; however, the lethal dose of alcohol remains the same (Matuschka, 1985).

There are actually two different forms of tolerance. In the first form of tolerance, which is called *physical tolerance*, the individual's body adapts to the effects of the drug so that it takes more and more in order to achieve the same effect. In the case of alcohol, an inexperienced drinker might be quite intoxicated after five or six mixed drinks, while the chronic drinker might hardly have started to feel the effects of alcohol after "only" six drinks.

In the second form of tolerance, known as *behavioral tolerance*, the chronic drinker might *appear* quite sober, in spite of the fact that she or he is intoxicated. If judged only on the basis of physical appearance, many chronic alcoholics are able to appear relatively sober, at least to the untrained observer, in spite of the fact that blood tests would reveal that the individual is quite intoxicated.

Alcohol, like the other CNS depressants, is capable of bringing about a state of both psychological and physical *dependence* (Segal & Sisson, 1985). Psychological dependence refers to a pattern of repeated self-administration of alcohol because the individual finds it rewarding. Physical dependence refers to a characteristic withdrawal syndrome, which comes about after the body adapts to the drug's effects. Over time, the alcoholic's body learns to function *in spite of the use of alcohol*. When the body adapts to the constant presence of alcohol, it will take a period of time before the body functions return to normal if the person stops drinking.

This period of adjustment from the intoxicated state to the normal state involves a great deal of discomfort. This is the phase of *withdrawal*, which many alcoholics attempt to avoid through the use of more alcohol. The severity of the withdrawal from alcohol depends on: (a) the intensity with which the individual used alcohol, (b) the duration of time during which the individual drank, and (c) the individual's state of health. In other words, the longer the period of alcohol use and the greater the amount ingested, the more severe the alcohol withdrawal syndrome, all other things being equal.

Long-term use of alcohol at high dosage levels affects every body system (Schuckit, 1984). Many alcoholics speak of a "craving" for the alcohol long after they had stopped drinking. It was postulated that this was because chronic alcohol use can significantly reduce the brain's production of a group of opiatelike neurotransmitters, the *endorphins*, the *enkephalins*, and the *dynorphins* (Trachtenberg and Blum, 1987). These neurotransmitters function in the brain's pleasure center to help moderate an individual's emotions and behavior.

Blum (1988) reported that a by-product of alcohol metabolism, *tetrahydroisoquinoline* (TIQ), is capable of binding to opiatelike receptor sites within the brain's pleasure center. In so doing, the individual experiences a sense of well-being (Blum and Trachtenberg, 1988). This mechanism seems to be the reason why alcohol use is rewarding to the individual; however, TIQ's effects are short-lived, and the individual must drink more alcohol in order to regain or maintain the initial pleasurable feeling.

Chronic use of alcohol causes the brain to reduce its production of enkephalins, as the ever-present TIQ is substituted for naturally produced neurotransmitters (Blum and Trachtenberg, 1988). Furthermore, animal research suggests that the chronic use of alcohol reduces the amount of available dopamine and serotonin in the brain. The cessation of alcohol intake results in a neurochemical deficit, according to Blum and Trachtenberg, which the individual attempts to relieve through further chemical use. If the individual does not use chemicals, this deficit is experienced as the craving for alcohol commonly reported by recovering alcoholics.

Recent research has also uncovered mechanisms by which alcohol seems to alter the brain's chemistry following both short-term and chronic alcohol use. The changes in the brain chemistry underscore the potency of alcohol, a chemical that has long been thought to be relatively harmless. Obviously, alcohol is more potent than was once thought.

SCOPE OF THE PROBLEM OF ALCOHOLISM

It has been estimated that 100 million Americans drink alcohol at least occasionally. The American Psychiatric Association (1985) estimated that approximately 10 million adults and another 3 million children and adolescents are addicted to alcohol. Beasley (1987) presented a higher figure, reporting that between 10 and 15 million Americans are currently alcoholic, with an additional 10 million being "on the cusp of alcoholism" (p. 21).

Franklin (1987) reported that alcoholism accounts for an astounding 85% of drug addiction. According to the American Psychiatric Association (1985), another 30 to 40 million people were indirectly affected by alcoholism either through family ties to the alcoholic or as victims of the alcoholic. Obviously, as these figures demonstrate, for a significant number of people alcohol is more than a social drink: it is a drug of addiction. Alcoholism affects us all, either directly or indirectly.

EFFECTS OF CHRONIC ALCOHOL USE

First, it is necessary to understand that the distinction between alcohol "abuse," and alcohol "dependency" is often at best an artificial one, as Schuckit, Zisook, and Mortola (1985) have observed. Indeed, the authors found that a group of men identified as alcohol abusers was *virtually identical* to another group of men diagnosed as being alcohol dependent.

The only major difference was that the latter group of men took more drinks when they did drink, and were more likely to have had more alcohol-related medical problems. The authors concluded that "It is not clear whether the distinction between alcohol abuse and alcohol dependence carries any important prognostic or treatment implications . . ." (p. 1403).

On the Digestive System

Segal and Sisson (1985) note that there is no simple formula by which to calculate the amount of damage done by drinking. As Segal and Sisson (1985) noted:

> Some heavy drinkers of many years' duration appear to go relatively unscathed, while others develop complications early (e.g., after five years) in their drinking careers. Some develop brain damage; others liver disease; still others, both. The reasons for this are simply not known. (p. 145)

It has been known for many years that the chronic use of alcohol will result in a higher risk of many forms of cancer. Schuckit (1984) noted that ". . . alcohol is associated with high rates of cancer of all levels . . . especially the esophagus and the stomach as well as the head and neck" (p. 52).

Nelson (1989) warned that the combination of cigarettes and alcohol is especially dangerous, as alcoholics who smoke tend to have "especially high rates of throat cancers" (p. 8 Ex).

In speaking of the impact of the chronic use of alcohol on the digestive system, Nace (1987) observed that ". . . the organ most commonly thought to be affected by alcohol is the liver" (p. 23). He went on to note that the human liver "bears the brunt of ridding the body of alcohol" (p. 24). The first manifestation of liver problems is the development of a *fatty liver*, a condition in which the liver becomes enlarged and does not function at full efficiency (Nace, 1987; Willoughby, 1984). This can usually be detected by physical examination, or through various blood tests (Schuckit, 1984).

If alcohol consumption continues, the individual is likely to develop *alcoholic hepatitis*, which Nace characterized as "a slow, smoldering process which may proceed or coexist with cirrhosis" (p. 25). Symptoms of this condition include a low-grade fever, malaise, jaundice, an enlarged and tender liver, and dark urine (Nace, 1987). A physical examination may reveal characteristic changes in the blood chemistry (Schuckit, 1984). Although it is thought that alcoholic hepatitis precedes the development of cirrhosis of the liver, this has not been proven.

Cirrhosis of the liver is the sixth leading cause of death in the United States (Nace, 1987). Over time, if the person continues to drink, scar tissue and fat deposits form in the liver, and large areas of the liver are permanently damaged. A physician will discover a hard, nodular liver; an enlarged spleen; testicular atrophy; "spider" angiomas; tremor; jaundice; and confusion, as well as a number of other symptoms in many chronic alcoholics (Nace, 1987).

Cirrhosis can bring about severe complications, including liver cancer, and sodium and water retention, (Nace, 1987; Schuckit, 1984). Furthermore, the scar tissue and fat deposits prevent the liver from filtering the blood as efficiently as before, causing toxins to build up in the blood. This then adds to the damage being done to the brain by the alcohol (Willoughby, 1984; Julien, 1981).

At the same time, the now-enlarged liver puts a greater work load on the heart. Swelling of the liver puts pressure on the blood vessels that pass through it, causing the pressure to build up within the vessels. This condition is known as *portal hypertension*, and in turn may contribute to a swelling of the blood vessels in the esophagus. When the blood vessels in the esophagus swell, weak spots form on the walls of the vessels, much like weak spots form on an inner tube of a tire. These weak spots in the walls of the blood vessels of the esophagus may rupture, leading to massive bleeding (Willoughby, 1984; Schuckit, 1984). This is a medical emergency that carries about a 33-% mortality rate.

As if that were not enough, alcohol has been implicated in approximately one-third of the cases of *pancreatitis*, a painful inflammation of the pancreas. Nace notes that this condition "usually occurs after 10 to 15 years of heavy drinking" (p. 26). The chronic use of alcohol has also been shown to cause *gastritis,* or an inflammation of the lining of the stomach. This may result in bleeding from the stomach lining or may contribute to the formation of ulcers (Willoughby, 1984). It has been estimated that about 30% of heavy drinkers will suffer from chronic gastritis (Matuschka, 1985).

If an ulcer forms over a major blood vessel, the individual may experience a "bleeding ulcer," as the stomach acid eats through the stomach lining and blood vessel walls. This is a severe medical emergency, which may and frequently does result in death. Willoughby (1984) notes that the medical treatment for this condition may include the partial removal of part of the stomach through surgery, a condition that contributes to the body's difficulties in finding and absorbing suitable amounts of vitamins.

This, either by itself or in combination with further alcohol use, helps to bring about a chronic state of malnutrition in the individual, which in turn makes them a prime candidate for the development of tuberculosis (TB) (Willoughby, 1984). The treatment of TB is rather slow and difficult and often requires that the individual take medication on a regular basis for up to 18 months.

Sometimes, further surgery is necessary to remove the infected tissue, a process that is both painful and life-threatening in itself. Willoughby estimated that about 95% of those alcoholics who have a portion of their stomach removed for bleeding ulcers and continue to drink will ultimately develop TB.

The chronic use of alcohol lowers the effectiveness of the digestive system, resulting in malabsorption syndromes, where vitamins and needed nutrition are not absorbed in the quantities needed. When the body breaks down alcohol, one of the by-products is a sugar, which the body then burns in the place of normal food. This results in a form of anorexia, as the body replaces the normal calorie intake with empty calories obtained from alcohol. This in turn contributes to the decline in the effectiveness of the immune system as a whole, as well as the general lack of required vitamins in the alcoholic's body. Beasley (1987) termed this condition a "leaky gut," a common finding for chronic alcoholics.

On the Heart and Circulatory System

Red-blood-cell formation is suppressed in the alcoholic, and both blood-clotting problems and anemia are common (Nace, 1987). Bacterial pneumonia is more than twice as common in alcoholics as nonalcoholics (Nace, 1987). This is true for several reasons. The chronic use of alcohol lowers the resistance to disease by lowering the effectiveness of the immune system. Second, the individual might aspirate some of the material vomited during and after periods of drinking, a process known as *aspirative pneumonia.*

Alcohol is also implicated in damage to the cardiovascular system itself. Alcohol is known to be *cardiotoxic,* which is to say that it is toxic to the muscle tissue of the heart. Prolonged exposure may result in permanent damage to the heart muscle tissue, resulting in hypertension (high blood pressure) and inflammation of the heart muscle known as *myocardiopathy.* Myocardiopathy is found in approximately *one-quarter* of chronic alcoholics (Schuckit, 1984).

On the Central Nervous System

Alcohol has been implicated in a deterioration of the peripheral nerves in the hands and feet known as *peripheral neuropathies.* This condition is found in 5 to 15% of chronic alcoholics and is rarely found in nonalcoholic individuals. Vitamin B deficiencies, secondary to poor nutrition and vitamin malabsorption syndromes, are thought to be the cause of this condition (Nace, 1987; Beasley, 1987). The chronic lack of proper vitamins causes nerve cells to die over time, with those in the hands and feet being the first affected (Schuckit, 1984).

Alcohol has also been implicated in damage to the brain tissue itself, and alcohol-induced brain damage may become so severe as to result in the need for nursing-home placement. Indeed, Schuckit (1984) estimated that between 15 and 30% of *all* nursing-home patients were there because of permanent alcohol-induced brain damage. Beasley (1987) identified alcoholism as the single most preventable cause of dementia in the United States at this time. Berg, Franzen, and Wedding (1987) reported that one could detect signs of alcohol-induced brain damage even before the development of alcohol-related liver damage.

One of the most frequent symptoms found in heavy drinking is that of memory disturbance, especially during that period when the person is drinking most. The person may find it impossible to remember events that took place while they were intoxicated, a condition that is known as *blackout.* These periods of amnesia might last several days, although for the most part they involve shorter periods of time (Segal and Sisson, 1985; Willoughby, 1984).

During a memory blackout, the individual is able to carry out many complex tasks, often with great efficiency; however, they will not have any memory of having done these tasks at a later time. The exact mechanism through which alcohol is able to bring about a memory blackout is unknown, but is "among the most frequently reported symptoms in the progression of alcoholism" (Zucker and Branchey, 1985, p. 296).

Alcohol, as noted previously, is implicated in avitaminosis (Willoughby, 1984). Avitaminosis is caused either by a lack of adequate vitamin intake, or an inability on the body's part to use the vitamins effectively (Beasley, 1987). This process depletes the body's reserves of many vitamins and over a period of time can result in a form of brain damage known as *Wernicke's encephalopathy* (Reuler, Girard, and Cooney, 1985).

Wernicke's encephalopathy is a condition that develops when the body is deprived of adequate amounts of thiamine, one of the *B* family of vitamins, for extended periods of time. This chronic thiamine deficiency results in brain damage, which has been associated with a 10 to 20-% mortality rate (Reuler, et al. 1985). The individual suffering from Wernicke's encephalopathy may be confused to the point of being delirious and disoriented. Of those who survive this condition, up to 80% will develop a condition known as *Korsakoff's psychosis* or *Korsakoff's syndrome* (Reuler, et al., 1985; Kolb and Brodie, 1982).

Korsakoff's syndrome is marked by an inability to remember the past accurately or to learn new information. The person who has Korsakoff's syndrome tends to fill in these gaps in memory by making up answers to questions. This process is called *confabulation*.

One individual who was suspected of suffering from Korsakoff's syndrome reported that he was "53," when the record demonstrated that he was almost 58 years old. He was able to correctly identify his date of birth, when asked to do so, but could not correctly recall his current age. He repeatedly confabulated an age, in this case 53, in place of the actual age that he could no longer recall.

Confabulation may involve different areas of memory and is sometimes difficult to spot without collateral information or objective background data. Sacks (1970) noted that, occasionally, the individual will lose virtually all memories after a certain period of their lives, and will almost be "frozen in time." The example that he offered was of a man who, in the mid 1970s, was convinced that it was just after World War II, and was unable to recall anything after the late 1940s. This example of confabulation, while extremely rare, can result from chronic alcoholism. More frequent are the less pronounced cases, where significant portions of memory are lost, but the individual retains *some* memory.

Such behavior is thought to reflect brain damage, and it is of interest to note that Schuckit (1984) estimated that between 40 and 70% of all alcoholics who were detoxified demonstrated evidence of brain damage, either on psychological testing or CAT scans. DeFranco, Tarbox, and McLaughlin (1985) noted that long-term alcoholics demonstrated greater cognitive deficits on psychometric tests than did less chronic alcoholics, supporting Schuckit's (1984) hypothesis.

Grant (1987), however, questioned whether this was permanent brain damage, or if some *limited* degree of recovery was possible for the chronic alcoholic. Grant noted that research in the area of brain damage and alcoholism used recently detoxified alcoholics for the most part, and found evidence suggesting a degree of improvement in alcoholics who were abstinent from alcohol for extended periods of time. This would seem to be true both for women (Fabian and Parsons, 1983) and men (Grant, 1987). Most certainly, however, chronic alcohol use has been implicated in some degree of brain damage for many individuals.

As was noted in Chapter 2, alcohol interferes with the normal sleep cycle. As a result of chronic alcohol use, the individual may experience a decrease in dream time, which takes place during the rapid eye movement (REM) phase of sleep. When people stop drinking, they enter a period of abnormal sleep known as "REM rebound."

This is a pattern of sleep where the person will dream more intensely and more vividly, often to the point of frequent nightmares. REM rebound can last for up to six months after the person has stopped drinking. These rebound dreams may be so frightening that the individual might return to the use of alcohol in order to "get a decent night's sleep."

On the Emotions

As stated many times earlier, alcohol is a CNS depressant. Willoughby (1984) noted that the depressant effects from *one* drink may last as long as 96 hours. Segal and Sisson (1985) noted that the effects of an alcohol binge of only one or two days might last for several weeks after abstinence. Obviously, alcohol is more potent than is generally recognized.

Chronic alcohol use often results in a range of neurotic and even psychotic symptoms, which are thought to be secondary to the malnutrition and toxicity found in alcoholism (Beasley, 1987). These symptoms might include depressive reactions (Schuckit, 1984), generalized anxiety disorders, and panic attacks (Beasley, 1987). Indeed, Beasley observed that of those patients who were diagnosed as having a generalized anxiety disorder, more than 20% were alcoholics.

These anxiety attacks are often treated by physicians through the use of antianxiety agents, which are potentially addictive. If the physician fails to obtain an adequate history and physical (or if the patient lies about his or her alcohol use), there is a risk that the alcoholic might combine the use of the antianxiety medication with alcohol; the potential for an overdose is created. Also, as Beasley (1987) noted, the family of antianxiety agents known as benzodiazepines might, when combined with alcohol, bring about a *paradoxical rage reaction.* This condition results when a drug that is normally a depressant brings about an unexpected period of rage in the individual, which may in turn result in physical harm to others.

As noted above, alcohol has been implicated in depressive reactions for chronic alcoholics. Surprisingly, many people who are clinically depressed will use alcohol in order to *numb* the depressive feelings that they experience. This is a form of *self-medication* that tends to add to the feelings of depression in the long term. Many people are unaware of this, thus setting up a vicious cycle where the individual feels depressed, turns to alcohol to deal with the feelings of depression, then ends up feeling even more depressed at least in part because of his or her drinking.

Schuckit (1983) estimated that between one-third and one-half of alcoholics would display symptoms of depression at some point in their lives.

However, in the vast majority of cases, the individual will be found to suffer from an *alcohol-induced* depression, which will clear shortly after detoxification (Schuckit, 1983; Willenbring, 1986).

Primary depression in alcoholics is rare. It has been estimated that only 2–3% (Powell, Read, Penick, Miller, and Bingham, 1987), or perhaps as many as 5% (Schuckit, 1984), of the cases of depression seen in alcoholics is actually a primary depression. The rest of the depressions seen in chronic alcoholics are thought to be alcohol-induced. Furthermore, it is well known that depression is significantly related to suicide, and Schuckit (1986) noted that the lifetime risk for suicide among alcoholics, whether their depression was primary to or secondary to their drinking, was almost 15%.

Alcohol Withdrawal for the Chronic Alcoholic

Unlike the social drinker, who might recover from a night's drinking with little more than a hangover, withdrawal after chronic alcohol use may result in the *delirium tremens* (DT's) . This is an acute brain syndrome that develops within 72 to 96 hours after the last drink (Schuckit, 1984). In rare cases this condition will develop up to ten days after the last drink (Slaby, Lieb, and Tancredi, 1981).

It has been estimated that only about 5% of alcoholics will develop the DT's (Slaby, et al., 1981) but they are certainly to be feared. The DT's involve a period of delirium, hallucinations, delusional beliefs that one is being followed, and possible withdrawal seizures. Historically, 5 to 25% of the cases of individuals going through alcohol withdrawal syndrome die from exhaustion (Schuckit, 1984).

In recent years, the benzodiazepines have been found quite useful in the alcohol withdrawal process. The judicious use of benzodiazepines has been found to control the tremor, hyperactivity, convulsions, and anxiety associated with alcohol withdrawal (Miller, Frances, and Holmen, 1988). After the withdrawal symptoms have been controlled, the dosage level of benzodiazepines should be reduced by 10-20% each day, until the drug is discontinued (Miller, Frances, and Holmen, 1988). In this manner, a gradual withdrawal from alcohol may be accomplished with minimal discomfort to the client.

Other Complications From Chronic Alcohol Use

Indirectly, alcohol contributes to a large number of head injuries (Slaby et al., 1981), as the intoxicated individual falls and strikes his or her head on coffee tables, magazine stands, or whatever happens to be in the way. Schuckit (1984) observed that chronic alcohol use may reduce the individual's life expectancy by 15 years, with the leading causes of death being (in decreasing order of frequency) heart disease, cancer, accidents, and suicide. Siegel (1989) reported that 100,000 Americans die each year from alcohol-related diseases.

In addition to this, women who drink while pregnant run the risk of causing alcohol-induced birth defects, a condition known as the *fetal alcohol syndrome*. This condition will be discussed in detail in the chapter "Hidden Victims of Chemical Dependency." The reader should be aware at this point, however, of a connection between alcohol use during pregnancy and birth defects.

Chronic alcoholism has been associated with a premature aging syndrome, where the chronic use of alcohol causes individuals to appear much older than they actually are. In many cases, the overall physical condition of the individual corresponds to that of a person between 15 and 20 years older than the chronological age of the alcoholic. One individual, a man in his 50s, was told by his physician that he was in good health . . . for a man about to turn 70!

Admittedly, every alcoholic will not suffer from every consequence reviewed above. Some alcoholics will never suffer from stomach problems, for example, but may suffer from advanced heart disease. However, Schuckit (1984) noted that in one research study, *93% of those alcoholics admitted to treatment had at least one important medical problem in addition to their alcoholism.*

Research has demonstrated that, in most cases, the first alcohol-related problems are experienced when the person is in their late 20s or early 30s. Schuckit (1984) observed that by the age of 31 approximately half of those who will fit the criteria for alcoholism will have done so. However, this means that a significant number of known alcoholics—again, approximately half—do not follow this *classic* picture.

IS THERE SUCH A THING AS AN ADDICTION-PRONE PERSONALITY?

Kamback (1978) observed that alcoholism (and other forms of drug dependence) usually emerges over a period of years. The time span necessary for addiction to develop, and express itself, obscures the foundation upon which the addiction comes to rest. At this point in time, however, there are two schools of thought concerning alcoholism.

The first school of thought holds that there are clear-cut personality and genetic patterns that predispose one to alcoholism. This school of thought might be called the "determinist" viewpoint, in the sense that alcoholism is viewed as a unitary phenomenon, and that the same forces that brought about alcoholism in one individual also brought about alcoholism in every other individual.

The second school of thought holds that alcoholism is a "final common pathway," which is the outcome of a wide range of possible environmental/genetic/personality/chance factors. In other words, this school of thought holds that the "alcoholic personality" is a product of the disease process, not a cause of it. To understand *alcoholism*, from such a viewpoint, would mean that one must understand the various forces that made *this* individual alcoholic; alcoholism would have different meanings for different individuals.

Butcher (1988) observed that personality factors have long been suspected to play a role in the development of addiction. As such, Butcher's position is strongly deterministic. Tarter (1988) advanced still another deterministic theory, noting that personality characteristics, such as the antisocial personality disorder and certain neurotic traits, might increase the risk of subsequent addiction. However, such theoretical models do not allow for more than a general statement that such personality characteristics might increase the long-term risk that a person will become addicted.

One research project that tried to identify a preexisting "alcoholic personality" was conducted by Hoffmann, Loper, and Kammeier (1974). The authors examined the Minnesota Multiphasic Personality Inventory (MMPI) scores of known alcoholics who had taken the MMPI years before, while they were students in college. These scores were then compared with MMPI profiles obtained from the same individuals following their admission to a chemical dependency treatment program. The results indicated that there were measurable personality patterns that predated the development of alcoholism.

Nathan (1988) challenged this deterministic viewpoint, however, noting that there is no consistent pattern of personality or psychometric pattern that might reliably differentiate future alcoholics from those who will not become alcoholic. Nathan postulated that the characteristics of the so-called addictive personality found by earlier researchers actually reflected a misdiagnosis, in the sense that previous research confused the antisocial personality disorder with a prealcoholic personality pattern.

Bean-Bayog (1988) postulated that the so-called alcoholic personality emerged as a *result* of the impact of chronic alcoholism on the personality pattern, which is to say that *the personality characteristics often noted to exist in the alcoholic were a result of the disease process*, not a factor that aided in the initial development of the disease. Thus, the debate over whether there is a preexisting alcoholic personality that might be detected prior to the emergence of alcoholism continues to rage.

One confounding factor in the research into the nature of alcoholism is that there does not seem to be *one* pattern of alcoholism. One person might be unquestionably alcoholic before their eighteenth birthday and others, in spite of a long history of abusive drinking, are in their fifties and still do not fit the criteria for a diagnosis of alcoholism.

Research has cast doubt on the popular stereotype of the "typical" alcoholic. Rather, there are a number of different drinking patterns, many of which might be classified as a form of alcoholism (Franklin, 1987). This frequently causes some degree of confusion in the literature, since different authors define the problem of alcoholism in different ways.

Along these lines, Morey, Skinner, and Blashfield (1984) noted that while traditional thought has considered alcoholism a "unitary phenomenon" (p. 408), several subtypes of alcoholics emerged from their research. The first subtype were those who "showed evidence of alcohol abuse but who had not accrued symptoms of physical dependence on alcohol" (p. 415). In contrast to this first group of drinkers, there was a second group of drinkers who were "more gregarious and socially oriented, [tending] to prefer beer, and [tending] to drink in a sustained manner" (p. 415).

The last group of alcoholics were those individuals who were "socially withdrawn and schizoid, [preferring] wine or liquor [tending] to drink in binges, had more somatic complaints, and [having] more psychological difficulties" (p. 415). Each of these three groups seemed to respond to a different treatment approach than did the others, suggesting that one must consider the form of alcoholism when developing a treatment program for the individual.

To further compound the problem, there is evidence (Zucker and Gomberg, 1986) that would suggest that the factors bringing about alcohol dependency are not the same factors as those supporting the continued use of alcohol after alcohol addiction develops. This is to say that the initial use of alcohol during adolescence or adulthood might be brought about by one set of factors, which are only dimly understood; however, after alcoholism has developed, the person might *continue* to use alcohol for a number of totally unrelated reasons.

THE EVOLUTION OF ALCOHOLISM: A STUDY OF THE RISK FACTORS

Leigh (1985) postulated that there were five elements, or factors, supporting drug addiction. These were the: (1) biological factors (genetic, physiological, and biochemical), (2) cultural factors (customs, social attitudes, and social policy toward chemical use), (3) environmental factors (conditioning, learning, and life events), (4) interpersonal factors (social and family situations), and (5) intrapersonal factors (developmental forces, personality, sex differences, and emotional status). Various combinations of these factors might result in different forms of chemical addiction in different individuals, according to Leigh (1985), who speaks of a "multidimensional" nature of chemical dependency (p. 34).

Research attempting to identify the factors leading to addiction would thus have to factor out those traits predating the addiction from those traits resulting from the addiction. Furthermore, one must factor out the influences of genetics from the environmental, social, interpersonal, and intrapersonal influences. This is a difficult task; however, research has started to offer some clues as to the possible causes of alcoholism.

Cloninger, Gohman, and Sigvardsson (1981) used the adoption records of some 3000 individuals from Sweden, as well as histories of their natural and adoptive parents. They found that the children of alcoholics were likely to be alcoholic themselves, even in cases where the children were reared by adoptive parents almost from birth. The individuals studied fell into two groups. The first group comprised the majority of individuals, almost three-quarters of which were alcoholic, and as a general rule they had begun by drinking in moderation. It was only later in life that these individuals could be classified as alcoholic. Even so, these individuals tended to function within society and were only rarely involved in anti-social behavior.

Environment played a strong role for this group. Even if the child's genetic inheritance seemed to predispose the child to alcoholism, if that child had been adopted by a middle-class family in infancy, his or her chances of actually being alcoholic in adulthood were no greater than normal. If the child were adopted into a poor family, the chances were greater that this child would grow up to be an alcoholic.

The second, smaller, group of subjects were more violent and tended to be male. These individuals tended to be both alcoholic and involved in criminal behavior. A male child born to a "violent" alcoholic ran almost a 20% chance of himself becoming alcoholic, no matter what social status the child's adoptive parents were. There thus would seem to be a clear-cut, genetic predisposition toward alcoholism, based on the work of Cloninger, Gohman, and Sigvardsson (1981). However, they also found that, at least for some alcoholics, environmental factors also seem to play a role in the development of alcoholism.

Ackerman (1983) noted that children of alcoholic parents are perhaps *four times* as likely to become alcoholic than are children of nonalcoholics. Schuckit (1987) noted that there "is evidence that alcoholism is a genetically influenced disorder" (p. 301), although he concedes that there are also environmental factors—some of which have yet to be identified—that play a strong role in the development of alcoholism.

Schuckit (1987) also noted that some of these environmental factors include an unstable home environment early in life, a relatively low-status occupation for the father, and an extended neonatal hospital stay for the infant who later grows up to be alcoholic. Kolb and Brodie (1982) postulated that there is both a genetic predisposition as well as environmental factors necessary for alcoholism to exist. The authors concluded that ". . . genetics, constitution, and the child's emotional experiences in its family transactions all contribute to the predisposition to alcoholism" (p. 619).

The importance of environmental factors is demonstrated by Schuckit's (1987) observation that in identical twins, the concordance rate for alcoholism in both twins when one twin was alcoholic was still only 58%. This is to say that where one identical twin is alcoholic, there is only a 58% chance that the other twin will also be alcoholic, in spite of the fact that these individuals are genetically identical. For fraternal twins, when one twin is alcoholic, the concordance rate was only 28%.

If alcoholism were mediated only by the individual's genetic inheritance, then you would expect that identical twins would have a concordance rate of nearly 100%, since they are genetically the same. However, even in the case where you have two different individuals with the exact same genetic makeup, there is only about a 60-% probability that both twins will be alcoholic when one twin is alcoholic. Clearly, while there is a strong genetic component to alcoholism there also are other factors that influence the development of alcoholism as well.

There is, thus, no "typical" alcoholic. Nor are there clearly identified risk factors that might be used to identify the person who is likely to become alcoholic. But, one might safely say that the longer a person drinks, and the greater the amount of alcohol ingested, the more likely he or she is to become addicted or to develop some of the medical complications associated with alcoholism. I speak here of the steady, abusive alcohol use that is the hallmark of alcoholism, and not of social drinking. Indeed, by definition, if the person has developed any of the complications associated with alcoholism, they are not drinking on just a social basis.

Thus, about the only generalization that can be made about the risk factors for alcoholism is that the children of alcoholics have a three- to fourfold increase in their own risk of becoming alcoholic (Schuckit, 1987; Ackerman, 1983; Vaillant, 1983). This is because of a genetic predisposition toward alcoholism, and evidence suggests that this genetic predisposition also requires certain environmental factors to trigger the development of alcoholism.

However, if the individual has *ever* had an addiction disorder, be it to another drug, sex, food, or any of the other forms of addiction, then this person should certainly be considered *at risk* for alcoholism.

SUMMARY

In this chapter we have explored how alcohol affects the body and some of the more common complications of alcohol use and addiction. The course of alcoholism is fluctuating, according to Schuckit (1984), and in all too many cases the alcohol addiction is not recognized until too late. Alcohol at least contributes to numerous diseases, if it is not the sole causal agent of these different diseases.

We have also explored various theories about the nature of addiction to alcohol. To date, there is no clearly identified factor, or combination of factors, that seems to bring about alcoholism. Rather, based on the current literature, one gets the impression that there are various forms of alcoholism, each of which might have a different set of supporting factors.

CHAPTER 4

Barbiturates and the CNS Depressants

It is safe to assume that man has suffered from the symptoms of anxiety for thousands of years. Indeed, as Gelenberg (1983) observed, anxiety is a universal human experience in response to the stress of day to day living. Each year, some 11% of the adults in this country use an antianxiety agent at least once (Sussman, 1988). The most commonly used antianxiety agents today are the benzodiazepines (Sussman, 1988).

Anxiety can range from a mild sense of irritability and uneasiness to severe panic states where the individual might feel a sense of impending doom or a fear that they are about to die (Gelenberg, 1983). Until recently, alcohol was perhaps the only chemical agent that could be used in the control of the symptoms of anxiety. It was only in the last century that a number of other drugs became available for the treatment of anxiety. These new antianxiety[1] agents included the bromides, the barbiturate family of chemicals, meprobamate, and the various members of the benzodiazepine chemical group (Feighner, 1987).

These chemicals, despite superficial differences in chemical structure, are all CNS depressants. They all share common characteristics, and to a significant degree potentiate the effects of other CNS depressants. Although such drugs have a proven potential for abuse, they are also the treatment of choice by physicians for the control of the symptoms of anxiety.

The prevalence of sedative abuse in this country "probably exceeds that of the opiates" (Mirin and Weiss, 1983, p. 237). Sedative abuse, however, has not received the same publicity as narcotic addiction. Thus, the chemical dependency counselor or mental health professional will be working with people who are using these drugs on a regular basis, either legally or illegally. We will begin our review of the antianxiety agents with the barbiturates.

HISTORY OF THE BARBITURATES

The history of alcohol is a long one, and has been discussed elsewhere (see chapter two). In brief, however, the major reason alcohol was regard-

[1]Occasionally, mental health professionals will use the term *anxiolytic* rather than antianxiety. In this section, however, the term antianxiety will be utilized.

ed as a medicine was that it could be used both to induce sleep and (if the person drank enough) to control pain. For much of history, alcohol was one of the few chemical agents that could be used with consistent, and usually predictable, results by physicians.

The barbiturates, as a class of drugs, are relative newcomers when compared to alcohol. Barbiturates were discovered in the last half of the 19th century, by a German scientist. However, it was not until the year 1903 that the first barbiturate—Veronal—was introduced for human use (Peluso and Peluso, 1988). Since then, some 2500 *different* barbiturates have been isolated in laboratories.

But for the most part only about fifty forms of barbiturates are used today (Lingeman, 1974), and the barbiturates have largely been replaced by the benzodiazepines (Schuckit, 1984). In spite of the introduction of newer drugs, there are still some areas of medicine where the barbiturates remain the drug of choice. Thus, in spite of the introduction of newer drugs over the years, pharmaceutical companies continue to manufacture barbiturates, and mental health professionals still encounter individuals who are either using prescribed barbiturates or are abusing barbiturates.

The barbiturates have a considerable abuse potential. It has been estimated that between one-fifth (Lingeman, 1974) to as much as *one-half* (Matuschka, 1985) of the 300 tons of barbiturates manufactured in the United States each year is diverted to the black market. Peluso and Peluso (1988) reported that a recent list of the twelve most frequently abused prescription drugs included three barbiturates and two barbituratelike drugs. Barbiturates thus represent a significant part of the drug abuse problem.

PHARMACOLOGY OF THE BARBITURATES

Julien (1981) observed that barbiturates fall into four different classes.[2] Barbiturates are classified by their *duration of action*. That is, the length of time the drug will continue to affect the person taking it.

First, there are the *ultrashort-acting* barbiturates, the effects of which last for less than one hour. Examples of such ultrashort barbiturates include Pentothal and Brevital (Schuckit, 1984). Such drugs are often used in surgical procedures, where a short duration of action is desirable.

Second, there are the *short-acting* barbiturates, the effects of which will last for less than three hours. Barbiturates that fall into this classification include Nembutal, among others (Schuckit, 1984). Third, there are the *intermediate-acting* barbiturates, the effects of which last three to six hours. Included in this group are such drugs as Amytal. Fourth, there are the *long-acting* barbiturates, the effects of which last longer than six hours

---

[2]Other authors might use different classification systems for the barbiturates, usually classifying them as ultrashort, intermediate, and long acting. Again, such classification systems are based on the duration of action of the various barbiturates.

(Abel, 1982). Phenobarbital is perhaps the most commonly encountered drug in this class.

The barbiturates, as a class, are chemically similar and thus tend to have similar effects on the person using them. The only major difference between the barbiturates is the length of time that it takes the individual's body to absorb, metabolize (break down), and excrete the different forms of barbiturate. Other than this, they have remarkably similar effects on the human body. Gelenberg (1983) noted that the short-term barbiturates were rapidly inactivated by the liver, where the long-term barbiturates such as phenobarbital were eliminated from the body largely unchanged by the kidneys, which allowed the long-term barbiturates to remain active for a longer period of time.

The barbiturate molecule is rapidly and completely absorbed through the stomach and small intestine, and barbiturates are usually administered orally (Julien, 1981). Rarely, however, one of the ultrashort-acting barbiturates might be administered intravenously for use as an anesthetic in surgery. This is a dangerous procedure, which requires *immediate* access to life-support systems in case of adverse side effects.

The barbiturates, like alcohol, are well absorbed from the stomach and small intestine. The *Harvard Medical School Mental Health Newsletter* (1988) noted that, with the exception of the fact that barbiturates have a longer effect than does alcohol, the action of this class of drugs was very similar to that of alcohol. The barbiturates are distributed throughout the body and affect all body tissue to some degree. Matuschka (1985) noted that at normal dosage levels the barbiturates depress not only the activity of the brain, but also to a lesser degree the activity of muscle tissues, the heart, and respiration.

The barbiturates are able to reach the brain itself rather quickly, and depending on the dose of the particular barbiturate used, it will act either as a sedative or a hypnotic. Like alcohol, the barbiturates are *global* in action, which is to say that the barbiturates will affect the entire central nervous system (Sheridan, Patterson, and Gustafson, 1982). However, at normal dosage levels the barbiturates have the greatest impact on the cortex itself, as well as the reticular activating system of the brain (which is responsible for awareness) and the medulla oblongata (which controls respiration) (Matuschka, 1985).

The *primary* use for barbiturates today is to produce sedation, or sleep, although the barbiturates have also been found useful in the control of epilepsy (Julien, 1981; Ray, 1983). Schuckit (1984) notes that the short-acting class of barbiturates, that is to say that class of barbiturates whose effects last less than three hours, are the barbiturates most frequently abused. Jenike (1987) warned, however, that as tolerance to the barbiturates develops, there is no concomitant increase in the lethal dose. Thus, as the person abusing the barbiturates increases the dosage levels to achieve the same effect, he or she will come closer and closer to the lethal dose.

The effects of the CNS depressants in general and barbiturates in particular will vary depending on the amount of the drug ingested and the potency of the specific drug being used. At normal dosage levels, the effects of the barbiturates are very similar to those seen with alcohol (Peluso and Peluso, 1988). Cross-tolerance between alcohol and the barbiturates is common, as is some degree of cross-tolerance between the barbiturates and the opiates, which also have a depressant effect on the central nervous system (Matuschka, 1985).

Withdrawal from CNS depressants is dangerous, and should only be attempted in a medical setting (Matuschka, 1985; Kauffman, Shaffer, and Burglas, 1985; Schuckit, 1984). They should *never* be abruptly withdrawn, as to do so "entails a substantial risk of sensory confusion, seizures, functional brain damage, and even death" (Kauffman, et al., 1985).

Ray (1983) noted that abrupt withdrawal from the barbiturates without medical supervision may result in death in approximately 5% of the cases, a figure Lingeman (1974) agrees with. Thus, barbiturate withdrawal, like alcohol withdrawal, carries with it a risk of death, which is not usually true for opiate withdrawal.

SUBJECTIVE EFFECTS OF BARBITURATES

At Normal Dosage Levels

At low doses, the barbiturates reduce feelings of anxiety and create a sense of euphoria. These effects are thought to reflect the disinhibition effect of the barbiturates on the cortex (Abel, 1982). The exact mechanism by which barbiturates bring this about is not known (Sheridan, Patterson, and Gustafson, 1982), although there are many theories as to how these drugs work.

The physical sensations brought about by low doses of barbiturates are very similar to those of alcohol, and the subjective effects are "practically indistinguishable from alcohol's" (Peluso and Peluso, 1988, p. 54). This is to be expected, since both alcohol and the barbiturates affect the cortex of the brain. Clinically, the effects of the barbiturates might be indistinguishable from the effects of alcohol, especially when above-normal doses are used.

The *Harvard Medical School Mental Health Letter* (1988) reported that barbiturate intoxication closely resembles alcohol intoxication. Sheridan, Patterson, and Gustafson (1982) reported that, at low dosage levels, the barbiturates bring about decreased motor activity, sedation, and possibly a feeling of elation or euphoria. Patients who are intoxicated by barbiturates will demonstrate such behaviors as slurred speech and unsteady gait (Jenike, 1987). Like alcohol, the barbiturates are capable of causing both tolerance and physical dependence (Jenike, 1987).

As the dosage level of barbiturates is increased, the reticular formation of the brain is affected. This is the part of the brain thought to be responsible for screening out unwanted sensory stimuli, and is involved in attending to our environment. In a sense, the reticular formation helps us to maintain contact with the relevant parts of our environment, while screening out information that is not immediately relevant.

An example of this would be a mother who could sleep through a thunderstorm, but who awakens immediately when her child starts to cry. Even during sleep, the reticular formation continues to function. In the example given above, the reticular formation will screen out the distracting sounds of the thunderstorm to allow sleep to continue; however, as soon as the infant starts to cry, the mother awakens.

When the reticular formation is affected by a low dose of one of the barbiturates, the drug will function as a sedative. If the dose is increased, hypnosis (sleep) is achieved. Indeed, the barbiturates had long been used in the treatment of insomnia, until the introduction of the benzodiazepines in the 1960s.

However, Abel (1982) notes that the sleep one achieves through the use of barbiturates is not the same as the normal state of sleep. The barbiturates suppress the REM state of sleep (Abel, 1982; Peluso and Peluso, 1988). Research has demonstrated that about one-quarter of a young adult's sleep time is spent in REM sleep (Foulkes, 1979). Adequate, and appropriate, sleep patterns seem to play a role in emotional as well as physical health (Fiss, 1979). Thus, through the interference with normal sleep patterns, barbiturate-induced sleep may have an impact on the emotional and physical health of the individual.

Furthermore, Gelenberg (1983) observed that tolerance begins to develop to the hypnotic effect of the barbiturates within a matter of days. When used for long periods of time as a sleep aid and then discontinued, the barbiturates cause the person to enter a state of REM rebound. This is where the person will dream more intensely and more vividly for a period of time, as the body tries to catch up on lost REM sleep time (Abel, 1982).

These dreams have been described by individuals as nightmares strong enough to tempt the individual to return to the use of drugs in order to get a "good night's sleep again." This rebound effect lasts for several nights, after which there is a gradual return to a normal sleep pattern. Further, the barbiturates have been found to add only about 20 to 40 minutes to the individual's actual sleep time (Ray, 1983).

Another drawback of the barbiturates is what is called drug "hangover" (Govoni and Hayes, 1985). The physical experience of barbiturate hangover is similar to that of an alcohol hangover, in that the individual is simply "unable to get going" the next day. Barbiturates often require an extended period of time for the body to completely metabolize and excrete.

The time necessary for the individual's body to metabolize one-half of the original dose ingested is called the *half-life* of the drug. The process of detoxification is *not instantaneous*. Small amounts of the barbiturates will remain in the person's bloodstream for hours, or even days, after one dose of the drug. Julien (1981), for example, noted that the effects of the barbiturates on judgment, motor skills, and behavior *might last for several days after a single dose of a barbiturate.*

If the person continually adds to this reservoir of unmetabolized drug by taking repeated doses of the drug, there is a greater chance that the individual will experience a drug hangover. However, whether because of a single dose or repeated doses, the drug hangover is caused by traces of unmetabolized barbiturates remaining in the individual's bloodstream when he or she wakes up the next day. The individual might feel "not quite awake," or drugged, as she or he attempts to meet the demands of the day. In some cases, individuals have been known to use CNS stimulants such as the amphetamines to counteract the effects of the depressants used the night before.

At Above-Normal Dosage Levels

If the dosage level is increased beyond that normally necessary to induce sleep, or if the individual has used different CNS depressants at once, several things will happen to the individual. There is a progressive loss of reflex activity, and depression of respiratory and vasomotor functions as the barbiturates interfere with the normal function of the medulla oblongata, the part of the brain that maintains respiration. If not corrected, the barbiturates may cause coma and death (Jenike, 1987).

When used for an extended period of time, these drugs may also bring about physical dependence and a characteristic withdrawal syndrome, very similar to that seen in alcohol withdrawal. Honigfeld and Howard (1978) note that after tolerance to the effects of the barbiturates has developed, the individual's body becomes more efficient in breaking down the barbiturates and at functioning in spite of the continued presence of the drug.

Lingeman (1974) observed that while tolerance might develop to the effects of the barbiturates, this physical tolerance does not alter the lethal dose of the drug to any significant degree. Which is to say that while the individual might need more and more of the drug to achieve the same effect once achieved at a lower dose, because of the tolerance factor, the amount of the drug necessary for an overdose—and death—does not change significantly.

The barbiturates are involved in some 3000 drug-related deaths each year, many of which may be unintentional overdoses (Julien, 1981). Peluso and Peluso (1988) reported that barbiturates accounted for about three-quarters of all drug-related deaths as recently as a few years ago.

The barbiturates present a significant withdrawal danger. Schuckit (1984) notes that the severity of the withdrawal syndrome "in general parallels the strength of the drug, the doses taken, and the length of administration" (p. 22). As a general rule, abuse of 500 mg per day of barbiturates, *or the equivalent dose of other drugs*, will result in a significant risk of withdrawal seizures in the normal individual after a period of time (Schuckit, 1984). Withdrawal from the barbiturates is dangerous and potentially fatal (Slaby, Lieb, and Tancredi, 1981).

As noted above, the barbiturates have a significant potential for physical dependence, as well as tolerance. A pregnant woman may transmit the barbiturates to the fetus through the placenta, and nursing mothers should not use this class of drugs unless under a physician's care. It is possible for the infant to be born with an addiction to barbiturates if the mother has used this class of drugs prior to delivery. Barbiturate withdrawal in the newborn is more complicated than narcotic withdrawal in the newborn (Peluso and Peluso, 1988).

The elderly, or those with impaired liver function, are especially likely to have difficulty with the barbiturates. This is because it will take longer for their bodies to metabolize the drug. Sheridan, Patterson, and Gustafson (1982) advised that older individuals who receive barbiturates be started at one-half the usual adult dosage, because their livers might not be able to metabolize larger doses.

The mixture of alcohol with barbiturates is especially dangerous, because each drug potentiates the effects of the other, by "competing" with the other drug in the liver (Schuckit, 1984). In other words, each drug interferes with the metabolism of the other in the liver, allowing the toxic effects of both drugs to continue with greater intensity than one would expect. Death often results from an overdose combination of alcohol and barbiturates, or barbiturates and another CNS depressant.

With the introduction of the benzodiazepines in the 1960s, barbiturates seem to have fallen into some disfavor, especially as an antianxiety agent and a sleep aid. The *Harvard Medical School Mental Health Letter* noted that the barbiturates are "now generally considered obsolete" (p. 1). They continue to be useful as a surgical anesthetic and in the control of epilepsy. It should be noted, however, that there are exceptions to this rule, and one will still occasionally encounter a person who continues to abuse barbiturates.

BARBITURATELIKE DRUGS

Because of the many adverse side effects of the barbiturates, pharmaceutical companies have long searched for substitutes that might be effective, yet safe to use. During the 1950s, a number of other drugs were introduced to treat the same conditions for which the barbiturates were used. These drugs included Quaalude and Sopor (both brand names of methaqualone),[3] Doriden (glutethimide), Placidyl (ethchlorvynol), and Noludar (methyprylon).

[3]The *brand name* of each drug is given first, with the generic name in parentheses.

Julien (1981) notes that the chemical structure of many of these drugs is very similar to that of the barbiturates. Not surprisingly, these drugs also have an abuse potential that is very similar to that seen with barbiturates. Schuckit (1984) observed that Placidyl (ethchlorvynol) and Doriden (glutethimide) are especially dangerous, and recommends that neither drug be used. Kauffman, et al. (1985), note that because the range between the therapeutic dosage level and the toxic dose of the drug is extremely small, Doriden is extremely dangerous. Harvey (1985) noted that Doriden has "little to recommend its continued use as a sedative-hypnotic" (p. 363).

Methaqualone has achieved significant popularity in the drug world, and is purported to have aphrodisiac properties (which have not been proven) (Mirin and Weiss, 1983). Although this drug was withdrawn from the market in America, there are addicts who claim to have used methaqualone manufactured in Mexico and smuggled into this country.

Individuals who have used methaqualone report feelings of euphoria, well-being, and behavioral disinhibition. The usual hypnotic dose is between 150 and 300 mg, but some individuals have been known to use 2000 mg in a single day (Mirin and Weiss, 1983). Death from methaqualone overdose has occurred, especially when the drug is taken with alcohol.

THE BENZODIAZEPINES

In the 1960s, the first of a new class of drugs, the *Benzodiazepines* were introduced. Since then, the benzodiazepines have become the treatment of choice for the control of anxiety (Rickels, Giesecke, and Geller, 1987). Some of the drugs in this family include Valium (diazepam), Librium (chlordiazepoxide), Dalmane (flurazepam), Xanax (alprazolam), Ativan (lorazepam), and a range of others. Schuckit (1984) noted that each of these drugs was initially introduced as "nonaddictive and safe" (p. 23) substitutes for the barbiturates.

Over the years, however, many researchers have found that the benzodiazepines present some danger of addiction (Schuckit, 1984). Jenike (1987) reported that a person who took 80 to 120 mg of diazepam a day for 40 to 50 days would become addicted to this benzodiazepine, while between 300 and 600 mg of chlordiazepoxide a day for 60 to 180 days would result in addiction to this benzodiazepine. The author reported that the time required for dependence to develop to the other benzodiazepines is not known at this time.

Juergens and Morse (1988) reported that withdrawal symptoms for alprazolam (or other benzodiazepines) will be observed in patients who have taken prescribed dosage levels for longer than four months. The authors noted that the pharmacological characteristics of Xanax, which reaches peak blood levels in 1–2 hours and is fully metabolized in 6–16 hours, make it especially attractive as a drug of abuse.

The authors offered case histories on seven patients, six of them women, who became addicted to alprazolam after receiving prescriptions for the treatment of anxiety or depression. Juergens and Morse (1988) reported that all seven patients had withdrawal symptoms when the medication was discontinued and concluded that six of the patients demonstrated some degree of tolerance to the drug's effects. Given this fact, it is quite disturbing to note that the journal, *American Druggist* (1989), reported that Xanax (alprazolam) was the third most commonly prescribed drug in the United States during 1988.

Peluso and Peluso (1988) estimated that *ten million Americans* have used benzodiazepines for nonmedical purposes at some point, and that four million Americans are estimated to have done so in the last year alone. Woods, Katz, and Winger (1988) suggest that about 1% of the population uses benzodiazepines for nonmedical purposes each year, and in general downplayed the danger of addiction to the benzodiazepines.

Medical Uses of the Benzodiazepines

The benzodiazepine family of drugs is one of the most frequently prescribed classes of drugs (Rickels, Schweizer, and Lucki, 1987). Valium (diazepam) is often used as a muscle relaxant, while Clonopin (clonazepam) has been found useful in the control of some forms of epilepsy. Some other members of the benzodiazepine family of drugs have been found useful as *short-term* sleep aids. Such benzodiazepines include Restoril (temazepam), Halcion (triazolam), and Dalmane (flurazepam).

The benzodiazepines have been found to be most useful in the *short-term* control of the symptoms of anxiety and are "by far the most widely used of the anxiolytics and hypnotics" (Rickels, Schweizer, and Lucki, 1987, p. 781). Specific benzodiazepines that are used in the treatment of anxiety include: Valium (diazepam), Librium (chlordiazepoxide), Tranxene (clorazepate), Xanax (alprazolam), and Ativan (lorazepam).

Schuckit (1984) noted that the antianxiety effects of the benzodiazepines last about two to three weeks, and that these drugs are not useful in treating anxiety continuously over a long period of time. The *Harvard Medical School Mental Health Letter* (1988) did not support this conclusion, however, concluding that while patients might develop some tolerance to the sedative effects of benzodiazepines, they did not become tolerant to the antianxiety effects of these medications.

Woods, et al. (1988), noted that there is some controversy as to whether the benzodiazepines are effective in the long-term control of anxiety. The authors estimated that 15% of those who use benzodiazepines take the medication on a daily basis for a year or longer. Woods, et al., observed that those who take benzodiazepines for extended periods of time tend to be older, have a history of treatment by mental health professionals, and suffer from multiple health problems.

The possibility of suicide through a drug overdose is a very real concern for the physician. The benzodiazepines are considered to be a very "safe" drug because there is a large range between the normal therapeutic dose and the lethal dose. Of some 8000 benzodiazepine overdoses, involving *only* benzodiazepines, only one death was reported. Rickels, Schweizer, and Lucki (1987) reported that while the benzodiazepines were implicated in one-fourth to one-half of all drug overdoses, in virtually every case where the overdose resulted in death another drug was also involved.

(NOTE: Because of the danger of potentiation brought on by combinations of various drugs, such as combinations of a benzodiazepine and another CNS depressant such as alcohol or opiates, *any suspected drug overdose should **always** be treated by a physician*.)

Pharmacology of the Benzodiazepines

Where the barbiturates depress the normal function of the *entire* neuron, the benzodiazepines are more selective in their action. Clinical research has suggested that the benzodiazepines will affect only the action of a single neurotransmitter. This neurotransmitter, which is known as Gamma aminobutyric acid (GABA), serves as a biochemical "brake". GABA serves to shape and slow neurotransmitter activity in the brain. Neurons that utilize GABA are widely distributed throughout the central nervous system, including the cortex and the hippocampus areas of the brain (Angevine and Cotman, 1981).

The benzodiazepines facilitate the action of GABA, allowing this neurotransmitter to reduce the level of nerve excitement without blocking the other activities of the brain. Recently, researchers suggested that the benzodiazepines work by blocking the neuron action of a specific portion of the brain, the locus coeruleus (Upjohn Company, 1989). Nerve fibers from this portion of the brain connect with other parts of the brain thought to be involved in fear and panic reactions. By blocking the stimulation of the neurons of the locus coeruleus, the benzodiazepines are thought to reduce anxiety levels.

The barbiturates, in contrast, depress the *entire* range of activity of neurons in many different parts of the brain, including the cortex. The barbiturates achieve a more global reduction in nerve cell activity, and tend to cause sedation along with a reduction in anxiety levels.

Because their action is more selective than that of barbiturates, the benzodiazepines have become the drug of choice for the treatment of anxiety and as an aid to sleep. The *Harvard Medical School Mental Health Letter* (1988) noted that the benzodiazepines are very similar in their actions, differing mainly in the duration of action. Unlike the barbiturates, excessive sedation at normal dosage levels of the benzodiazepines is rare.

Rickels, Schweizer, and Lucki (1987) note that when CNS depression *is* observed with benzodiazepines, it is usually a result of too large a dose being used for that particular person. Sussman (1988) suggested that advancing age may make the individual more susceptible to the sedation, impaired motor coordination, memory loss, and respiratory depression occasionally found as a side effect of benzodiazepine use.

Benzodiazepine Abuse and Addiction

It has been reported that the benzodiazepines are frequently over-prescribed. Peluso and Peluso (1988) stated that three-quarters of the prescriptions written for benzodiazepines are for conditions inconsistent with the recommended uses of these drugs. Woods, Katz, and Winger (1988) challenged this conclusion. The authors stated that in the vast majority of cases, the benzodiazepines are appropriately prescribed and used according to instructions (Woods, et al. (1988).

It was claimed that *1.5 million* Americans were addicted to benzodiazepines, with the vast majority of these people being women (Peluso and Peluso, 1988). Indeed, *65%* of the Valium (just one of the benzodiazepine family of drugs) users are women (Peluso and Peluso, 1988). Schuckit (1984) noted that with the exception of differences in the potency of the various antianxiety agents, virtually all of the CNS depressants have demonstrated tolerance and withdrawal patterns that are quite similar to those of the barbiturates.

The *Harvard Medical School Mental Health Letter* (1988) admitted that at normal dosage levels, physical dependence to the benzodiazepines was possible in four to six weeks, in some cases. However, in most cases it would require four to six months for dependence to develop to this class of medication. It was noted that "most" (p. 3) patients would experience withdrawal symptoms after eight months of benzodiazepine use at normal dosage levels, and "after a year almost all" (p. 3) patients would experience some symptoms of withdrawal from benzodiazepines.

Woods, et al., (1988) agreed that the benzodiazepines had some abuse potential, and warned physicians that

> . . . a mild degree of physiological dependence is likely to develop in some patients taking benzodiazepines on a regular basis for several months (p. 3478).

In general, the authors downplayed the abuse potential of benzodiazepines except for individuals with a history of drug abuse. Woods, et al. (1988), also concluded that the benzodiazepines possessed no significant reinforcement potential and claimed that most patients do not increase the dosage levels above what was prescribed, even if they were addicted to these drugs. The only exception were those people who had a history of abusing CNS depressants.

Complications Caused by Benzodiazepine Use at Normal Dosage Levels

The benzodiazepines are not perfect drugs. Harvey (1985) notes that tolerance to the anticonvulsant effects of benzodiazepines is possible, and because of this the benzodiazepines are of only limited value in the control of epilepsy. Also, while the benzodiazepines at normal dosage levels are not general neuronal depressants, as are the barbiturates, excessive sedation is occasionally seen even at normal dosage levels.

The elderly, for reasons that are not clearly understood, are especially vulnerable to being oversedated by benzodiazepines (Rickels, Schweizer, and Lucki, 1987). The same is often true for persons with liver damage. Patients on benzodiazepines who are also using other CNS depressants such as antihistamines, narcotics, or alcohol are also at risk of oversedation because of the potentiation between different CNS depressants.[4]

When oversedation occurs, the individual is likely to experience feelings of drowsiness, fatigue, light-headedness, dizziness, and mental or physical slowing. By adjusting the dosage schedule, or the amount of the specific drug being used, it is usually possible to avoid such problems.

Occasionally, at normal dosage levels, the benzodiazepines bring about a degree of irritability, hostility, or aggression. Beasley (1987) reported that it is common for the combination of alcohol and benzodiazepines to bring about this paradoxical rage reaction, noting that ". . . hundreds of reports on the so-called 'paradoxical rage reaction' in individuals combining alcohol and diazepam are now on file . . ." (p. 123). However, the *paradoxical rage reaction* is also seen on occasion in persons using only benzodiazepines at therapeutic doses.

Hand (1989) noted that since the benzodiazepine Halcion (triazolam) was introduced, some 2300 adverse reactions have been reported to the manufacturer, Upjohn Pharmaceuticals. The author concluded that:

> . . . compared with other benzodiazepines, triazolam causes more agitation, confusion, amnesia, hallucinations, and bizarre or abnormal behavior. Suicides, attempted suicides, deaths, and violent crimes have been associated with triazolam administration. In most of the adverse reaction reports, the drug was taken as recommended (p. 3).

This paradox, that of a rage reaction in a person who has used a tranquilizer, is thought to be the result of the disinhibition effects of the benzodiazepines. Which is to say that, as the benzodiazepine lowers social inhibitions, the person is more likely to engage in behavior that they successfully controlled previously. A similar effect is often seen in persons who drink alcohol.

The possibility that the benzodiazepines will contribute to memory

---

[4]When in doubt about whether two or more medications should be used together, *always* consult a physician or the local poison control center.

problems has also been suggested (Schuckit, 1984; Rickels, Giesecke, and Geller, 1987). Indeed, evidence exists that even at therapeutic dosage levels, the benzodiazepines may interfere with the formation of memory patterns (Plasky, Marcus, and Salzman, 1988; Harvey, 1985). Hand (1989) reported that one benzodiazepine commonly used as a sleep aid, Halcion (triazolam), could cause memory disturbance when used at therapeutic dosage levels.

This process is termed *anterograde amnesia,* which is a form of amnesia that involves the formation of memories after a specific event (Plasky, Marcus, and Salzman, 1988). A person with anterograde amnesia might be unable to remember information presented to them after the ingestion of the drug. At normal dosage levels, the benzodiazepines might also disrupt the normal psychomotor skills necessary to drive an automobile or work with dangerous power tools.

This effect is not as apparent in situations where the individual is "allowed to compensate on a difficult task by performing it more slowly" (Rickels, Schwiezer, and Lucki, 1987, p. 784). However, tasks that require vigilance or speed of motor performance might be affected by benzodiazepine use. Rickels, Schwiezer, and Lucki (1987) report that "caution should be exercised" (p. 785) by patients who use benzodiazepines and who also drive. Woods, et al., (1988), suggested that such changes in psychomotor coordination might persist for several days following the initial use of benzodiazepines.

The benzodiazepine family of drugs occasionally will produce mild respiratory depression, even at normal therapeutic dosage levels. These results are seen most often in persons with pulmonary disease; however, the use of the benzodiazepines should be avoided in patients who suffer from sleep apnea, chronic lung disease, or other sleep-related breathing disorders (Rickels, Schwiezer, and Lucki, 1987). Doghramji (1989) warned against the use of CNS depressants by patients who suffer from Alzheimer's disease, as such medications might potentiate preexisting sleep apnea problems.

Graedon (1980) warned that Dalmane, which is often used in the treatment of insomnia, tends to build up in the individual's system. If the person uses Dalmane for even a few days he or she might experience significant levels of CNS depression. If this person ingests alcohol, or possibly an over-the-counter cold remedy after using Dalmane for even a few days, the remaining Dalmane could combine with the depressant effects of the alcohol or cold remedy to produce serious levels of CNS depression.

Gold (1988) observed that CNS depressants such as alcohol, barbiturates, and the benzodiazepines, may interfere with spinal-cord-mediated reflexes necessary for erection and orgasm in the male. Women on CNS depressants might experience a decrease in vaginal secretion in spite of sexual excitement. These effects might be found even when these drugs are used at normal dosage levels.

Subjective Experience of Benzodiazepine Agent Use

When used as an antianxiety agent at normal dosage levels, the benzodiazepines will induce a gentle state of relaxation. When used in the treatment of insomnia, the benzodiazepines initially reduce the sleep latency period and the number of times a person might awaken during the night (Harvey, 1985). This effect is often greatest in those persons who experience some degree of insomnia (Harvey, 1985). At first, persons who use the benzodiazepines to help them sleep often report a sense of deep and refreshing sleep.

However, the benzodiazepine family of drugs also interferes with the normal sleep cycle, reducing the amount of REM sleep. It is during the REM phase of sleep that we dream, and experimental research suggests that dreaming is necessary for mental health (Hobson, 1989). Alcohol, the barbiturates, and the benzodiazepines have all been proven to interfere with the amount of REM sleep the user achieves.

When a person discontinues the use of a CNS depressant he or she will experience the REM rebound effect (Woods, et al., 1988) described earlier in this chapter, in which the individual experiences an increase in the amount of sleep time spent in REM sleep, accompanied by more vivid and often frightening dreams. It is as if the brain is attempting to make up for lost REM sleep by making the person dream more often and more intensely. Under normal conditions, such as the night after a bad night's sleep, REM rebound will result in an insignificant increase in total REM sleep; however, chronic use of the CNS depressants, or even limited use of CNS depressants in certain individuals, can cause a significant rebound effect. The *Harvard Medical School Mental Health Letter* (1988) observed that rebound anxiety and insomnia lasting from three days to three weeks had been reported in some cases where the individual had used a benzodiazepine as a sleep aid for only one or two weeks.

This finding is unusual, and most people will experience REM rebound only after a more protracted period of drug use. The vivid dreams that are experienced when the person is going through a period of severe REM rebound are often quite frightening. There are cases on record where these nightmares have motivated the person to return to drug use in order to "get a good night's sleep" again.

Long-Term Consequences of Chronic Benzodiazepine Abuse

Although introduced as safe and nonaddicting substitutes for the barbiturates, it has been found that the benzodiazepines do indeed have a significant abuse potential. As noted above, Peluso and Peluso (1988) estimated that some 4 million Americans have used Valium for nonmedical purposes in the last year, and that 10 million have done so at some point in their lives. Dietch (1983) explored the nature of benzodiazepine abuse and outlined several criteria to aid in the recognition of benzodiazepine abuse.

These criteria included: (1) taking the drug after the medical/psychiatric need for its use had passed, (2) symptoms of physical or psychological dependence on one of the benzodiazepines, (3) taking the drug in amounts greater than the prescribed amount, (4) taking the drug to obtain an euphoriant effect, and (5) using the drug in order to decrease self-awareness.

The development of physical dependence on the benzodiazepines is a function of the dosage level of the drug being used, and the length of time that the person has used the drug. Kauffman et al. (1985), noted that Valium (diazepam) might produce minimal withdrawal symptoms in the first five days for the heavy user, and that withdrawal symptoms from Valium seem to reach their peak between the fifth and ninth days (p. 119).

Dietch (1983) noted that abstinence symptoms of benzodiazepine addiction might include anxiety, insomnia, dizziness, nausea and vomiting, muscle weakness, tremor, confusion, convulsions (seizures), and a drug-induced withdrawal psychosis. In addition to the problems of physical dependence, Dietch noted that it is possible to become psychologically dependent on benzodiazepines. Indeed, Dietch noted that "Psychological dependence on benzodiazepines appears to be more common than physical dependence" (p. 1140). Psychologically dependent persons might either take the drug continuously, or intermittently, because they *believe* they need benzodiazepines in spite of their actual medical requirements. The actual numbers of persons who are psychologically dependent on benzodiazepines is unknown.

There is a tendency, at least among some users of the benzodiazepines, to increase dosage levels above that prescribed by physicians. This phenomenon is not well understood, as there is no clear-cut development of tolerance to benzodiazepines. However, it was noted that, ". . . the magnitude of such increases appears to be small . . ." and that in general ". . . subjects tended to titrate their dose according to the level of environmental stress" (Dietch, 1983, p. 1141).

The limited information on this phenomenon is based on patients who were prescribed one of the benzodiazepines for medical/psychiatric reasons. There is virtually no information on how drug abusers might use this class of drugs or what dosage level might be preferred by drug addicts. Woods, et al. (1988), postulated that the person who was most likely to abuse benzodiazepines was one who had a history of polydrug abuse.

All of the CNS depressants, including the benzodiazepines, are capable of producing a *toxic psychosis,* especially in overdose situations. This condition might also be called an *organic brain syndrome* by some professionals. Schuckit (1984) notes that this toxic psychosis includes auditory hallucinations and/or paranoid delusions, and notes that this drug-induced psychosis should clear in 2 to 14 days.

As with the barbiturates, withdrawal from benzodiazepines should only be attempted under the supervision of a physician. Severe withdrawal symptoms may include hyperthermia, delirium, convulsions, a drug-

induced psychosis, and possible death (Jenike, 1987). Detoxification may be necessary on an inpatient basis in some cases, although Woods, et al. (1988), noted that most patients can be slowly withdrawn from benzodiazepines with few or no side effects.

Surprisingly, in spite of all that is known about the barbiturates and the CNS depressants in general, people still abuse them in significant numbers. It has been reported that many individuals who abuse the amphetamines and cocaine (see the chapter on CNS stimulants) will use depressants either to control some of the side effects of their stimulant use, or to "come down" from the stimulants in order to sleep (Peluso and Peluso, 1988). Alcoholics will often use CNS depressants during the daytime, to avoid the telltale smell of alcohol at work (Peluso and Peluso, 1988).

In the time since their introduction in the 1960s, the benzodiazepines have become one of the most frequently prescribed medications. As a class, the benzodiazepines are the treatment of choice for the control of anxiety. They have also become a significant part of the drug abuse problem. In spite of the fact that many of the benzodiazepines were first introduced as "nonaddicting and safe" substitutes for the barbiturates, there is evidence to suggest that they have an abuse potential similar to that of the barbiturate family of drugs.

ENTER BUSPIRONE: A NEW ERA IN THE CONTROL OF ANXIETY?

Recently, a new medication, BuSpar (buspirone) was introduced. BuSpar is an antianxiety agent that is not a member of the benzodiazepine family. It is chemically unrelated to currently available antianxiety compounds, presents a clinical picture of fewer side effects, but is "comparable with . . . both diazepam and clorazepate" (Feighner, 1987, p. 15).

Clinical testing would suggest that buspirone does not cause significant sedation or fatigue (Feighner, 1987), and there was no evidence of potentiation between buspirone and select benzodiazepines, or alcohol and buspirone (Feighner, 1987).[5] Research has found that buspirone use might result in gastrointestinal problems, drowsiness, decreased concentration, dizziness, headache, feelings of lightheadedness, nervousness, diarrhea, excitement, sweating/clamminess, nausea, and feelings of fatigue (Newton, Marunycz, Alderdice, and Napoliello, 1986; Feighner, 1987).

Unlike the benzodiazepine family of drugs, buspirone has no anticonvulsant action, nor is it useful as a muscle relaxant (Eison and Temple, 1987). The mechanism of action for buspirone is thought to differ from that of the benzodiazepines (Eison and Temple, 1987).

Buspirone is not immediately effective, but must be used for several

---

[5]This is *not*, however, a recommendation that these substances be mixed. As before, alcohol should not be mixed with medication, no matter what the purpose of the medication, or how safe it appears to be.

days before maximum effects are seen. Research has suggested that buspirone has "failed to demonstrate any abuse liability in either animal or human studies" (Lader, 1987, p. 25). Furthermore, there is no evidence of a withdrawal syndrome such as that seen in chronic benzodiazepine abuse (Lader, 1987). Rickels, Giesecke, and Geller (1987) found that buspirone failed to demonstrate any impact on memory in a sample of 39 subjects suffering from generalized anxiety disorder, as measured by psychological tests.

Rickels, Schweizer, Csanalosi, Case, and Chung (1988) noted that buspirone has not been shown to lessen the intensity of withdrawal symptoms experienced by patients who were addicted to benzodiazepines. The authors attempted to identify the long-term effects of buspirone, and found no evidence of tolerance to buspirone's effects over a six-month period of time. The authors also failed to identify any evidence of a physical dependence or withdrawal syndrome from buspirone in that time frame.

Thus, buspirone appears to offer many advantages over the benzodiazepines in the treatment of anxiety states. The reader is cautioned that this is a new drug and much has yet to be learned about it; however, at this point in time, buspirone would seem to be the drug of choice in the treatment of anxiety states in the addiction-prone individual.

CHAPTER 5

Cocaine

The CNS stimulants include such drugs as cocaine, the amphetamine family of drugs, and amphetaminelike drugs such as Ritalin. The behavioral effects of these drugs are remarkably similar, in spite of the specific chemical differences between the various drugs (Gawin and Ellinwood, 1988). Cocaine will be discussed in this chapter, while the other CNS stimulants will be reviewed in the next chapter.

INTRODUCTION TO COCAINE

Cocaine is obtained from the coca bush *Erythroxylon coca*, which grows in the higher elevations of Peru, Bolivia, and Java (Lingeman, 1974). For thousands of years natives have chewed the leaves of the coca plant (Byck, 1987). The drug was, and still is, used as a stimulant to help the natives reduce feelings of fatigue and hunger, so that they may function in the high mountains of South America (Abel, 1982). Prior to the invasion of Peru by the Spanish conquistadores in the 16th century, cocaine was used in religious ceremonies and as a medium of exchange (Ray, 1983). Byck (1987) described cocaine as "a mysterious gift of the gods, used in ancient burials" (p. 5).

White (1989) reported that the modern natives of the mountain regions of Peru chew the leaves mixed with lime, which is obtained from sea shells. The lime works with saliva to release the cocaine from the leaves and also helps to reduce the bitter taste of the coca leaf (White, 1989). Indeed, *some* coca bushes are still grown for native use, although in recent years the majority of such bushes have been grown for the international cocaine trade. White (1989) reported that 60% of the world's supply of the coca plant is grown in Peru, 22% in Bolivia, and 15% in Colombia.

Jaffe (1985) noted that the natives of Peru who continue to chew coca on a regular basis "appear to have little difficulty in discontinuing use of the drug when they move to lower altitudes" (p. 552). Byck (1987) challenged this conclusion, however, noting that "appreciable blood levels" of cocaine might be achieved through the oral use of coca, and that "coca chewers are *de facto* users" (p. 4, italics in original). White (1989) reported that recent research found that chewing coca leaves was not as harmful as was once thought and suggested that the practice might actually help the chewer absorb some of the phosphorus, vitamins, and calcium contained in the mixture.

COCAINE IN MODERN HISTORY

Although coca has been in use for thousands of years, Schuckit (1984) reported that the active agent of coca was only isolated in 1857. Following the isolation of the drug, researchers began to concentrate large amounts of relatively pure cocaine for human use. The newly developed hypodermic needle also made it possible to introduce cocaine directly into the bloodstream for the first time. This was to prove a dangerous combination.

During the late 1800s, Sigmund Freud himself experimented with the drug, at first thinking it a cure for depression (Rome, 1984). [Surprisingly, subsequent research (Post, Weiss, Pert, and Uhde, 1987) has cast doubt on the antidepressant properties of cocaine]. At that time, cocaine was easily available without a prescription. Freud also advocated cocaine as a "cure" for the withdrawal symptoms associated with opiate addiction (Lingeman, 1974; Byck, 1987). However, when Freud discovered the drug's previously unsuspected addictive potential, he discontinued his research on cocaine.

In the late 1800s and early 1900s, cocaine found its way into a wide variety of products and medicines, often without it being mentioned on the label as an active ingredient. The new drink "Coca-cola" was one of many beverages and elixirs that contained cocaine (White, 1989). Following the passage of the Pure Food and Drug Act of 1906, however, it became necessary to list the ingredients of a patent medicine or elixir on the label. As a result of this law, cocaine was removed from many patent medicines.

With the passage of the Harrison Narcotics Act of 1914, nonmedical cocaine use was prohibited (Maranto, 1985). This served to drive recreational cocaine use underground, where it remained until the late 1960s. By then, cocaine had the reputation of being the "champagne of drugs" (White, 1989, p. 34) for those who could afford it. Since the 1960s, cocaine has become increasingly popular, and in the last few years, cocaine use has reached epidemic proportions.

There are many reasons why cocaine became so popular in the late 1960s. During this period in time, there was a growing disillusionment with the amphetamines, which were known killers. Drug users would warn each other that "speed kills," a reference to the fact that the amphetamines could kill the user in a number of ways. However, cocaine had the reputation of bringing about many of the same sensations found in amphetamine use without the risk of addiction (Gawin and Ellinwood, 1988; Maranto, 1985).

Cocaine was almost all but forgotten since the Harrison Narcotics Act of 1914, and the bitter truth about the dangers of cocaine use were either forgotten, or dismissed as "moralistic exaggerations" (Gawin and Ellin-wood, 1988, p. 1173). Jaffe (1985) observed that

> . . . when the popularity of cocaine began to increase in the early 1970's, there was again a tendency to underestimate its toxicity and the seriousness of the dependence that it induces (p. 551).

In the late 1960s and early 1970s, a few respected pharmacologists even attested—incorrectly—to the fact that cocaine was nonaddicting (Maranto, 1985).

In addition to the reputation that cocaine was a "nonaddicting" substitute for the amphetamines, it was also known as a special drug, a "society high" (Doweiko, 1979). These features added to the glamour of cocaine use (White, 1989). Concurrently, during the late 1960s and early 1970s increasing restrictions on the amount of amphetamines manufactured served to tighten the supply of available amphetamines (Lingeman, 1974). As a result, a smaller amount of amphetamines were diverted to illegal markets, which added to a growing demand for a substitute.

It should be noted that, until the latter half of the 1960s, amphetamines were *the* stimulant of choice, and there was little cocaine use being reported. Thus, few professionals had first-hand experience with cocaine addiction. The lessons so painfully learned almost three-quarters of a century earlier about the nature of cocaine addiction were easily forgotten.

In retrospect, by the late 1960s there was a trend away from the amphetamines to cocaine. This is the reverse of what had happened a half century earlier, when cocaine was replaced by the recently introduced amphetamines as the stimulant of abuse. The trend away from cocaine to the amphetamines was brought about by several factors.

First, there was the fact that it was so difficult to obtain cocaine. Second, there was the high cost of cocaine as compared to the amphetamines. Third, there were the known dangers of cocaine use, which in the late 1920s and early 1930s were well documented in the medical literature. Fourth and finally, the effects of cocaine would last only a short time, while the effects of the amphetamines tended to last for hours (Weiner, 1985).

MEDICAL USES OF COCAINE

Cocaine is used by physicians as a topical anesthetic in the ear, nose, throat, rectum, and vagina. On occasion, cocaine is also included in a mixture called *Brompton's cocktail*, which is used to control the pain of cancer (Govoni and Hayes, 1985). The onset of cocaine's action, when used as a local anesthetic, is approximately one minute, with a duration of effect that might last as long as two hours (Govoni and Hayes, 1985).

In the brain, cocaine is thought to block the reabsorption of certain neurotransmitters, after these chemicals have been released across the synapse (Potter, Rudorfer, and Goodwin, 1987). The neurotransmitters involved include dopamine, which is one of the neurotransmitters thought to play a role in the activation of the brain's reward system. By blocking the reabsorption of these neurotransmitters, cocaine will gradually cause the brain to enter a state of neurotransmitter-depletion, which is experienced as a depression by the individual.

SCOPE OF THE PROBLEM OF COCAINE ABUSE

Perhaps 22 million Americans have tried the drug at some point and about 4 million might use the drug on a daily basis (Maranto, 1985). Peluso and Peluso (1988) gave a higher figure, noting that as many as 24 million Americans are regular users of cocaine. L. Siegel (1989) reported that between 500,000 and 750,000 Americans use cocaine daily.

It is estimated that, in 1985 (the last year for which figures are available), Americans consumed an estimated 72 metric tons of cocaine (Lamar, 1987). Decker, Fins, and Frances (1987) estimated that 5000 people a day are introduced to cocaine. Kirsch (1986) reported that "$60 to $70 billion" (p. 46) is spent annually for cocaine. Obviously, in spite of the "war" on drugs, and in spite of the many dangers associated with cocaine use, there is a thriving demand for the drug. As depressing as these figures are, however, White (1989) reported that there was evidence suggesting that the number of Americans using cocaine has either leveled off, or possibly even declined, in recent years.

HOW COCAINE IS ABUSED

Cocaine is used in one of a number of ways. First, cocaine hydrochloride powder might be "snorted" (the powder is inhaled through the nose). Cocaine hydrochloride is a water soluble form of cocaine and thus is well adapted to either intranasal or intravenous use (Sbriglio and Millman, 1987). Gold and Verebey (1984) observed that snorting is the most common method through which recreational users will abuse cocaine.

Schuckit (1984) notes that when used in this manner (that is, intranasally), cocaine powder is usually arranged on a glass in thin lines 3–5 cm long, each of which contains approximately 25 mg of cocaine. The powder is diced, usually with a razor blade, on a piece of glass or a mirror. This is called a "line" by users. The powder is then inhaled through a drinking straw or rolled paper. When it reaches the nasal passages, which are richly supplied with blood vessels, the cocaine is quickly absorbed. This allows the cocaine to gain rapid access to the blood stream, usually in three to five minutes (Gonzales, 1985; Gold and Verebey, 1984).

The second manner in which cocaine might be used is by intravenous injection. Cocaine hydrochloride powder is mixed with water, then injected into a vein, where it will rapidly reach the brain. Jones (1987) reported that cocaine administered intravenously will take approximately 15–20 seconds to reach the brain. The results of injecting cocaine are similar to results reported by those who use freebase. The user will experience a rapid, intense, feeling of euphoria. This will be discussed in more detail in the section on the subjective effects of cocaine in this chapter.

The third form of cocaine use, sublingual, is becoming increasingly popular especially when the hydrochloride salt of cocaine is utilized (Jones, 1987). The sublingual administration of a drug involves placing the drug under the tongue where there is a rich supply of blood vessels. This method of administration will result in large amounts of the drug entering the bloodstream quickly. When cocaine is used sublingually, the results are similar to those seen in intranasal administration of cocaine.

The fourth major method of cocaine use involves the fumes being inhaled. The practice of burning or smoking different parts of the coca plant dates back to at least 3000 B.C. Siegel (1984) noted that the Incas would burn coca leaves at religious festivals. In the late 1800s, coca cigarettes were used to treat hay fever and opiate addiction, and by the year 1890 cocaine was being used for the treatment of whooping cough, bronchitis, asthma, and a range of other conditions (Siegel, 1984). However, the practice of smoking cocaine for recreational purposes is apparently a relatively new phenomenon.

Kirsch (1986) observed that in the mid 1960s it was discovered that it was easier to smoke freebase cocaine than cocaine hydrochloride. This was because the freebase form is more volatile and will decompose less when heated than does the cocaine hydrochloride. This is the practice known as "freebasing".

Gonzales (1985) described the process as involving the separation of the cocaine from its hydrochloride salt. Siegel (1984) noted that this is done by treating cocaine hydrochloride with various solutions, then filtering out the precipitated cocaine-freebase. This will increase the purity of the obtained powder, but will not burn off the impurities in the cocaine (Siegel, 1984). The process of preparing cocaine freebase is quite long and complicated, and as a result smoking cocaine freebase was limited to a small proportion of those who abused cocaine (Gawin, Allen, and Humblestone, 1989).

When heated, the cocaine powder vaporizes, and the person inhales the fumes, a process that allows the cocaine to take effect in just *seven seconds* (Gonzales, 1985). Dr. Ronald Siegel (quoted in Gonzales, 1985) notes that ". . . there is no such thing as a social-recreational free-baser" (p. 200). In effect, by the time a person has begun freebasing cocaine, he or she is addicted to the drug. So potent is the process of freebasing cocaine that Gold and Verebey (1984) called it "tantamount to intravenous administration without the need for a syringe" (p. 714).

The fifth way in which cocaine might be used is also through smoking.

The form of cocaine known as "crack" or "rock" is used for this purpose. The solid crystals will, when smoked, provide "an intense, wrenching rush in a matter of seconds" (Lamar, Riley and Smghabadi, 1986, p. 16). The process is similar to that of freebase, in that the crack is cocaine base, freed from its hydrochloride salt. Crack is sold in ready-to-use form, in containers that allow the user one or two inhalations for a relatively low price (Gawin, Allen, and Humblestone, 1989).

This feature makes it a preferred form of cocaine (Kirsch, 1986). The cost of crack is also lower than freebase, making it more attractive to the under-eighteen crowd (Bales, 1988).

Breslin (1988) described how one crack "factory" worked:

> Curtis and his girlfriend dropped the cocaine and baking soda into the water, then hit the bottle with the blowtorch. The cocaine powder boiled down to its oily base. The baking soda soaked up the impurities in the cocaine. When cold water was added to the bottle, the cocaine base hardened into white balls. Curtis and Iris spooned them out, placed them on a table covered with paper, and began to measure the hard white cocaine. . . . (p. 212)

The effects of crack are short-lived, lasting only a few minutes (Breslin, 1988; Lamar, et al. 1986). The person must use more crack to try to reachieve the initial "rush." Eventually, the person experiences a period of severe postcocaine depression, which encourages further use of cocaine in order to feel normal again.

SUBJECTIVE EFFECTS OF COCAINE

Cocaine will bring about a feeling of "quick, intense euphoria" (Lingeman, 1974, p. 46), as well as an indifference to pain and fatigue, and a decrease in hunger (Abel, 1982; Lingeman, 1974). Weiner (1985) noted that the intravenous administration of cocaine will result in a "rush" that is "somewhat akin to sexual orgasm" (p. 552). Freebasing cocaine, or using crack, will result in the same subjective experience. This rush, however, does not result from oral or intranasal administration of cocaine.

Gold and Verebey (1984) observed that the rush experience is so intense "it alone can replace the sex partner of either sex" (p. 719). Indeed, some male users have experienced spontaneous ejaculation without direct genital stimulation after either injecting cocaine or freebasing cocaine. Cocaine users in the author's experience have been known to speak of cocaine in the same terms as a lover; however, as tolerance develops to the effects of cocaine, the individual will begin to experience impotence (for males) or frigidity (in females).

Siegel (1984) noted that within seconds the initial rush is replaced by a period of excitation that lasts for several minutes. During this period the individual will feel an increased sense of competence or energy (Gold and Verebey, 1984). Schuckit (1984) notes that there is no objective evidence suggesting that a person under the effects of cocaine is actually stronger, although because of the effects of cocaine on the nervous system, the person is likely to *feel* more powerful.

This euphoria, however, lasts a few minutes (Byck, 1987), an estimated 20 minutes, or up to an hour (Gonzales, 1985), depending on the method by which the cocaine is used. Kirsch (1986) reported that although crack contains the same adulterants and impurities found in cocaine,

> it feels purer because smoking the concentrated alkaloid gives a more immediate, intensified rush. This happens because the smoke is absorbed into the blood-stream through the lung tissue—the most direct route to the brain (p. 46).

The rush obtained from crack begins almost instantly, and subsides quickly. This makes the drug *seem* more pure than when cocaine is used intranasally. When snorted, cocaine must be absorbed through the mucous membranes of the nose, which is a slower process than smoking crack, and the high is less intense (Kirsch, 1986).

Cocaine's effects are very short-lived. Julien (1981) noted that the body starts to metabolize cocaine in only 5 to 15 minutes. To maintain the initial effect, the user must repeatedly use the drug (Lingeman, 1974). Eventually, the person is using cocaine not to gain the initial euphoria, but simply to avoid the postcocaine-use depression that is ultimately experienced by every cocaine user.

To complicate matters, Schuckit (1984) notes that tolerance to cocaine may develop within "hours or days" (p. 86). Thus, the individual will begin to require more and more cocaine in order to achieve the same effect that was initially experienced. This urge to increase the dosage and continue using the drug can reach the point where it "may become a way of life and users become totally preoccupied with drug-seeking and drug taking behaviors" (Siegel, 1984, p. 731).

At this point, the person is addicted to cocaine. Gold and Verebey (1984) termed cocaine "deceptively addictive" (p. 720), while Kirsch (1986) called crack "extraordinarily addictive" (p. 47).

Some individuals have been known to routinely administer huge amounts of cocaine in a day's time, as a result of their tolerance to the drug's effects (Schuckit, 1984; Gonzales, 1985). Siegel (1984) reported that some cocaine users would use up to 30 grams (there are 1000 mg per gram) in a day, using the cocaine as frequently as once every five minutes. It should be pointed out that these dosage levels are quite toxic, and would be fatal to the naive drug user. In this case, "naive" means that the person has not had time to develop a tolerance to the drug's effects.

Surprisingly, although cocaine is a potent CNS stimulant, it also functions as an effective local anesthetic. This property of cocaine was discovered about 100 years ago (Byck, 1987). It is thought that cocaine acts as an anesthetic by blocking the nerve signals, or impulses, of the peripheral nerves. Cocaine changes the electrical potential of these peripheral nerves, preventing them from passing on their nerve impulses to the brain. The body is unable to sense pain from the part of the body under the influence of cocaine, at least for a period of time. However, because of its addictive potential, cocaine is rarely used in medicine (Schuckit, 1984).

PSYCHOLOGICAL EFFECTS OF COCAINE

Julien (1981) notes that in man the cortex is the first part of the brain to be affected by cocaine, followed by the brain stem at higher doses. This is true no matter how the drug first enters the body. The drug is thought to cause the nerve cells in the brain to release vast amounts of the neurotransmitters normally used in small amounts to carry messages between neurons (Lamar, et al., 1986), and then blocks the reabsorption of these chemicals (Potter, Rudorfer, and Goodwin, 1987). This overstimulation serves to lower the amount of stimulation needed to activate the brain's reward system (Kornetsky and Bain, 1987).

Cocaine causes the brain's reward system to function more easily, with less than normal stimulation. This experience is, needless to say, quite pleasurable for the individual. Cocaine is thought to accomplish this by blocking "the reuptake of released monoamines including norepinephrine, dopamine and serotonin" (Woods, Winger, and France, 1987, p. 23). These are neurotransmitters thought to be involved in the normal function of the human brain.

Normally, after the neurons in the brain release neurotransmitters, they are reabsorbed for future use. As noted above, smoking (or injecting) cocaine can bring about an intense rush that has been described in terms of a sexual orgasm (Gold and Verebey, 1984). The effects are such that, according to one cocaine addict quoted by Lamar, et al. (1986), "It feels like the top of your head is going to blow off" (p. 16). However, cocaine blocks the reabsorption process, gradually depleting the supplies of neurotransmitters, causing the person to fall deeper and deeper into a cocaine-induced depression.

Cocaine is self-reinforcing. The person who uses cocaine is likely to experience pleasurable effects and will want to repeat the experience. Remember that freebasing will result in the person feeling the euphoria from the drug in just seven seconds, and this immediacy of reinforcement is quite powerful. To achieve this, the person might go into a cycle of continuous cocaine use known as "coke runs," using cocaine for hours, or days at a time. Individuals have been known to use cocaine until they cannot stay awake any longer or until the available supply of cocaine is exhausted (Siegel, 1984; Weiner, 1985).

Animal research has demonstrated that rats who are given intravenous cocaine for pushing a bar set in the wall of their cage will do so repeatedly, ignoring food or even sex (Maranto, 1985; Hammer & Hazleton, 1984). These rats will continue to use the drug to the point of death from convulsions or infection (Hammer & Hazleton, 1984). This is a reflection of how potent a reinforcer cocaine is and how addictive cocaine is.

COMPLICATIONS OF COCAINE ABUSE

Cocaine is hardly a safe drug. Indeed, Cohen (1984) reported that cocaine was the fifth most frequently mentioned drug in emergency room reports in 1982. Cocaine can kill through a variety of mechanisms. A small percentage of the population simply cannot detoxify cocaine, no matter how small the dosage level used. The livers of such people are unable to produce an essential enzyme necessary to break down the chemical. For these people, the use of even a small amount of cocaine could result in serious, if not fatal, complications.

Even for the individual whose body is able to metabolize cocaine, it is a dangerous drug. Estroff (1987) reported that "cocaine is much more deadly than heroin when abused in unlimited quantities" (p. 25). Death may be brought about by uncontrolled seizures following cocaine use, or from paralysis of breathing muscles (Estroff, 1987). Cocaine may cause strokes, which may kill or cause paralysis. Indeed, death can come about so quickly that "the victim never receives medical attention other than from the coroner" (Estroff, 1987, p. 25).

Although the exact cause is not known, cocaine is known to bring about damage to the heart muscle—and death through heart failure (Maranto, 1985). Whether used intranasally or injected, cocaine can cause cardiac arrhythmias (irregularities in the heartbeat), which may be fatal (Schuckit, 1984), as well as heart attacks and sudden death from cardiac arrest (Maranto, 1985).

Decker, et al. (1987), noted that the question of whether cardiac complications associated with cocaine use were due to the cumulative effects of cocaine or impurities in the cocaine were unclear. However, cocaine use was reported to be associated with

> profound cardiovascular effects such as sudden death from cardiac arrest, pericardial chest pain, myocardial infarction, hypertension, ventricular tachyarrhythmias, and angina pectoris (Decker, et al., 1987, p. 464).

Cocaine can bring about pain in the region over the heart, and the lower thorax *(pericardial chest pain).* Cocaine is also able to bring about the death of heart muscle usually by disrupting the blood supply to the affected tissue (a *myocardial infarction*). The term *ventricular tachyarrhythmias* refers to a pattern of abnormally fast contractions of the ventricles of the heart, usually in excess of 150 contractions per minute (Friel, 1974), which may rapidly prove fatal (Cohen, 1984).

It was also reported by Decker, et al. (1987), that increased use, the reexposure to cocaine after a period of abstinence, or even the first exposure to cocaine might predispose the individual user to myocardial infarction, angina pectoris, or both. The authors went on to observe that there is

a danger that chest pain in some of these young people may be misinterpreted as being of psychogenic etiology when it actually may signal cardiac damage resulting from remote or recent drug use (p. 465).

In addition to this, chronic intranasal use of cocaine can result in sore throats, inflamed sinuses, hoarseness, and on occasion a breakdown of the cartilage of the nose (Cohen, 1984). Cocaine use has also been implicated in damage to the surface lining of the nose and sinuses (Maranto, 1985) in those individuals who snort the drug.

If the person who injects cocaine uses a "dirty" needle, or fails to use sterile techniques, she or he will be exposed to endocarditis (Burden and Rogers, 1988), Hepatitis B, AIDS, various other blood infections, and skin abscesses (Cohen, 1984). Wetli (1987) observed that in addition to these infections, there are occasional, isolated reports of unusual infections, such as fungus infections of the brain, associated with intravenous cocaine use.

Opiate addicts frequently are forced to inject medications intended for oral use. Oral medications often include *fillers*, substances that are added to the active agent of an oral medication to give it form and make it easier to handle. These fillers were never intended to enter the bloodstream, and are harmless when the medication is taken orally. The repeated injections of these foreign materials cause extensive scarring at the site of injection, forming the characteristic "tracks" of chronic opiate addicts (Wetli, 1987). In contrast to this, however, cocaine addicts usually inject soluble materials, and are thus less likely to develop extensive scars at the site of injection (Wetli, 1987).

There is a danger of adverse interactions between cocaine and medications being used to treat other conditions or other drugs being abused by the individual (Cohen, 1984). Macdonald (1988) noted that cocaine is often used in conjunction with marijuana, and that both drugs are capable of increasing heart rate "above levels seen with either drug alone" (p. 459), a matter of some consequence for persons whose heart muscle has been damaged.

Cocaine has also been implicated as causing panic reactions and a drug-induced psychosis (Maranto, 1985; Schuckit, 1984). Chronic use of cocaine has been implicated in the development of a drug-induced paranoia. This condition is known as "coke paranoia," and usually clears within a few hours (Davis and Bresnahan, 1987) to a few days (Schuckit, 1984) after the person has stopped using cocaine. On occasion, however, the paranoid state seems to become permanent (Maranto, 1985).

Drug-induced periods of rage (Gonzales, 1985), or outbursts of anger and violent assaultive behavior (Kauffman, Shaffer, and Burglass, 1985) have been reported, following chronic use of cocaine. Cocaine often brings about seizures in the person using the drug, which may be fatal without proper medical intervention. Finally, Maranto (1985) noted that either a few hours after snorting the drug, or within 15 minutes if the person has injected it, the person slides into a state of depression, which after prolonged use might reach suicidal proportions (Cohen, 1984).

This depression is the result of cocaine's depleting the nerve cells in the brain of the neurotransmitter *norepinephrine,* one of the chemical messengers passed between nerve cells. In many cases, this period of depression will resolve itself in a few hours to a few weeks.

In addition to this, freebasing may result in significant lung damage (Gonzales, 1985; Maranto, 1985), and one encounters the possibility of liver damage from cocaine use in *any* form (Maranto, 1985). Evidence exists that cocaine may cause a withdrawal syndrome (Hammer & Hazleton, 1984), which Gawin and Ellinwood (1988) thought was "comparable to the acute withdrawal of the alcohol hangover" (p. 1176).

After periods of extended use, some people have experienced the "cocaine bugs," a hallucinatory experience where the person will feel as if bugs were crawling on, or just under, the skin of their bodies (Gonzales, 1985). The technical term for this is *formication* (Hinsie and Campbell, 1970), and there are case reports involving people burning their arms or legs with matches or cigarettes, or scratching themselves repeatedly, in an attempt to rid themselves of these unseen bugs (Gonzales, 1985; Lingeman, 1974).

Animal research has suggested that, after repeated exposures to cocaine, it was possible for the animal to develop seizures at a dose that previously had not brought on such convulsions. This process was termed a "pharmacological kindling" (Post, et al., 1987), and it was found that while cocaine itself might have a short half-life (the period of time in which the body is able to metabolize one-half of a given dose of a chemical), "the sensitization effects are long lasting" (p. 113).

The authors went on to observe that

> Repeated administration of a given dose of cocaine without resulting seizures *would in no way assure the continued safety of this drug **even for that given individual*** . . . (p. 159) (italics and boldface added for emphasis).

Thus, while the *immediate effects* of cocaine might last only a short time, the body might become hypersensitive to cocaine for long periods of time. If this should happen, the person could suffer serious—possibly fatal—side effects from a dosage level of cocaine that was once easily tolerated.

Cocaine is clearly addictive. After a long period of use, users reach the point where they are not using the drug to feel good; rather, they are using the drug "just to maintain a feeling of being normal" (as one cocaine addict expressed it). It has been reported (Lamar, et al., 1986) that individuals who snort cocaine will develop an addiction in three to four years, while those who smoke crack might be fully addicted in 6 to 10 *weeks.*

Gawin and Kleber (1986) found that the postcocaine-binge recovery process moved through several stages. In the early part of the first stage, which lasted from one to four days, the person experienced feelings of agitation, depression, and anorexia (loss of desire to eat), as well as a strong craving for cocaine. As the person progressed through the first phase, he or she lost the craving for cocaine, but experienced insomnia and exhaustion, combined with a strong desire for sleep.

After the first week of abstinence, the person returned to a normal sleep pattern, and gradually experienced stronger cravings for cocaine and higher levels of anxiety. Conditioned cues exacerbated the individual's craving for cocaine, drawing the person back to cocaine use. If the person could withstand the environmental and intrapersonal cues for further cocaine use, she or he moved into the "extinction" phase of cocaine use, where a more normal level of function was gradually reached.

The extinction phase began after ten weeks of abstinence. If the person were unable to maintain sobriety, he or she would again go on a cocaine binge, and the cycle would repeat itself. If she or he is able to withstand the craving, there is a good chance that she or he might achieve sobriety; however, it was noted that cocaine addicts might suddenly experience craving for cocaine "months or years after its last appearance" (Gawin and Ellinwood, 1988, p. 1176), long after the last period of cocaine use.

Cocaine has been implicated in the deaths of a large number of individuals, often by causing seizures and hyperthermia, in both men and women. Women who are pregnant and who use cocaine have been found to suffer from a higher incidence of spontaneous abortions, premature labor, and *abruptio placentae*. These are all complications to pregnancy that might prove fatal to the fetus and possibly the mother (Sbriglio and Millman, 1987). Peluso and Peluso (1988) noted that there is evidence that infants born to women who used cocaine during pregnancy may suffer small strokes prior to birth as a result of the rapid changes in the mother's blood pressure.

WOMEN AND COCAINE

Peluso and Peluso (1988) observed that women tend to develop a different pattern of cocaine use than do men, an observation supported by Griffin, Weiss, Mirin, and Lang (1989). Research data suggest that women begin to use cocaine at an earlier age than men (Griffin, Weiss, Mirin, and Lang, 1989; Peluso and Peluso, 1988). Further, women who use cocaine seem to use approximately twice as much as do male cocaine users (Peluso and Peluso, 1988).

Griffin, Weiss, Mirin, and Lang (1989) found that women who abused cocaine tended to enter treatment at an earlier age than did their male counterparts. Finally, Atkinson (1986) noted that cocaine has become part of a courtship scene. Some women accept a gram of cocaine in much the same way that their mothers and grandmothers would accept flowers or candy. Kolodny (1985) reported that the offer of cocaine to an individual by another is viewed by many as an invitation to engage in sexual relations.

There is evidence to suggest that women are introduced to cocaine by men, but that once they begin to use cocaine, women tend to do so in a different manner than do men. Peluso and Peluso (1988) suggest that cocaine's impact on the lifestyle of the woman is also more devastating than it is for the man, but there is little research into the impact of cocaine use on the lifestyle of the user.

THE TREATMENT OF COCAINE ADDICTION

Although the treatment process will be discussed in more detail in later chapters of this text, brief mention of the treatment of addiction should be made here. Unfortunately, although a great deal is known about the manifestations of cocaine addiction, Weiner (1985) noted that "very little is known about the natural history of cocaine dependence" (p. 553).

Gawin and Ellinwood (1988) reported that "of 30 million Americans who have tried cocaine intranasally, 80 percent have not become regular users, and 95 percent are not addicted to the drug" (p. 1174). There is little research into the factors that bring about addiction to the CNS stimulants; however, it is not possible to determine which person who abuses cocaine is likely to become addicted. Furthermore, in contrast to the research into the genetics of alcoholism, "research on genetic factors in stimulant abuse has not been pursued" (Gawin and Ellinwood, 1988, p. 1177).

The confusion surrounding the treatment of cocaine addiction might be seen in the debate over whether to use antidepressants to curb the craving that many cocaine addicts encounter during the earliest stages of detoxification. It has been reported (Wilbur, 1986) that the antidepressant imipramine is effective in curbing the postwithdrawal craving for cocaine. Gawin, Kleber, Byck, Rounsaville, Kosten, Jatlow, and Morgan (1989) also concluded that, when used at therapeutic dosage levels, the anti-depressant desipramine was able to reduce the craving for cocaine ex-perienced by addicts in the early stages of recovery.

However, Decker, Fins, and Frances (1987) noted that

> Little attention has been given to the possible cardiac risks of using antidepressants to prevent cocaine intoxication or to treat "crashes" or withdrawal symptoms (p. 465).

Another problem with the use of tricyclic antidepressants to control the craving for cocaine is that it typically takes 7–14 days for the antidepressant to begin to reduce the craving (Gawin, Allen, and Humblestone, 1989). The authors have experimented with a drug currently available in Europe, the Far East, and Carribean—but not in the United States—in the control of the craving for cocaine that many addicts experience during the initial period of sobriety. This drug, flupenthixol, was found to be quite effective in the control of postcocaine craving by Gawin, Allen, and Humblestone (1989), who called for further research into the use of this drug in the treatment of cocaine addicts.

Kolb and Brodie (1982) postulate that cocaine dependence is even more resistive to treatment than is opiate addiction. However, this is only a theory, and it has not been tested in clinical practice. Siegel (1984) outlined the difficulties of treating cocaine addiction, which include the fact that the cocaine addict has often forgotten what a drug-free life is like.

Concerning the physical withdrawal from cocaine, Gold and Verebey (1984) observed that there are "no severe withdrawal symptoms such as those seen in opiate withdrawal" (p. 720) in cases of cocaine addiction. However, cocaine withdrawal was marked by such complaints as paranoia, depression, fatigue, craving and agitation, chills, insomnia, nausea, and vomiting.

The authors also point out that evidence suggests cocaine addiction might lead to vitamin deficiencies, especially of the B complex and C vitamins. Indeed, the authors found that 73% of a sample of cocaine abusers tested had at least one vitamin deficiency. It was concluded that these vitamin deficiencies reflected the malnutrition found in cocaine abuse, since cocaine causes anorexia (Gold and Verebey, 1984).

The authors went on to suggest that *total abstinence is essential* in the treatment of cocaine addiction, and that follow-up treatment should include behavior modification and psychotherapy (Gold and Verebey, 1984).

The first phase of recovery from amphetamine or cocaine addiction is the phase of the "crash." Within one to four hours after the last use of the drug following a binge, the individual experiences intense depression, agitation, and anxiety (Gawin and Ellinwood, 1988), as well as a craving for sleep. This sleep might, in some cases, be either initiated or supplemented by the use of CNS depressants, marijuana, or alcohol.

The next phase, withdrawal, lasts for a period of weeks. During this phase, the individual will experience decreased energy and a limited ability to experience pleasure, as well as a craving for additional use of the drug. This period will resolve itself in 6 to 18 weeks if there is no additional drug use (Gawin and Ellinwood, 1988). However, this is the phase where the individual might initiate new periods of drug use in an attempt to self-medicate the poststimulant depression.

If the individual is able to avoid further chemical use, however, she or he will enter into a period of extinction. Brief periods of craving might be experienced from time to time, usually situationally provoked (Gawin and Ellinwood, 1988), which gradually become less and less frequent. However, as with the other forms of drug addiction, the individual is at risk for addiction to other chemicals and needs to avoid other drug use for the rest of his or her life.

SUMMARY

In the past 150 years, the active agent of the coca bush has been isolated, and methods devised to concentrate large amounts of cocaine have been developed. The concurrent development of the hypodermic needle allowed for the intravenous injection of large amounts of relatively pure cocaine into the body. Almost immediately, cocaine became a popular drug of abuse, which by the turn of the century was known to be both potent, and deadly.

It remained a common drug of abuse until government regulations limited the availability of cocaine. The development of the amphetamines, a family of drugs which have effects on the central nervous system similar to those of cocaine, allowed addicts to substitute amphetamines for the increasingly rare cocaine. In time, the dangers of cocaine were forgotten.

In the late 1960s and early 1970s, government regulations began to limit the availability of the amphetamines. In the generation since then, addicts have returned to cocaine. The drug has further been refined through experimentation for use not only as an injected drug, but also for smoking. The concentrated "rocks" of cocaine are known as "crack," a potent and dangerously addictive form of cocaine that is currently flooding the streets.

CHAPTER 6

The Amphetamines

The CNS stimulants include such drugs as cocaine, the amphetamine family of drugs, and amphetaminelike drugs such as Ritalin. The behavioral effects of these drugs are remarkably similar, in spite of the specific chemical differences between the specific drugs (Gawin and Ellinwood, 1988). Cocaine was discussed in the last chapter, while the other CNS stimulants will be reviewed in this chapter.

Lingeman (1974), noted that the amphetamine family of chemicals were first discovered in the year 1887; however, it was not until 1927 that these drugs were found to be useful to medicine. It was in that year that Benzedrine was introduced, in an inhaler similar to smelling salts, for use in the treatment of asthma (Grinspoon and Bakalar, 1985). The ampoule, which could be purchased over-the-counter, would be broken, releasing the concentrated amphetamine liquid into the surrounding cloth. The Benzedrine ampoule would then be held under the nose and inhaled, much like smelling salts are.[1]

The amphetamines were also initially used in the treatment of depression and to heighten one's capacity to work (Grinspoon and Bakalar, 1985). It was not long, however, before it was discovered that these ampoules of Benzedrine could be unwrapped, carefully broken open, and the concentrated Benzedrine used for injection. Street drug users quickly discovered that the effects of the amphetamines were quite similar to those of cocaine. Amphetamines came to be viewed by many as a "safe" replacement for cocaine, which by the early 1920s was known to be a very dangerous drug.

During World War II, the amphetamines were used by American, British, German, and Japanese armed forces to counteract fatigue and heighten endurance (Brecher, 1972). Following the war, American physicians routinely prescribed amphetamines for the treatment of depression and for weight loss. By 1970, some *8% of all prescriptions were for some form of amphetamines* (Peluso and Peluso, 1988). Indeed, so popular were the amphetamines that by the early 1970s, some *31* different amphetamine preparations were being marketed either alone or in combination with other drugs (Brecher, 1972).

It is ironic that, just a generation later, drug users would be drifting away from the amphetamines and all of the dangers associated with

[1]Needless to say, amphetamines are no longer sold over the counter.

amphetamine use (Estroff, 1987), to the "safe" "Society high" (Doweiko, 1979) of cocaine. Chronic users of the amphetamines found that the drug ultimately came to dominate their lives. The drug would bring about agitation when used at high doses and would result in a drug-induced depression when one's supply ran out. Martin (1971) characterized the chronic use of amphetamines as being "even more psychologically destructive than heroin" (p. 334).

Eventually, people began to understand that "speed kills," either directly (through its impact on the heart and vascular system) or indirectly (by causing a deterioration in the person's self-care activities). However, while we have not returned to the levels of amphetamine use seen in the late 1960s and early 1970s, the amphetamines are second only to marijuana as the most commonly abused illicit drug among high school seniors (Peluso and Peluso, 1988).

MEDICAL USES OF AMPHETAMINES

The amphetamine family of drugs is one of the more powerful groups of CNS stimulants (Jaffe, 1985). The amphetamines' and similar drugs' (Ritalin, for example) effects are caused by improvement of the action of the smooth muscles of the body (Weiner, 1985). These drugs also have been known to improve athletic performance to some degree and are often abused for this purpose; however, these effects are not uniform, and overuse of the CNS stimulants can actually bring about a *decrease* in athletic abilities (Weiner, 1985).

Amphetamines were once thought to be useful in the control of weight (Martin, 1971). This was due to the *anorexic* side effect of the amphetamines. Anorexia is a condition in which the individual has lost his or her desire to eat. Subsequent research, however, has demonstrated that the amphetamines are only minimally effective as a weight-control agent, and they are no longer recognized as effective in weight control (Julien, 1981; Weiner, 1985).

Although the amphetamines were once thought to be antidepressants, they are no longer used as such (Potter, Rudorfer, and Goodwin, 1987); however amphetamines, and related compounds, do have a limited medical value. First, in a limited number of cases, these drugs have been found useful in the control of the symptoms of hyperactivity in children (Abel, 1981; Martin, 1971). Surprisingly, although the amphetamines are CNS *stimulants*, they have a calming effect on children who are hyperactive as a result of a condition known as *minimal brain damage*, which is also known by the terms *hyperactivity* or the *attention deficit syndrome*.

The amphetamines help hyperactive children by enhancing the function of the reticular activating system (RAS) of the brain. This is the portion of the brain thought to be involved in focusing one's attention (Gold and Verebey, 1984). The RAS is thought to "screen out" extraneous stimuli, so that one might concentrate on a specific task. In children who suffer from hyperactivity, the RAS is thought to be underactive, allowing the children to be easily distracted. The amphetamines are believed to stimulate the RAS to the point where the child is able to function more effectively.

Second, the amphetamines have been found to be the treatment of choice for a rare neurological condition known as *narcolepsy*, a lifelong condition that causes the person to fall asleep during waking hours (Martin, 1971). Doghramji (1989) described narcolepsy as an incurable disorder that is thought to reflect a chemical imbalance within the brain. One of the chemicals involved, dopamine, is the neurotransmitter that amphetamines cause to be released from neurons in the brain. Current thinking is that the amphetamines may at least partially correct the dopamine imbalance that causes narcolepsy.

PHARMACOLOGY OF AMPHETAMINES AND SIMILAR DRUGS

The amphetamines are thought to impact on many parts of the central nervous system and muscles of the body. In the brain, the medulla (which is involved in the control of respiration) is stimulated, causing the individual to breathe more deeply and more rapidly. At normal dosage levels, the cortex is also stimulated, resulting in reduced feelings of fatigue and possibly increased concentration (Abel, 1982; Mirin and Weiss, 1983).

The amphetamines are absorbed from the gastrointestinal system following oral doses (Mirin and Weiss, 1983), and the effects are first noticed about thirty minutes after the individual takes the drug. The amphetamine molecule bears a close resemblance to the dopamine molecule and impacts on the dopamine receptors in the brain. Drugs that block dopamine receptor sites within the brain, such as the phenothiazines, are often effective in the control of some of the symptoms of an amphetamine overdose (Honigfeld and Howard, 1978).

The amphetamines are metabolized by the liver; however, after an oral dose of an amphetamine, at least 50% of the drug will be excreted unchanged by the kidneys (Mirin and Weiss, 1983). The half-life of the amphetamines is 10–30 hours, and the half-life depends at least in part on the acidity of the individual's urine (Govoni and Hayes, 1985).

METHODS OF AMPHETAMINE ABUSE

Amphetamine powder may be "snorted," in a manner similar to the way in which cocaine is used. Because of the ease with which they can be manufactured, amphetamines are often sold in homemade tablet form for oral use. These tablets are often white, with crossed score lines on one side, resulting in a street name of "white cross" (Doweiko, 1979). Occasionally, amphetamines are diverted from legitimate sources, and such pharmaceutical amphetamines will come in a variety of capsules or tablets. The tablets (or powder, if purchased in powder form) may be prepared for intravenous use, as is done with heroin. There is little evidence that amphetamines are intentionally smoked.

Chronic users of amphetamines will often embark on "speed runs," repeatedly using amphetamines in order to recapture and maintain the elusive euphoria that was initially experienced with the drug. Indeed, long-term users of amphetamines have been known to inject up to 1700 mg per day in divided doses, gradually building up to this total daily dosage level as their tolerance for the drug increases (Weiner, 1985).

SUBJECTIVE EXPERIENCE OF AMPHETAMINE USE

The amphetamine experience is, to a large degree, very similar to that seen with cocaine. Among the major differences between these two classes of drugs are: (1) where the effects of cocaine might last from a few minutes to an hour at most, the effects of the amphetamines may last many hours (Schuckit, 1984), (2) unlike cocaine, the amphetamines are effective when used orally, and (3) unlike cocaine, the amphetamines have only a small anesthetic effect (Weiner, 1985).

Brecher (1972) also noted that the amphetamines were relatively cheap, with a thousand tablets costing a pharmaceutical company only *seventy-five cents* to manufacture in the late 1960s. They are also easily transported, since the amphetamines are available in either tablet or capsule form. These additional features added to the tendency for drug users to substitute amphetamines for the more expensive, and frequently unavailable, cocaine that they might otherwise have used.

Finally, the amphetamines are easily manufactured and the process does not require specialized training in chemistry. This makes amphetamine manufacturing especially tempting in a college chemistry class, a fact not unknown to faculty and law enforcement officials. The financial rewards for the illegal manufacturing of amphetamines are quite high, with a $1000 investment eventually yielding a return of as much as $40,000 for methamphetamine (Peluso and Peluso, 1988).

The effects of the amphetamines on an individual will depend on that individual's mental state, the dosage level used, the relative potency of the specific amphetamine, and the manner in which the drug is used. The usual oral dosage level is between 15 and 30 mg per day (Lingeman, 1974); however, this depends on the potency of the amphetamine or amphetamine-like drug being used (Julien, 1981).

At low to moderate oral dosage levels, the individual will experience feelings of increased alertness, an elevation of mood, a mild euphoria, less mental fatigue, and an improved level of concentration (Julien, 1981; Weiner, 1985). Gawin and Ellinwood (1988) noted that the amphetamines and cocaine will produce "a neurochemical magnification of the pleasure experienced in most activities" (p. 1174) when initially used.

The authors went on to note that the initial use of amphetamines or cocaine would

> produce alertness and a sense of well-being . . . they lower anxiety and social inhibitions, and heighten energy, self-esteem, and the emotions aroused by interpersonal experiences. Although they magnify pleasure, they do not distort it; hallucinations are usually absent (p. 1174).

Some people will experience insomnia and anxiety, as well as irritability and hostility (Grinspoon and Bakalar, 1985) during periods of initial use. It is not uncommon for illicit drug users to try to counteract these side effects through the use of alcohol or benzodiazepines. Indeed, Peluso and Peluso (1988) estimated that *half* of all regular users of amphetamines may also be classified as heavy drinkers, individuals who attempt to control the side effects of the amphetamines through the use of alcohol.

As the individual experiments with the drug, he or she will discover that, initially, higher doses also intensify the euphoria experienced (Gawin and Ellinwood, 1988); however, higher dosage levels of amphetamines might also result in confused behavior, irritability, fear, suspicion, hallucinations, and delusions (Julien, 1981; Weiner, 1985). Davis and Bresnahan (1987) reported that a "single large injection of amphetamine can produce a paranoid psychosis within hours in nonpsychotic amphetamine abusers," a condition that will continue as long as the amphetamine remains in the body.

As tolerance to the euphoria brought about by the amphetamines develops, there is a tendency for the person to use higher and higher dosage levels (Peluso and Peluso, 1988). Eventually, the obsessive user substitutes intravenously administered amphetamines for the orally administered forms of stimulants. Individuals who "graduate" to the intravenous use of amphetamines usually do so when they are no longer able to achieve the desired effects through oral or intranasal use of the drug. The intravenous user of amphetamines will, if she or he fails to use proper sterile technique, run the risk of endocarditis (Burden and Rogers, 1988) as well as any of a wide range of other blood infections, including the AIDS virus (Wetli, 1987).

At the same time, however, there is evidence that most amphetamine users will not progress to the level of addiction (Gawin and Ellinwood, 1988). Thus, the question of what percentage of those who begin to experiment with amphetamines will ultimately become dependent on these drugs has not been answered.

The development of tolerance to the effects of the amphetamines is not inevitable. When the amphetamines are used in the treatment of narcolepsy, a person may be maintained on a specific dosage level for years, without the development of tolerance (Weiner, 1985; Brecher, 1972). Tolerance does, however, develop to the euphoria effect of the amphetamines, making it necessary for the individual to increase the dosage in order to try and regain the same initial euphoria.

High dosage levels of the amphetamines may result in a drug-induced psychosis often indistinguishable from schizophrenia (Wurmser, 1978). At one time it was thought that the amphetamines essentially brought on a latent schizophrenia in a person who was vulnerable to this condition. It has now been suggested, however, that the amphetamines are able to cause a drug-induced psychosis even in essentially normal people (Grinspoon and Bakalar, 1985; Kolb and Brodie, 1982). This drug-induced state often includes confusion, suspiciousness, hallucinations, and delusional thinking, as well as "acute episodes of violence" (Wurmser, 1978, p. 398). Under normal conditions, this psychosis clears up within days after the drug is discontinued (Schuckit, 1984; Kolb and Brodie, 1982). In some cases, the drug-induced psychosis seems to become permanent (Jaffe, 1985).

CONSEQUENCES OF PROLONGED USE OF AMPHETAMINES

The consequences of prolonged amphetamine use, like that of cocaine, include the drug-induced psychosis previously mentioned, as well as various complications caused by dietary neglect or inadequate sleep over time. Gold and Verebey (1984) noted that vitamin deficiencies were commonly found in chronic amphetamine abusers, a side effect of malnutrition.

Julien (1981) notes that "fatalities directly attributable to the use of amphetamines are rare" (p. 84), and observed that naive drug users have survived doses of 400–500 mg. Long-term users of amphetamines have been known to use up to 1700 mg per day in "speed runs," gradually building up to this total daily dosage level as their tolerance for the drug increases (Weiner, 1985).

Weiner (1985), reported that chronic use of the amphetamines might result in confusion, assaultiveness, irritability, weakness, insomnia, anxiety, delirium, paranoid hallucinations, panic states, and suicidal and homicidal tendencies. As with cocaine, prolonged use of the amphetamines may result in the individual experiencing formication, the sensation of having unseen bugs crawling either on, or just under, the skin (Hinsie and Campbell, 1970).

Amphetamine addicts, like cocaine addicts, have been known to scratch or burn the skin, in an attempt to rid themselves of these unseen bugs. In addition to these consequences, prolonged use of the amphetamines may result in vomiting, anorexia, cardiac arrhythmias, anginal pain, and diarrhea. Convulsions, coma, and death are possible from amphetamine use, even if somewhat rare (Schuckit, 1984).

Fatigue and depression follow prolonged periods of amphetamine use, with the depression often reaching suicidal proportions (Slaby, Lieb, and Tancredi, 1981). Kauffman, Shaffer, and Burglas (1985) noted that marked feelings of depression could persist for *months* following cessation of amphetamine or cocaine use. Gawin and Ellinwood (1988) noted that prolonged use of the amphetamines seems to bring about a "sustained neurophysiologic change" in the brain of the user (p. 1178).

Thus, evidence now exists that prolonged use of the amphetamines might bring about actual physical damage to the cells of the brain, which in turn affects how the brain functions. Research in this area is quite limited, however, and there is no research into the long-term impact of amphetamine use on brain function.

Gawin and Ellinwood (1988) observed that the periods of drug-induced euphoria experienced in the amphetamine or cocaine binge might create "vivid, long-term memories" (p. 1175). These memories, in turn, form part of the foundation of the craving that many cocaine or amphetamine users reported when they stopped using the drug. The recovery process from prolonged amphetamine use follows the same pattern seen for cocaine.

THE TREATMENT OF AMPHETAMINE ADDICTION

Amphetamine abuse has waxed and waned several times and was last a significant part of the drug problem in the late 1960s and early 1970s. At that time, the dangers of amphetamine abuse became clear, and there was a trend away from amphetamines to the supposedly safer drug, cocaine. There is little systematic research into the factors that bring about addiction to the CNS stimulants. In contrast to the research into the genetics of alcoholism, ". . . research on genetic factors in stimulant abuse has not been pursued" (Gawin and Ellinwood, 1988, p. 1177).

Although it has been suggested that antidepressants might be of value in curbing the craving that many cocaine addicts encounter during the earliest stages of detoxification, no research has been conducted to determine whether the antidepressants would be of value in the treatment of amphetamine addiction.

There is evidence suggesting that amphetamine addiction might lead to vitamin deficiencies, especially of the B complex and C vitamins. It has been found that 73% of a sample of cocaine abusers tested had at least one vitamin deficiency. It was concluded that these vitamin deficiencies reflected the malnutrition found in cocaine abuse, since cocaine causes anorexia (Gold and Verebey, 1984). Since the amphetamines also cause anorexia, one would suspect that similar vitamin deficiencies would develop in the chronic amphetamine user.

The first phase of recovery from amphetamine addiction is the "crash." Within one to four hours after the last use of the drug following a binge, the individual experiences intense depression, agitation, and anxiety (Gawin and Ellinwood, 1988), as well as a craving for sleep. This sleep might, in some cases, be either initiated or supplemented by the use of CNS depressants, marijuana, or alcohol, especially when the individual abuses other illicit drugs.

The next phase, withdrawal, lasts for a period of weeks. During this phase, the individual will experience decreased energy and a limited ability to experience pleasure, as well as a craving for additional use of the drug. This period will resolve itself in 6–18 weeks if there is no additional drug use (Gawin and Ellinwood, 1988). However, this is the phase where the individual might initiate new periods of drug use in an attempt to self-medicate his or her poststimulant depression.

If the individual is able to avoid further chemical use, however, she or he will enter into a period of extinction. Brief periods of craving might be experienced from time to time, usually situationally provoked (Gawin and Ellinwood, 1988), which gradually become less and less frequent; however, as with the other forms of drug addiction, the individual is at risk for addiction to other chemicals and needs to avoid other drug use for the rest of his or her life (Gold and Verebey, 1984). Self-help groups such as Narcotics Anonymous or Cocaine Anonymous are of value in treating the amphetamine addict.

SUMMARY

Although they were discovered in the 1880s the amphetamines were first introduced as a treatment for asthma some 40 years later, in the 1920s. The early forms of amphetamine were sold over the counter in cloth covered ampules that were used in much the same way as smelling salts are today. Within a short time, however, it was discovered that the ampules were a source of concentrated amphetamine, which could be injected. The resulting "high" was found to be similar to that of cocaine—which had gained a reputation as being a dangerous drug to use—but lasted much longer.

The amphetamines were used extensively both during and after World War II. Following the war, American physicians prescribed amphetamines for the treatment of depression, and as an aid for weight loss. By the year 1970, amphetamines accounted for 8% of all prescriptions written. However, in the time since then, physicians have come to understand that the amphetamines present a serious potential for abuse. The amphetamines have come under increasingly strict controls, which limit the amount of amphetamine manufactured and the reasons why a person may receive any of these drugs.

Unfortunately, the amphetamines are easily manufactured, and there has long been an underground manufacture and distribution system for these drugs. In the late 1970s and early 1980s street drug users drifted away from the amphetamines, to the supposedly safe stimulant of the early 1900s: cocaine. Recent evidence would suggest that the pendulum has started to swing back in the opposite direction. A new generation has discovered the amphetamines, and use of this class of drugs is increasing as drug addicts steer away from the known dangers of cocaine back to the amphetamines.

CHAPTER 7

Marijuana

The marijuana plant, *Cannabis sativa*, has been used for recreational and medicinal purposes for many centuries and currently is a popular recreational drug (Mirin and Weiss, 1983). In exploring its history as a medicinal agent, Grinspoon and Bakalar (1985) noted that as late as the 19th century marijuana was used as an analgesic, a hypnotic, and an anticonvulsant. Gazzaniga (1988) reported that, with the beginning of Prohibition in the post-World War I era, the working class turned to growing or importing marijuana as a substitute for alcohol. Its use declined with the end of Prohibition, but marijuana again became a popular drug of abuse in the 1960s and 1970s.

It has been estimated that marijuana is currently the fourth most commonly used psychoactive agent worldwide, following nicotine, caffeine, and alcohol (Berger and Dunn, 1982). Surprisingly, marijuana did not become a serious drug of abuse in the United States until the 1960s (Bloodworth, 1987). Currently, marijuana is "the most frequently used drug in the United States" (Nahas, 1986, p. 82). In recent years, there has been interest in the possible medical use of marijuana to control the nausea sometimes found in cancer chemotherapy patients (Grinspoon and Bakalar, 1985) and to control glaucoma.

In a recent article in its "Forum Newsfront" section, *Playboy* (1988) reported that the Asthma and Allergy Foundation of America had examined air samples from the Los Angeles area. This was done in order to determine which pollen particles were drifting in the air. Surprisingly, it was found that 40% of the pollen was from marijuana plants. The implication is that somebody is growing a lot of marijuana in and around the Los Angeles area, a finding that underscores the popularity marijuana has achieved as a drug of abuse.

SCOPE OF THE PROBLEM
AND PATTERNS OF MARIJUANA USE

It is difficult to obtain a clear picture of marijuana use in America, at least in part because the pattern keeps changing. Oliwenstein (1988) estimated that approximately 6 million Americans between the ages of 18 and 25 smoke marijuana on a daily basis, while another 16 million use it occasionally. Mirin and Weiss (1983) reported that 40–45 million Americans have used marijuana at some point in their lives, including 60% of those between the ages of 18 and 25.

Jenike (1987) reported that 60% of the population of the United States has used marijuana at least once, with 20 million Americans using it on a regular basis. L. Siegel (1989) also reported that approximately 20 million Americans use marijuana on a regular basis. Peluso and Peluso (1988) advanced a different figure, noting that more than *60 million* Americans used marijuana in a recent month, while the number of regular users is around 30 million people.

Obviously, different researchers have failed to agree on the number of Americans who have used, or are currently using, marijuana. This is because, as Peluso and Peluso (1988) have noted, "A few puffs on a joint is this generation's social martini" (p. 110). Social sanctions against marijuana use have been replaced by more liberal laws, and in many states possession of a small amount of marijuana has been decriminalized. So, over time, a growing percentage of the population has tried marijuana. A percentage of those who try it will go on to use the drug on a regular basis.

The majority of marijuana users, perhaps as many as 60%, experiment with the drug briefly and then discontinue further use of marijuana. Another 35% might use the drug once or twice a week, while perhaps 5% of those who use marijuana do so more frequently than twice weekly (Mirin and Weiss, 1983).

Research would thus suggest that the majority of those who have used marijuana do so as part of a phase, after which they will rarely, if ever, use the drug again. However, for perhaps 40% of those who try the drug, it becomes a regular part of their lifestyle for at least a while.

METHODS OF ADMINISTRATION

The marijuana plant contains over 400 compounds, but the active ingredient of marijuana appears to be a chemical known as THC[1] (Mirin and Weiss, 1983; Schwartz, 1987; Bloodworth, 1987). The highest concentrations of THC are found in the small upper leaves and flowering tops of the marijuana plant (Mirin and Weiss, 1983). Berger and Dunn (1982) reported that the term *marijuana* is used to identify the relatively weak preparations of the cannabis plant that are used for smoking or eating, while the term *hashish* is used to identify a preparation with a higher concentration of THC.

In the United States, the primary method of marijuana use is smoking, although users will occasionally ingest marijuana. Marijuana cigarettes, which are called "joints," contain 5–20 mg of THC. These cigarettes usually contain between 500 mg and 750 mg of marijuana, which for "street pot" contains approximately 4.1% THC (Schwartz, 1987).

[1]Which is short for *delta-9-tetrahydrocannabinol*.

The technique of smoking a marijuana cigarette is somewhat different from the technique used when smoking a regular cigarette (Schwartz, 1987). Users inhale the smoke deeply into their lungs, then hold their breath for 20–30 seconds in an attempt to get as much THC into the blood as possible (Schwartz, 1987). Through this method, about half of the available THC is absorbed through the lungs into the blood (Mirin and Weiss, 1983; Schwartz, 1987).

When smoked, the effects begin almost immediately, usually within ten minutes (Bloodworth, 1987). The effects reach peak intensity within 30 minutes and begin to decline within an hour. Estimates of the duration of the subjective effects of marijuana range from less than three hours (Brophy, 1985) up to four hours (Grinspoon and Bakalar, 1985; Bloodworth, 1987). The half-life of THC in the body has been estimated at approximately three days (Schwartz, 1987) to a week (Bloodworth, 1987).

When marijuana is ingested by mouth, the user will absorb only a small percentage of the available THC. Schwartz (1987) estimated that the user would have to ingest three times as much THC in order to achieve the same effects achieved by smoking one joint. Also with ingestion by mouth the user will not experience the immediate effects of smoking marijuana, but usually require 30–60 minutes (Mirin and Weiss, 1983), to perhaps two hours (Schwartz, 1987), before they begin to feel the effects of the drug. Estimates of the duration of marijuana's effects when ingested range from 3–12 hours (Mirin and Weiss, 1983) (Grinspoon and Bakalar, 1985).

SUBJECTIVE EFFECTS OF MARIJUANA

At moderate dosage levels, marijuana will bring about a two-phase reaction (Brophy, 1985). The first phase begins shortly after the drug enters the bloodstream, when the individual will experience a period of mild anxiety, followed by a sense of well-being, or euphoria, as well as a sense of relaxation and friendliness (Mirin and Weiss, 1983).

Friedman (1987) reported that evidence has been uncovered suggesting that marijuana causes "a transient increase in the release of the neurotransmitter dopamine" (p. 47), a chemical thought to be involved in the experience of euphoria. Individuals who are intoxicated on marijuana will also experience mood swings as well as an altered sense of time (Mirin and Weiss, 1983). Grinspoon and Bakalar (1985) attributed marijuana with the ability to cause a splitting of consciousness, in which the user will possibly experience the sensation of observing themselves while under the influence of the drug.

Marijuana users have often reported the feeling of being on the threshold of a significant personal insight but being unable to put this insight into words. These reported drug-related insights seem to come about during the first phase of the marijuana reaction. The second phase of the marijuana experience begins when the individual becomes sleepy, which takes place following the acute intoxication caused by marijuana (Brophy, 1985).

There are few immediate adverse reactions to marijuana (Mirin and Weiss, 1983). Marijuana users occasionally experience panic reactions (Berger and Dunn, 1982). Factors that influence the development of marijuana-related panic reactions are the individual's prior experience with marijuana, the individual's expectations for the drug, the dosage level being used, and the setting in which the drug is used. Such panic reactions are most often seen in the inexperienced marijuana user (Mirin and Weiss, 1983; Bloodworth, 1987).

Nahas (1986) noted that marijuana use might trigger an underlying psychosis in an individual who has suffered a previous psychotic episode or who may be predisposed to psychosis. Nahas (1986) also noted that the role of marijuana in the emergence of these psychotic episodes has not been determined, but there is evidence suggesting that marijuana may trigger psychotic episodes.

However, Grinspoon and Bakalar (1985) disagreed with Nahas' (1986) conclusion. The authors reported that marijuana may cause the individual to experience some distortion of the body image, as well as paranoid reactions and increased anxiety but noted that marijuana tends to sedate, rather than stimulate, the user.

PHARMACOLOGY OF THC

The active agent of marijuana, THC, is first detoxified by the liver, after which about 65% is excreted in the feces, and the rest excreted in the urine (Schwartz, 1987). Tolerance to the effects of THC develop rapidly, and in order to continue to achieve the initial effects, the chronic marijuana user must use "more potent cannabis, deeper, more sustained inhalations, or larger amounts of the crude drug" (Schwartz, 1987, p. 307).

Because the liver is unable to immediately metabolize all of the THC in the system, and because the THC binds to fat cells, significant amounts of THC may be stored in the body's fat reserves. The THC may then be slowly released back into the blood after the person has stopped using marijuana (Schwartz, 1987). This can account for the phenomenon in which heavy marijuana users have been known to test positive for THC in urine toxicology screens for weeks after their last use of the drug (Schwartz, 1987). The casual user of marijuana will usually test positive only for three days after the last use of the drug.

CONSEQUENCES OF CHRONIC MARIJUANA USE

As previously noted, the marijuana plant has been shown to contain about 400 different chemicals (Mirin and Weiss, 1983), some of which have not yet been identified (Bloodworth, 1987). Tests have shown that more than 2000 separate metabolites of these chemicals may be found in the body after marijuana has been smoked (Jenike, 1987), many of which may remain present for weeks. In addition to this, if the marijuana is adulterated (as it frequently is), the various adulterants will add their own contribution to the flood of chemicals being admitted to the body when the person uses marijuana.

Jenike (1987) noted that marijuana may be adulterated with PCP (to be discussed in the section on hallucinogenics); insect spray; dried, shredded cow manure (which may expose the user to salmonella bacteria); or herbicide sprays such as paraquat. The chemicals in these substances also gain admission into the user's body when the marijuana is smoked and must be considered when one attempts to measure the impact of marijuana on the user.

The active agent of marijuana, THC, may cause lung damage and reduce the effectiveness of the body's immune system. Smoking marijuana can also cause increased levels of carbon monoxide in the blood (Oliwenstein, 1988). Indeed, it has been reported that the marijuana smoker will absorb *five times* as much carbon monoxide per joint as would a cigarette smoker who smoked a single regular cigarette (Oliwenstein, 1988).

Furthermore, marijuana users who smoked even just a few joints a day seemed to develop the same type of damage to the cells lining the airways as do cigarette smokers who develop lung cancer (Oliwenstein, 1988). Mirin and Weiss (1983) observed that chronic use of marijuana often brings about obstructive pulmonary diseases similar to those seen in cigarette smokers. Bloodworth (1987) noted that marijuana smoke contains 5–15 times the amount of a known carcinogen, benzopyrene, as does tobacco smoke.

It was reported that marijuana smokers have an increased frequency of bronchitis and other upper respiratory infections (Mirin and Weiss, 1983), and Peluso and Peluso (1988) reported that marijuana suppresses part of the immune system. Bloodworth (1987) observed that there is conflicting evidence that marijuana will impact on the immune system but pointed out that even a weak immuno-suppressant effect could have "a devastating effect on AIDS patients" (p. 180).

Marijuana has been implicated in reduced sperm counts in men (Brophy, 1985), and a 50% lower blood testosterone level in men has been reported for the chronic user of marijuana (Bloodworth, 1987). Bloodworth (1987) also reported that chronic marijuana use in women could result in abnormal menstruation, failure to ovulate, and possible fetal damage if the woman was pregnant. Wray and Murthy (1987) reported that chronic marijuana use could result in fertility problems for women.

Persons who have previously used hallucinogenics may also experience marijuana-related "flashback" experiences (Mirin and Weiss, 1983; Jenike, 1987). Such "flashbacks" are usually limited to the six-month period following the last marijuana use.

It has been postulated that there is no known evidence of marijuana-related brain damage, even in the heavy user of marijuana (Berger and Dunn, 1982; Jenike, 1987); however, Peluso and Peluso (1988) have challenged this conclusion, noting that evidence suggests that chronic marijuana use may result in physical changes in the brain similar to those seen in aging. Bloodworth (1987) reported that marijuana was found to cause microscopic changes in the synaptic cleft in the brain of animals; however, the significance of this finding for humans was not clear.

Friedman (1987) reported that THC changes the way in which the brain handles sensory information and may also disrupt memory (Wray and Murthy, 1987). Furthermore, Friedman (1987) reported that chronic exposure to THC "damages and destroys nerve cells and causes other pathological changes in the hippocampus" (p. 47), a portion of the brain thought to be involved with processing sensory information. Wray and Murthy (1987) reported that marijuana use seems to interfere with the retrieval mechanisms of memory. Thus, there does appear to be evidence that the chronic use of marijuana can cause brain damage.

Jenike (1987) reported that marijuana may cause impaired reflexes, decreased short-term memory, and decreased attention spans. Mirin and Weiss (1983) noted that automobile drivers under the influence of marijuana will frequently misjudge the speed and length of time required for braking, factors that may contribute to accidental death while using marijuana.

Schwartz (1987) reported that marijuana use may impair coordination and reaction time for 12 to 24 hours after the euphoria from the last marijuana use has ended and noted that teenagers who smoked marijuana as often as six times a month "were 2.4 times more likely to be involved in traffic accidents" (p. 309). The exact significance of these findings is not clear at this time, but this study does suggest that marijuana's effects on coordination might be longer lasting than was once thought.

Marijuana use can cause a significant increase in heart rate, a matter of some consequence to persons who suffer from heart disease (Macdonald, 1988; Bloodworth, 1987). Cocaine users will often smoke marijuana concurrently with their use of cocaine in order to counteract the excessive stimulation caused by the cocaine. The combination of marijuana and cocaine can increase heart rate above that seen from either drug alone, raising the heart rate an additional 50 beats per minute (Macdonald, 1988). Again, this is a matter of some importance to persons with heart disease, although it should be pointed out that marijuana by itself does not apparently cause heart disease (Brophy, 1985; Jenike, 1987).

There is conflicting evidence as to whether chronic marijuana use might bring about an *amotivational syndrome*. Mirin and Weiss (1983) noted that some researchers have described this condition as consisting of a decreased drive and ambition, short attention span, easy distractability, and a tendency not to make plans beyond the present day. Although the existence of this syndrome has been challenged (Mirin and Weiss, 1983),

Schwartz (1987) argued that further research is necessary to determine once and for all whether chronic marijuana use can cause this amotivational syndrome.

In terms of immediate lethality, marijuana is a "safe" drug. Nahas (1986) noted that there were no clearly documented cases of a lethal overdose involving marijuana alone. Weil (1986) noted that marijuana was "among the least toxic drugs known to modern medicine" (p. 47). In contrast to the estimated 346,000 deaths in this country each year from tobacco, and the total of 125,000 yearly fatalities from alcohol use, marijuana causes only an estimated 75 deaths each year, mainly from accidents (Crowley, 1988). Grinspoon and Bakalar (1985) estimated that the effective dose is between 1/20,000th and 1/40,000th the lethal dose, which is to say that marijuana is a very safe drug in terms of immediate toxicity.

MARIJUANA AND PREGNANCY

Research into the effects of marijuana on pregnant women or the fetus is difficult to conduct, at least in part because it is difficult to separate the effects of the marijuana from other chemicals that the pregnant woman might use (Nahas, 1986). However, evidence suggests that marijuana use during pregnancy might contribute to "intrauterine growth retardation, poor weight gain, prolonged labor, and behavioral abnormalities in the newborn" (Nahas, 1986, p. 83).

Roffman and George (1988) noted that several research studies have found evidence that marijuana use during pregnancy might result in developmental problems for the fetus, including lowered birth weight and possible nervous system abnormalities; however, as the authors noted, these findings cannot be directly attributed to marijuana use during pregnancy. Roffman and George (1988) called for further research into the effects of marijuana on pregnancy.

ADDICTION POTENTIAL OF MARIJUANA

As the reader will recall from earlier chapters, two of the cardinal symptoms of addiction to any chemical are the development of tolerance to that chemical and the existence of a withdrawal syndrome when that drug is discontinued. Bloodworth (1987) reported that smoking as few as three marijuana cigarettes a week may result in tolerance to the effects of marijuana.

Bloodworth (1987) also noted that, because of marijuana's long half-life in the human body, one did not usually see the same severity of withdrawal symptoms as found in narcotic or barbiturate withdrawal. Nahas (1986) reported that there was evidence of a withdrawal syndrome from the heavy use of marijuana, including sweating, vomiting, nausea, and sleep disturbance. Bloodworth (1987) supported this conclusion and went on to suggest that the chronic marijuana user might experience feelings of irritability, anxiety, anorexia, and a general malaise when the drug was abruptly discontinued.

TREATMENT OF MARIJUANA ABUSE

Short-term, acute reactions to marijuana do not require any special intervention (Brophy, 1985). Panic reactions to marijuana usually respond to "firm reassurance in a nonthreatening environment" (Mirin and Weiss, 1983, p. 278), but the patient should be watched to ensure that no harm comes to the patient or to others (Mirin and Weiss, 1983). Grinspoon and Bakalar (1985) noted that marijuana may cause transient feelings of anxiety, which is experienced only during the initial period following the drug's use.

Bloodworth (1987) noted that marijuana users usually do not present themselves for treatment unless there is some form of coercion. Even when the marijuana user does enter treatment, the specific therapeutic methods for working with the chronic marijuana user are not well developed (Mirin and Weiss, 1983). Roffman and George (1988) suggested that this is because of the mistaken belief that, since marijuana is not as toxic as other drugs of abuse, its use by adults is not a cause of major concern to health care providers. Thus, health care providers have not addressed the issue of how to deal with the chronic marijuana user.

Total abstinence from all psychoactive drugs is required if treatment is to work (Bloodworth, 1987). A treatment program that identifies the individual's reason(s) for continued drug use, and helps the individual find alternatives to further drug use, is thought to be most effective. Supplemental groups that focus on vocational rehabilitation and socialization skills are also of value in the treatment of the chronic marijuana user (Mirin and Weiss, 1983). Jenike (1987) reported that treatment efforts should focus on understanding the abuser's disturbed psychosocial relationships.

In working with the marijuana addict, Bloodworth (1987) concluded that "family therapy is almost a necessity . . ." (p. 183). Group therapy as a means of dealing with peer pressure to use chemicals is necessary, in this author's opinion, and the importance of self-help support groups such as Alcoholics Anonymous or Narcotics Anonymous "cannot be overemphasized" (Bloodworth, 1987, p. 183).

SUMMARY

Marijuana has been the subject of controversy for the last generation. In spite of its popularity as a drug of abuse, surprisingly little is actually known about marijuana. In spite of this fact, some groups have called for marijuana's complete decriminalization. Other groups maintain that marijuana is a serious drug of abuse with a high potential for harm. Even the experts differ on the potential for marijuana to cause harm. Where Weil (1986) classified marijuana as one of the safest drugs known, Oliwenstein (1988) termed marijuana a dangerous drug.

The available evidence at this time would suggest that marijuana is not as benign as it was once thought. Marijuana, either alone or in combination with cocaine, will increase heart rate—a matter of some significance to those with cardiac disease. There is evidence that chronic use of marijuana will cause physical changes in the brain, and the smoke from marijuana cigarettes has been found to be even more harmful than tobacco smoke. One may expect that, in the years to come, marijuana will remain a most controversial drug.

CHAPTER 8

Narcotic Analgesics

> The addict sees nothing as his fault—not his addiction, not his degrada-
> tion, nor his desperation. He is convinced he has been thrown into life
> without the armor and weapons that others have. Heroin enables him to
> escape from the unfair battle. It deadens his desire for friends, for achieve-
> ment, for wealth, for strength, for sex, and even for food (Bassin, 1970, p.
> 117).

Man has known about narcotic analgesics for thousands of years. Indeed,
opium, the dried juice from the opium poppy plant *Papaver somniferum,* has
been used for medicinal purposes for at least 2500 years (Jaffe, 1985b).
Berger and Dunn (1982) observed that Sumerian records hint at the possible use of opium even earlier, around the year 4000 B.C. It is thus safe to
assume that opium has been a part of civilization for quite some time.

Abel (1982) defined an analgesic as being a drug that is able to bring
about the "relief of pain without producing general anesthesia" (p. 192).
There are two such groups of drugs. The first are those drugs that bring
about a *local anesthesia* and the second are those that change the perception
of pain, the *global analgesics.*

Cocaine, for example, is a local anesthetic, and as such will block the
transmission of nerve impulses from the site of the injury to the brain. In so
doing, cocaine (or any of the other local anesthetics developed after
cocaine) prevents the brain from receiving the nerve impulses that would
transmit the pain message from the site of the injury.

The global analgesics change the person's perception of pain. This
group of analgesics was further divided into two subgroups by Abel (1982).
The first of these is the *narcotic* family of drugs, which have both a CNS
depressant capability as well as an analgesic effect. The second subgroup
of global analgesics are nonnarcotic analgesics such as aspirin, acetaminophen, and similar agents.

The nonnarcotic analgesics are thought to interfere with the action of .
chemicals released by injured tissues of the body, which reduces pain and
inflammation. They are useful in the control of fever and do not have a
major impact on the central nervous system. The nonnarcotic analgesics
will be discussed in detail in chapter 10.

Many of the narcotic analgesics may be traced either directly or indirectly to opium. Indeed, the term *opiate* was once used to designate those
drugs derived from opium (Jaffe and Martin, 1985). Recently, a number of

either synthetic or semisynthetic opiatelike painkillers have been introduced. The generic term *opioid* is used to refer to any drug that is similar to morphine in its actions, although others use the terms opiate and opioid interchangeably (Jaffe and Martin, 1985). In this text, the terms *opiate*, or *narcotic* will be used.

As previously noted, opium has been used for medicinal purposes for at least 2500 years (Jaffe, 1985b). Berger and Dunn (1982) observed that Sumerian records hint at the use of opium around the year 4000 B.C. However, it was not until 1803 that a German scientist isolated a pure alkaloid base from opium, a chemical that was later called *morphine* after the Greek god of sleep Morphius.

Ray (1983) noted that for thousands of years, opium was perhaps the only chemical that physicians could use with predictable results. Opium was useful in the control of mild to severe levels of pain and (in an era before modern sanitation) could be used to treat dysentery. Since the discovery of aspirin and similar analgesics, the narcotics are no longer used in the treatment of mild to moderate levels of pain.

The narcotics are still used in the control of severe pain and severe diarrhea. In spite of the medical advances of the past century, the narcotics continue to be one of the more powerful, and useful, family of drugs available to physicians today.

NARCOTIC ADDICTION IN HISTORY

The invention of the hypodermic needle by Alexander Wood in 1857 made it possible to inject drugs into the body quickly and relatively painlessly. This, combined with the availability of relatively large amounts of pure morphine, produced a rather severe outbreak of morphine addiction (Jaffe and Martin, 1985). Furthermore, as Ray (1983) points out, injected morphine was not thought to be addicting, at least during the early 1850s, and was freely available without a prescription.

This is not to say that the opiate family of drugs had not been abused before this time. Indeed, Ray (1983) noted that there is evidence from 1500 B.C. that opium was used to prevent the excessive crying of children, while Galen (129–199 A.D.) spoke of opium cakes being sold in the streets of Rome. By the year 1729 China had found it necessary to outlaw opium smoking and within a little more than a century fought a major war with England over England's importation of opium to China (Franklin, 1985; Ray, 1983).

Morphine was used freely in battlefield hospitals during the American Civil War, as well as the Franco-Prussian and Prussian-Austrian wars in Europe (Ray, 1983). Intravenous morphine was found to be an effective way to provide relief from battlefield wounds. Because morphine slowed the wavelike contractions of the muscles surrounding the intestines, it was also used to control the dysentery encountered in crowded, unsanitary army camps.[1] So many soldiers on both continents became addicted to morphine that morphine addiction came to be called the "soldier's disease" (Ray, 1983, p. 332).

During the last half of the 19th century, the United States suffered from a wave of opiate addiction. Both opium and morphine were freely available without prescription. Like cocaine, morphine was included in patent medicines. Many people unknowingly became addicted to the opiates in various patent medicines.

Further, the practice of smoking opium was brought to this country by Chinese, many of whom came to this country to work on the railroad in the late 1800s. While the practice did not become very popular, it was reported that by the year 1900 a quarter of the opium imported into this country was for smoking (Ray, 1983).

It has been estimated that, by the year 1900, approximately *1% of the total population of this country* (Brecher, 1972) was addicted to narcotics. This included people who had become addicted to opiates as a result of medical treatment, through various patent medicines, and through the practice of smoking opium. It should be recalled that opiates were freely available through mail-order houses and over-the-counter.

Concern over the growing numbers of people addicted to cocaine, the opiates, or both prompted passage of the Pure Food and Drug Act of 1906. This law required that the contents of medicines be printed on the labels so that the purchaser might know what was contained in the medicine. Eight years later, the Harrison Narcotics Act of 1914 was passed, which prohibited the use of certain drugs without a prescription. These laws were passed to help contain the growing drug addiction problem in the United States. Since then, various legal restrictions have been used as the drug abuse problem has waxed and waned; however, the problem of narcotic abuse and addiction has never entirely disappeared.

MEDICAL USES OF THE NARCOTIC ANALGESICS

The opiates are used to control acute, severe pain and as cough suppressants (Reiss and Melick, 1984). Because they suppress the motility of the gastrointestinal tract, the opiates continue to be used in the control of *severe* diarrhea. This will be discussed in more detail in the section "Complications Caused by Narcotic Analgesic Use At Normal Dosage Levels."

Several forms of opiates, with various potencies and duration of effects, have been developed over the years. Some of these are natural opiates, while others are semisynthetic or totally synthetic, opiatelike chemicals. Morphine is still considered the prototype of the opiates,

[1] Dysentery is an infection of the lower intestinal tract that causes a great deal of pain and severe diarrhea mixed with blood and mucus. The organisms causing it are found in contaminated water (as was often found in crowded army camps) and it can prove rapidly fatal. Dehydration is the usual cause of death.

however, and it continues to be the standard against which other opiates are measured (Jaffe and Martin, 1985). Surprisingly, because the synthesis of morphine in the laboratory is difficult, most morphine is still obtained from the opium poppy.

The opiates have very similar actions, and except for differences in potency the effects of the opiates might be considered as a class of drugs. Heroin is one of the preferred narcotics among addicts and is illegal in the United States. In England, heroin is used to control severe pain, especially the pain caused by cancer. More potent than morphine (Lingeman, 1974), heroin is converted into morphine by the body after injection (Bazell, 1988). Heroin will not be discussed separately, since its actions are similar to the actions of other opiates.

MECHANISMS OF ACTION

Reiss and Melick (1984) note that the analgesic effect of the opiates is attributed to a number of factors. First, the opiates seem to mimic the actions of the body's natural painkillers, a group of three opiatelike neurotransmitters: the *endorphins*, the *enkephalins*, and the *dynorphins*. These chemicals are thought to be used by the brain to control pain and moderate the emotions. The opiates seem to use the same receptor sites in the brain to reduce the patient's awareness of pain. Jaffe and Martin (1985) noted that the morphinelike drugs are able to achieve analgesia without a significant loss of consciousness, a decided advantage in many cases.

The opiates also appear to be able to reduce the individual's anxiety level, promote drowsiness, and allow sleep in spite of severe pain (Brown, 1987; Govoni and Hayes, 1985). When therapeutic doses of morphine are given to a patient in pain, he or she will usually report that the pain is less intense, less discomforting, or entirely gone (Jaffe and Martin, 1985). Brown (1985) observed that some of the factors influencing analgesia achieved through the use of morphine included the route by which the medication was administered, the interval between doses, and the dosage level.

The cough suppressant action of codeine, a close chemical relative of morphine (Reiss and Melick, 1984), is thought to result from the ability of codeine to suppress the cough reflex. This is controlled by the medulla, a portion of the brain responsible for the maintenance of the body's internal state (Jaffe and Martin, 1985).

SUBJECTIVE EFFECTS OF NARCOTICS AT NORMAL DOSAGE LEVELS

At normal dosage levels, in the person who is using narcotics for medical reasons, these drugs will change the individual's perception of pain

(Julien, 1981). In order to understand how this is achieved, one must understand that pain is a multifaceted phenomenon. The individuals' experience of pain is, at least to some degree, influenced by their anxiety level, their expectations, and by their level of tension. The more tense, frightened, and anxious a person is, the more likely she or he is to experience pain in response to a given stimuli.

The opiates are able to raise the individual's pain threshold by moderating some of the fear, anxiety, and tension that normally accompany pain states (Jaffe and Martin, 1985). The individual will thus not attach the same importance to the pain felt and will experience less distress than before. Narcotic analgesics produce some drowsiness and some sedation (Schuckit, 1984) without a general loss of consciousness (Jaffe and Martin, 1985).

Narcotic analgesics will cause the pupils of the eyes to constrict. Govoni and Hayes (1985) noted that some patients experience constriction of the pupils even in total darkness and observed that this class of drugs will alter the pupil's response to light. Some patients also report a sense of euphoria (Jaffe and Martin, 1985) after using one of the narcotic analgesics, which will be discussed in more detail.

These effects are seen in a normal individual who is experiencing some degree of pain. However, when pain-free individuals receive the same dose of morphine, they are likely to experience nausea, vomiting, some degree of drowsiness, and an inability to concentrate (Jaffe and Martin , 1985). Many people will experience a sense of euphoria. Unlike alcohol, however, even large doses of morphine will not cause slurred speech or significant motor incoordination (Jaffe and Martin, 1985).

The mechanism by which opiates are able to produce a sense of euphoria is not well understood. However, since the discovery of the endorphins in 1975, it is believed that the opiates may mimic the actions of this family of neurotransmitters (Kirsch, 1986). The endorphins are thought to be responsible for stress management and are also thought to be "natural painkillers." When flooded with opiates, the brain reacts as if massive amounts of endorphins were released. Where there is no stress or pain, the individual will often experience a sense of euphoria.

Franklin (1987) postulated that this mechanism might also account for the addictive potential of the opiates. Franklin thought that the future opiate addict was a person who suffered a great deal of emotional distress throughout life, possibly because of a biological deficit. It was postulated that such a person would lack normal levels of endorphins. Since this person had always known psychological suffering, he or she would have no way of knowing that this situation was not normal and would not seek help in dealing with this pain.

When opiates were injected, that person's brain would be flooded with a substitute for the missing endorphins and suddenly gain release from the emotional pain that she or he had always felt. When the opiates began to wear off, the individual would seek out more opiates to regain the euphoria and comfort that had only just been discovered through the use of opiates.

Over time, as the body reduces production of natural endorphins, the individual must continue to use narcotics to avoid the painful withdrawal symptoms that are the hallmark of narcotic addiction.

COMPLICATIONS CAUSED BY NARCOTIC ANALGESICS AT NORMAL DOSAGE LEVELS

Even at therapeutic dosage levels, the opiates will cause some degree of constriction of the pupils and will depress respiration. Indeed, following therapeutic doses of morphine (or a similar agent), respiration might be affected for four to five hours. It is advised that opiates be used with extreme caution (Eisenhauer and Gerald, 1984, p. 229) in individuals suffering from respiratory problems such as asthma, emphysema, chronic bronchitis, and pulmonary heart disease.

When used at therapeutic dosage levels, morphine and similar drugs can cause nausea and vomiting (Brown, 1985). Research has demonstrated that, at normal dosage levels, approximately 40% of ambulatory patients using morphine will experience some degree of nausea—approximately 15% will vomit (Jaffe and Martin, 1985). Brown (1985) noted that ambulation increases the chances that a patient will experience nausea or vomiting and suggested that patients not walk around immediately after receiving medication. These side effects are dose-related, which is to say that as the dosage level increases, these side effects are seen in a greater percentage of the population.

At therapeutic dosage levels, morphine and similar drugs may decrease the secretion of hydrochloric acid in the stomach. The muscle contractions of peristalsis (which push food along the intestines) are restricted (Govoni and Hayes, 1985), possibly to the point of spasm in the muscles involved (Jaffe and Martin, 1985). This is the side effect that made morphine so useful in the treatment of dysentery.

The opiates are well absorbed through the gastrointestinal tract, but when used orally, there is a great variation in the levels of narcotics found in the blood (Govoni and Hayes, 1985). Thus, the oral route is not the most effective method of administration and is used only in cases of moderate levels of pain. The narcotics are well absorbed through the lungs (as when opium is smoked) and the nasal mucosa (as when heroin powder is "snorted").

In addition to the uneven absorption rates obtained from oral doses of narcotics, Brown (1985) pointed out that the liver will metabolize at least 50% of the morphine absorbed through the gastrointestinal tract before it reaches the brain. It is thus difficult to determine how much of an oral dose of morphine will reach the blood or how much will actually reach the brain before being metabolized by the liver. For this reason, larger doses are prescribed when narcotics are taken orally.

Because a greater degree of control over the amount of narcotics that reach the blood is achieved when narcotics are injected, the opiates are most often injected when used for medical purposes (Jaffe and Martin, 1985). (For this same reason, the most common method of narcotic abuse also involves the injection of narcotics.) However, on occasion, the opiates are still administered orally.

METHODS OF OPIATE ABUSE

Although the narcotic analgesics are quite useful in the control or treatment of a range of conditions, there are those who will abuse this family of drugs by self-administering narcotics for personal pleasure. These individuals will usually inject the narcotic, either under the skin ("skin-popping"), or into a vein ("mainlining"). The practice of smoking opium is not commonly found in this country, where supplies of opium are limited. However, in parts of the world where supplies of opium are more plentiful, the practice of smoking opium is more common.

It is not known what percentage of those who experiment with opiates will stop further use of the drug without ever being addicted. Some users claim to be able to remain only occasional abusers of the narcotics. The narcotic family of drugs does present a significant danger of dependency, however, and many users will develop a formal addiction to narcotics after a period of abuse. Jenike (1987) observed that it was possible to become addicted to narcotics in "less than two weeks" (p. 13), if the drugs were used on a daily basis in regularly increasing doses.

Narcotics are obtained from many sources. The user generally buys "street" narcotics—narcotics that have been smuggled into this country, then distributed for sale on the local level. The narcotics are usually sold in a powder form, in small packets that are sold individually. The powder is mixed with water, then the mixture is heated in a small container (usually a spoon) over a small flame such as from a cigarette lighter or candle. The mixture is then injected.

Another source of narcotics are pharmaceuticals intended for legal use. The tablet is crushed or the capsule taken apart, and the powder is mixed with water. Again, the mixture is heated in a small container (usually a spoon) over a small flame (usually a match, candle, or cigarette lighter), which helps dilute the powder. The resulting mixture is then injected.

The method of injection used by narcotic addicts differs from the manner in which a physician or nurse will inject medication into a vein. Lingeman (1974) observed that the technique is called "booting," and described the process as one in which the narcotic is injected into the vein a little at a time, letting it back up into the eye dropper, injecting a little more, letting the blood-heroin mixture back up, and so on. The addict believes that this technique prolongs the initial pleasurable sensation of the heroin as it first takes effect—a feeling of warmth in the abdomen, euphoria, and sometimes a sensation similar to an orgasm (p. 32).

In the process, however, the hypodermic needle, and the syringe (or the eye dropper attached to a hypodermic needle, a common substitute) become contaminated with the individual's blood. When other addicts use the same needle, as is commonly done by both cocaine and opiate addicts, contaminated blood from one individual is passed to the next, and the next, and the next. . . .

Furthermore, as was noted by Wetli (1987), intravenous narcotic addicts who inject medication intended for oral use will inject directly into the bloodstream starch or other "fillers" that were not intended for intravenous use. These fillers are mixed with the medication to give it body and form. They are usually destroyed by stomach acid when the medication is taken orally but cannot be destroyed by the body's defenses when injected. Repeated exposure to these agents can cause extensive scarring at the point of injection, which forms the "tracks" caused by repeated injections of street opiates.

Jaffe (1986; 1985b) noted that it is not clear how the opiates function as a reinforcer, as the opiates impact on different parts of the brain. But animal research and clinical evidence with human subjects suggest that the opiates are indeed powerful reinforcers. Kirsch (1986) noted that opiates are thought to activate the same reward system of the brain that cocaine does; however, this is not known for certain.

It is known, however, that a single dose of opiates will reduce anxiety and provide a feeling of increased self-esteem. When abused through injection, many opiates will bring about a sensation of a "rush" or a "flash." This is a sudden, brief, pleasurable sensation that has been described as similar to the sexual orgasm (Lingeman, 1974; Jaffe, 1986; 1985b) that lasts 30–60 seconds (Mirin and Weiss, 1983). Following this, the individual will experience a feeling of drowsiness and euphoria that lasts for several hours (Mirin and Weiss, 1983).

As tolerance to the opiates develops, however, the individual will no longer experience the initial rush with the same intensity, and the opiates lose the initial antianxiety effect. Kline (1985) observed that the opiates cause the brain's natural endorphine system, which is involved in regulation of the emotions, to at least partially shut down. In other words, over time, the brain substitutes the chemical opiates for natural endorphins.

When the supply of opiates is eliminated from the body, the brain no longer has the necessary amounts of either natural endorphins or opiates needed to regulate the emotions and pain. In time, the brain will again start to produce endorphins on its own. However, until it does, the individual will experience withdrawal symptoms. Withdrawal from the opiates will be discussed in a later section.

Over time, the individual will become tolerant to some of the effects of the opiates, but tolerance does not develop equally to each of the effects of the opiates (Jaffe, 1985). The individual can develop "remarkable tolerance" (Jaffe, 1985b, p. 990) to the analgesic and respiratory depressant effects of the opiates but less to the constipation that can result from opiate use. Thus, chronic use of narcotics can (and often does) result in significant problems with constipation.

OPIATE ADDICTION

The narcotic family of drugs possess a significant potential for addiction. Indeed, the potential for addiction is so serious that it is one of the major factors limiting the medical use of narcotics (Jaffe and Martin, 1985).

In spite of the addiction potential of the narcotics, only a fraction of those who briefly experiment with opiates will become addicted (Jaffe, 1985b). Jenike (1987) reported that ". . . about half of the individuals who engage in opioid abuse develop opioid dependence" (p. 13). However, there is no way at this time to determine whether a given person who is abusing opiates will ultimately become addicted.

It has been suggested (Khantzian, 1985) that there is a dynamic interaction between the psychological distress that a person might experience and the vulnerability of that person to develop an addiction. Khantzian suggested that opiate addicts were drawn to the drug because of its ability to help them control powerful feelings of rage and anger, as opposed to cocaine addicts, who struggled with feelings of depression and hypomania.

Franklin (1987) postulated that some individuals were "at risk" for opiate addiction because they were in "constant psychic pain" (p. 87). It is of interest to note that there is a significant interrelationship between the experience of pain and the experience of depression, and Franklin (1987) postulates that for the individual, this inner pain might be a reflection of depression.

Research has not identified the primary cause of this inner pain. Possibilities include a lack of proper maternal love during a critical phase of childhood or a biological deficit. However, since those individuals grew up with this inner pain, they would never have known an existence without it. They would, in other words, accept it as "normal." That is, until they began to experiment with opiates.

At this point, Franklin (1987) postulated that the opiate-addict-to-be would suddenly and forcefully learn what life without the constant psychic pain could be. Such a person would, in Franklin's (1987) words, "be instantly and forever addicted" (p. 87).

It is of interest to note that Maddux, Desmond, and Costello (1987) found that active opiate addicts were significantly more depressed than were those who would only occasionally abuse opiates. Further, Maddux et al. (1987) found that narcotic abusers were more depressed than those who were abstinent. This is the opposite of what one would expect based on Franklin's (1987) work, raising an interesting chicken-or-the-egg question.

The evidence indicates a significant relationship between depression and opiate addiction; however, the evidence does not suggest which condition precedes the other. It is possible, as Franklin (1987) hypothesized, that depression develops first, setting the foundation for subsequent addiction. However, it is equally possible that the observed depression is a *result* of prolonged chemical use, not a cause of it. There is no clear answer to this problem.

Whatever the actual reason, it should be recalled that *all* opiates possess the potential for abuse and to various degrees are capable of causing tolerance, psychological dependence, and physical addiction (Eisenhauer and Gerald, 1984). In addressing the question of the diagnosis of opiate addiction, Jaffe (1986) noted that current diagnostic criteria for opiate dependence usually require only the existence of tolerance or opiate withdrawal symptoms following use of the opiates.

Following an extended period of use, the exact length of which is unknown, the opiates are able to bring about an addiction and a classic pattern of withdrawal symptoms. Jenike (1987) suggested that a person could become addicted to narcotics in less than two weeks of daily use at ever increasing dosage levels.

Jaffe (1986) observed that after addiction has developed, withdrawal from narcotics will vary in intensity as a result of these factors: (a) the potency of the specific opiate being abused, (b) the length of time that the person has used the drug, and (c) the speed with which withdrawal is attempted.

In theory an opiate addict who has been using the equivalent of 50 mgs of morphine a day for three months will have an easier detoxification than would another individual who has been using the equivalent of 50 mgs of morphine a day for three years. Also, an opiate addict who is gradually withdrawn from opiates at the rate of the equivalent of 10 mgs of morphine a day will have an easier detoxification than would an addict who suddenly stops using the drug ("cold turkey").

The narcotics, like a large number of other drugs, cross the placenta. Thus, when a pregnant woman uses narcotics, both the mother and the fetus are exposed to opiates. These infants are, in a very real sense, hidden victims of addiction and will be discussed in more detail in the chapter "Hidden Victims of Chemical Dependency."

EXTENT OF THE PROBLEM OF NARCOTIC ADDICTION

It has been reported that there are over 500,000 known heroin addicts in the United States (L. Siegel, 1989; American Psychiatric Association,

1985). Peluso and Peluso (1988) agree with this figure, noting that perhaps one-fifth of these heroin addicts are women. Another 1 million women are thought to be using heroin on an occasional basis, but have not become addicted (Peluso and Peluso, 1988). All together, some six metric tons of heroin were consumed by addicts in America in 1984 (Peluso and Peluso, 1988).

Lingeman (1974) noted that the number of people who occasionally abuse opiates but never graduate to the intensive, compulsive use of opiates that is the hallmark of addiction, is simply not known. It was hypothesized, however, that "the majority go on to mainlining" (p. 106). Jaffe (1985b) challenged this conclusion, noting that only a fraction of those who briefly experiment with opiates will become addicted.

However, little information exists as to the number of persons who: (a) once were addicted to opiates, but are now drug-free, (b) once were addicted to opiates, but whose drug of choice is now something other than opiates, (c) were abusing narcotics, but could not be classified as *addicted* at this point in time, or (d) were using a narcotic other than heroin. Nor is information available to determine the male/female ratio for narcotic addicts.

DuPont (1987) reported that although there are those who are only just starting to develop an addiction to narcotics, the number of heroin users in this country peaked in 1971. Chasnoff and Schnoll (1987) observed that, of those women abusing chemicals, the greatest number use drugs other than the narcotics.

The figure of 500,000 known heroin addicts previously cited is an estimate that may not accurately reflect the true scope of narcotic addiction in America. However, this author has worked with former narcotic addicts who now are addicted to cocaine, alcohol, or other chemicals. These individuals, while perhaps technically not opiate addicts any longer, were still addicted and admitted that they would return to narcotic use if it were possible for them to regain the euphoria they experienced from these drugs a decade or more ago.

There are those individuals who claim to have used narcotics only on a weekend basis for years but deny the compulsion to use any chemicals during the week. Further, there are individuals who claim to be using narcotics other than heroin—narcotics that are usually obtained through pharmaceutical supply houses or from other sources. If this information is accurate, these individuals would not be identified as *heroin* addicts, but are certainly part of the spectrum of narcotics use in America.

Thus, the figure of 500,000 known heroin addicts must be viewed only as a baseline figure, which may not accurately reflect the narcotic addiction problem in America. The nature of narcotic addiction is to avoid the spotlight of scientific inquiry, and there is little accurate data about the extent of this problem.

SYMPTOMS OF OPIATE
WITHDRAWAL IN THE NARCOTIC ADDICT

As a general rule, opiate withdrawal symptoms begin 8–12 hours after the last dose of the drug is administered. This depends on the speed with which the individual's body is able to metabolize the specific chemical being used, and in some cases withdrawal symptoms might be seen sooner than 8–12 hours after the last dose. In order to avoid these withdrawal symptoms, the addict must either inject the drug again or substitute the use of another drug.

Schuckit (1984) noted that these withdrawal symptoms might include tearing, running nose, repeated yawning, sweating, restless sleep, dilated pupils, anorexia, irritability, insomnia, weakness, abdominal pain, ejaculation in male addicts, and gastrointestinal upset. Constipation is a significant problem, which can result in fecal impaction and, in rare cases, intestinal obstruction. (Jaffe, 1986).

It has been suggested that, once addiction develops, these withdrawal symptoms might make the person so uncomfortable as to reinforce the tendency toward continued drug use (Bauman, 1988). This is true even if the initial "rush" is no longer experienced because of drug tolerance (Jaffe, 1986). Jenike (1987) reported that ". . . as many as one-third of addicts have a pathologic fear of detoxification" (p. 13), apparently because of a fear of the distress of withdrawal. In other words a circular pattern of drug use is established where the individual initially uses the drug because it is pleasurable. However, after awhile, the pleasure is no longer there, and the individual is forced to continue the drug simply to postpone as long as possible the symptoms of narcotic withdrawal.

Opiate addicts in a medical setting will often emphasize the distress they experience during withdrawal, possibly as a ploy to obtain additional medications from medical staff. Jenike (1987) gave several examples of the manipulativeness demonstrated by addicts in maintaining their drug habits. However, as Eisenhauer and Gerald (1984) noted, the abstinence syndrome "produces extreme distress in the dependent individual . . ." but ". . . it does not represent a threat to life" (p. 229). Symptoms of the opiate withdrawal syndrome will abate, even in the absence of treatment (Eisenhauer and Gerald, 1984).[2]

Opiate addiction, and the lifestyle required to maintain the addiction, carries with it a significant risk of death. Mirin and Weiss (1983) estimated that there is a 1% per year death rate for urban addicts. Schuckit (1984) reported that the annual mortality rate for opiate addicts is 5–10 per 1000, with the leading causes of death being suicide, homicide, accidents, and disease. Jenike (1987) gave an even higher figure, stating that about 10 per 1000 narcotics addicts die each year.

---

[2]This assumes that the individual is addicted *only* to opiates. If the individual is addicted to other chemicals, this will complicate the withdrawal process. Withdrawal from chemicals should *always be attempted only under medical supervision.*

Opiate addicts often share needles, on occasion each waiting in turn to use the same needle to inject drugs. Wetli (1987) noted that intravenous drug users, who usually fail to practice proper sterile technique, are in danger of developing such problems as "peripheral cellulitis and abscesses, viral hepatitis, endocarditis (infection of the heart valves), pneumonia, lung abscesses, tetanus, and malaria" (p. 49), in addition to AIDS. Burden and Rogers (1988) identified the use of intravenous drugs as one of the risk factors for endocarditis. Heyward and Curran (1988) reported that AIDS was now the leading cause of death for intravenous drug users.

OPIATE OVERDOSE

Jaffe and Martin (1985) note that "In man, death from morphine poisoning is nearly always due to respiratory arrest. . . ." (p. 501), a view that is supported by Eisenhauer and Gerald (1984). However, this is only for cases of overdose with pharmaceutical opiates. There is some question whether fatal overdoses from "street" narcotics are caused by the narcotics or by the multitude of chemicals added to them (Kirsch, 1986). In any case, *known or suspected opiate overdose is a life-threatening emergency, which **always** requires immediate medical support and treatment.*

There are several "street" myths about the treatment of opiate overdose. There is the myth that cocaine (or another CNS stimulant) will help in the control of an opiate overdose. Another myth, known to this author, is that it is possible to control the symptoms of an overdose by putting ice packs under the arms and on the groin of the overdose victim. Unfortunately, the treatment of an opiate overdose is a complicated matter, which does not lend itself to such easy solutions.

Even in the best-equipped hospital, a narcotics overdose may result in death. Sheridan, Patterson, and Gustafson (1982) indicated that the prescription medication Narcan (naloxone hydrochloride) is the treatment of choice for known or suspected opiate overdose. Naloxone is thought to bind at the narcotic receptor sites within the brain, preventing the narcotic molecules from reaching the receptors and causing respiratory depression.

Even with the use of naloxone, oxygen and possibly mechanical ventilation may also be necessary (Sheridan, Patterson, and Gustafson, 1982). The effects of naloxone are short-lived, as the drug has a half-life of only 60–90 minutes (Sheridan, Patterson, and Gustafson, 1982). In cases of severe overdose, more than one dose of naloxone may be necessary. The reader must thus keep in mind that *known or suspected opiate overdose is a life-threatening emergency, which **always** requires immediate medical support and treatment.*

A WORD ON FENTANYL AND "DESIGNER" DRUGS

In recent years, a new synthetic narcotic known as Sublimaze (fentanyl is the generic name of this drug) has been introduced. Like other opiates, fentanyl is intended for the control of pain. Because of its short duration of action, this drug is especially useful as an analgesic during surgery (Govoni and Hayes, 1985).

Fentanyl is extremely potent, but there is some controversy over exactly how potent fentanyl actually is. Kirsch (1986) noted that fentanyl is "approximately 3,000 times stronger than morphine, [and] 1,000 times stronger than heroin" (p. 18). Kirsch went on to note that the active dose in man is *one microgram*, and offered as a basis of comparison the observation that the average postage stamp weighs 60,000 micrograms.

The *1987 Physician's Desk Reference* (Medical Economics Company, 1987) noted that *one-tenth of a milligram* (0.10 mg) of fentanyl is as potent as 10 milligrams of morphine. Gallagher (1986) reported that fentanyl is 100 times as potent as morphine, and 20–40 times as potent as heroin. Govoni and Hayes (1985) estimated that fentanyl is 80 times as potent as morphine.

By manipulation of the chemical structure of fentanyl, Gallagher (1986) observed that it was possible to produce a drug that was 2000–6000 times as potent as morphine. It is obvious from this information that, while the true potency of fentanyl has yet to be determined, it is a very potent drug.

Fentanyl, when used in a medical setting, is used only by injection. There are no oral forms of this drug on the market. Kirsch (1986) noted that evidence suggests that some people who abuse the drug might be smoking or "snorting" it.

As previously noted, fentanyl is so potent a drug that extremely small doses are effective in humans. Its detection is extremely difficult, and routine drug toxicology screens might overlook the presence of such small amounts of fentanyl in the blood or urine of a suspected drug user (Kirsch, 1986; Gallagher, 1986). Thus, even a "clean" urine or blood drug screen might not rule out fentanyl use.

Adverse Effects of Fentanyl

Among the side effects of fentanyl are respiratory depression, constipation, and, because of its potency, a significant risk of fatal overdose. Kirsch (1986) reported that fentanyl was able to produce a 25% decrease in heart rate and a 20% drop in blood pressure. He also noted that some addicts have been known to die so rapidly after using fentanyl that they were found with the needle still in their arms.

This phenomenon is well documented in cases of narcotic overdoses but is not understood by medicine. Some researchers attribute the rapid death to the narcotic itself, while others postulate that death is brought on by the various chemicals added to the drug to "cut" or dilute it on the street.[3]

[3]It is a common practice to "cut" or dilute opiates sold on the street in order to increase their value. The highly concentrated drug is mixed with other chemicals, which usually have little or not psychoactive potential, several times in the distribution process. The relative potency of the final form of the drug that results from this process is lowered, with volume increasing at each stage of the process. Lingeman (1974) observed that heroin is often "cut" from four to seven times before it is finally sold to addicts on the street.

Govoni and Hayes (1985) noted that, when used in a medical setting, some of the side effects of fentanyl include blurred vision, a sense of euphoria, nausea, vomiting, dizziness, delirium, lowered blood pressure, and possible respiratory depression or respiratory arrest. Cardiac arrest is a possible side effect of fentanyl (Govoni and Hayes, 1985).

Subjective Effects of Fentanyl

Fentanyl, although entirely a synthetic drug, is still a member of the opiate family of drugs. As such, fentanyl will produce analgesia, for which it is used in medical settings. It will also, when abused, produce a sense of drowsiness and euphoria. Addicts also report a short-lived rush experience that seems to be of a shorter duration than that found in heroin abuse (Kirsch, 1986).

Fentanyl has a rather short half-life in the body. The *1987 Physician's Desk Reference* noted that the analgesic effects of this drug last only one to two hours but the effects of fentanyl on respiration might last longer than the analgesia produced by the drug.

It is difficult to understand the addictive potential of fentanyl. Dr. William Spiegelman (quoted in Gallagher, 1986) observed that ". . . it can take years to become addicted to alcohol, months for cocaine, and one shot for fentanyl" (p. 26). To further complicate matters, "street chemists" are manipulating the chemical structure of fentanyl, adding a few atoms to the basic fentanyl chain here, snipping a few atoms there, to produce what are known as "drug analogs."

These street chemists are taking advantage of the fact that laws that identify both legal and illegal drugs are highly specific. The exact location of each atom in the drug molecule is identified, and its relationship to every other atom in the drug's chemical chain is identified and recorded. In cases where the drug is a legitimate medical agent, this chemical structure is then used to register the copyright of that drug with the government. If the drug is illegal, this chemical chain is then used to identify the drug as a "controlled" substance.

Let us say, for the sake of discussion, that a drug with a chemical structure A-B-C-D is registered as a "new" drug by its manufacturer. This hypothetical drug is used to control pain, but it also has a high addiction potential. The manufacturer recommends that this new drug be used only to control *extreme* pain, and the drug is not easily obtained by street addicts. The chemical structure A-B-C-D is registered as the chemical structure of this new drug, and a copyright is granted for its manufacture.

However, a drug with the chemical structure A-B-C-E, even though it retains the core structure "A-B-C" from the parent drug and produces effects similar to those of that drug, would still technically be a "different" drug since its molecular structure is not *exactly* the same as the drug A-B-C-D. This is called a drug "analog".

Drug analogs vary both in terms of potency, and safety. When drug analogs are manufactured, their regulation by the courts is extremely difficult. This is because each drug analog must be registered as an illegal substance, with the exact location of each atom on the drug molecule identified. When this finally is accomplished (and it sometimes can take months to identify the chemical structure of an unknown chemical) a law that identifies the specific chemical structure of that particular analog (in this case A-B-C-E) must be passed. This is a complicated, and often lengthy, process. At such time, it would be a simple matter for the illicit drug chemists to change the basic chemical structure of the parent drug just a little bit, build a new analog, perhaps with the chemical structure A-B-C-G this time, and start the whole cycle over again.

The new analog might be more or less potent than the parent molecule. Kirsch, (1986) identified nine drug analogs to fentanyl that are known, or suspected, to have been sold on the streets. These drug analogs range in potency from 1/10th that of morphine for the analog benzylfentanyl to approximately 3000 times more potent than morphine for 3-methyl fentanyl.

Fentanyl and its analogs are rapidly becoming a significant part of the drug abuse problem in this country. Gallagher (1986) observed that, in California, fentanyl analogs are currently being used by 20% of the opiate addicts. The problems and techniques of treatment will be discussed in the chapter "Treatment of Chemical Dependency." However, the mental health professional should have a basic understanding of opiate addiction, including the new "designer" drugs, to better serve the public.

THE TREATMENT OF OPIATE ADDICTION

The man on the street seems to believe that once an opiate addict, always an addict, and is quite pessimistic about treatment for narcotic addiction. Research has indeed suggested that some 90% of those addicts who achieve abstinence will return to chemical use within six months (Schuckit, 1984), confirming the layman's dismal opinion about the treatment of narcotic addiction.

However, on the positive side, more than a third of all opiate addicts will ultimately be able to achieve and retain sobriety. Jenike (1987) reported that for those addicts who survive their addiction, abstinence from opiate use is finally achieved about nine years after the addiction first developed. This is a far brighter picture than is generally assumed by health care professionals. The treatment of opiate addiction will be discussed in more detail in the section on treatment methods.

SUMMARY

The narcotic family of drugs have been effectively utilized by physicians for untold thousands of years. Indeed, after alcohol, the narcotics might be man's oldest drug. The narcotics have been found to be useful in the control of severe, acute pain, as well as in the control of the symptoms of severe cough and diarrhea. The only factor that limits their application is the addiction potential that this family of drugs presents.

This addiction potential has been known for thousands of years. Indeed, even more than alcohol, the narcotics have been recognized as addicting drugs. In spite of this, the narcotics have presented a major problem as drugs of abuse for generations. With the advent of the chemical revolution, synthetic narcotics have been developed which promise to be major abuse problems in the decades to come.

CHAPTER 9

Inhalants and Aerosols

Although rarely encountered by chemical dependency professionals, there are a small number of people who use and abuse the anesthetic gases commonly associated with either general or dental surgery (Julien, 1981). In addition, there are a wide variety of cheap, easily concealed chemical agents such as various forms of nail polish remover, cleaning agents, gasoline fumes, and some forms of glue that may be used to bring about a sense of euphoria and various short-term mental changes (Schuckit, 1984; Westermeyer, 1987). These chemicals are inhaled, and thus are called *inhalants*.

Cohen (1977) identified several reasons why the inhalants are abused by teenagers. First, these chemicals have a rapid onset of action, usually within a few seconds. Second, inhalant users report pleasurable effects, including a sense of euphoria, when they use these chemicals. Third, and perhaps most important, the inhalants are relatively inexpensive and are easily available to teenagers.

Most of the commonly used agents may be easily purchased by teenagers because no legal restrictions are placed on their sale.[1] The inhalants are usually available in small, easily hidden packages. Brunswick (1989) identified some of the more popular inhalants as being:

> . . . accessible and cheap. They are found at the corner drug store, in the garage, or under the kitchen sink. They take the form of magic markers, glue and fingernail polish. They produce a short but intense high that some have likened to the rush from rock cocaine, or "crack" (p. 6A).

The inhalants are thus easily available, inexpensive, and easily hidden. Inhalant abuse tends to be a cyclical phenomenon, which is on the increase in some parts of the United States (Brunswick, 1989).

GLUE SNIFFING AND SIMILAR CHEMICAL USE

Brecher (1972) noted that certain chemical agents reach the brain more rapidly and efficiently when they are inhaled, rather than ingested or injected. Such chemicals enter the bloodstream in an extremely short

[1]Obviously, this does not apply to anesthetic gases, but refers to more commonly abused inhalants.

period of time, usually within seconds, and do so without their chemical structure being altered by the liver (Berger and Dunn, 1982).

There have been historical references to the practice of inhalant abuse in the past century. However, these references were usually to the use of anesthetic gases, and it was not until the 1960s that much attention was paid to the practice of glue sniffing (Brecher, 1972; Westermeyer, 1987), where the individual will use model-airplane glue as an inhalant, the active agent of which is usually toluene.

Berger and Dunn (1982) suggested that the practice of glue sniffing began in California, when teenagers accidentally discovered the intoxicating powers of model-airplane glue. The first known reference to this practice was in 1959, in the magazine section of a Denver newspaper (Brecher, 1972). Local newspapers soon began to carry stories on the dangers of inhalant abuse, in the process giving explicit details of how to use airplane glue to become intoxicated and what effects to expect. Within a short time, a "Nationwide Drug Menace" (Brecher, 1972, p. 321) emerged.

Brecher (1972) observed that a "problem" was essentially manufactured through distorted media reports. The author pointed out that in response to media reports of deaths due to glue sniffing, one newspaper researched several stories and found only nine deaths that could be attributed to glue sniffing. Of this number, six deaths were due to asphyxiation: each victim had used an airtight plastic bag and had suffocated.

In the seventh case, there was evidence that asphyxiation was also the cause of death, while in the eighth case there was no evidence that the victim had been using inhalants. Finally, in the ninth case, the individual was found to have been using gasoline as an inhalant but was in poor health to begin with. Furthermore, Brecher noted that ". . . among tens of thousands of glue-sniffers prior to 1964, no death due unequivocally to glue vapor had as yet been reported. The lifesaving advice children needed was not to sniff glue with their heads in plastic bags" (p. 331).

In reading Brecher's (1972) work, one is left with the question of how serious the glue-sniffing problem was before the news media began to publish reports of it. Although one is left with the impression that this "problem" was manufactured by the media, subsequent research has found that the use of inhalants may introduce into the body toxic chemicals that might damage many parts of the body (Brunswick, 1989).

Extent of the Problem

The sporadic use of inhalants usually lasts for a year or two, and is generally a fad among teenagers (Schuckit, 1984; Lingeman, 1974) . It has been suggested (Newcomb and Bentler, 1989), that these agents are usually the first consciousness-altering agents used by children. Mirin and Weiss (1983) noted that inhalants tend to be most popular among boys in their early teens, especially in poor or rural areas where more expensive drugs of abuse are not easily available.

McHugh (1987) suggested that the inhalants are most often abused by grade-school children and agreed with Newcomb and Bentler (1989) that these chemicals are often the first consciousness-altering chemicals used by children. Furthermore, after a year or two, and certainly by adolescence, the user tends to abandon the use of inhalants (McHugh, 1987). Unfortunately, as Brunswick (1989) reported, approximately one-third of the children who abused inhalants were found to be using traditional drugs of abuse four years later. Thus, for some, inhalants may be "gateway" chemicals that lead the way to further drug use in later years.

Schuckit (1984) noted that some individuals continue the use of inhalants for 15 years or more, an observation supported by Westermeyer (1987). These people are apparently a minority, and it would appear that the majority of those who use inhalants either go on to other forms of drug use in later years or discontinue further experimentation with chemicals.

The actual percentage of those persons who are using solvents remains unknown. But Schuckit (1984) noted that one study found that 20% of the adolescent girls and 33% of the adolescent boys questioned admitted to using solvents *at least once*. Thus, it is safe to say that a sizable minority of teenagers will experiment with inhalants.

Method of Administration

McHugh (1987) noted that inhalant abuse is "a group activity" (p. 334). Lingeman (1974) observed that the most common method of abuse was for the user of glue to squeeze some into a paper bag. The user then "holds the bag tight over his nose, and inhales the fumes" (p. 85) to introduce the chemical into his or her lungs.

Mirin and Weiss (1983) noted that volatile gases are inhaled from a handkerchief or rag that has been soaked with the chemical, or that glue fumes are inhaled after the glue has been squirted into a paper bag. Brunswick (1989) reported that children using inhalants will often simply squirt the chemical onto a rag and inhale the fumes from the rag. The effects may last up to 45 minutes, depending on the individual's exposure to the chemical being abused (Mirin and Weiss, 1983).

Subjective Effects of Inhalants

The effects of inhalant fumes on the individual might include a feeling of hazy euphoria, or what Berger and Dunn (1982) called a "floating euphoria" (p. 105). The intoxication from an inhalant is somewhat like that caused by alcohol, followed by double vision, ringing in the ears, and hallucinations (Lingeman, 1974). Occasionally, according to Lingeman (1974), the user of glue fumes will "erupt into violence or have delusions of grandeur, during which they think they can fly, or lie on railroad tracks . . ." (p. 85).

One of the initial experiences of inhalant abuse is a feeling of euphoria, although nausea and vomiting may also occur (McHugh, 1987). As the individual continues to abuse the chemical, depression of the central nervous system develops. The individual may become confused, disoriented, and experience a loss of inhibitions (McHugh, 1987). If the individual continues to inhale the fumes, stupor, seizures, and cardiorespiratory arrest may develop (McHugh, 1987). After 30–60 minutes, the person will usually return to a normal state of consciousness, if he or she has an adequate air supply.

Schuckit (1984) noted that in most cases, the mental change following inhalation of glues, solvents, or aerosol gases from spray cans "disappears fairly quickly, and, with the exception of headache, serious hangovers are usually not seen" (p. 161). Westermeyer (1987) noted that the impairment of the central nervous system resulting from the use of inhalants usually clears "in minutes to a few hours" (p. 903).

Complications From Inhalant Abuse

There is no evidence of withdrawal symptoms from the use of these substances (Lingeman, 1974). Schuckit (1984) noted that there is a possibility of "residual organic brain syndromes" (p. 163), which is to say possible organic brain damage, as a result of using such agents (which might be detected by EEG studies). Other symptoms might include a coarse tremor, staggering gait, and speech difficulties.

Evidence suggests that these agents might also bring about toxic reactions involving respiratory depression, cardiac arrhythmias (irregularities in the heart beat), kidney damage, and possibly liver damage (Brunswick, 1989; Schuckit, 1984). Seizures and death are possible from inhalant abuse, depending on the agent being abused (Mirin and Weiss, 1983). Parras, Patier, and Ezpeleta (1988) noted that gasoline sniffing by children has resulted in occasional cases of lead poisoning, a serious condition that may have long-term consequences for the child's physical and emotional growth.

Westermeyer (1987) observed that the use of various inhalants might result in liver damage, bone marrow suppression, sinusitis (irritation of the sinus membranes), erosion of the nasal mucosal tissues, and laryngitis, among other things. He concluded that these problems usually resolve after some weeks of abstinence (p. 903). Schuckit (1984) agreed that permanent organ damage is rare, but pointed out that there have been cases of permanent organ damage as a result of inhalant use. McHugh (1987) noted that various inhalants may cause coma, ataxia, convulsions, brain damage, or death.

Sharp and Behm (1977) reported that their study of 37 chronic inhalant users found that 40% had scored in the brain-damaged range on a test designed to detect neurological dysfunction. However, the authors hesitated to conclude that their findings were a result of chronic use of inhalants. The authors termed their research findings preliminary, noting that their results might reflect preexisting brain damage rather than the effects of inhalant abuse. In spite of this fact, Westermeyer (1987) suggested to physicians that patients known to abuse inhalants should be routinely assessed for damage to the central nervous system, peripheral nervous system, kidneys, liver, lungs, heart, and bone marrow.

It has been reported (Mirin and Weiss, 1983) that a condition similar to the DT's of alcoholism exists in some chronic users of inhalants. This condition might reflect inhalant-induced brain damage, although there is a need for further study in this area.

ANESTHETIC MISUSE

Berger and Dunn (1982) reported that *nitrous oxide* and *ether*, the first two anesthetic gases to be used, were introduced as recreational drugs prior to their use as surgical anesthetics. Indeed, these gases were routinely used as intoxicants for quite some time before they were used by medicine. Horace Wells, who introduced medicine to nitrous oxide, noticed the pain-killing properties of this gas when he saw a person under its influence trip and gash his leg without any apparent pain (Brecher, 1972).

As medical historians know, the first planned demonstration of nitrous oxide as an anesthetic was something less than a success. The patient returned to consciousness in the middle of the operation and started to scream in pain. However, the use of nitrous oxide spread as medicine gradually accepted this anesthetic gas (Brecher, 1972).

The use of nitrous oxide, chloroform, and ether is confined, for the most part, to dental or general surgery. Very rarely, however, one will encounter a person who has abused, or is currently abusing, these agents. There is little information available concerning the dangers of this practice, nor is there much information as to the side effects of prolonged use.

Julien (1981) noted that the pharmacological effects of the anesthetic gases are the same as the effects of the barbiturates. Depending on the dosage, the anesthetics produce a variety of effects ranging from an initial period of sedation and relief from anxiety to analgesia and sleep. Furthermore, Julien (1981) reported that nitrous oxide is often misused because it is incapable of inducing unconsciousness, *if the person has an adequate oxygen supply.*

For this reason Lingeman (1974) reported that nitrous oxide is rarely used as an anesthetic unless it is combined with other agents. However, unless the person uses a special mixture of oxygen and nitrous oxide, he or she may run the danger of *hypoxia* (a decreased oxygen level in the blood that can result in permanent brain damage if not corrected immediately). In surgery, the anesthesiologist takes special precautions to ensure that the patient has an adequate oxygen supply. But, when a person is using nitrous oxide for recreational purposes, she or he will lack the support resources available to a surgical team and will run the risk of serious injury or even death. It is possible to achieve a state of hypoxia from virtually any of the inhalants (Julien, 1981), including nitrous oxide (McHugh, 1987). Recreational users of nitrous oxide report that the gas causes a feeling of euphoria, giddiness, hallucinations, and a loss of inhibitions (Lingeman, 1974).

Abel (1982) noted that the volatile anesthetics are not metabolized by the body to any significant degree, but enter and leave the body essentially unchanged. Once the source of the gas is removed, the concentration of the gas in the brain begins to drop and normal circulation brings the brain to a normal state of consciousness within moments. While the person is under the influence of the anesthetic gas, however, the ability of the brain cells to react to painful stimuli seems to be reduced (Abel, 1982).

SUMMARY

The use of inhalants seems to involve mainly teenagers. Inhalant use seems to be a phase, and individuals who use these agents do not usually do so for more than one or two years. There are a few individuals who will continue to inhale the fumes of gasoline, solvents, certain forms of glue, or anesthetic gases for many years. The effects of these chemicals on the individual seem to be rather short-lived. There is evidence, however, that prolonged use of certain agents can result in permanent damage to the kidneys, brain, and liver. Death, through either hypoxia, or prolonged exposure to inhalants is possible. Very little is known about the effects of prolonged use of this class of chemicals.

CHAPTER 10

Over-the-Counter Analgesics

Medications used in the control of pain can be classified into three groups. First, there are the local anesthetics, which interfere with the transmission of pain messages from the site of the injury to the brain. When used properly, cocaine is one such agent. In spite of the fact that cocaine is now viewed with disfavor, it is still the local anesthetic of choice for certain procedures.

Second are the global analgesics, which work within the brain to alter the perception of pain. The narcotic family of drugs are most frequently used as global analgesics, and these drugs work to alter the individual's perception of pain within the brain. Third, there are the nonnarcotic analgesics, which are thought to interfere with the chemical sequence that results in pain at the site of an injury. This latter class of medications includes aspirin,[1] ibuprofen, and acetaminophen, chemicals that are normally considered *over-the-counter* (OTC) medications.[2]

Until the introduction of aspirin in the late 1800s, physicians were forced to use opiates in the control of mild to moderate levels of pain. However, the opiates are addictive and have a depressant effect on the central nervous system. These factors limit the usefulness of the opiates in the control of mild to moderate levels of pain (Giacona, Dahl, and Hare, 1987).

Aspirin, or *acetylsalicylic acid*, does not present the clinician with the potential for addiction found with the narcotic family of analgesics. For this reason, aspirin has become the drug of choice in the control of mild to moderate levels of pain (Flower, Moncada, and Vane, 1985). In addition to its ability to control or reduce inflammation, aspirin may also reduce fever, in part by causing peripheral vasodilation and sweating (Govoni and Hayes, 1985; Sheridan, Patterson, and Gustafson, 1982). Martin (1971) noted that aspirin is *the* most commonly used drug in this country.

Since the 1950s a number of other aspirinlike, nonnarcotic analgesics have also been introduced (Reiss and Melick, 1984). Many of these medications share characteristics or applications with aspirin. While these medications are useful, each offers the potential for adverse side effects even at

---

[1]Aspirin is one of a family of related compounds, many of which have analgesic, anti-inflammatory, antipyretic (or antifever) actions. However, none of these aspirinlike drugs appears as powerful as aspirin, and they will not be discussed in this chapter.
[2]An *over-the-counter* medication is one that can be legally purchased without a prescription.

normal dosage levels (Aronoff, Wagner, and Spangler, 1986), and thus should be understood by the chemical dependency professional. In this chapter, we shall discuss three of the more commonly used OTC analgesics: aspirin, ibuprofen, and acetaminophen.

MEDICAL USES OF THE OTC ANALGESICS

The analgesics aspirin, ibuprofen, and acetaminophen are used in the control of mild to moderate pain (Reiss and Melick, 1984; Giacona, et al., 1987). Giacona, et al. noted that aspirin is also effective in treating common headaches, neuralgia, the pain associated with oral surgery, and other musculoskeletal pain. Aspirin, ibuprofen, and acetaminophen are also useful in controlling fever (Eisenhauer and Gerald, 1984). While acetaminophen only has a minor anti-inflammatory action (Mitchell, 1988), both aspirin and ibuprofen have been found most useful in the control of inflammation caused by arthritis (Giacona et al., 1987; Graedon, 1980).

Aspirin is quite popular as a home remedy and has been in use for nearly 85 years (Graedon, 1980). Flower, Moncada, and Vane (1985) estimated that Americans consume 10–20 *thousand tons* (40 million pounds) of aspirin a year. Graedon (1980) reported that *19 billion* doses of aspirin are sold every year. Indeed, aspirin is so popular that many people underestimate its usefulness (Jaffe and Martin, 1985; Graedon, 1980) and tend to underestimate its potential for causing serious side effects (Reiss and Melick, 1984).

PHARMACOLOGY OF THE OTC ANALGESICS

Each cell in the human body produces chemicals called the prostaglandins. When the cell is injured, these chemicals are released, causing inflammation and pain. Eisenhauer and Gerald (1984) observed that aspirin's analgesic effect might be attributed to its power to inhibit the production of prostaglandins, an observation supported by others (Giacona et al., 1987; Aronoff, Wagner, and Spangler, 1986; Sheridan, Patterson, and Gustafson, 1982). By blocking the action of the prostaglandins, aspirin helps control mild to moderate levels of pain and inflammation caused by injury to the body.

Aspirin also inhibits the clotting of blood platelets, reducing the ability of the blood to form clots. This side effect is of value in the control of *transient ischemic attacks* (TIAs or "mini-strokes") (Eisenhauer and Gerald, 1984), and either the initial or subsequent heart attacks (Govoni and Hayes, 1985; Graedon, 1980).

Acetaminophen is thought to have a mechanism of action very similar to that of aspirin (Giacona et al., 1987). The exact manner by which acetaminophen reduces pain is unknown (Govoni and Hayes, 1985), but it is thought that this drug, like aspirin, interferes with the synthesis of prostaglandins. Unlike aspirin, acetaminophen does not possess significant anti-inflammatory potential, nor does it interfere with the normal clotting of the blood (Govoni and Hayes; Eisenhauer and Gerald, 1984).

Ibuprofen was, until recently, available only by prescription. However, in the past few years, this medication has been approved for OTC use in modified dosage forms. This medication, like aspirin, has been found to be effective in the control of mild to moderate levels of pain, and the control of fever (Govoni and Hayes, 1985). In addition, depending on the dose, ibuprofen has been found to be about one-fifth to one-half as irritating to the stomach as aspirin (Giacona et al., 1987). This is not to say that ibuprofen is totally free of side effects. Graedon (1980) noted that 4–14% of those who use this medication will experience gastrointestinal irritation.

Although ibuprofen has an anti-inflammatory action, higher doses are necessary before the anti-inflammatory action of ibuprofen becomes effective (Govoni and Hayes, 1985). Graedon (1980) pointed out that ibuprofen is *only as effective as aspirin* at dosage levels of between 1600 and 2400 mg per day.

NORMAL DOSAGE LEVELS OF OTC ANALGESICS

There is conflicting evidence as to whether aspirin's analgesic effects are dose-related (Giacona et al., 1987), and there is mixed evidence suggesting little or no additional analgesic benefits from increasing the dosage levels above 600 mg every four hours. Seymore and Rawlins (1982) reported that 1200 mg of aspirin seemed to provide a greater degree of relief from dental pain than did 600 mg in a single dose. However, Aronoff, Wagner, and Spangler (1986) postulated that there was a "ceiling effect" (p. 769) for aspirin, beyond which higher dosage levels would not provide greater pain relief. The authors reported that this ceiling level was "approximately 1000 mg every 4 hr" (p. 769).

The United States Pharmacopeial Convention (1983) recommends a normal adult oral dosage level for aspirin of 325 to 650 mg every four hours, as needed for the control of pain. Furthermore, this text warns that aspirin should not be continuously used for longer than ten days by an adult or longer than five days by a child under the age of twelve, except under a doctor's orders (The United States Pharmacopeial Convention, 1981, 1983).

(Note: When used in the treatment of arthritis, aspirin may be used at higher than normal dosage levels. These dosage levels are usually used under a doctor's direct care and supervision, and as such represent a specialized application of aspirin. This application of aspirin, because it is carried out under the supervision of a physician, will not be discussed here.)

Aspirin is rapidly and completely absorbed through the gastrointestinal tract, although the speed with which aspirin is absorbed depends on the acidity of the stomach contents (Sheridan, Patterson, and Gustafson, 1982). When taken on an empty stomach, the rate at which aspirin is absorbed depends on how quickly the tablet crumbles (Rose, 1988). The aspirin will pass through the stomach lining and begin to reach the bloodstream in as little as one minute (Rose, 1988). While food may slow the rate at which aspirin is absorbed, it does not reduce the amount that is absorbed. Peak blood levels are achieved in one to two hours when a single dose is ingested (Sheridan, Patterson, and Gustafson, 1982), or 5–18 hours when repeated dosage levels are used (Govoni and Hayes, 1985).

Aspirin is sold alone and in combination with agents designed to reduce the irritation that aspirin might cause to the stomach. Govoni and Hayes (1985) reported that time-release and enteric-coated tablets have been known to bring about erratic absorption rates. Graedon (1980) warned that when antacids were taken along with aspirin to reduce stomach irritation, blood levels of aspirin were found to be 30–70% lower than when aspirin was used without antacids.

The United States Pharmacopeial Convention (1983) noted that the usual adult dose of acetaminophen is also 325–650 mg every four hours, as needed for the control of pain. Aronoff, Wagner, and Spangler (1986) observed that acetaminophen's antipyretic and analgesic effects are equal to those of aspirin and that the ceiling level of acetaminophen is the same. Peak blood concentrations were achieved in 30–120 minutes after an oral dose of acetaminophen (Govoni and Hayes, 1985), and the half-life of an oral dose was one to four hours. Persons with significant liver damage might experience a longer half-life of acetaminophen because it is metabolized by the liver.

Because acetaminophen is metabolized by the liver, chronic use of alcohol may lower the dosage level necessary for the person to become toxic from acetaminophen (Mitchell, 1988). Indeed, Mitchell (1988) noted that there have been reports that a few chronic alcoholics have become toxic on acetaminophen at dosage levels only slightly higher than the normal recommended dose.

The author concluded that, when used at recommended dosage levels, acetaminophen was "unlikely to produce liver injury in patients with chronic alcoholism" (p. 1602). Both Govoni and Hayes (1985), and Graedon (1980) disagreed with this conclusion, however, and neither recommended the use of acetaminophen with alcoholic patients.

Govoni and Hayes (1985) recommended that 300–600 mg of ibuprofen be used 3–4 times a day for the control of rheumatoid arthritis, while 200–400 mg every 4–6 hours may be used to control mild to moderate pain. The Upjohn Company, the manufacturer of Motrin (a brand of ibuprofen), does not advise total daily dosage levels higher than 3200 mg, in divided doses (Medical Economics Company, 1989).

Ibuprofen is rapidly absorbed when used orally, with peak blood plasma levels being achieved one to two hours following ingestion of the drug. Within four hours after the drug is ingested, blood plasma levels will fall to about half that of the peak blood plasma level, when used at normal therapeutic dosage levels (Govoni and Hayes, 1985). The drug is metabolized by the liver, and only 10% is excreted unchanged (Govoni and Hayes).

COMPLICATIONS CAUSED BY USE OF OTC ANALGESICS

Approximately 0.2% of the general population is allergic to aspirin; however, of those individuals with a history of allergic disorders, about 20% will be allergic to aspirin. Symptoms of an allergic reaction to aspirin might include both rash and asthmalike reactions, which may be fatal (Eisenhauer and Gerald, 1984; Graedon, 1980). Govoni and Hayes (1985) warned that patients with the "aspirin triad" (p. 104), which is to say those individuals with a history of nasal polyps, rhinitis, and asthma, should not use aspirin.

Martin (1971) cautioned that aspirin was the most common drug that brought on asthma attacks, often within 20 minutes of ingestion. These attacks "may be severe, prolonged, and occasionally fatal" (p. 363). Graedon (1980) reviewed the symptoms of an allergic reaction to aspirin, noting that these symptoms included wheezing, abdominal pain, and breathing problems. Govoni and Hayes (1985) warned that patients who are sensitive to aspirin are also likely to be sensitive to ibuprofen, as cross-sensitivity between these two drugs is common.

Reiss and Melick (1984) observed that aspirin use can result in gastric irritation and bleeding. Sheridan, Patterson, and Gustafson (1982) warned that aspirin's side effects include anorexia, nausea, and vomiting. The United States Pharmacopeial Convention (1983) noted that aspirin should not be used by persons with a history of ulcers, bleeding disorders, or other gastrointestinal disorders. Martin (1971) observed that up to 70% of those patients who repeatedly ingest aspirin will experience some degree of gastrointestinal bleeding. Such bleeding may be severe, especially if the patient has some form of underlying gastrointestinal pathology.

Because of their effects on blood clotting, neither aspirin or ibuprofen should be used by persons with a bleeding disorder such as hemophilia (Govoni and Hayes, 1985; United States Pharmacopeial Convention, 1983). Govoni and Hayes reported that a single dose of aspirin can affect bleeding time for three to seven days. Persons who are undergoing anticoagulant therapy, which reduces the ability of the blood to form clots, obviously should not use aspirin except when directed by a physician.

Aspirin should not be used by persons with a history of chronic rhinitis (Govoni and Hayes, 1985). Patients being treated for hyperuricemia (a buildup of uric acid in the blood often found in gout as well as other conditions) should also not use aspirin. At therapeutic dosage levels, this drug inhibits the action of probenecid, one of the drugs used to treat hyperuricemia, and reduces the body's ability to excrete uric acid. Acetaminophen is a suitable substitute for patients who suffer from gout and need a mild analgesic (Govoni and Hayes, 1985).

Prolonged use of aspirin can result in iron deficiency anemia in some patients (Govoni and Hayes, 1985; Sheridan, Patterson, and Gustafson, 1982). Both aspirin and ibuprofen can bring about a loss of hearing and a persistent ringing in the ears known as tinnitus. If this occurs, *the aspirin or ibuprofen should be immediately discontinued, and a physician contacted.* The patient's hearing will usually return to normal when the aspirin or ibuprofen is discontinued (Govoni and Hayes, 1985).

The elderly are especially susceptible to toxicity from aspirin and similar agents because their bodies are unable to metabolize and excrete this family of drugs. Sussman (1988) warned that one common cause of anxiety states in the elderly is the use of aspirin or similar drugs.

Aspirin or related compounds should *not* be used by children who are suffering from a viral infection. Research strongly suggests that aspirin might increase the possibility of the child developing Reye's syndrome. Reye's syndrome is a serious, potentially fatal condition that includes swelling of the brain, seizures, disturbance of consciousness, and a fatty degeneration of the liver (Friel, 1974).

Surprisingly, aspirin has been implicated in the failure of intrauterine devices (IUDs) to prevent pregnancy. The anti-inflammatory action of aspirin is thought to be the cause of its ability to interfere with the effectiveness of intrauterine devices.

Graedon (1980) warned that patients on ibuprofen who experience changes in their vision should discontinue the medication and consult with their physician *immediately*. In addition to the 3–9% of the patients using ibuprofen who experience skin rashes or hives as a side effect of this medication, ibuprofen has been implicated in the formation of cataracts (Graedon, 1980). The Upjohn Company, which manufactures and markets Motrin, warned that it has been found to cause a number of side effects, including heartburn, nausea, diarrhea, vomiting, nervousness, hearing loss, congestive heart failure in persons who had marginal cardiac function, changes in vision, and elevation of blood pressure (Medical Economics Company, 1989).

Aspirin, ibuprofen, and acetaminophen have all been identified as the cause of death in cases of overdose. Flower, Moncada, and Vane (1985) estimated that aspirin is involved in approximately 10000 overdoses each year, mainly by children. The authors noted that an overdose of aspirin is a serious medical emergency that may, even with the best of medical care and support, result in death.

Symptoms of aspirin toxicity, such as those found in patients who use large doses of aspirin, include headache, dizziness, tinnitus, mental confusion, increased sweating, thirst, dimming of sight, and hearing impairment (Sheridan, Patterson, and Gustafson, 1982). Other symptoms of aspirin toxicity include restlessness, excitement, apprehension, tremor, delirium, hallucinations, convulsions, stupor, coma, and possible death (Sheridan, Patterson, and Gustafson).

Mitchell (1988) noted that there is limited information available on the actual incidence of acetaminophen overdoses in any country. It was reported by Mitchell (1988) that in Great Britain, aspirin overdoses resulted in an estimated 200–250 deaths per year, while acetaminophen poisoning caused an estimated 150 deaths per year. Acetaminophen poisoning may cause death through liver failure.

Michell (1988) also observed that when *N-acetylcysteine* is administered within several hours of the initial overdose, it is quite effective in the treatment of acetaminophen poisoning. However, as Graedon (1980) noted; the symptoms of an overdose of acetaminophen might not be observed for up to 48 hours after the overdose itself. In the case of an overdose of acetaminophen, treatment must begin *immediately*, not when signs of liver toxicity are noted.

COMPLICATIONS OF OTC ANALGESICS WHEN USED DURING PREGNANCY

Women who are, or who suspect that they might be pregnant, should not use aspirin except under the supervision of a physician (Eisenhauer and Gerald, 1984). Aspirin has been implicated as a cause of decreased birth weight in children born to women who used it during pregnancy. Evidence suggests that aspirin may be a cause of stillbirth and increased perinatal mortality (United States Pharmacopeial Convention, 1983).

Briggs, Freeman, and Yaffe (1986) explored the impact of maternal aspirin use on the fetus, and on infants whose mothers were breast feeding. The authors reported that the use of aspirin by the mother during pregnancy might produce "anemia, antepartum and/or postpartum hemorrhage, prolonged gestation and prolonged labor" (p. 26a). Aspirin has also been implicated in significantly higher perinatal mortality and retardation of intrauterine growth when used at high doses by pregnant women (Briggs, Freeman, and Yaffe).

The authors noted that maternal use of aspirin in the week before delivery might interfere with the infant's ability to form blood clots following birth. The United States Pharmacopeial Convention (1981) went further than this, warning that women should not use aspirin in the last two weeks of pregnancy. Sheridan, Patterson, and Gustafson (1982) went further still, stating that aspirin should not be used during the last month of pregnancy. Aspirin has been found to cross the placenta, and research has suggested that maternal aspirin use during pregnancy might result in higher levels of aspirin in the fetus than in the mother (Briggs, Freeman, and Yaffe, 1986).

Chasnoff (1988) noted that since the liver of the fetus is not fully developed, it is often difficult to predict the fate of any drug in the fetus's body. Furthermore, the fetus often lacks the highly developed renal function of the mother, making it difficult for a drug to be excreted by the fetus even if it could metabolize the drug. These factors make it difficult to predict the impact of any drug on the fetus. Govoni and Hayes (1985) do not recommend *any* use of aspirin by pregnant women, especially in the last trimester of pregnancy.

Briggs, Freeman, and Yaffe (1986) observed that, in addition to the more traditional forms of aspirin, many "hidden" forms of this drug are also consumed during pregnancy. Chasnoff (1988) reported that 50–60% of pregnant women use some form of analgesic during their pregnancy. Such a large number of women using various chemicals, under poorly controlled conditions, makes it most difficult to assess the impact of aspirin use on the fetus or on nursing infants, according to Briggs, Freeman, and Yaffe (1986).

However, the authors warn that pregnant women should not use aspirin or products that contain aspirin on the grounds that the benefit/risk ratio of such drug use has not been established. Although there have been no proven problems in women who breast feed their children, the use of aspirin in women who choose to breast feed is also not recommended (United States Pharmacopeial Convention, 1983; Briggs, Freeman, and Yaffe, 1986).

Acetaminophen was found to be "safe for short-term use" at recommended dosage levels by pregnant women (Briggs, Freeman, and Yaffe, 1986, p. 2a). There have been no reports of serious problems in women who have used acetaminophen during pregnancy. The authors noted, however, that the death of one infant from kidney disease was attributed to the mother's continuous use of acetaminophen at high dosage levels during pregnancy. Although this drug is excreted in low concentrations in the mother's milk, Briggs, Freeman, and Yaffe (1986) found no evidence suggesting that this had adverse effects on the infant.

The manufacturers of ibuprofen do not recommend that this drug be used during pregnancy. When used at therapeutic dosage levels, this drug was not reported to cause congenital birth defects (Briggs, Freeman, and Yaffe, 1986). However, similar drugs have been known to inhibit labor, prolong pregnancy, and potentially cause other problems for the developing child. Research would suggest that ibuprofen does not enter into human milk in significant quantities when used at normal dosage levels (Briggs, Freeman, and Yaffe), and is considered "compatible with breast feeding" (p. 217 i).

SUMMARY

Over-the-counter analgesics are often discounted by many as being "real" medications. Indeed, aspirin is perhaps America's most popular drug, with more than 20,000 *tons* of aspirin being manufactured and consumed in this country alone. Aspirin, acetaminophen, and ibuprofen are quite effective in the control of mild to moderate levels of pain, without the side effects found with narcotic analgesics. But these drugs, in spite of the fact that they are available over-the-counter, do carry significant potential for harm.

Acetaminophen has been implicated in toxic reactions in chronic alcoholics at near-normal dosage levels. Acetaminophen has also been implicated as the cause of death in people who have taken overdoses. Aspirin and ibuprofen have been implicated in fatal allergic reactions, especially in those who suffer from asthma. The use of aspirin in children with viral infections is not recommended. The use of some of these drugs in pregnant women is not advised. Women who are nursing are advised to check with their physician to determine if they should avoid the use of any of the OTC analgesics during lactation.

CHAPTER 11

The Hallucinogenics

It has been estimated that about 6000 different species of plants might be used for their psychoactive properties (Brophy, 1985). Jaffe (1985a) noted that humans have used hallucinogenics for centuries. Berger and Dunn (1982) observed that such substances were used by ancient cultures in religious ceremonies, in healing rituals, and for predicting the future. Kolb and Brodie (1982) noted that hallucinogens were also used to produce euphoria and as aphrodisiacs in many parts of the world.

By the middle of this century, hallucinogenic substances were the subject of much scientific inquiry. The effects of lysergic acid diethylamide-25 (LSD-25 or simply, LSD), a substance obtained from the rye fungus ergot *Claviceps purpurea* (Lingeman, 1974), were first recorded in 1943. At that time, a scientist accidentally ingested a small amount of LSD-25 and experienced the hallucinogenic effects of this drug for the first time.

Following World War II there was a great deal of scientific interest in hallucinogenics, especially in light of the similarities between the actions of these chemicals and various forms of mental illness. In the 1960s, use of the hallucinogenics moved from the laboratory into the streets, and hallucinogens became drugs of abuse (Brown and Braden, 1987).

The widespread abuse of LSD in the 1960s prompted the classification of this drug as a controlled substance in 1970 (Jaffe, 1985a). While the prevalence of hallucinogen abuse has declined in recent years, it is still common (Mirin and Weiss, 1983). Indeed, the use of one hallucinogen, *phencyclidine* (PCP) has become so popular that it has reached "epidemic proportions" (Brophy, 1985, p. 674). Recently, another drug, N, alpha-dimethyl-1,3-benzodioxole-t-ethanamine (MDMA), has become quite popular as a chemical of abuse. This drug is frequently sold on the streets under the name of "Ecstasy." Both PCP and MDMA will be discussed in later sections of this chapter.

SCOPE OF THE PROBLEM

Mirin and Weiss (1983) noted that the majority of those who have used LSD only experimented with the drug a few times, possibly out of curiosity or the desire to intensify a certain experience. Jaffe (1985a), noted that one study found that 21% of Americans between the ages of 18 and 25 admitted to having used hallucinogenics at one time but that only 1 or 2% admitted to having used them in the month preceding the interview. Jaffe's (1985) observations would support those of Mirin and Weiss (1983).

The American Psychiatric Association (1985) noted that it is difficult to estimate the number of drug abusers in this country. This is true in part because the use of many drugs is illegal. Individuals who use chemicals are thus unlikely to readily admit to this practice. But it is also difficult to estimate the number of drug abusers because opinions differ among experts as to exactly what constitutes experimental, casual, or abusive use of chemicals. Thus, the above figures should be regarded as estimates of a problem that, by its very nature, will tend to remain hidden.

PHARMACOLOGY OF THE HALLUCINOGENS

Mirin and Weiss (1983) observed that the commonly abused hallucinogenics might be divided into two major groups on the basis of their pharmacology. First, there are the hallucinogens that bear a structural resemblance to a neurotransmitter known as *serotonin*. Hallucinogenics in this group include LSD, psilocybin, and the drug dimethyltryptamine (DMT).

A second group of hallucinogenics is chemically related to the neurotransmitters dopamine and norepinephrine. The chemical structure of these agents also resembles that of the amphetamine family of drugs (Mirin and Weiss, 1983). These hallucinogenics include, among others, mescaline, MDMA, and DOM (STP).

In spite of the chemical differences between hallucinogens, the effects of the various hallucinogenics are remarkably similar. All hallucinogens alter the users' perception of the external world and of their bodies. These chemicals produce hallucinations that are usually recognized by the user as being drug-induced (Lingeman, 1974).

In order to avoid duplication of material, the major focus of this chapter will be on the hallucinogens LSD, MDMA, and PCP. Other hallucinogens will only be briefly discussed.

Pharmacology of LSD

Neither LSD nor any of the other hallucinogenic drugs have any legitimate medical use at this time. LSD is quite potent, being effective at doses as low as 50 micrograms (Mirin and Weiss, 1983).[1] Lingeman (1974) noted the usual dose used by illicit drug users was from 100 to 700 micrograms.

When taken orally, LSD is rapidly absorbed and is quickly distributed

[1]There are 1000 micrograms in 1 milligram.

to all body tissues (Mirin and Weiss, 1983). Lingeman (1974) noted that only about 0.01% of the drug ingested actually reaches the brain. Thus, of a 50 microgram dose of LSD, only *five-tenths of a microgram actually reaches the brain*. This makes it quite difficult to trace the drug once it reaches the brain.

The exact mechanism of action for LSD is unknown (Jaffe, 1985a), although this drug is thought by Mirin and Weiss (1983) to inhibit the activity of serotonin in the midbrain. This view was challenged by Jaffe, who reported that LSD is now thought to have actions at various sites in the central nervous system, ranging from the cortex of the brain to the spinal cord, including the midbrain sites identified by Mirin and Weiss.

LSD is usually administered orally, and the effects are first experienced within 20 minutes (Mirin and Weiss, 1983) to an hour (Lingeman, 1974) after the drug is ingested. Some of the physical effects noted after the use of LSD include tachycardia, increased blood pressure, increased body temperature, pupillary dilation, nausea, and muscle weakness (Mirin and Weiss). Jaffe (1985a) reported that after LSD has been ingested there is an exaggeration of normal reflexes (known as hyperreflexia), dizziness, and some degree of tremor. Lingeman characterized these changes as "relatively minor" (p. 133).

Factors that influence the speed with which LSD begins to act include the amount of the drug ingested and the development of tolerance to the drug (Mirin and Weiss, 1983). Tolerance to the effects of LSD develop quickly, often within two to four days (Brown and Braden, 1987; Mirin and Weiss), and abates just as rapidly (Lingeman, 1974). Cross-tolerance between the different hallucinogens is common (Lingeman).

In terms of direct physical mortality, LSD is a relatively safe drug (Brown and Braden, 1987). Weil (1986) classified LSD as one of the safest drugs known to modern medicine. Lingeman (1974) reported that the lethal dose of LSD in humans was not known, but observed that an elephant given a massive dose of LSD (297,000 micrograms, or 5940 doses at 50 micrograms each) died.[2] Other hallucinogenics are not as benign, however, and LSD has been known to *indirectly* contribute to a number of fatalities.

The plasma half-life of LSD is rather short, with approximately half of the drug being metabolized into nonhallucinogenic substances by the liver in two to three hours (Mirin and Weiss, 1983; Jaffe, 1985a). Surprisingly, the effects of LSD in man seem to last about 8–12 hours (Jaffe), a phenomenon that is not understood at this time.

Research has discovered that LSD is a complex, often surprising chemical. It is active in extremely small doses, yet appears to affect many body systems. Only a small portion of the LSD that is ingested actually enters the brain. Yet, as will be discussed in the next section, the drug has a profound impact on consciousness.

[2] Lingeman (1974) did not, however, identify how the elephant happened to ingest the LSD in the first place.

SUBJECTIVE EFFECTS OF LSD

The effects of LSD vary, depending on the individual's mental state at the time the drug is ingested and the setting in which the drug is used (Lingeman, 1974). Brophy (1985) reported that the hallucinogenic "trip" passes through several distinct phases. First, within a few minutes of taking LSD, there is a release of inner tension. This stage, which will last one to two hours (Brophy, 1985) is characterized by laughing or crying, and a feeling of euphoria (Jaffe, 1985a).

The second stage usually begins between 30–90 minutes (Brown and Braden, 1987) to 2–3 hours (Brophy, 1985) following the ingestion of the drug. During this portion of the LSD experience, the individual will experience perceptual distortions such as visual illusions and hallucinations. Mirin and Weiss (1983) described this phase as being marked by "wavelike perceptual changes" (p. 267), and noted that synesthesia is often experienced during this phase. Synesthesia is a phenomenon where information from one sense may "slip over" into another sensory system. A person who is experiencing synesthesia may report that they are able to "taste" colors, or "see" music.

The third phase of the hallucinogenic experience will begin three to four hours after the drug is ingested (Brophy, 1985). During this phase of the LSD "trip," the person will experience a distortion of the sense of time. The person may experience marked mood swings and a feeling of ego disintegration. Feelings of panic are often experienced during this phase as are occasional feelings of depression (Lingeman, 1974). During this stage, LSD users may express a belief that they possess quasi-magical powers or that they are magically in control (Jaffe, 1985a). This loss of contact with reality has resulted in fatalities, as individuals have jumped from windows or attempted to drive motor vehicles.

If the person *does* develop a panic reaction to the LSD experience, she or he will often respond to calm, gentle reminders from others that these feelings are caused by the drug and will pass. Brophy (1985) reported that medical personnel may administer antipsychotic medications such as Haldol in low doses until the individual regains control. Jenike (1987) recommended the use of benzodiazepines to help the individual deal with the anxiety, while phenothiazines were found useful in aborting the LSD experience. Even with such intervention, some patients remain psychotic and require weeks to months of psychiatric care.

Kolb and Brodie (1982) warned that many hallucinogens are adulterated with belladonna, or other anticholinergics. These substances, when mixed with phenothiazines, may bring about coma and death through cardiorespiratory failure. Thus, it is imperative that the physician treating a "bad trip" know what drug(s) have been used and, if possible, be provided with a sample to determine what medication is best in a given case.

Mirin and Weiss (1983) reported that the likelihood of a "bad trip" is determined by the individual's expectations for the drug (which is known as the "set"), the setting in which the drug is used, and the psychological health of the user. Inexperienced users are more likely to experience a "bad trip" than are experienced LSD users (Mirin and Weiss, 1983). As a result of the drug's effects on the user, LSD is thought to be capable of activating a latent psychosis (Lingeman, 1974; Mirin and Weiss), that may require long-term psychiatric care.

The effects of LSD start to wane four to six hours after ingestion. As the individual begins to recover, he or she will experience "waves of normalcy" (Mirin and Weiss, 1983, p. 267), with a gradual return to a normal waking state. Within 12 hours, the acute effects of LSD have cleared, although a "sense of psychic numbness may last for days" (Mirin and Weiss, p. 267).

PHENCYCLIDINE (PCP)

Phencyclidine (PCP) was first developed in the 1950s, and was initially used as a "highly potent, but relatively nontoxic" (Berger and Dunn, 1982, p. 98) anesthetic for animals. Research into its possible use in man was discontinued in 1965, when it was discovered that patients who had received PCP experienced a drug-induced delirium (Brown and Braden, 1987). In 1978, all legal production of PCP was discontinued, and the drug was declared a controlled subtance as defined by the Comprehensive Drug Abuse Prevention and Control Act of 1970 (Slaby, Lieb, and Tancredi, 1981).

Nonetheless, by the mid-1970s PCP had become one of the most frequently abused drugs in the United States (Jaffe, 1985a). Mirin and Weiss (1983) reported that approximately one in six adults between the ages of 18 and 25 had *knowingly* used PCP. Berger and Dunn (1982) observed that approximately half of those who knowingly use PCP do so on at least a weekly basis. The person who uses PCP will usually abuse other drugs, including alcohol (Berger and Dunn).

The operative term in the above paragraph is "knowingly" used PCP. The drug is easily manufactured (Slaby, Lieb, and Tancredi, 1981), and thus may be produced by amateur chemists. Because it is so easily manufactured, PCP is often mixed into other "street" drugs or sold under the guise of other chemicals (Brophy, 1985; Kauffman, Shaffer, and Burglas, 1985). It is quite common for a person buying LSD to unknowingly purchase PCP. The drug is also often mixed with marijuana to increase its effects.

Phencyclidine is an unusual drug in that, depending on the dosage level and the route of administration, it will demonstrate anesthetic, stimulant, depressant, or hallucinogenic effects (Brown and Braden, 1987; Jaffe, 1985; Mirin and Weiss, 1983). The drug may be smoked, used intranasally, taken by mouth, or injected intravenously (Brown and Braden, 1987; Slaby, Lieb, and Tancredi, 1981). Tolerance is not known to develop to PCP

(Jenike, 1987), and there is no evidence of physical dependence to PCP (Newell and Cosgrove, 1988).

The absorption of PCP after smoking is rapid, and one will begin to experience symptoms within minutes (Brophy, 1985) to an hour (Mikkelsen, 1985). Jaffe (1985a) observed that ". . . few drugs seem to induce so wide a range of subjective effects" (p. 566). Mirin and Weiss (1983) observed that ". . . most regular users report unwanted effects . . ." (p. 271) from this drug, including feelings of anxiety, restlessness, and disorientation.

Berger and Dunn (1982) observed that PCP users report the drug would bring them either to "the heights, or the depths" (p. 100) and noted that drug-induced depression is common. Other negative effects of PCP include disorientation, mental confusion, assaultiveness, anxiety, irritability, and paranoia (Berger and Dunn, 1982). Indeed, so many people have experienced so many undesired effects from PCP that researchers are at a loss to explain why the drug is so popular (Berger and Dunn, 1982).

Small doses of PCP, usually less than 5 mg, will produce a state resembling that of alcohol intoxication (Mirin and Weiss, 1983). The individual will experience a loss of muscle coordination, staggering gait, slurred speech, and numbness of the extremities (Jaffe, 1985a). The acute effects last 4–6 hours, after which the user will "come down," or gradually return to normal, over a period of 6–24 hours (Berger and Dunn, 1982).

As the dosage level increases to the 5–10 mg range, many users will experience a disturbance of body image; different parts of their bodies will no longer seem "real" (Jaffe, 1985a; Brophy, 1985). Assaultiveness is common at the higher dosage levels (Jaffe), and individuals who have ingested PCP are often capable of unusual feats of strength (Brophy, 1985; Jaffe, 1985).

As the dosage level reaches the 20 mg range, coma, seizure, hypertension, and severe psychotic reactions are possible (Brophy, 1985). Jaffe (1985a) observed that there was one case on record where a single dose of PCP brought about a psychotic reaction that continued for several weeks.

Jaffe (1985a) noted that cigarettes containing PCP powder may contain as much as 100 mg of PCP. Death from respiratory arrest, convulsions, and hypertension have all been reported in cases of PCP overdose (Brophy, 1985). Jaffe reported that the half-life of PCP following an overdose may be as long as 72 hours, but that it is possible to reduce the half-life to 24 hours by changing the acidity of the blood. The coma that is brought on by an overdose of PCP may last up to 10 days (Mirin and Weiss, 1983).

PCP Psychosis

Phencyclidine has been implicated in a drug-induced psychosis that may last for days, or weeks, following the last use of the drug (Mirin and Weiss, 1983; Jaffe, 1985a; Jenike, 1987). This PCP psychosis seems to be most likely in those persons who either have suffered a previous schizophrenic episode (Mirin and Weiss, 1983), or who are vulnerable to such an episode (Jaffe). There is no way to predict in advance who might develop a PCP psychosis.

Mirin and Weiss (1983) observed that the PCP psychosis usually progresses through three stages, each of which lasts approximately five days. The first stage of the PCP psychosis is usually the most severe and is characterized by paranoid delusions, anorexia, insomnia, and unpredictable assaultiveness. During this phase, the individual is extremely sensitive to external stimuli (Mirin and Weiss, 1983; Jaffe, 1985a), and the "talking down" techniques that might work with an LSD "bad trip" will not usually work with a PCP psychosis (Jaffe).

The second phase is marked by continued paranoia and restlessness, but the individual is usually calmer and in intermittent control of his or her behavior (Mirin and Weiss, 1983). This phase also usually lasts five days, and will gradually blend into the final phase of the PCP-psychosis recovery process. The third phase is marked by a gradual recovery over 7 to 14 days; however, in some patients the PCP psychosis may last for months (Mirin and Weiss; Slaby, Lieb, and Tancredi, 1981). Social withdrawal and severe depression are also common following chronic use of PCP (Jaffe, 1985a).

Kauffman, Shaffer, and Burglas (1985) observed that there is no withdrawal syndrome following even prolonged periods of hallucinogen use. Jaffe (1985a) noted that chronic PCP users reported memory problems, which would clear when they stopped using the drug. Recent evidence (Newell and Cosgrove, 1988) would suggest that chronic PCP users demonstrate the same pattern of neuropsychological deficits found in other forms of chronic drug use. However, when the individual discontinues PCP use, there is a significant recovery of memory function (Newell and Cosgrove, 1988).

ECSTASY: LATEST IN A LONG LINE OF "BETTER" HALLUCINOGENS

In recent years, a "new" hallucinogenic has been growing in popularity among college students (Barnes, 1988). The drug MDMA is called "Ecstasy," "XTC," or "Adam" on the streets (Barnes, 1988). Although classified by some as a new "designer" drug, it was actually first synthesized in 1914 (Climko, Roehrich, Sweeney, and Al-Razi, 1987).

MDMA did not gain popularity as a chemical of abuse until approximately 15 years ago (Hayner and McKinney, 1986), and thus was not classified as a controlled substance in the 1960s. Since it was not a controlled substance, its manufacture was legal until the Drug Enforcement Administration classified MDMA as a controlled substance, on July 1, 1985 (Climko et al., 1987).

MDMA is chemically related to another hallucinogen, known as MDA (Kirsch, 1986), and MDMA's structure resembles that of the amphetamines (Kirsch, 1986). MDMA briefly surfaced, then disappeared, during the 1960s (Kirsch, 1986). Because LSD was more potent and did not cause the nausea or vomiting that MDMA does, LSD became the popular drug of abuse, and MDMA was all but forgotten for 20 years.

Then, during the mid-1970s, illicit drug manufacturers "decided to resurrect, christen, package, market, distribute, and advertise" (Kirsch, 1986, p. 76) MDMA. Marketing plans and possible product names were discussed (Kirsch, 1986). For a period of time, the possible name of "Empathy" was considered; however, Ecstasy finally was selected (Kirsch, 1986). Unknown drug manufacturers first created a demand for a "product," which was then conveniently met by the very people who had first manipulated the public into clamoring for the product.

Kirsch (1986) noted that original samples of Ecstasy included a "package insert" (p. 81) that "included unverified scientific research and an abundance of 1960s mumbo-jumbo" (p. 81). However, these same package inserts warned the user not to mix Ecstasy with other chemicals (including alcohol), to only occasionally use the drug, and reminded the user that care should be taken to ensure a proper "set" in which to use the chemical (Kirsch, 1986).

Scope of the Ecstasy Problem

Hayner and McKinney (1986) observed that "No one is sure how many doses . . ." of MDMA had been taken, but noted that ". . . the number is in the hundreds of thousands" (p. 341). This estimate may be low. Kirsch (1986) noted that in 1976 one drug "lab" was known to have manufactured and distributed an estimated 10,000 doses of MDMA per month. By the year 1984, this same lab was manufacturing and distributing approximately 30,000 doses of the drug per month. In 1985, the year that the manufacture of MDMA was declared illegal, the same lab was thought to be producing 500,000 doses per month. Unfortunately, more than one drug lab is known to have produced MDMA.

On July 1, 1985, the Drug Enforcement Administration (DEA) classified MDMA a controlled substance (Climko et al., 1987). Kirsch (1986) noted that ". . . trafficking in MDMA [was made] punishable by fifteen years in prison and a $125,000 fine . . ." (p. 84). Several labs were immediately shut down by the DEA, and other people stopped making or selling MDMA.

The demand was still there, however, fueled by news stories in the popular press about Ecstasy's supposed value in psychotherapy. This demand was met, to a large degree, by drug dealers who (either knowingly or unknowingly) sold other substances as Ecstasy (Kirsch, 1986). Hayner and McKinney (1986) noted that

> . . . substances intended for popular recreational use are most often
> produced in clandestine laboratories with little or no quality control, so
> generally speaking users cannot be sure of the purity of what they are
> ingesting (p. 341).

It should be pointed out that, with illegal drugs, one cannot be sure that
the drug purchased was what she or he wanted! For, as Brown and Braden
(1987) observed, "Misrepresentation is the rule with illicit drugs" (p. 341).

In spite of these problems, however, Peroutka (1989) reported that "a
significant number of students" (p. 191) on one college campus admitted to
having used MDMA at least once. The median number of doses per
student was 4.0, with an average number of doses reported being 5.4 per
student who admitted using the drug. The dosage levels being reported
were between 60–250 mg, a dosage level found to cause neurotoxicity in
animals, and the author identified MDMA or related compounds as being
the cause of death in at least five cases (Peroutka, 1989).

Ecstasy's Effects on the User: Subjective and Objective Impact

Climko et al. (1987), noted that ". . . preclinical research on MDMA is
. . . scant" (p. 365). There is little objective research into the behavioral
effects of MDMA in humans. Barnes (1988) noted that there has never been
"a controlled clinical trial with the drug, making its precise toxicity or
efficacy in people impossible to determine" (p. 239).

Some psychiatrists advocate the use of MDMA as an aid to psychotherapy (Price, Ricaurte, Krystal, and Heninger, 1989). Climko et al.
(1987), reported that one "uncontrolled study" (p. 365) found that MDMA
brought about a positive change in mood, but the authors also pointed out
that MDMA has been reported to cause

> . . . tachycardia, an occasional "wired" feeling, jaw clenching, nystagmus,
> a nervous desire to be in motion, transient anorexia, panic attacks, nausea
> and vomiting, ataxia, urinary urgency . . . insomnia, tremors, inhibition of
> ejaculation, and rarely, transient hallucinations (p. 365).

Hayner and McKinney (1986) reported that, at normal doses, MDMA
caused an increased heart rate, tremor, tightness in jaw muscles, bruxism
(grinding of teeth), nausea, insomnia, headache, and sweating. People
who were "particularly sensitive" (p. 341) to MDMA might experience
numbness and tingling in extremities of the body, vomiting, increased
sensitivity to cold, visual hallucinations, ataxia, crying, blurred vision,
nystagmus, and the experience of having the floor appear to shake.

Peroutka (1989) observed that recreational users of MDMA tend to use
the drug only once every two to three weeks, if not less frequently. This
rather unusual drug-use pattern reflects the fact that the desired effects of

the drug become weaker, while the individual becomes more likely to experience the negative side effects of the drug. Taking a double dose of the drug does not increase the desired effects of MDMA, but rather makes it more likely that the individual will experience unpleasant side effects (Peroutka, 1989).

Interestingly, at normal dosage levels, Ecstasy may cause the users to "relive" painful, often suppressed, memories (Hayner and McKinney, 1986). Thus, the individual might relive an experience that she or he did not want to remember. This action, which many psychotherapists thought might prove of benefit in the confines of the therapeutic relationship, seems to be so frightening as to be "detrimental to the individual's mental health" (Hayner and McKinney, 1986, p. 343).

Furthermore, Hayner and McKinney (1986) reported that symptoms of an MDMA overdose included tachycardia, hypertension, hypotension, heart palpitations, hyperthermia (elevation of body temperature, possibly to dangerous levels), renal failure, and visual hallucinations. MDMA, it was noted "can potentially kill at doses that were previously tolerated in susceptible individuals" (p. 342). The exact mechanism of death is still not certain. The drug also brought about residual effects, including anxiety attacks, persistent insomnia, rage reactions, and a drug-induced psychosis (Hayner and McKinney, 1986).

Climko et al. (1987), noted that the exact mechanism of action for MDMA was not clear, but animal research suggests that the drug influences the action of serotonin, a neurotransmitter in the brain. Hinsie and Campbell (1970) noted that serotonin is thought to function in the

> regulation of centers in the brain concerned with wakefulness, temperature regulation, blood pressure regulation, and various other autonomic functions (p. 695).

Barnes (1988) reported that recent clinical research using animals demonstrates that MDMA is *neurotoxic* to a certain group of neurons. Animal research has found that MDMA damages certain brain cells, specifically those that use serotonin as a neurotransmitter.

Ecstasy is a rather toxic drug when compared to the traditional hallucinogens such as LSD. Where a rat might receive 10,000 times the normal human dose of LSD and not demonstrate neurotoxicity, monkeys that received only two or three times the normal dose of MDMA were found to have developed symptoms of neurotoxicity (Price et al., 1989; Barnes, 1988).

Clinical evidence now suggests that Ecstasy is neurotoxic in humans as well as animals, although there is no information on whether this brain damage is permanent (Barnes, 1988). Peroutka (1989) argued that while there was no evidence to suggest that MDMA was addictive, there *was* evidence to suggest "a long-term, and potentially irreversible, effect of MDMA on the human brain" (p. 191).

Price et al. (1989), found indirect evidence suggesting that MDMA indeed causes neurotoxicity in humans. It was found that MDMA users responded differently to a test designed to measure serotonin levels in the body. The measured differences between MDMA users and normal control subjects were not statistically significant in the study conducted by Price et al. (1989); however, the authors concluded that the results were indeed suggestive of neurotoxicity caused by Ecstasy use.

In recent years, MDMA has become a rather popular hallucinogen. Research suggests that MDMA is toxic to certain brain cells in animals. By extension, one would expect that MDMA is also toxic to portions of the human brain, especially those portions that use serotonin as a neurotransmitter. The latest drug to emerge from the nation's illicit laboratories may very well cause organic brain damage in the user.

SUMMARY

Weil (1986) suggested that people initially use chemicals in order to alter the normal state of consciousness. Hallucinogen use in the United States, at least in the last generation, has followed a series of waves, as first one drug and then another becomes the drug of choice for achieving this altered state of consciousness. In the sixties, LSD was the major hallucinogen, and in the seventies and early eighties, it was PCP. Currently, MDMA seems to be gaining in popularity as the hallucinogen of choice.

If we accept Weil's (1986) hypothesis, it is logical to expect that other hallucinogens will emerge over the years as people look for a more effective way to alter their state of consciousness. One might expect that these drugs will, in turn, slowly fade as they are replaced by newer hallucinogenics. Just as cocaine faded from the drug scene in the 1930s and was replaced for a period of time by the amphetamines, so one might expect wave after wave of hallucinogen abuse as new drugs become available. Thus, chemical dependency counselors will have to maintain a working knowledge of an ever-growing range of hallucinogens in the years to come.

CHAPTER 12

Cigarettes and Nicotine

The use of tobacco was well known in the New World for many hundreds of years before Europeans arrived. Tobacco was used in religious ceremonies, and Schuckit (1984) suggested that the tobacco in use then was "more potent and may have contained high concentrations of psychoactive substances" (p. 190). Within a few years of its introduction to Europe by Columbus's men, the use of tobacco spread across Europe and into Asia (Schuckit). Tobacco use spread in spite of harsh opposition from the Church and various governments. Berger and Dunn (1982) reported that in Germany, public smoking was once punishable by death, while in Russia castration was the sentence for the same crime.

Smoking soon became at least moderately acceptable in society. Over the years, society's view of tobacco use has changed. Tobacco was, in the years following its introduction to Europe, thought to be a medicine. During the last two centuries, its use has been interpreted as a mark of sophistication. Only in the last generation or two has tobacco use been widely associated with public criticism.

The face of tobacco use has changed over the years. Starting in the mid-nineteenth century, several forces combined to change the shape of tobacco use in the United States. First, new varieties of tobacco were planted, allowing for a greater yield than in previous years. Second, new methods of curing the leaf of the tobacco plant were found. Third, the advent of the industrial age brought with it machinery capable of manufacturing the cigarette, a smaller, less expensive, neater way to smoke than cigars.

Prior to the introduction of the cigarette, the major method of tobacco use was chewing. The practice of chewing tobacco, then spitting into the ever present cuspidor, contributed to the spread of tuberculosis and other diseases (Brecher, 1972). Public health officials began to campaign against the practice of *chewing* tobacco after the year 1910. The new cigarette, manufactured in large numbers by the latest machines, provided a more sanitary alternative to chewing tobacco.

Unlike cigar smoke, the smoke of the new cigarette was so mild that it could be inhaled (Jaffe, 1985a). This allowed the nicotine to enter the lungs, and from there the circulatory system. For many, cigarette smoking became the method through which their nicotine addiction might be serviced. The world hasn't been the same since.

SCOPE OF THE PROBLEM

The use of cigarettes grew in popularity following World War I and peaked in the mid-1960s (Schuckit, 1984). At that time, some 600 *billion* cigarettes were being manufactured in the United States each year (Jaffe, 1985a). Schuckit (1984) estimated that in the mid-1960s approximately 52% of adult American males and 32% of adult American females were cigarette smokers.

In 1964, the Surgeon General of the United States released a report stating that cigarette smoking was a danger to the smoker's health and outlined the various problems that might be caused by smoking. Since then, the number of adults who continue to smoke has gradually declined. In spite of a growing body of information on the dangers of tobacco use, some 4000 cigarettes *per person per year* are still consumed in the United States (Berger and Dunn, 1982).

It is difficult to determine the exact percentage of Americans who continue to smoke cigarettes. The American Psychiatric Association (1985) estimated that *44 million* American adults still smoke cigarettes. Henning-field and Nemeth-Coslett (1988) gave a higher figure, reporting that 50 million Americans continue to smoke, while another 10 million used "smokeless" tobacco products.

Hughes, Gust, and Pechacek (1987) estimated that 33% of all Americans currently smoke. L. Siegel (1989) reported that some 60 million Americans continue to smoke. In his exploration of adolescent drug use patterns, Jaffe (1985a), found that one-fifth of current high school seniors smoke on a regular basis.

PHARMACOLOGY OF SMOKING

The primary method by which tobacco is used is by smoking (Schuckit, 1984), although in recent years chewing tobacco has made a comeback. The exact pharmacology of tobacco smoking is quite complicated. Jaffe (1985a) outlined several variables that influenced the composition of tobacco smoke, including: (a) the exact composition of the tobacco being used, (b) how densely the tobacco is packed, (c) the length of the column of tobacco (for cigarette or cigar smokers), (d) the characteristics of the filter being used (if any), (e) the paper being used (for cigarette smokers), and (f) the temperature at which the tobacco is burned.

When smoked, some 4000 different compounds are generated by tobacco, and these chemicals are inhaled into the body (Jaffe, 1985a; Schuckit, 1984). A partial list of these compounds would include:

> carbon monoxide, carbon dioxide, nitrogen oxides, ammonia, volatile nitrosamines, hydrogen cyanide, volatile sulfur-containing compounds, nitrites and other nitrogen-containing compounds, volatile hydrocarbons, alcohols, and aldehydes and ketones (e.g., acetaldehyde, formaldehyde and acrolein) (Jaffe, 1985a, p. 555).

Some of the chemicals obtained from tobacco smoke are documented carcinogens. Thus, cigarette use introduces known carcinogenic chemicals directly into the body. Cigarette smoke also contains radioactive compounds such as polonium 210 (Jaffe, 1985).

Rustin (1988) noted that tobacco smoke contains nicotine, which reportedly has "properties similar to those of cocaine and amphetamine" (p. 18). However, tobacco smoke also includes *acetaldehyde*, a chemical that is also the first metabolite produced by the liver when alcohol is metabolized. Acetaldehyde is more potent than alcohol and, like alcohol, has a sedative effect on the user (Rustin, 1988).

Nicotine itself is a powerful reinforcer. It is thought to be less powerful than cocaine or the amphetamines (Jaffe, 1985a), although Weil (1986) claimed that nicotine is a more powerful reinforcer than amphetamines. Henningfield and Nemeth-Coslett (1988) reported that *intravenous* nicotine was five to ten times more potent than intravenous cocaine, in terms of its reward potential. Bertone, Gomez, Jacques, and Mattiko (1988) reached a similar conclusion, noting that "Milligram for milligram, nicotine is more potent than cocaine in modifying behavior" (p. 14).

Smoking cigarettes delivers nicotine to the brain more effectively than intravenous injection (Weil, 1986). When smoked, the nicotine will reach the brain in just seven (Lichtenstein and Brown, 1980) to eight (Jaffe, 1985a) seconds.

Once in the body, nicotine will be rapidly distributed to virtually every blood-rich tissue in the body, including the brain (Henningfield and Nemeth-Coslett, 1988). In the digestive system, nicotine causes a decrease in the strength of stomach contractions (Schuckit, 1984), while its action on the brain may cause the smoker to experience nausea and vomiting (Jaffe, 1985a).

Cigarette smoke can cause irritation of the tissues of the lungs and pulmonary system, deposit potentially harmful chemicals into the lungs, and cause a decrease in the motion of the cilia (small hairlike projections that help to clean the lungs). Nicotine will cause an increase in heart rate, blood pressure, and the strength of heart contractions, while reducing peripheral blood flow (Schuckit, 1984).

The mechanism by which nicotine effects the central nervous system is unknown. Smokers are known to experience stimulation of the brain (Schuckit, 1984), and decreased muscle tone (Jaffe, 1985a). Animal research would suggest that nicotine stimulates the release of the neurotransmitters norepinephrine and dopamine (Jaffe). According to Henningfield and Nemeth-Coslett (1988), research has discovered that nicotine binds selectively to the neurons in the rat brain that are thought to be responsible for stimulation of the central nervous system and a decrease in muscle tone.

Drug interactions between nicotine and various therapeutic agents are well documented. Cigarette smokers, for example, will require more morphine for the control of pain and may experience less sedation from benzodiazepines than do nonsmokers (Jaffe, 1985a). Nicotine also seems to counteract some of the sedation seen with alcohol use, and Schuckit (1984) has suggested that this may be one reason why alcoholics seem to smoke so much. Tobacco also interacts with many anticoagulants, as well as propranolol, and caffeine (Schuckit, 1984).

NICOTINE ADDICTION

It is difficult to determine what percentage of those who use tobacco are actually *addicted* to nicotine. In their research into tobacco dependence, Hughes, Gust, and Pechacek (1987) found that ". . . many, but not all, smokers are behaviorally or physically dependent on tobacco" (p. 207). Henningfield and Nemeth-Coslett (1988) support this statement, noting that

> Simple exposure to tobacco does not ensure that dependence will develop, nor is everyone who uses tobacco dependent on nicotine (p. 38 s).

It is well known, however, that many, perhaps most, cigarette smokers demonstrate the classic symptoms of addiction, including tolerance (Jaffe, 1985a) and withdrawal (Schuckit, 1984). Rustin (1988) did not address the issue of what percentage of those who used tobacco would become addicted. He did conclude that nicotine addicts demonstrated all of the characteristics necessary for a diagnosis of a drug addiction, including: (a) tolerance, (b) withdrawal symptoms, and, (c) drug-seeking behaviors. In addition to this, Rustin (1988) noted that tobacco users will develop drug-using rituals that seem to provide the individual with a sense of security in an insecure world.

It is difficult to break the nicotine habit. To place the strength of nicotine addiction in perspective, Kozlowski, Wilkinson, Skinner, Kent, Franklin, and Pope (1989) asked some 1000 individuals in treatment for a drug addiction to rate the relative difficulty of quitting smoking, as compared to their drug of choice. Surprisingly, 74% rated the task of quitting cigarette use at least as difficult as giving up their drug of choice, a finding that underscores the addiction potential of tobacco.

Some researchers believe that chronic smokers tend to smoke in such a way as to regulate the nicotine level in the blood. Smokers will increase or decrease their cigarette use to achieve, and then maintain, an individually specific blood level of nicotine (Lichtenstein and Brown, 1980). Jaffe (1985a) observed that, when given cigarettes of a high nicotine content, smokers will use fewer cigarettes, while the reverse is true when a smoker is given low-nicotine cigarettes.

Henningfield and Nemeth-Coslett (1988) challenged this conclusion, however, noting that research suggests that cigarette smokers are "remarkably insensitive" (p. 45 s) to changes in nicotine levels in the blood. The authors noted that the hypothesis that cigarette smokers will regulate their use to maintain a constant blood plasma level of nicotine has "never been convincingly demonstrated" (p. 46 s). The authors, in reviewing the rapid changes in blood plasma nicotine levels across the span of a single day, concluded that the research data does not support the constant-level hypothesis.

Withdrawal symptoms usually begin within hours of the last use of tobacco (Schuckit, 1984). The exact nature of the withdrawal symptoms vary from person to person, and Jaffe (1985a) noted that higher daily intake of nicotine is associated with stronger withdrawal symptoms. Jaffe also reported that women tend to experience more withdrawal symptoms following chronic cigarette smoking than do men.

The symptoms of withdrawal include decrease in heart rate and blood pressure, increased peripheral blood flow, decrease in attentiveness, and an increase in aggressiveness (Jaffe, 1985a). Insomnia, hunger, tremulousness and a strong craving for tobacco have also been reported (Jaffe). Other symptoms of tobacco withdrawal include drowsiness, anxiety, headache, fatigue, tremor, and heart palpitations (Brecher, 1972). Former smokers often report an increase in weight over time, although the exact mechanism by which this comes about is unknown.

COMPLICATIONS OF
THE CHRONIC USE OF TOBACCO

Because of the various factors that influence the exact effects of tobacco smoke, the impact on the individual smoker is much more difficult to determine. Jaffe (1985a) noted the exact amount of nicotine, "tar," and carbon monoxide obtained from a specific brand of cigarette is determined when the cigarette is "smoked" by a test machine. However, the various smoking methods used by individuals causes significant variability in the chemical combinations generated by each cigarette. Thus, it is difficult to determine exactly what chemicals, and in what concentrations, might be introduced into the body of an individual smoker.

Cigarettes are, however, a known health hazard. By the year 1909, approximately 4.2 billion cigarettes were manufactured in the United States (Brecher, 1972). Carcinoma (cancer) of the lung was a relatively rare disorder during this period (Bloodworth, 1987). However, following the growing popularity of cigarette smoking, there was a gradual increase in the mortality rates that researchers believe could be attributed to tobacco.

By the year 1980, Lichtenstein and Brown (1980) reported that in any given year cigarette smoking causes some 80,000 deaths from lung cancer, 22,000 deaths from other forms of cancer, 225,000 deaths from various other cardiovascular diseases, and an additional 19,000 deaths from various other pulmonary diseases.

Henningfield and Nemeth-Coslett (1988) estimated that cigarette smoking contributed to more than 300,000 deaths a year in the United States alone. L. Siegel (1989) gave a higher estimate yet, reporting that tobacco use resulted in 320,000 deaths each year. DeAngelis (1989) quoted the Surgeon General of the United States, who concluded that cigarette use resulted in 390,000 annual deaths in the United States. Klag and Whelton (1987) found that cigarette smoking significantly increased the chance of stroke in males, and called for a program to "promote smoking cessation on a national, as well as on an individual, level" (p. 628).

After alcohol, tobacco use results in the highest annual death rate of any abused substance (Schuckit, 1984). Scott (1987) went further than this, stating that nicotine-related deaths exceeded even those caused by alcohol. Nelson (1989) concluded that cigarette smoking "takes more than three times as many lives as alcohol, and 10 times as many lives as all other drugs combined" (p. 8 Ex).

Chronic cigarette smokers are known to suffer increased rates of cancer of the lung, the mouth, the pharynx, the larynx, and the esophagus; increased rates of cardiovascular disease; and increased mortality from pulmonary disease (Schuckit, 1984). Lichtenstein and Brown (1980) noted that 35-year-old men who smoked two packs of cigarettes a day experienced twice the mortality of nonsmokers. Nelson (1989) reported that alcoholics who also smoke cigarettes are especially vulnerable to cancer of the throat.

DeAngelis (1989), in reviewing the Surgeon General's report on cigarette smoking in the United States, reported that *one-sixth* of all deaths in this country were related to smoking. This figure, more than one-third higher than past estimates, included deaths from certain forms of stroke and cancer of the cervix, conditions that the Surgeon General's report concluded were also caused by cigarette smoking.

TREATMENT OF NICOTINE ADDICTION

As many thousands of people may attest, it is extremely difficult to stop smoking. Lichtenstein and Brown (1980) reported that only one person in four is able to permanently stop smoking before the age of 60. Weil (1986) advanced the hypothesis that it was easier to withdraw from heroin than it was from nicotine and noted that "I have never seen anyone have as much physical trouble giving up heroin as I have seen many people have giving up cigarettes" (p. 42).

Jaffe (1985a) noted that, of those who attempt to stop smoking, two-thirds may stop for a very few days, but that only 20–40% will be tobacco free a year later. Jaffe also noted that, unlike opiate addicts, cigarette smokers who try to gradually cut down on the frequency with which they smoke in order to reduce the severity of their withdrawal may actually extend their withdrawal symptoms. The reason for this phenomenon is, as yet, unknown.

Nicotine-containing gum has been shown to be helpful (although not totally effective) in controlling both the craving for cigarettes and the irritability associated with withdrawal from cigarettes (Jaffe, 1985a; Schuckit, 1984). A nasal spray that contains nicotine has been developed for use in the control of tobacco craving. The preliminary results suggest that blood plasma levels of nicotine obtained from this nasal spray are similar to blood plasma levels obtained from smoking, but its effectiveness as an aid to stop smoking has not been demonstrated.

Gottlieb, Killen, Marlatt, and Taylor (1987) found that when subjects were led to expect nicotine-containing gum, they reported fewer withdrawal symptoms, regardless of whether the gum they chewed actually contained nicotine. The individual's *expectations* as to whether they received nicotine gum seemed to moderate their withdrawal symptoms from cigarettes (Gottlieb, et al.). This report raises questions about the role of the individual's expectations on the tobacco withdrawal process.

Glassman, Stetner, Walsh, Raizman, Fleiss, Cooper, and Covey (1988) explored the application of an antihypertensive drug, Catapres (clonidine) to the craving for nicotine often reported by former cigarette smokers. This medication has been found to be of value in the control of drug-craving in narcotics withdrawal, and Glassman et al. (1988), found that more than twice as many subjects who received clonidine were able to stop smoking and remain abstinent over a four-week span than were subjects who received a placebo.

Bertone et al. (1988), advanced a treatment program that is based on the fact that nicotine addiction is similar to other forms of chemical addiction. First, this program includes a detoxification component involving the use of clonidine and nicotine chewing gum for a controlled withdrawal over a ten-day period.

Second, Bertone et al. (1988), used a controlled dietary intervention program, on the theory that "Eating and drinking behaviors play an important role in the activation of the smoking response" (p. 15). The authors noted that there is often an association between eating and smoking. Emphasis on proper diet thus helps to control the weight gain often reported by former smokers.

The third component of the treatment program is a "therapeutic activities program" (p. 16) designed to help the individual enhance cardiovascular fitness. Stress management techniques are used as the fourth component of the treatment program, while individual and group therapy is the fifth component. Finally, a twelve-step program known as Smokers Anonymous is used as the sixth component of treatment.

Although the treatment program advocated by Bertone et al. (1988), certainly makes clinical sense, the authors failed to provide long-term statistics demonstrating the usefulness of their approach to nicotine addiction. Thus, while this treatment approach appears attractive, it has not demonstrated a superior "cure" rate than other, less involved, treatment programs. Indeed, Kozlowski et al. (1989), concluded that "Most cigarette smokers give up smoking without formal treatment" (p. 901), raising the question of whether extensive treatment programs are necessary for tobacco dependence.

SUMMARY

Tobacco use, once limited to the New World, was first introduced to Europe by Columbus's men. Once the practice of smoking or chewing tobacco reached Europe, tobacco use rapidly spread. Following the introduction of the cigarette around the turn of the century, smoking became more common, rapidly replacing tobacco chewing as the accepted method of tobacco use.

The active agent of tobacco, nicotine, has been found to have an addiction potential similar to that of cocaine or narcotics. A significant percentage of those who are currently addicted to nicotine will attempt to stop smoking cigarettes, but will initially be unsuccessful. Current treatment methods have been unable to achieve a significant cure rate, and more comprehensive treatment programs have been suggested for nicotine addiction. These comprehensive programs are patterned after chemical addiction treatment programs, but have not demonstrated a significantly improved cure rate over more traditional treatment programs for cigarette smoking.

CHAPTER 13

A Short Primer on Theoretical Models of Addiction

A respected instructor once shared a story about how a hypothetical automobile accident might be viewed by different professionals. The automobile, according to the story, skidded off of a wet road and smashed into a tree. The driver was ejected from the vehicle and was killed. Several vehicles immediately stopped, and the drivers of these vehicles rushed to the wreckage.

A physician happened to reach the victim first and pronounced the driver dead at the scene of the accident from massive head trauma. A highway safety expert was next on the scene of the accident and announced that the cause of death was an unsafe road design, combined with the fact that the tree was allowed to grow in a dangerous position at the side of the road. A meteorologist came upon the scene of the accident and blamed the death on the weather conditions at the time of the crash. Finally, when the police officer who was called to the scene of the accident arrived, he saw numerous empty cans of beer in the back of the car and blamed the death on the driver's use of alcohol.

The point illustrated by this story is that one event—the accident—could be viewed differently by different professionals. Chemical dependency is much like this hypothetical automobile accident; the compulsive use of drugs can be viewed differently by different professionals.

This is unfortunate because the beginning student often finds that chemical dependency is confusing simply because it is a new field of study. The student's confusion is compounded by the fact that chemical dependency experts are unable to agree even on the definition of what constitutes drug abuse, as opposed to experimental or casual drug use (American Psychiatric Association, 1985).

In this chapter, we will review the major theoretical models of drug dependency in order to provide the student with an overview of how different professions view the problem of addiction. It is the belief of this author that each of the major schools of thought has something to offer to the understanding of drug abuse. Each of the following theoretical models provides a different "roadmap" that the reader might find helpful in his or her understanding of drug abuse and dependency.

THE COMPLEX NATURE OF ADDICTION

In the past, there have been numerous simplistic attempts to identify the "cause" of chemical dependency. These studies have consistently failed to identify such a causal agent. In addressing the earlier research, Tarter (1988) noted that

> . . . no single factor appears to cause the development of a substance-abuse problem. Rather, it is the aggregation of risk factors that best predicts alcoholism or substance-abuse outcome" (p. 189).

To further complicate matters, chemical dependency is quite often an "imposter." As was noted in chapter 1, drug addiction is much like syphilis because dependency can masquerade as any number of other, apparently unrelated, conditions. Only some of the manifestations of the addictive disorders are identified as social problems. Finally, different professions view the problem of addiction in different ways, with the result being that few professionals from one field understand the language or concepts that another profession might use in treating addiction.

For example, the person who buys heroin on the street is classified as an "addict," and as such is a social problem. The person who is markedly overweight is "obese," however, and this is at most an individual medical problem. The person who visits eight or nine different physicians and obtains prescriptions for Valium from seven or eight of these physicians, taking care to have the prescriptions filled at different pharmacies, is not called an "addict," but a "patient" (Peluso and Peluso, 1988).

Chemical dependency is indeed an imposter, able to hide behind a range of diagnostic classifications. For example, as has been discussed in preceding chapters, the various drugs of abuse may bring about periods of rage, memory loss, drug-induced psychotic reactions, and periods of depression that might reach the point of suicide. More than one cocaine addict has been hospitalized with a diagnosis of "Brief Reactive Psychosis," only to admit later that they did not tell the admissions officer they were using cocaine or amphetamines.

These are all psychiatric conditions that, without knowledge of the person's chemical use, might be misinterpreted by mental health professionals. If the condition is misdiagnosed, it will be difficult to provide the proper treatment. Indeed, Beasley (1987) contends that alcoholism is often misdiagnosed, and mistreated, by the health care profession.

Couples enter marital counseling with the presenting complaint of "arguments," spouse abuse, or sexual dysfunction. If the professional is knowledgeable, she or he might inquire about each partner's chemical use, and possibly discover that behind the presenting complaint was an addiction that was either unsuspected or at least unacknowledged. If the professional does not inquire about the possibility of drug/ alcohol addiction, many weeks, or months, may be invested in therapy without the root problem even coming to light. Addiction is thus an imposter that hides behind virtually the whole spectrum of human suffering.

THE DISEASE MODEL OF ADDICTION

Biological Theories

There are those who think that addiction is a reflection of a "disease," perhaps a genetic or metabolic disorder, but certainly an illness. Jellinek (1960) is credited with presenting a comprehensive disease model of the prototypical addiction: alcoholism. Jellinek advanced the theory that alcoholism was actually a disease, with symptoms, and a progressive course, in an era when the predominant school of thought was that alcoholism was a moral weakness (Kolb and Brodie, 1982).

The key elements to the Jellinek model were: (a) a *loss of control* over one's drinking, and (b) the belief that alcoholism was a *progressive* disorder. In other words, Jellinek proposed that the alcoholic was *unable to consistently predict* in advance how much he or she would drink at any given time. Alcoholism, like other disease states, was also viewed as a progressive disorder that would, if not arrested, result in the individual's death.

Jellinek viewed alcoholism as a disease that might take any of many different forms, or styles, of drinking. Jellinek classified several subgroups of alcohol-drinking patterns. The first of these was the *Alpha* alcoholic. Jellinek thought that the *Alpha* alcoholic was psychologically dependent on alcohol but believed that this individual could abstain for periods of time from the use of alcohol, if this were necessary.

The element of loss of control was found in the *Alpha* alcoholic's psychological dependence on alcohol, which might manifest itself in regular drinking. The *Alpha* alcoholic was viewed by Jellinek as possibly suffering from the nutritional disorders brought about by alcoholism, as well as family conflict caused by his or her alcohol use. But, the *Alpha* alcoholic was not viewed as being physically dependent on alcohol.

Alpha alcoholism was not thought to be *automatically* progressive by Jellinek. Rather, Jellinek thought that the *Alpha* form of alcoholism might be a stable pattern of drinking. If the *Alpha* drinking pattern were to evolve into another form of alcoholism, Jellinek believed that the *Alpha* alcoholic would evolve into the *Gamma* form of alcoholism. However, as previously stated, the *Alpha* form of alcoholism was thought to be relatively stable.

Jellinek also classified some drinkers as *Beta* alcoholics. The *Beta* alcoholic was described as not being psychologically or physically dependent on alcohol. But the *Beta* alcoholic might demonstrate medical symptoms of chronic alcohol use such as gastritis and cirrhosis of the liver. If the *Beta* alcoholic progressed, it was also to the *Gamma* form of alcoholism, according to Jellinek.

The *Delta* alcoholic was thought to demonstrate physical dependence on alcohol but few or no physical problems from chronic drinking. In contrast to this, the *Gamma* alcoholic was seen as demonstrating both physical symptoms from drinking and physical dependence on alcohol.

The *Gamma* alcoholic also demonstrated a progressive loss of control over alcohol use, according to Jellinek. As noted above, both the *Alpha* and, less frequently, *Beta* alcohol-use patterns could progress to the *Gamma* pattern of alcohol use over time.

Finally, the *Epsilon* alcoholic might best be classified as the binge drinker. This form of alcoholism was least frequently encountered in the United States according to Jellinek where the *Alpha* and the *Gamma* drinking patterns were most common. Jellinek noted that there were other culturally related patterns of drinking (for example, "fiesta drinking") that were worthy of study but were possibly not true forms of alcoholism.

Jellinek's model of alcoholism offered a number of advantages to physicians. First, it provided a diagnostic framework within which physicians could classify different patterns of drinking, as opposed to the restrictive dichotomous "is or isn't he or she an alcoholic?" view that had previously prevailed. Second, Jellinek's model helped to classify alcoholism as a physical disease, worthy of medical treatment. Prior to this, as likely as not, alcoholism was viewed as a moral weakness.

However, Jellinek's (1960) model does contain a number of flaws. For example, Vaillant (1983) observed that the Jellinek model fails to take into account the fact that, over time, drinking patterns often change. Thus, when used in longitudinal research, the Jellinek model begins to break down. Also, Vaillant's research has challenged the idea that alcoholism is a progressive disorder. (Although, Vaillant's conclusions have also been challenged by other researchers in the field of addiction.)

Peele (1984) observed that a number of investigations have failed to confirm Jellinek's theory that there is a loss of control associated with chronic alcoholism. Indeed, there is strong evidence that alcoholics tend to regulate their drinking, but that they demonstrate only *inconsistent control* over their drinking. Finally, Peele concluded that "there is no distinct point at which genuine alcoholism or addiction to alcohol can be said to exist" (p. 1342).

One component of a biological theory of disease is that there is a biophysical foundation to the disorder. In infectious diseases, this is the bacteria, virus, or fungus that invades the organism. Another class of diseases are caused by a genetic disorder. As noted in previous chapters, there is strong evidence suggesting that there is a genetic predisposition to alcoholism. The case for a genetic predisposition to other forms of addiction is not clear at this time, but one might assume that such a genetic predisposition exists. As such, chemical dependency is very much like a number of other physical disorders where there is a genetic predisposition, and in this sense might be said to be a "disease."

Levenson, Oyama, and Meek (1987) identified three groups of individuals who were thought to be "at risk" for alcoholism by reason of having an alcoholic parent, a "prealcoholic personality pattern" as measured by psychological tests, or a combination of the two. The authors then administered an alcoholic beverage, the exact strength of which was based on the subject's weight.

This was done to compare the responses to a standard drink of alcohol of these three high-risk groups with control subjects who lacked these risk factors. It was found by Levenson, Oyama, and Meek (1987) that the high-risk subjects demonstrated a significantly different response pattern to a given dose of alcohol than did those individuals who were judged to be low-risk subjects. This study suggested a basic biological/personality difference between those individuals thought to be at risk for alcoholism as compared to those individuals who were not.

Ackerman (1983) suggested that without intervention 40–60% of the children of alcoholics will themselves become addicted to alcohol in adult life. Schuckit (1987) noted that ". . . there is evidence that alcoholism is a genetically influenced disorder" (p. 301), noting that research has demonstrated "a threefold to fourfold increased risk for this disorder in sons and daughters of alcoholics" (p. 301).

Tarter (1988) postulated that there were "inherited behavioral traits" (p. 189) that predisposed an individual to substance abuse, including alcoholism. Cloninger, Gohnan, and Siguardsson's (1981) cross-cultural adoption studies were strongly suggestive of a genetic component to alcoholism. Robertson (1988), in exploring the biological roots of addictive behavior, postulated that there was a neurochemical foundation to the various compulsions, including chemical addiction. He offered as evidence of such a neurochemical foundation to compulsive behavior the observation that compulsive gamblers excrete more of the neurotransmitter norepinephrine in their urine than did normal subjects.

However, although evidence does seem to point to a biological foundation to drug addiction, research has not been able to identify the specific nutritional deficit or genetic pattern that will bring about addiction. Nathan (1980) observed that

> . . . no differences have been found in the rate of metabolism, route of metabolism, site of metabolism, or susceptibility to the effects of drugs between people who become addicts and those who do not (p. 243).

In a similar vein, Schuckit (1987) observed that while there are several biological "markers" that show promise in the early detection of individuals at risk for alcoholism, ". . . no generally accepted biological marker of a vulnerability toward alcoholism has yet been identified" (p. 307). Schuckit concludes that "The final development of this disorder probably depends on the interaction between biological and environmental factors" (p. 307).

Meyer (1989) viewed addiction as resulting from the interaction between several factors, including: (a) social forces, (b) the psychological resources of the individual, and (c) the genetic inheritance of the individual. In addition to these three factors, Meyer identified an additional risk factor that may shape drug addiction. Although this factor is often overlooked, Meyer pointed out that the "pharmacological characteristics" (p. 189) of a drug also serve as a risk factor in the development of chemical dependency.

In exploring the interaction between environmental factors and genetic heritage, Loranger and Tulix (1985) concluded that

> There is some evidence from adoption studies that given a genetic pre-disposition to either mild or severe alcohol abuse, environmental factors largely determine the severity of the abuse (p. 156).

Swinson (1980), in addressing the issue of genetic and family influences in the development of chemical dependency, concluded that genetic inheritance appeared to be the strongest influence in men, while environmental influences were strongest in women.

Thus, research has provided strong evidence suggesting a biological predisposition toward alcoholism. The case for a biological predisposition toward other forms of addiction is less clear. It is not possible at this time to make more than a general statement that there apparently are some strong biological components to alcoholism. Hopefully, in the next few years, a biological marker will be identified that will aid in the diagnosis of alcoholism and other forms of drug addiction.

SHORTCOMINGS OF THE DISEASE MODEL OF ADDICTION

In spite of the evidence pointing to drug dependency as a disorder with a genetic predisposition, drug addiction remains a most curious "disease." For, *unlike other genetic disorders, drug addiction also requires some measure of active participation by the individual* in the disease process.

Addicts will consciously and unconsciously distort or deny the truth, project responsibility for their problems onto others, and rationalize away anything that stands between them and their drug of choice. The book Alcoholics Anonymous (1976) noted that alcoholism would bring:

> . . . misunderstanding, fierce resentment, financial insecurity, disgusted friends and employers, warped lives of blameless children, sad wives and parents . . . (p. 18).

Yet, to many addicts, all of this is excused on the grounds that, "I have a disease." This is, in part, a reflection of the medical model. B. Siegel (1989) noted that modern medicine "always gives the credit to the disease rather than the person" (p. 12). The addict who hides behind the disease label is a challenge to the chemical dependency professional. The label offers the addict a potential rationalization that excuses him or her from personal responsibility for his or her behavior. "Sure I went out and used drugs again" the addict often cries, "I have a disease!"

However, and this is the point often overlooked by addicts, *with the power to label oneself diseased come certain responsibilities toward the care and treatment of that disease.* When the addict attempts to hide behind the disease label, it is up to the chemical dependency counselor or human services professional to confront the addict with the fact that *the label "disease" does not absolve the individual from responsibility for the treatment of his or her affliction*. Rather, this underscores the issue of personal responsibility in the control and treatment of the disorder.

A person who unknowingly has a highly contagious disease, such as a flu virus, might be excused for walking into a crowded room. However, if the person *knowingly* exposes others to this same disease, that person is morally responsible for his or her behavior. Thus, with the knowledge that one is addicted comes a definite responsibility to work toward sobriety.

Viktor Frankl (1978) addressed the issue of psychosis, another disorder in which there appears to be a strong genetic component, which in some ways is similar to drug addiction. Frankl noted that psychosis was

> . . . a matter of the bodily system's biochemistry. However, what the patient makes of his psychosis is entirely the property of his human personality. The psychosis that afflicts him is biochemical, but how he reacts to it, what he invests in it, the content with which he fills it—all this is his personal creation, is the human work into which he has molded his suffering (p. 60).

Much the same might be said of chemical addiction. Evidence suggests a strong biological predisposition toward alcoholism, a "matter of the bodily system's biochemistry," in Frankl's (1978) words. However, the individual's reaction toward the addiction, what she or he invests in the addiction, how she or he fills the addictive void within, all of this is the personal creation of the addict. In other words, the individual may fight against the addiction within, or use it as an excuse for further drug use.

Vaillant (1983) observed that:

> . . . once patients understand that they have a "disease," they become more, not less, responsible for self-care. This is why the self-help group Alcoholics Anonymous places such single-minded emphasis on the idea that alcoholism is a disease (p. 19).

The disease model, or biological theories of addiction, thus postulate that there is an as yet unidentified genetic or metabolic "cause" to drug addiction. A central tenet of the biological theories is that addiction is, at its heart, the result of a biological condition. But there are those who challenge the disease concept of addiction.

For example, Vaillant (1983), in addressing the disease model of one specific form of chemical dependency—alcoholism—noted that even if alcoholism was a disease, "both its etiology and its treatment are largely social" (p. 4). Thomas Szasz (1972) termed alcoholism a "bad habit" (p. 84), noting that "if we choose to call bad habits 'diseases,' there is no limit to what we may define as a disease" (p. 84).

In a later essay, Szasz (1988) termed drug abuse a "mythical disease" (p. 319), and noted that drugs are, essentially, neutral. Some are natural substances, while others are the invention of human ingenuity, but *by themselves drugs are neither good nor bad*. It is the use to which these chemicals are put, the manner in which the individual might choose to use them, that determines whether a certain drug is "good" or "bad".

In his essay, Szasz (1988) pointed out that society has made an arbitrary decision to classify some drugs as dangerous, and others such as alcohol and tobacco, as being acceptable for social use. Yet the basis for these decisions are not scientific studies, but "religious or political (ritual, social) considerations" (p. 316). Szasz charged that the "war on drugs" is essentially a "war on human desire" (p. 322). The problem is not so much the chemicals, but the disorder of desire that prompts people to use chemicals for personal pleasure.

Dreger (1986) challenged the concept that alcoholism is a disease. He noted that

> . . . alcohol drinking is promoted by every Madison Avenue technique and by every type of peer pressure one can imagine. No other disease is thus promoted (p. 322).

Fingarette (1988), in addressing the disease concept of addiction, postulated that the disease model of addiction has become "big politics and big business" (p. 64). Peele (1988), in his essay on the disease model of addiction, concluded

> The disease model has been so profitable and politically successful that it has spread to include problems of eating, child abuse, gambling, shopping, premenstrual tension, compulsive love affairs, and almost every other form of self-destructive behavior. . . . From this perspective, nearly every American can be said to have a disease of addiction (p. 67).

SUMMARY OF THE DISEASE MODEL OF ADDICTION

Currently, there is significant evidence to suggest that alcoholism has a biological basis, although research has failed to clearly identify the biochemical flaw that results in drug dependency. The disease model of addiction, while useful, has also been seriously challenged by many as being too restrictive, or even as being an artificial construct. Some, especially Szasz (1988) and Weil (1986), have challenged the disease model, in that the core issue seems to be an artificial distinction between the use of one chemical over another. There are those within the medical community who view the addictive disorders as being a disorder of normal desire, rather than a true "disease" (Szasz, 1988).

PSYCHOSOCIAL MODELS OF ADDICTION

In the previous section, we briefly explored the medical model of addiction. In this section, we will discuss the psychosocial theories of addiction.

These theoretical models of drug dependency maintain that the individual is drawn to chemicals in large part because of internal (psychological) or external (social or cultural) forces. The psychosocial models of addiction have contributed much to our understanding of drug abuse and addiction.

SOCIAL/CULTURAL THEORIES OF CHEMICAL DEPENDENCY

The *social/cultural* theories of drug dependency focus on the forces in the individual's interpersonal environment that bring about, or support, drug addiction. Such environmental forces include the culture in which the individual is raised and such social factors as family, peer group, and social expectations for chemical use.

In discussing alcoholism, Vaillant (1983) observed that "cultural patterns of alcohol *use* are very important" (p. 6, italics in original) in the determination of normal and abnormal drinking patterns. Leigh (1985) noted that each society has a certain set of attitudes and feelings about the use of specific chemicals within that culture. Meyer (1989) pointed out that such social attitudes toward the use of specific chemicals is but one of several factors that help shape the individual's drug-use patterns.

Meyer (1989) also pointed out that the society within which the individual lives and the psychological resources of the individual are associated with drug addiction. The pharmacological potential of the drug and the individual's genetic inheritance also play a role in the development of a drug problem. However, as Meyer observed

> . . . the significance of these factors varies over time depending on the general availability of a drug and society's attitude toward its use (p. 189).

Thus, social attitudes toward chemical use are significant determinants of a drug addiction problem. In his paper on the social impact of social rules on the use of one chemical, alcohol, Peele (1984) reported that ". . . styles of drinking and attitudes toward alcohol vary tremendously across cultures" (p. 1337). But, while there might be significant variation across cultures, the individual's culture helps to shape the individual's drug-use patterns.

For middle-class American values in effect at this time, excessive use of recreational drugs, or the use of recreational drugs besides alcohol (and *possibly* marijuana), will result in social disapproval (Peele, 1984). Alcohol use is acceptable, within certain limits, but heroin use is not. This reality has helped to spawn the formation of subcultures in which different patterns of recreational drug use may be more acceptable. The essential point to recall is that cultural values help to shape chemical-use patterns.

Cahalan (1978) reported that, for both the Jewish and Italian-American cultures, drinking was limited mainly to religious or family celebrations. In these cultures, excessive drinking was strongly discouraged, and proper drinking behavior was modeled by the adults. Because of this, Cahalan hypothesized that first-generation Jewish-Americans and Italian-Americans had low rates of alcoholism.

Pelle (1984) noted that the Chinese-American adults would model proper drinking behavior, and that peer groups would maintain social customs. Alcohol was not viewed as a rite of passage into adulthood, nor was its use associated with social power. In contrast to this, however, the Irish-American culture viewed alcohol use far more liberally; alcohol use was viewed as a rite of passage, and peer groups encouraged the use of alcohol. For this reason, Pelle concluded that the Irish-American sub-culture subsequently demonstrated higher rates of alcoholism than the Chinese-American subculture.

Kunitz and Levy (1974) explored the different drinking patterns of the Navaho and Hopi Indian tribes. This study is significant in that both cultures coexist in the same part of the country and share similar genetic histories. However, Navaho tribal customs hold that public group drinking is acceptable, while solitary drinking is a mark of deviance. For the Hopi, however, drinking is more likely to be a solitary experience.

Nathan (1980) concluded that while cultural patterns might predispose the individual to alcoholism, social influences play a role in the translation of this potential into actual drug dependency. For example, it is well known that the environment in which a person uses drugs, and his or her expectations for the drugs (both of which are social variables), strongly influence the impact of the drug experience on the individual.

Greenblatt and Shader (1975), pointed out that the setting (which includes being in an unfamiliar place, being alone, or being with unfamiliar people) can often bring about a "bad trip." The reverse also appears to be true: if the person comes to associate a drug experience with a certain set of people, or with certain positive experiences, she or he is more likely to experience pleasant feelings when using drugs with those people.

Franklin's (1987) observation, outlined in chapter one, was that there were class-specific patterns of drug abuse, at least prior to the Viet Nam conflict. The implication is that the influence of one's social class was reflected in the individual's drug use, with different social groups having a different drug of choice. Nathan (1980) also concluded that social in-fluences play a role in determining what drug(s) a person will use. A multitude of other social influences might affect a person's chemical use.

For example, after the individual has used drugs, the environment will provide cues to remind the individual of previous drug use. A friendly pat on the back from a "drinking buddy" after a night on the town can communicate acceptance of one's drinking. Other sources of social feed-back include newspaper advertisements, television programs, conver-sations with friends or co-workers, casual observations of others using the same chemicals, and so on.

The individual's previous experience with a particular drug can have a strong impact on how the individual reacts to that chemical. Research repeatedly has demonstrated that the individual not only has to be "taught" what to look for in the drug experience but also how to enjoy the drug's effects. This feedback comes from significant others in the person's environment: family and peer group members, the news media, advertising, school, and so on.

Kandel and Raveis (1989) concluded that peer influences played a significant role in the individual's initiation to marijuana, a conclusion that underscores the importance of the peer group on the evolution of specific drug-use patterns. Indeed, when the influence of a spouse's drug use was compared with the influence an individual's peer group had on his or her chemical use, Kandel and Raveis found that the peer group had the more significant impact on the individual.

It is well known that adolescents often look upon drinking as a sign of entry into adulthood (Leigh, 1985), and the adolescent peer culture strongly encourages repeated episodes of chemical abuse (Millman, 1978; Swaim, Oetting, Edwards, and Beauvais, 1989). Leigh, in addressing the role of social forces on the evolution of the individual's drug use, noted that chemical use "is learned from those who have the most social influence" (p. 14).

The family is certainly powerful in teaching social rules and expectations (Erikson, 1963), and this is nowhere more true than in the evolution of chemical addiction. Bowen (1985) noted that alcoholism is a family disorder, in which each member of the family "system" plays a role in the maintenance of the alcoholism.

Stanton, Todd, Heard, Kirschner, Kleiman, Mowatt, Riley, Scott, and van Deusen (1978) found a similar pattern for heroin addiction. The authors found that the heroin addiction process came about as part of a very complex family interaction pattern, in which heroin addiction on the part of one family member seemed to take the stress off of other dysfunctional family members.

SHORTCOMINGS OF THE SOCIAL/CULTURAL MODEL OF ADDICTION

The social/cultural theories of addiction have provided a valuable perspective on the environment within which the individual learns socially transmitted rules of drug-use behavior. The social/cultural school of thought has also outlined the process by which social pressure is used to either reward or punish drug-using behavior. Unfortunately, the social/cultural theorists have advanced few, if any, treatment methods that might be used by the chemical dependency professional. This is a major weakness of the social/cultural theories of drug addiction, which has limited their application to the field of drug addiction.

SUMMARY OF THE SOCIAL/CULTURAL THEORIES OF DRUG ABUSE AND ADDICTION

The social/cultural research conducted to date has done much to help identify the specific social and cultural influences on a person's decision to use chemicals. In a general sense, it has been found that the culture helps to identify standards of behavior for the individual, including which drugs are acceptable and what pattern of drug use is appropriate for that culture. Initially, the family defines rules for socially acceptable drug use. Ultimately, as the child grows up, peer groups help identify which behaviors are to be rewarded. The social/cultural model of drug addiction has failed, however, to propose a form of treatment for drug addiction.

PSYCHOLOGICAL THEORIES OF ADDICTION

The Inter/Intrapersonal Theories

The psychological theories of drug addiction are subdivided into two groups. First, there are the interpersonal theories of addiction, which in many ways are quite similar to the social/cultural model just reviewed. Second, the intrapersonal theories of addiction might better be classified as the *conflict* models of addiction, for these theories maintain that addiction rests on conflict within the individual.

The Interpersonal Theories
The interpersonal theories of drug dependency are based at least in part on the social and familial factors that play a role in the development and maintenance of an addiction to chemicals. These interpersonal forces, which overlap with the social/cultural theories previously reviewed, help shape the manner in which individuals perceive and react to the drug experience.

As the individual learns about chemical abuse through social-feedback mechanisms, she or he will establish certain expectations about the drug's effects. These expectations are then modified or rejected on the basis of personal experience and on feedback from the environment. Social psychologists believe drug-use behavior is shaped by the individual's society.

Rohsenow and Bachorowski (1984) conducted a series of experiments where subjects believed they were to receive alcohol. Some of the subjects did, in fact, receive alcohol, while others received only nonalcoholic beverages. In each case, care was taken to ensure that the volunteer did not know whether his or her drink contained alcohol.

The authors found that ". . . expectancies of alcohol consumption were the primary determinant of the subjects' evaluations . . . subjects who were led to believe that alcohol had been consumed were significantly *less* aggressive than were those who believed that only tonic had been consumed" (p. 429, italics in original). Rohsenow and Bachorowski (1984) went on to report that "Eighty-eight percent of the subjects reported expecting more pleasurable effects than aggressive effects from alcohol . . ." (p. 430).

In other words, 88% of the subjects reported that they anticipated alcohol would make them less aggressive and more relaxed. Subjects who *thought* they had received a nonalcoholic tonic were more likely to act aggressively than were those subjects who thought they had received an alcoholic beverage, in spite of what they actually drank. The expectations of the individuals helped to shape their reaction to the drink they *thought* they received.

Brown, Goldman, Inn, and Anderson (1980) explored peoples' expectations for alcohol and found that there were six different areas where people had preconceptions about alcohol's effects. The authors reported that subjects expected positive effects from alcohol use on life experiences, that alcohol use would enhance social and physical pleasure, and that it would enhance sexual performances. The authors also found that their subjects thought moderate alcohol use would increase social aggressiveness, increase assertiveness, and reduce tension.

These expectations, many of which are learned through social interactions, then help to shape the individual's subjective interpretation of alcohol's effects. The phenomenon of individual expectations has been found to have a powerful impact on the human body, one that is not limited to the individual's interpretation of the effects of alcohol.

B. S. Siegel (1986) noted that the individual's expectations for chemotherapy in the treatment of cancer influence their physical reaction to the medication. Siegel observed that those individuals who expected little or no nausea from their chemotherapy actually experienced significantly less nausea than did those persons who expected a great deal of discomfort.

The literature thus demonstrates that expectations for alcohol, and by extension the other drugs of abuse, influence the individual's subjective interpretation of the drug's effects. These expectations are learned from various sources in the environment. Significant others in the environment also provide important feedback (either positive or negative) to the individual concerning his or her drug use. All of this environmental feedback helps to shape the individual's expectations for further drug use.

An often overlooked point is that, while the environment might play a significant role in the evolution and maintenance of drug abuse/addiction, the individual also helps to shape his or her interpersonal environment. Leigh (1985) observed that there is a "potentially reinforcing interactive effect" (p. 10) between the individual and his or her drug-using environment, which includes the social group to which one belongs.

By choosing her or his associates, the individual becomes an active part

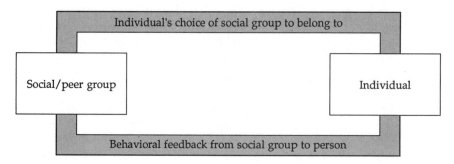

FIGURE 13-1

of the environment, not just a helpless victim of external forces. Stuart (1980), in exploring this point, observed that

> The individual is thus seen as both the partial cause and the partial result of an interaction between his or her covert and overt actions and the reactions that these behaviors elicit in others (p. 44).

There is a subtle, often unrecognized feedback mechanism between the individual and his or her interpersonal support system. While the individual will have his or her behavior shaped at least in part by the behavioral expectations of the social group, the individual will also help to shape the behavioral expectations of the social support system by associating with certain individuals and avoiding others. Figure 13-1 is a graphic representation of this feedback mechanism.

A reflection of this process might be seen in the observation that alcoholics (and other addicts) seem to drift toward social groups where drug use is tolerated and encouraged. At the same time, addicts avoid social groups where their drug use will be discouraged.

By avoiding those sections of society where drug use is discouraged, addicts are able to avoid much of the negative feedback that their chemical use might generate. For example, Kandel and Raveis (1989) found that one important determinant of the individual's cocaine-use pattern was whether she or he had friends who also used cocaine. Kandel and Raveis found that individuals who used cocaine tended to associate more with individuals who also used cocaine.

Simpson, Crandall, Savage, and Pava-Krueger (1981) noted that, before treatment, 60% of their sample of opiate addicts spent "a lot" (p. 38) of time engaged in "street" leisure activities, while only 13% of their sample did so at follow-up. Before treatment, the most frequent companions of the addicts studied were also opiate addicts, a pattern that changed following treatment.

This study illustrates both the shift in interpersonal relationship patterns that follows treatment, and the process by which individual addicts will surround themselves with people who are congruent with their life-style (drug using or chemically free). The individual, at least to some degree, chooses the environment in which to live, by choosing his or her associates, which in turn supports his or her drug use.

The Intrapersonal Conflict Theories

Virtually every major school of psychotherapy has offered theoretical models of addiction. In general, psychological theories have postulated that chemical abuse and drug dependency were outgrowths of the individual's attempts to come to terms with internal conflicts. The phenomenon of a businessman having a drink after "a tough day at the office" is a classic example of how some people use chemicals to deal with internal stress. Other theorists, viewing human behavior as being shaped by the society within which the individual lives, adopted a modified social viewpoint as to the causes of addiction.

Among the major schools of individual psychotherapy, both Harry Stack Sullivan (1953) and Karen Horney (1950), both prominent psychiatrists in their own right, viewed alcohol use as an attempt by the individual to deal with internal anxiety. Edwards (1982) viewed addiction as a response by the individual to come to terms with one's ultimate helplessness and the threat of abandonment. Connelly (1980) viewed alcoholism, and Frederick (1980) viewed drug abuse, as forms of "indirect" suicide.

Alcohol is also associated with such dysfunctional interpersonal relationships as incest, and child and spouse abuse. But research into the factors that bring about incest has demonstrated that, although alcohol "is frequently cited as a contributing factor in the instigation of incestuous activity, most of these men are not alcoholics" (Swanson and Biaggio, 1985, p. 669). Although alcohol is frequently mentioned as playing a role in incest, most men who are involved in incestuous activity are not *addicted* to alcohol.

Victims of incest often experience shame as a result of the incestuous activities or sexual assault (that is, rape or attempted rape). Clinical evidence also suggests that there is a strong relationship between the pervasive feeling of shame and addiction (Bradshaw, 1988; Fossum and Mason, 1986). Not surprisingly, chemical dependency professionals frequently encounter clients who have been victimized in early life.

Coleman (1982) reported that an estimated 33–62% of female alcoholics had either been neglected or sexually abused. Fossum and Mason (1986) reported an even higher figure, noting that some adolescent chemical dependency treatment centers have found that *three-quarters* of their female clients reported having been sexually abused.

Clinical evidence would strongly suggest that sexual or physical abuse on the part of the parents or significant others can leave deep emotional scars on the child. In adult life, these battered children might turn to drugs to deal with the pain of having been physically, emotionally, and/or sexually abused. This may be because, as Bradshaw (1988) observed, all compulsive behavior reflects the individual's attempt to escape the shame experienced in the family of origin.

Based on personal experience, Bradshaw (1988) included chemical addiction within his definition of compulsive behaviors. Indeed, Bradshaw noted that, in response to the shame and pain of growing up in his family, "I felt sane only when I was drunk" (p. 89). However, when a person compulsively uses one, and only one, method of escaping from shame, they become addicted to that system of control. Furthermore, as Beattie (1989) pointed out, although ". . . compulsive behaviors may help us temporarily avoid feelings or problems, they don't really stop the pain" (p. 14).

Evidence suggests that alcohol and drug addiction might, at least initially, be an attempt at self-medicating emotional distress. Khantzian (1985) explored this hypothesis and suggested that some people are drawn to the narcotics because these drugs help control internal feelings of rage and aggression, while others are drawn to cocaine in an attempt to relieve depression (Kandel and Raveis, 1989).

Brown (1985), who addressed the treatment of alcoholism, noted that the chemical a person uses provides *an illusion of control* over the harsh, painful feelings encountered in life. Franklin (1987) made a similar observation, noting the opiates' ability to lift the addict from an ongoing depression. Franklin postulated that before the individual's drug use, this lifelong depression was perceived by the individual as his or her normal emotional state.

After being introduced to drugs, however, the individual would come to learn that his or her distress was not "normal," and that there is at least a chemical escape from continuous emotional pain. The narcotics then provide at least the illusion of control over the depression that the individual has known throughout his or her life. However, ultimately, the method of "control" comes to dominate the individual's life, and the person becomes addicted.

Alcohol is occasionally used in an attempt to self-medicate depression. However, because alcohol is itself a depressant, it can bring about a drug-induced depression through chronic use. Research suggests that in the vast majority of cases, the feelings of depression reported by alcoholics is alcohol-induced (Willenbring, 1986). But, in about 5% of the cases, there is a primary depression that the person is attempting to self-medicate through alcohol.

The tendency to use (or not use) drugs is governed by well known laws of behavioral learning. A rule of thumb, somewhat simplified from the laws of behavior as advanced by Rachlin (1970), holds that whenever a certain behavior *increases pleasure,* or *decreases discomfort,* it will function as a *reinforcer* for the individual. As such, the specific behavior that resulted either in a reduction in discomfort, or an increase in the level of comfort, is likely to be repeated.

The individual uses recreational drugs because the pharmacological properties of those drugs make their use pleasurable. To illustrate this point, consider that cocaine's effects have been likened to that of a sexual lover, and that the "rush" from intravenous opiate or cocaine use has been likened to the sexual orgasm. Indeed, so powerful is cocaine's effects that some users *prefer* cocaine to a lover!

The disturbing fact that drugs of abuse serve as powerful reinforcers is often overlooked by newcomers to the field of addiction. Crowley (1988), in a paper presented at the 1988 annual meeting of the American Psychological Association, noted that drugs serve as powerful reinforcers for both humans and animals. Meyer (1989) also pointed out that one must consider the pharmacological characteristics of a drug in order to understand the phenomenon of drug abuse or addiction.

Crowley (1988) noted that research suggests *the nature, magnitude, and schedule of the consequences of drug use may ultimately prove more important than the antecedents of drug use in shaping chemical dependency.* Indeed, Crowley noted that immediate consequences of chemical use (that is, the reward value of the drug) have a stronger impact on drug use than do the delayed consequences of chemical use.

For this reason, Crowley believes that smokers have difficulty breaking their addiction to cigarettes. The consequences of smoking, such as cancer, diseases of the lung, and heart disease, might not appear until after many years of cigarette use. These long-term consequences are potential modifiers of behavior; however, they carry less force than the immediate craving for a cigarette. In brief, nicotine seems to be an extremely addictive drug, which causes a great deal of craving in the individual who stops smoking.

Memory, itself a psychological phenomenon, often stimulates the addict to return to drug use, or "relapse." Johnson (1980) termed one form of this process "euphoric recall," which is the tendency for addicts to remember the "good" times, while overlooking the pain and suffering that their addiction caused. The addict will recall his or her drug use in positive terms, using denial or minimization to overlook the more negative consequences of the chemical use.

Drug-using memories can often bring about a relapse by reminding the individual of previous drug use. For example, one individual, who had been drug-free for a year, reported a sudden preoccupation with narcotics while at work. Detailed exploration of the exact circumstances under which this preoccupation took place revealed that, after dropping a spoon at a restaurant, the individual began to think about using drugs again. The spoon, which opiate addicts use to "cook" the mixture of water and opiates before injection, was the environmental trigger that brought this memory to the surface and started this individual thinking about drug use.

SUMMARY OF THE PSYCHOLOGICAL MODELS OF ADDICTION

At one point or another, virtually every major school of psychotherapy has attempted to come to terms with the problem of drug dependency. In recent years, it has been found that drug-taking behavior follows the same behavioral laws as other human activities. Various schools of psychotherapy have postulated that chemical abuse and dependency reflect the individual's attempts to come to terms with internal stress and anxiety.

SHORTCOMINGS OF THE PSYCHOLOGICAL MODEL OF ADDICTION

To date, although the psychological model of addiction has provided valuable insights into the individual forces at work that initiate and maintain addiction, no comprehensive overview of addiction has been offered that adequately explains the many faces of addiction. Further, as with the other schools of thought previously reviewed, the psychological model of addiction has failed to identify a clearly superior treatment approach that is both comprehensive and effective.

FINAL COMMON PATHWAY THEORY OF ADDICTION

The *final common pathway* theory of chemical dependency is, in a sense, a nontheory. This theory of addiction is not supported by any single group or profession. Rather, the final common pathway theory holds that there is an element of truth in each of the theories of drug addiction previously reviewed. Depending on the individual, the "cause" might be social forces, psychological conditioning, an attempt on the part of the individual to come to terms with internal pain, or some combination of other factors.

In the final analysis, the final common pathway model of addiction requires the professional to develop a comprehensive picture of the individual in order to answer the question: *what caused this individual to become addicted to chemicals?* The addicted individual uses drugs because she or he finds that the drugs fill a need within. Somehow, for the addict, chemical use feels "right."

At first, the individual uses chemicals because they feel good. The drugs provide an enjoyable experience for the user, which the individual wants to repeat over and over again. However, for some reason, this particular individual became addicted to drugs, while others from the same environment, perhaps even the same family, did not.

Was it some biological predisposition that brought about the addiction? Were there close relatives who were also addicted, suggesting a genetic predisposition to chemical dependency? Was the person raised in an environment where drug use was expected? Did the social forces of the individual's environment allow him or her to excel, or were they locked into a lifetime of frustration and failure? Is there a history of psychological suffering the person is attempting to treat through self-medication?

This, then, is the core element of addiction according to the final common pathway theory of addiction: the addict uses drugs for any of a number of reasons. These may include a biological predisposition, a shortcoming in the personality structure, or some reason yet to be discovered. The drug comes to fill a need for the addict, and continued use results in the growth of a compulsion to continue to use drugs.

In order to treat the addiction, the chemical dependency counselor must identify the forces that brought about and support this individual's addiction to chemicals. On the basis of this understanding, the chemical dependency counselor may establish a treatment program that will help the individual achieve and maintain sobriety.

SUMMARY

Each of the major theories of chemical dependency reviewed in this text offers a degree of insight into the nature of drug addiction. The medical/biological model holds that there is a biochemical foundation to addiction, and it is well known that addicts tend to come from families where there are addicted parents or grandparents. Yet, in spite of a significant amount of research into the exact nature of the biochemical fault that brings about drug addiction, no biological "marker" has been isolated that consistently identifies persons likely to become addicted to chemicals.

The social/cultural theories of addiction underscore the importance of one's social environment and the impact that the peer group can have on the development of the individual's values and beliefs. Indeed, by exploring how different social groups tend to have contrasting cultural rules concerning acceptable drug use, the social/cultural schools of thought have challenged some of the basic tenets of the biological school of thought. For example, it has been demonstrated that of two different Indian tribes who live in the same portion of a western state, one will encourage group alcohol use while the other strongly encourages solitary use of alcohol. But, the social/cultural school of inquiry has offered little in the way of treatment approaches.

The psychological schools have explored the interpersonal and intrapersonal roots of addiction. The intrapersonal school of inquiry has highlighted how individual trauma from childhood, and current psychopathology, may set the foundation for chemical dependency in later life. At the same time, the interpersonal schools of thought have underscored the impact of interpersonal relationships and learning on subsequent drug use. Both schools of thought have shed valuable light on the impact of emotional pain on subsequent drug use. However, the psychological schools of thought have not been able to provide the final answer to the question of how to deal with chemical dependency.

A more pragmatic system is the final common pathway school of thought, which requires an individualized approach to the problem of addiction. The final common pathway approach holds that addiction might arise from a number of causes, and that in order to adequately treat the addict, the counselor must identify which causes apply in this case. Then, the needs uncovered in the inquiry process must be addressed as part of a comprehensive treatment program.

CHAPTER 14

Addiction as a Disease of the Human Spirit

To understand the reality of addiction is, ultimately, to understand something of human nature. Modern society, especially modern medicine, tends to disparage matters of the spirit. Modern humanity turns away, as if embarrassed by a subject so primitive as that of the "spirit." Yet in so doing society denies that which makes us unique, for humans are first of all spiritual beings.

In humanity, life has become aware of itself (Fromm, 1956). With this self-awareness, however, comes the painful understanding that each of us is forever isolated from his fellows. Fromm (1956) termed this awareness of one's basic isolation an "unbearable prison" (p. 7), in which are found the roots of anxiety and shame. "The awareness of human separation," wrote Fromm (1956) "without reunion by love—is the source of shame. It is at the same time the source of guilt and anxiety" (p. 8).

The flowers, the birds, and the trees cannot help but be themselves, for that is their nature. A bird does not think about being a bird, and a tree does not think about being a tree. Each behaves according to its gifts to become a bird or a tree. But, we possess the twin gifts of *self-awareness,* and *self-determination.* Within certain limits, people are aware of themselves and can decide their fate. These gifts, however, carry a price. Fromm (1956) viewed the awareness of our fundamental aloneness as the price paid for the power of self-determination.

Through self-awareness, we have come to know that we are different from the animal world. With the awareness of "self" comes the power of self-determination. But, in becoming aware of ourselves, we also came to feel isolated from the rest of the universe. Humankind became aware of "self," and in so doing came to know loneliness. It is only through the giving of self to another through love that Fromm (1956) envisioned humanity as transcending its isolation, to become part of a greater whole.

Merton (1978) took a similar view on the nature of human existence. He clearly understood, on the basis of his own personal experience, that one could not seek happiness through the compulsive use of chemicals. He discovered that ". . . there can never be happiness in compulsion" (1978, p. 3). Rather, Merton believed that happiness may be achieved through love shared openly and honestly with others. Martin Buber (1970) took an even more extreme view, holding that it is only through our relationships that our life has definition. Each person stands "in relation" to another. The degree of relation—the relationship—is defined by how much of the self one offers to another and receives in return.

The reader might question what relevance this material has to a text on chemical dependency. The answer to this is found in the observation that the early members of Alcoholics Anonymous (AA) came to view alcoholism (and, by extension, the other forms of addiction) as a unique "disease." In their wisdom, the early members of AA came to view alcoholism not only as a disease of the body, *but also of the spirit*. In so doing, they transformed themselves from helpless victims of alcoholism into active participants in the healing process of sobriety.

Out of this struggle, the early members of AA came to share an intimate knowledge of the nature of addiction. They came to view addiction not as a phenomenon to be dispassionately studied, but as an elusive enemy that held each member's life in its hands. The early members of AA struggled not to find the smallest common element that might "cause" addiction, but to understand and share in the healing process of sobriety. In so doing, AA's early pioneers came to understand that recovery was a spiritual process through which the individual sought the spiritual unity that she or he could not find through chemicals.

Self-help groups such as AA and Narcotics Anonymous (NA).[1] do not postulate any specific theory of how chemical addiction comes about. Herman (1988) noted that, unlike either medical or mental health professionals, "Twelve-Step programs do not dwell on the causes of addiction" (p. 52). Rather, it is simply assumed that any person whose chemical use interferes with his or her life has an addiction problem. Either you are addicted to chemicals, or you are not.

Addiction itself was viewed as resting on a spiritual flaw. Such spiritual flaws are not uncommon. B. S. Siegel (1989) observed that "One cannot get through life without pain" (p. 41), a fact that many of us tend to forget. Another author, Peck (1976), noted that "Life is difficult" (p. 1). He went on to conclude that

> Some of us will go to quite extraordinary lengths to avoid our problems and the suffering they cause, proceeding far afield from all that is clearly good and sensible in order to find an easy way out, building the most elaborate fantasies in which to live, sometimes to the total exclusion of reality (p. 17).

In this, the addict is not unique, for we all tend to try and avoid acceptance of the pain and suffering that life offers to us, if this is at all possible. But the addict chooses a different path. Addiction might be viewed as an outcome of a process through which the individual comes to use chemicals to avoid recognition and acceptance of life's problems. The

---

[1]Although they share many common elements, AA and NA are not affiliated. The two organizations cooperate on many matters, but are not associated with each other.

chemicals lead the individual away from what he or she believes is good and acceptable in return for the promise of comfort and relief.

DISEASES OF THE MIND, DISEASES OF THE SPIRIT: THE MIND/BODY QUESTION

As B. S. Siegel (1986) and many others have observed, modern medicine has come to enforce an artificial dichotomy between the individual's "mind" and "body." As a result of this dichotomy, modern medicine has become rather mechanical, with the physician treating "symptoms," or "diseases," rather than the "patient" (B. S. Siegel, 1989). In a sense, the modern physician has become a very highly skilled technician, who often fails to appreciate the unique *person* who is now in the role of a patient.

Morton Reiser (1984), in exploring the relationship between mind and body, also acknowledged that society has come to view the mind and the body as being separate. May (1988) pointed out that neurologists are able to speak of the physical structure of the brain in precise terms, and that theologians are able to define terms with great clarity. Both groups face a difficult struggle, however, when speaking of the human spirit. Diseases of the body are viewed as falling in the realm of physical medicine, while diseases of the mind fall into the orbit of the psychological sciences. Diseases of the human spirit, according to this view, fall into a vague area that is the specialty of clergy.

But, the patient is not just a "spiritual being" *or* a "psychosocial being" *or* a "physical being," but a unified whole. Adams (1988) noted that "addiction and chemical dependency affect each person physically, emotionally, socially, and spiritually" (p. 20). Unfortunately, society has difficulty accepting that a disease of the spirit—such as addiction—is just as real as a disease of the physical body.

But humans are indeed spiritual beings, and self-help programs such as AA and NA view addiction to chemicals as a spiritual illness. Their success in helping people to achieve and maintain sobriety would argue that there is some validity to this claim. Even so, society struggles to adhere to the artificial mind/body dichotomy. In the process, society struggles to come to terms with the disease of addiction, which is neither totally a physical illness, nor exclusively one of the mind.

THE GROWTH OF ADDICTION: THE CIRCLE NARROWS

Brown (1985), in speaking of the role of alcohol in the alcoholic's life, noted that as the disease of alcoholism progresses, the alcoholic comes to center his or her life around the use of the chemical. Indeed, Brown speaks of alcohol as being the "axis" (p. 79) around which the alcoholic's life revolves. Alcohol comes to assume a role of "central importance" (p. 78) for both the alcoholic and the alcoholic's family.

It is difficult for those who have never been addicted to chemicals to understand the importance that the addict attaches to the chemical. The addicted person will demonstrate a preoccupation with his or her chemical use, and will protect his or her source of chemicals. To illustrate this point, it is not uncommon for cocaine addicts to admit that, if it came down to a choice, they would choose cocaine over friends, lovers, or even family.

This reality is hard for the nonaddict to understand. The grim truth is that the active addict is, in a sense, insane. One reflection of this moral insanity is that the drug has come to take on a role of central importance in the addict's life. Other people, other commitments, take on a role of secondary importance. Addicts, in a very real sense "never seem to outgrow the self-centeredness of the child" (*The Triangle of Self-Obsession*, 1983, p. 1).

In exploring this point, the book *Narcotics Anonymous* (1982) noted that

> Before coming to the fellowship of N.A., we could not manage our own lives. We could not live and enjoy life as other people do. We had to have something different and we thought we found it in drugs. We placed their use ahead of the welfare of our families, our wives, husbands, and our children. We had to have drugs at all costs. . . . (p. 11, italics in original).

Kaufman, (1985), in his elegant introduction to Buber's (1970) text, spoke of those whose all-consuming interest is themselves. In this sense, chemical addiction might be viewed as a form of self-love, perhaps as a perversion of self-love. This is true in the sense that it is through the use of chemicals that addicts cheat themselves of the experience of reality, to replace it with their distorted desires of reality.

The addict demonstrates an ongoing preoccupation with chemical use. There is an exaggerated concern about maintaining one's supply of the drug and an avoidance of those who threaten the addict's further drug use. The alcoholic who, with six or seven cases of beer in storage in the basement, goes out to buy six more cases "just in case," demonstrates this preoccupation with chemical use.

Other people, when their existence is recognized at all, are viewed by the addict as being either useful in the further use of chemicals or as being impediments to drug use. But nothing is allowed to come between the individual, and his or her drug, if at all possible.

THE CIRCLE OF ADDICTION: ADDICTED PRIORITIES

The authors of the book *Narcotics Anonymous* concluded that addiction was a disease composed of three elements. These were the elements of: (a) a compulsive use of chemicals, (b) an obsession with further chemical use, and (c) a spiritual disease that is expressed through a total self-centeredness on the part of the individual. It is this total self-centeredness, the spiritual illness that causes the person to demand "what I want when I want it!", that makes the individual vulnerable to addiction.

As the disease of addiction progresses, the individual comes to center his or her life around continued use of the chemical. This is a reflection of the obsession with drug use, and chemical dependency professionals will often speak of the addict's *preoccupation* with drug use. But for the addict to admit to this would be to accept the reality of personal addiction. So, the persons who are addicted to chemicals will begin to use the defense mechanisms of denial, rationalization, projection, or minimization to justify their increasingly narrow range of interests both to themselves, and to significant others.

To support his or her addiction, the individual must renounce more and more of his or her self in favor of new beliefs and behaviors that make continued drug use possible. This is the spiritual illness that is found in addiction, for the individual comes to believe that "nothing should come between me and my drug use!". No price is too high, nor is any behavior unthinkable if it allows further drug use.

As the economic, personal, and social cost of continued drug use mount, the individual will lie, cheat, and steal to maintain his or her addiction. Addicted persons have been known to sell prized possessions, steal money from trust accounts, misdirect medications prescribed for patients, deny any significant feelings for a spouse or family members, and engage in theft—all in order to maintain the addiction.

Many addicts have gone to great pains to hide the evidence of their drug addiction. More than one "hidden" alcoholic has ultimately confessed to "taking the dog for a walk" at night, in order to hide empty bottles in neighbors' trash cans. Addicts have been known to hide drug supplies under rocks in the countryside, behind books in the living room, under the sink in the kitchen, behind the headboard of the bed, and in a multitude of other places. They have done so in order to maintain the illusion that they are not using chemicals.

Even the addict is confused about what caused this personality change. The book *Alcoholics Anonymous* (1976) noted that, when asked *why* they use alcohol addicts are unlikely to divulge the real reason. At the same time, the addict is likely to envy, and be mystified by, the normal individual's ability to say "no" to chemical use. Addicts simply do not know why they started, or why they continue to use drugs. They are, in a very real sense, spiritually blind.

As the addiction comes to control more and more of the individual's life, greater and greater effort must be expended by the addict to maintain the illusion of normalcy. Gallagher (1986) related how one physician, addicted to fentanyl, ultimately bought "street" drugs because it was no longer possible to divert enough drugs from hospital sources to maintain his habit. When the tell-tale scars from repeated injections of "street" drugs began to form, this same physician intentionally burned himself on the arm with a spoon to hide them.

The addict also finds that, as the drug comes to control more and more of his or her life, significant effort must be invested in the maintenance of the addiction itself. More than one cocaine or heroin addict has had to engage in prostitution (homosexual or heterosexual) in order to earn enough money to buy more chemicals. Everything is sacrificed in order to obtain and maintain a supply of the chemicals.

To combat the deception inherent in addiction, AA and NA place a heavy emphasis on the issue of honesty in their respective self-help programs. For drug dependency hides behind a wall of deception. Honesty breaks through this deception to bring addicts face to face with their addiction.

SOME GAMES OF ADDICTION

Jenike (1987) spoke at length of the manipulative games that addicts are likely to use in order to maintain their drug habits. Physicians were warned that addicts were likely to "use ploys such as outrage, tears, accusations of abandonment, abject pleading, promises of cooperation, and seduction" (p. 13) in order to manipulate others. The same warning holds true for other professionals who work with the addicted person.

Narcotic addicts have been known to visit hospital emergency rooms (Klass, 1989) or physicians' offices, in an attempt to seek medication. Sometimes, the presenting complaint is "kidney stones," or a story about how other emergency rooms have not been able to help the patient, who now faces a weekend without relief from some painful condition. The object of this "game" is to obtain a prescription for narcotics.

When asked for a urine sample, which would show traces of blood if the person suffered from a real kidney stone, addicts have been found secretly pricking their finger with needles to squeeze a few drops of blood into the urine. Another common practice is for the addict to insert foreign objects, such as darning needles, into the urethra to irritate the lining of the urethra. This will cause a small amount of blood to be released by the injured tissues, thus providing a sample of bloody urine.

Addicts have been known to visit several physicians for treatment of the same legitimate illness in order to obtain prescriptions for drugs from different sources. It is not unusual for addicts to study medical textbooks to learn what symptoms to fake, and how to provide a convincing presentation of these symptoms to health care professionals. The object of this "game," again, is to convince the physician to prescribe the desired drug.

Psychiatrists have been "conned" into keeping addicts' supplies of cocaine. In each case, the therapist thought the addict was actually interested in therapy. However, the real purpose of this "game" was to use the therapist to provide a safe "stash" for the cocaine. This allowed the addict to avoid the fear of being caught with cocaine by the police, or having it stolen by other addicts.

The only price the addicts had to pay for this deception was to show up three, four, or perhaps even seven days a week; confess their latest transgression of having purchased more cocaine; then reluctantly allow the therapists to take possession of all but that day's supply of the drug as an incentive to return. The addicts were then safe from police searches and other addicts looking for drugs. The therapists apparently thought they could out-manipulate the addicts into staying in therapy.

What the therapists did not realize was that, if the police were to search their office, *the therapists* (and not the addicts) would be in possession of a controlled substance. The addicts would not be responsible, since the cocaine was not in their possession. The addicts could deny any and all knowledge of the cocaine being there in the first place, since it was the addict's word against that of the therapist! The therapists could possibly face criminal charges, while the addicts looked for another place to stash their drugs.

A THOUGHT ON
PLAYING THE GAMES OF ADDICTION

A friend, who worked in a maximum security penitentiary for men, was warned by older, more experienced corrections workers not to try to "outcon a con." Which is to say that one should not try to out-manipulate a person whose entire life centers on the ability to manipulate others. "You should remember that, while you are home, watching the evening news, or going out to see a movie, these people have been working on perfecting their 'game.' It is *their* game, *their* rules, and in a sense *their whole life.*"

This is a good rule to keep in mind at all times when working with the addicted person. Addiction *is* a lifestyle, one that involves the manipulation of others into supporting the addiction. This is not to say that the addict cannot, if necessary, "change his spots," at least for a short time. This is especially true early in the addiction process, or during the early stages of treatment.

Often, addicts will go "on the wagon" for a few days or a few weeks, in order to prove to themselves and to others, that they can "still control it." Stuart (1980), in discussing this trait in the alcoholic, observed that

> . . . the alcohol-prone individual who passes up a drink so that he or she can later boast to a spouse about this major feat of self-management demonstrates not self-control but a choice between a lesser (alcohol) and a major (attention by a significant other) reinforcement (p. 31).

Unfortunately, addicts who go on the wagon overlook the fact that by attempting to "prove" control, they actually demonstrate their lack of control over the chemicals. They might, as Stuart (1980) observed, be able to give up the drug for a period of time, *if the reward is large enough.*

However, as the addiction progresses, it takes more and more to motivate addicts to give up their drug, even for a short time. Often, "a short time" becomes too long.

Vernon Johnson (1980) spoke at length of how the addict will even use compliance as a defense against treatment. Overt compliance is often used as a defense against acceptance of one's own spiritual, emotional, and physical deficits. In Johnson's essay on the subject, compliance is marked by a subtle defiance. It almost appears as if the client were "only going through the motions" in order to avoid further confrontation. In the struggle to avoid facing the reality of his or her addiction, the client will use a small piece of the truth as a defense against accepting the whole truth.

HONESTY AS A PART OF THE RECOVERY PROCESS

The authors of the book *Narcotics Anonymous* (1982) warned that the progression toward the understanding that one was addicted was not easy. Indeed, self-deception was part of the price that the addict paid for addiction. According to the NA "big book," it was "Only in desperation did we ask ourselves, 'Could it be the drugs?' " (p. 1–2).

Addicts will often speak with pride about how they have been more or less "drug free" for various periods of time. The "reasons" why the individual is drug free are virtually endless. This person is drug free because his or her spouse threatened divorce if the use of chemicals was continued. (But the individual secretly longs to return to chemical use, and will if he or she can find a way to do so.) Another person is drug free because his or her probation officer has a reputation for sending people to prison if their urine sample (drawn under strict supervision) tests positive for chemicals. (But this individual is counting the days until probation ends, and possibly sneaking an occasional pill when it is thought safe to do so).

In each instance, the person is drug free only because of an external threat. In virtually every case, as soon as the external threat is removed, the individual will gradually drift back to chemicals. It is simply impossible for one person to provide the motivation for another person to remain drug free forever.

Many addicts in treatment have admitted, often only after repeated and strong confrontation, that they had simply switched addictions in order to appear "drug free." It is not uncommon for an opiate addict in a methadone maintenance program to use alcohol, marijuana, or cocaine. The methadone does not block the euphoric effects of these drugs as it does the narcotics. Thus, the addict can maintain the appearance of complete cooperation, appearing each day to take his or her methadone without protest, while still freely using cocaine, marijuana, or alcohol.

In a very real sense, the addicted person has lost touch with reality. Over time, those who are addicted to chemicals come to share many personality traits. There is some question whether this personality type, the so-called addicted personality, predates addiction or evolves as a result of the addiction (Bean-Bayog, 1988; May, 1988; Nathan, 1988). However, this chicken-or-the-egg question does not alter the fact that, for the addict, the addiction *always* comes first. The addict centers his or her life around chemical use.

Many an addict has admitted to going without food for days on end, but few addicts willingly go without chemicals for even a short period of time. Cocaine addicts have spoken about how they would avoid sexual relations with their spouse, or significant other, in order to continue using cocaine. Just as the alcoholic will often sleep with an "eye opener" (that is, an alcoholic drink) already mixed by the side of the bed, addicts sometimes have a "rig" (that is, a hypodermic needle) loaded and ready for use so they can inject the drug even before they get out of bed for the day.

Many physicians boast that their patients have no reason to lie to them. One physician went so far as to boast that he *knew* a certain patient did not have prescriptions from other doctors, because the patient "told me so!". The chemical dependency professional needs to keep in mind at all times these two realities: (a) for the addict, the chemical comes first, and (b) the addict centers his or her life around the chemical. To lose sight of this reality is to run the danger of being trapped in the addict's web of lies, half-truths, and manipulations.

Recovering addicts will speak of how manipulative they were and will often admit that they were their own worst enemy. As they move along the road to recovery, addicts recognize that they deceived themselves as part of the addiction process. One inmate said, "Before I can run a game on somebody else, I have to believe it myself." As the addiction progresses, addicts do not question their perceptions, but believe what they need to believe in order to maintain their addiction.

For this reason, AA and NA place heavy emphasis on honesty. Recovered addicts recognize that honesty is their own defense against the self-deception they used in the past to support their addiction.

FALSE PRIDE: THE DISEASE OF THE SPIRIT

Every addiction is, in the final analysis, a disease of the spirit. Edmeades (1985) related a story about Carl Jung, who was treating an American, Rowland H., for alcoholism. Immediately after treatment, Rowland H. relapsed, but was not accepted back into analysis by Jung. His only hope of recovery, according to Jung, lay in a spiritual awakening, which he later found through a religious group in America.

Peluso and Peluso (1988) observed that Carl Jung identified alcoholism (and by implication all forms of addiction) as a disease of the spirit. The *Twelve Steps and Twelve Traditions of Alcoholics Anonymous* (1981) speaks of addiction as being a sickness of the soul. Peluso and Peluso reported that for each of the addicted persons in their book who had achieved sobriety, a spiritual awakening appeared to have been an essential element of their recovery. Kandel and Raveis (1989) found that a "lack of religiosity" (p. 113) was a significant predictor of continued use of cocaine and/or marijuana for young adults with previous experience with these drugs.

In speaking with addicts, one is impressed by how often they have suffered in their lifetimes. It is almost as if one could trace a path from the emotional trauma to the addiction. Yet the addict's spirit is not crushed at birth, nor does the trauma that precedes addiction come about overnight. The individual's spirit becomes diseased over time, as the addict-to-be loses his or her way in life.

Fromm (1968) observed that ". . . we all start out with hope, faith and fortitude" (p. 20). The assorted insults of life often join forces to bring about disappointment and a loss of faith, which are felt by the individual as an empty void within. Graham (1988) noted that at this point, if something is not found to fill the addict's "empty heart, he will fill his stomach with artificial stimulants and sedatives" (p. 14).

Few of us escape this moment of ultimate disappointment or ultimate awareness (Fromm, 1968). At this moment individuals are faced with a choice. They must choose whether they will "reduce their demands to what they can get and . . . not dream of that which seems to be out of their reach" (Fromm, 1968, p. 21). The NA pamphlet *The Triangle of Self-Obsession* (1983) observed that this process is, for most, a natural part of growing up.

But the person who is in danger of addiction refuses to reduce those demands. Rather, the addicted person comes to demand "What I want when *I* want it!" The NA pamphlet *The Triangle of Self-Obsession* (1983) noted that addicts tend to

> . . . refuse to accept that we will not be given everything. We become self-obsessed; our wants and needs become demands. We reach a point where contentment and fulfillment are impossible (p. 1).

Despair exists when the individual experiences true powerlessness. Existentialists speak of this void as one's awareness of one's nonexistence, of the utter futility of existence. When faced with the ultimate experience of powerlessness, one is faced with a choice: either accept one's true place in the universe or distort one's perceptions and thoughts to maintain an illusion of being more than this.

Peck (1976) identified the acceptance of one's true place in the universe, and the pain and suffering that life might offer, as being an essential ingredient of spiritual growth. When people reach this point of ultimate disappointment, many choose to turn away from reality because it does not offer them what they think they are entitled to. In so doing, these people become somewhat grandiose, and exhibit the characteristic *false pride* so frequently encountered in addiction.

One cannot accomplish the illusion of being more than what one is without an increasingly large investment of time, energy, and emotional resources. Merton (1961) observed that it is the lack of true humility, the acceptance of a distorted view of one's place in the universe, that allows despair to grow within. This despair grows with each passing day, as reality threatens time and again to force upon the individual an awareness of the ultimate measure of his or her existence.

In time, external supports are necessary to maintain this false pride. Brown (1985) identified one characteristic of alcohol as being its ability to offer the individual an *illusion of control* over his or her feelings. This is a common characteristic of every drug of abuse (May, 1988). If life does not provide the pleasure to which one feels entitled, at least one might find this comfort and pleasure in a drug, or combination of drugs.

When faced with this unwanted awareness of one's true place in the universe, the addicted person must increasingly distort his or her perception to maintain the illusion of superiority. Into this fight to avoid the painful reality of what *is*, the chemical injects the ability to seemingly choose one's feelings at will. The chemical, in effect, provides an illusion of control over the emotions, a kingly power to select what feeling one might wish to experience.

What the individual does not realize, often not until after the seeds of addiction have been planted, is that the chemical offers an *illusion* only. There is no substance to the self-selected feelings brought about by the chemical, only a mockery of deeper feelings possible through the humble acceptance of one's lot in life.

Humility is viewed by Merton (1961) as the honest acceptance of one's place in the universe, which includes the honest and open acceptance of one's strengths and weaknesses. At the moment the individual becomes aware of the reality of his or her existence, the individual may come to accept their lot in life, or struggle against existence itself.

When one struggles against this acceptance, one in effect places one-self above all else, to say "not as it is, but as *I* want it!". It is a cry against the ultimate knowledge (Fromm, 1968) that one is lost. This despair is often so all-inclusive that, ultimately, the self seems unable to withstand its attack. Addicts have described this despair as an empty, black void within. Then, as Graham (1988) noted, they have attempted to fill this void with chemicals.

The *Twelve Steps and Twelve Traditions* (1981) speaks of false pride as a sickness of the soul. In this light, chemical use might be viewed as a reaction against the ultimate despair of encountering one's lot in life: the false sense of being that says "not as it is, but as *I* want it!" in response to one's discovery of personal powerlessness.

Andrew Weil (quoted in Perrin and Coleman, 1988) noted that the person who uses drugs is essentially "seeking wholeness" (p. 58). But, in place of the spiritual struggle that Peck (1978) speaks of as being necessary to achieve this ultimate awareness, the addict seeks a shortcut. Tanner (1973) spoke of alcohol and drug use as a substitute for human contact. As such, the drugs dominate the individual's life, and the individual centers his or her life more and more on further chemical use, until at last the person believes that she or he cannot live without it.

In a sense, the false pride found in drug addiction is a form of narcissism. Narcissism is a reaction against perceived worthlessness, loss of control, and emotional and physical pain beyond description (Millon, 1981). Millon, in speaking of the narcissistic personality, observed that such persons have an exaggerated view of their own self-worth, and "they rarely question whether it is valid." The narcissistic personality tends to "place few restraints on either their fantasies or rationalizations, and their imagination is left to run free. . ." (p. 167).

While addicts are not usually narcissistic personalities in the pure sense of the word, there are significant narcissistic traits present in addiction. Narcissism, or false pride, is based on the lack of humility, a point Merton (1961) explored at length. Individuals come to distort not only their perceptions of "self," but also of "other," in the service of their pride.

Merton (1961), in speaking of the division that takes place within man's soul, noted that people

> . . . whose lives are centered on themselves, imagine that they can only find themselves by asserting their own desires and ambitions and appetites in a struggle with the rest of the world (p. 47).

In this quote are found the seeds of addiction. For the addicts' chemical of choice allows them to assert their own desires and ambitions on the rest of the world. Brown (1985) speaks at length of the illusion of control over one's feelings that alcohol gives to the user. The other drugs of abuse also give this same illusion of control to the user, a dangerous illusion that allows the individual to believe that he or she is asserting his or her own appetite on the external world.

Addicts often speak with pride of the horrors they have suffered in the service of their addiction. Johnson (1980) called this "euphoric recall", a process where the addicts recall the pleasant aspects of their drug use, while overlooking the pain and suffering they experienced during their chemical use. More than one addict, for example, has spoken at length of the quasi-sexual thrill experienced through cocaine or heroin. In the process, the addict dismisses the fact that the drug cost him or her a spouse, a family, and several tens of thousand dollars.

There is a name for the distorted view of one's self, and of one's world, that comes with chronic chemical use. It is called the insanity of addiction.

DENIAL, RATIONALIZATION, PROJECTION, AND MINIMIZATION: THE FOUR MUSKETEERS OF ADDICTION

Addiction, like all forms of insanity, rests in no small part on characteristic psychological defenses. In this case, these are the defenses of *denial, rationalization,* and *projection.* These defense mechanisms, like all psychological defenses, operate unconsciously in both the intrapersonal and interpersonal spheres. They operate as unconscious, automatic defense systems in order to protect the individual from the conscious awareness of anxiety.

Often without knowing it, addicts will use these defense mechanisms in an effort to avoid recognizing the reality of their addiction (May, 1988). Once the addiction is recognized, there is an implicit social expectation that the person deal with their addiction. Thus, to understand addiction, one must also understand each of these characteristic defense mechanisms.

Coleman, Butcher, and Carson (1980) defined the first of these defense mechanisms, *denial,* as:

> Probably the simplest and most primitive of all self-defense mechanisms
> . . . in which an attempt is made to "screen out" disagreeable realities by
> ignoring or refusing to acknowledge them (p. 151).

As part of the process, the person might utilize a selective perception (Coleman et al., 1984), which a person familiar with the AA twelve-step program (to be discussed in more detail in a later chapter) would term "tunnel vision." It is interesting to note that Perry and Cooper (1989) identified denial as being a rather immature defense mechanism that is associated with a lower level of function and with a greater number of symptoms.

The second of the psychological defense mechanisms commonly found in addiction is that of *projection.* This defense mechanism is defined by Coleman et al. (1984), as "Attributing one's unacceptable motives or characteristics to others" (p. 64). Johnson (1980) defined projection as "unloading *self*-hatred onto others" (p. 31, italics in original). Cameron (1963) reported that projection was the basis of *scapegoating,* a common defensive "game" used by addicts to justify their behavior. Perry and Cooper (1989) identified projection as being one of the more immature of defense mechanisms.

Finally, there is the defense mechanism of *rationalization,* which is defined by Coleman et al. (1984), as "Using contrived 'explanations' to conceal or disguise unworthy motives for one's behavior" (p. 64). Cameron (1963) went further in the definition of rationalization, noting that it is

> . . . the justification of otherwise unacceptable, ego-alien thought feeling
> or action, through the misuse and distortion of facts and through employ-
> ing a pseudo-logic. Rationalization is a common device . . . where people
> explain away their own defects, failures and misdeeds . . . (p. 243).

Anybody who has ever worked with an addicted person can recognize from personal experience how rationalization is one of the most important defensive devices used by the addict.

The defense mechanism of *minimization* operates in a different manner from the three defensive mechanisms reviewed above. In a sense, minimization operates like the defense mechanism of rationalization, but it is more specific than rationalization. The addicted individual who uses minimization as a defense will actively reduce, through a variety of mechanisms, the amount of chemical that she or he admits to using.

The alcoholic, for example, might drink out of an oversized container, perhaps the size of three or four regular glasses, and then admit to having "only three drinks a night!" (overlooking the fact that each drink is equal to three regular-sized drinks). The addict might claim to "only use once a day," and hope that whoever is doing the interview does not think to ask whether a "day" means a full, 24-hour day, or just during daylight hours. Another trick is for the addict to claim time when he or she was in treatment, in jail, or hospitalized, as "straight time" (that is, time when they were not using chemicals), overlooking the fact that they were unable to get drugs.

These defense mechanisms, as previously noted, operate automatically, and quite unconsciously, in order to protect individuals from a full realization of their addiction. The conscious awareness of one's addiction would be a painful awareness, and thus something to be avoided. For example, there is the rationalization, offered to this author by a number of different addicts, that marijuana use did not constitute addiction, since marijuana was "an herb," and thus was a natural substance.

You could only, or so the rationalization went, become addicted to *artificial* chemicals, such as alcohol, amphetamines, or heroin. Another popular rationalization is that it is "better to be an alcoholic than a needle freak . . . after all, alcohol is legal!". More than one alcoholic has denied his or her addiction, in spite of compelling evidence to the contrary, through the use of one or more of these common defense mechanisms.

SUMMARY

Many human service professionals who have had limited contact with addiction tend to have a distorted view of the nature of drug addiction. Having heard the term "disease" applied to chemical dependency, the inexperienced human service worker tends to think in terms of more traditional illnesses, and is often rudely surprised at the deception inherent in drug addiction.

While chemical dependency is a disease, it is a disease like no other. It is, as noted in an earlier chapter, *a disease that requires the active participation of the patient*. Further, self-help groups such as AA or NA view addiction as a disease of the spirit, and offer a spiritual program to help members achieve and maintain sobriety.

Addiction is, in a sense, a form of insanity. The insanity of addiction rests on the psychological defense mechanisms of rationalization, denial, and projection. These three defense mechanisms, plus minimization, keep the addict from becoming aware of the reality of his or her addiction until the disease has progressed quite far. To combat this deception, AA places emphasis on honesty. Honesty, both with self and with others, is the central feature of the AA program.

CHAPTER 15

Hidden Victims of Chemical Dependency

Addiction all too often involves not only the addicted person, but also a multitude of others. Even when one's view of addiction is limited only to the individual who has become dependent on chemicals, the disease is often hidden from view. It is the purpose of this chapter to explore some of the hidden faces of chemical dependency, so that the reader might be more sensitive to the many forms of drug addiction.

WOMEN AND ADDICTION: AN OFTEN UNRECOGNIZED PROBLEM

Peluso and Peluso (1988) offered some shocking statistics concerning the interrelationship between chemical use and gender. It was their contention that sedatives and "diet pills" have become "women's drugs" (p. 10), with women receiving 70% of the prescriptions for sedatives and 80% of the prescriptions for diet pills. The authors pointed out that *two-thirds* of the prescriptions written for mood-altering chemicals were for women and concluded that there are "millions of women whose dependence on prescriptions chemicals has been rendered invisible" (p. 9).

Research suggests that addiction to chemicals expresses itself differently in women than it does in men. Women usually obtain drugs in different ways, take them for different reasons, and experience different effects from the drugs than do men. In spite of these facts, however, ". . . the drug literature in general has paid relatively little attention to women" (Griffin, Weiss, Mirin, and Lang, 1989, p. 122), a point supported by Peluso and Peluso (1988), and Blume (1985).

Griffin et al. (1989), found that female narcotic addicts were likely to have started using opiates at a significantly older age and to have used drugs more heavily than their male counterparts. Griffin et al. also found that women addicted to narcotics were approximately the same age as men at the time of their first admission into drug treatment. In contrast, female cocaine abusers were found to have started drug use at an earlier age than did male cocaine abusers, and women were significantly younger at the time of their first admission to a drug treatment program. In spite of these differences, research into narcotic and cocaine addiction has failed to address the impact of these chemicals on women.

Blume (1985), in discussing alcoholism among women, noted that alcoholic women were different from alcoholic men in a number of ways. First, alcoholic women tend to have more variation in their response to alcohol than do men. Second, research suggests that women's menstrual cycles will influence their response to alcohol. Third, it has been reported that women alcoholics drink less alcohol, on the average day, than alcoholic men. In spite of this fact, alcoholic women first enter treatment at about the same age as alcoholic men.

Addicts have known for some time that women become addicted to chemicals. The text *Alcoholics Anonymous* (1976) reported that nearly one-quarter of the members of AA were women, and that for newer members the percentage of women was closer to one-third. Peluso and Peluso (1988) reported that in a recent year some 42% of those who called the "800-COCAINE" telephone hotline were women. These figures suggest that women are as deeply involved in the drug problem as are men.

Addiction is often more difficult to detect in working women, according to Pape (1988), and more difficult to confront in the workplace. Many women in the work force are working below capacity; thus, their chemical use is less likely to interfere with job performance than it is for men. Also, the threat of loss of employment is not as effective for women as it is for men, since many women work only to supplement their husbands' income. It is often easier for an addicted woman to quit her job than seek treatment (Pape, 1988).

It has been suggested (Hoard, 1988) that as many as 64% of female alcoholics suffer from premenstrual syndrome (PMS). As a result of PMS, these women present special symptoms, including anxiety, tension, insomnia, and mood swings. These feelings, in many cases, have been medicated through the use of alcohol or other psychoactive chemicals (Hoard, 1988). Following recovery from chemical dependency, PMS may place significant stress on the woman, and may contribute to relapse (Hoard, 1988).

To address this special problem, Hoard (1988) found that women who suffered from PMS needed to learn how to deal with it without resorting to abusable chemicals. Such nondrug coping methods might include dietary changes, appropriate use of certain forms of birth control medications, and individual counseling to help the woman understand, and cope with, the mood changes that are brought on by PMS.

Women are indeed hidden victims of addiction. Peluso and Peluso (1988) have suggested that society has hesitated to recognize the problem of addiction in women because of the important role women hold in society. The authors suggest that society has come to deny the reality of the problem, rather than address the issue of women's addiction, and thus help the issue remain a hidden problem.

Drug Addiction and Pregnancy

Chasnoff (1988) noted that most drugs taken by a woman during pregnancy easily cross over into the blood of the fetus. Thus, in most cases where the mother uses chemicals, the fetus is exposed to the same chemicals. If the mother is addicted, the child will share in the mother's addiction. Peluso and Peluso (1988) estimated that 80 of every 10,000 children born in New York City were addicted to chemicals at birth.

Chasnoff (1988) pointed out that since the fetus lacks the fully developed liver and excretory systems of the mother it is difficult to anticipate the impact that these chemicals will have on the fetus. Children may be born addicted to chemicals because of the mother's chemical use during pregnancy, or the drugs may have other effects on the child during pregnancy or following birth. The problem of drug use during pregnancy is often not immediately recognized, and the children are hidden victims of drug addiction. The effects of some specific drugs of abuse on pregnancy are discussed in more detail next.

Fetal Alcohol Syndrome

Women who drink on a regular basis while pregnant run the risk of causing alcohol-induced birth defects, a condition known as *fetal alcohol syndrome* (FAS). This condition is not found in every child of an alcoholic mother who drank during pregnancy (Chasnoff, 1988), and some infants demonstrate only some of the symptoms of FAS.

Alcohol crosses the placenta into the bloodstream of the fetus. Rose (1988) noted that when a pregnant woman drinks, the blood alcohol level of the fetus reaches the same level as that of the mother in only 15 minutes. Indeed, if the mother has been drinking immediately prior to childbirth, the smell of alcohol might be detected on the breath of the infant following birth (Rose, 1988).

Infants who suffer from FAS usually have a lower than normal birth weight, a pattern of characteristic facial abnormalities, and often will have a smaller brain at birth. Such children also exhibit slow growth patterns following birth, and are more likely to be retarded. Chasnoff (1988) reported that these children usually fall in the mild to moderately retarded range following birth, with an average IQ of 68.[1]

Gold and Sherry (1984) explored the impact of alcohol consumption during pregnancy on the child's subsequent school performance. The authors found that children whose mothers consumed alcohol during pregnancy were likely to suffer from learning disabilities, short attention span, emotional problems, or hyperactivity during childhood.

Beasley (1987) observed that FAS is the third most common cause of birth defects in the United States, and the only one that is *totally* preventable. Current research suggests that maternal alcohol use during the first

---

[1]The average IQ is 100. A person with an IQ of 68 would be classified as being mildly retarded.

trimester of pregnancy is associated with FAS (Chasnoff, 1988). Mirin and Weiss (1983) noted that seriously affected children might never achieve normal growth or intelligence, in spite of an optimal postnatal environment. Once the damage has been done during pregnancy, the child might be unlikely to recover, even if special efforts are made to help the child following birth.

Cocaine Use During Pregnancy

Women who use cocaine during pregnancy have been found to suffer from a higher incidence of spontaneous abortions, premature labor, and abruptio placentae (Chasnoff, 1988). All these complications of pregnancy might prove fatal to the infant and possibly the mother as well (Sbriglio and Millman, 1987). If the mother is addicted to cocaine at the time that she gives birth, the infant will also be addicted to cocaine, and will go through cocaine withdrawal at the same time that she or he is recovering from the trauma of birth.

Peluso and Peluso (1988) and Chasnoff (1988) noted that there is evidence that infants born to women who used cocaine during pregnancy may suffer small strokes prior to birth. These small strokes are thought to be a result of the rapid changes in the mother's blood pressure brought on by cocaine use. Chasnoff postulated that such strokes are similar to those occasionally seen in adults who use cocaine, and noted that there is evidence that cocaine use during pregnancy may result in cardiac and central nervous system abnormalities in the fetus.

Narcotic Use During Pregnancy

The narcotics, like a large number of other drugs, cross the placenta in the pregnant woman. Thus, both the mother and the fetus are exposed to opiates if the woman is using this family of drugs during pregnancy. Chasnoff (1988) listed the complications associated with narcotic use during pregnancy, including spontaneous abortions, premature delivery, neonatal meconium aspiration syndrome, neonatal infections acquired through the mother, lower birth weight, and neonatal narcotic addiction.

Chronic use of narcotics during pregnancy results in a state of chronic exposure to opiates for the fetus. Such infants are themselves physically dependent on narcotics at birth. Following birth, the infant will no longer be able to absorb drugs from the mother's blood, and will go through drug withdrawal shortly after birth.

In years past, this condition resulted in an almost 90% mortality rate in addicted infants (Mirin and Weiss, 1983). Peluso and Peluso (1988) reported that, in New York City, eight children per thousand are born addicted to heroin. In response to increased medical awareness of the special needs of the addicted infant (Mirin and Weiss, 1983), the mortality rate has dropped significantly in recent years. However, infants born to mothers who are themselves addicted to narcotics present special needs, and require specialized care, in order to survive the first few days of life.

Narcotics and breast feeding.   The woman who is using narcotics who is breast feeding her child will pass some of the drug on to the infant, through the milk (Sheridan, Patterson, and Gustafson, 1982). While the effects of a single dose of narcotics have only a minimal impact on the child, prolonged use of narcotics may cause the child to become sleepy, eat poorly, and possibly develop respiratory depression (Sheridan, Patterson, and Gustafson, 1982).

Marijuana and Pregnancy

It is difficult to isolate the effects of maternal marijuana use from other chemicals (that is, alcohol, aspirin, and possibly other drugs of abuse) that the expectant mother might also use (Nahas, 1986). Research suggests, however, that marijuana use during pregnancy might contribute to "intrauterine growth retardation, poor weight gain, prolonged labor, and behavioral abnormalities in the newborn" (Nahas, p. 83). Thus, at this time, there would appear to be significant consequences for the mother who uses marijuana during pregnancy.

Benzodiazepine Use During Pregnancy

Graedon (1980) warned that women who are pregnant, especially those in the first trimester of pregnancy, should not use any of the benzodiazepines. The benzodiazepines were once thought to contribute to the formation of cleft palates in children, a conclusion that has not been supported by research (Cohen, 1989). However, benzodiazepine use during pregnancy is not recommended (Cohen, 1989; Graedon, 1980). Further, since the benzodiazepines are found in the nursing mother's milk, Graedon suggests that nursing mothers also not use benzodiazepines.

Blood Infections

The woman who abuses injected drugs such as the narcotics or cocaine, and who shares intravenous needles, runs the risk of contracting any of a number of infections from other addicts. If the pregnant mother becomes infected, the fetus may be exposed to the same infection. Indeed, children born of mothers who use intravenously administered drugs may develop *any* of the blood infections commonly found in addicted persons.

It is even possible for the fetus to acquire AIDS through the mother's blood. In such cases, as Chasnoff (1988) pointed out, it is often necessary to wait a full year—if not longer—following delivery to determine whether the child is infected. During this period of time, the mother will not know whether she has a healthy child or a child infected with the AIDS virus. This makes it difficult for the mother to "bond" with the child, since she will not know whether the child is infected.

The transmission of blood-borne infections from mother to child is often not thought of as a common problem. Yet in some populations a significant percentage of the children born have been exposed to one or more infections as a result of the mother's use of intravenous drugs. These children are further hidden victims of drug addiction.

Summary of Drug Addiction and Pregnancy

Infants born to women who have used chemicals of abuse during pregnancy represent a special subpopulation. These children are often born addicted to the drugs the mother used during pregnancy. In many cases, the mother's use of chemicals during pregnancy has caused the child to experience physical complications, including stroke, retardation, lower weight at birth, and a number of other drug-specific complications. If the mother contracts an infection by sharing needles with other addicts, the fetus may also be infected.

CHEMICAL ABUSE IN CHILDREN AND TEENAGERS

Chemical use by children and adolescents is *not* a new phenomenon. Indeed, more than a century ago, in the time of Charles Dickens, alcoholism was rampant among the youth of England (Wheeler and Malmquist, 1987). There has always been a small percentage of adolescents who used alcohol or other chemicals for recreational purposes, but it was not until the last two generations that large numbers of adolescents have used other chemicals for recreational purposes.

It was once mistakenly thought that adolescents would outgrow, or become bored, with chemical use. Parents were assured by physicians that drug use was either a phase that the child would outgrow, or that the chemical use was a symptom of a deep-seated psychological problem. It has only been in recent years that professionals have recognized that chemical use among the young is a problem in its own right, and that children and adolescents are becoming addicted to the same chemicals adults are using.

The study of drug use and addiction among children and adolescents is limited by several factors. First, there is little research into possible chemical-use patterns by children (Newcomb and Bentler, 1989; Mikkelsen, 1985). This lack of information makes it quite difficult to identify which chemicals are being used by children in the first decade of life, or what the implications of this drug use might be for subsequent growth and development.

Second, on a similar note, there is only limited research into teenage drug-use patterns (Newcomb and Bentler, 1989; Mikkelsen, 1985). This lack of data makes it quite difficult to determine current drug abuse trends, the forces that motivate the individual adolescent to begin chemical use, or the impact that drug use might have on the adolescent's emotional adjustment.

A third factor contributing to the confusion surrounding child and adolescent drug use is that there is a tendency for some to equate virtually *any* use of a chemical during adolescence as being a sign of a serious drug-abuse problem (Newcomb and Bentler, 1989). This viewpoint causes some confusion into what constitutes "drug abuse" by adolescents and overlooks the fact that, for some, chemical use represents only a phase of experimentation or exploration.

During this phase of experimentation, an adolescent might demonstrate repeated and regular use of one or more chemicals, only to settle down in young adulthood to a more acceptable pattern of chemical use. Zarek, Hawkins, and Rogers (1987) reported that, of identified "problem drinkers" in adolescence, 53% of the men and 70% of the women were not judged to be problem drinkers seven years later. Thus, the adolescent who might have abused chemicals on a regular basis may not develop a problem with chemicals in young adulthood.

Fourth, and finally, drug-use patterns among children and adolescents may show rapid fluctuation, and variation, depending on the geographic location and the current drug-use "trends." The phenomenon of inhalant abuse is one such drug-use "fad," which rapidly waxes and wanes in a given geographic area as individuals embrace and then discard the use of these substances.

Virtually nothing is known about drug-use patterns of children. Newcomb and Bentler (1989) reported that inhalants are likely to be the first drug used by children to alter their state of consciousness but offered no statistical information about the epidemiology of childhood drug use. Schuckit (1984) reported that 20% of the adolescent girls and 33% of the adolescent boys questioned admitted to using inhalants *at least once* but did not offer more specific information than this.

Inhalant abuse, as previously noted, usually is a phase that will last one to two years at most. About one-third of the children who abuse inhalants move on to more traditional forms of drug abuse (Brunswick, 1989), which suggests that, for some, inhalants serve as a "gateway" chemical that leads to other forms of drug abuse.

For most adolescents, alcohol is possibly the first, and certainly the most common, mood-altering chemical used. However, parents are poor sources of information concerning their teenaged children's use of chemicals. It has been found that parents tend to *underestimate* their teenaged children's alcohol consumption by a factor of at least ten to one (Rogers, Harris, and Jarmuskewicz, 1987; Zarek, Hawkins, and Rogers, 1987). For this reason, much of what is known about adolescent drug-use patterns is based on information gathered through anonymous surveys of adolescents.

Rogers, Harris, and Jarmuskewicz (1987) reported that the average age at which the first drink of alcohol was consumed was 11.9 years for boys and 12.7 years for girls. The authors concluded that, in spite of isolated reports of alcohol abuse problems in children as young as 11 years of age, problem drinking was quite rare in preadolescence. The most popular form of alcohol for the adolescents surveyed was beer, although the recently introduced wine coolers were increasing in popularity. Those individuals who admit to even occasional experimentation with vodka, gin, whiskey, or bourbon should be considered to have an alcohol abuse problem, in the opinion of Rogers, Harris, and Jarmuskewicz (1987).

By early adolescence, 45% of adolescents sampled had smoked cigarettes and 56% had used alcohol at least once. Further, approximately 30% of the adolescents surveyed had used at least one illicit drug (usually marijuana) (Newcomb and Bentler, 1989). Zarek, Hawkins, and Rogers (1987) reported that about two-thirds of the adolescents in grades 7 through 12 have used alcohol at least once and concluded that "most adolescents become drinkers before entering high school" (p. 484).

Mikkelsen (1985) found that 9–42% of the high school students questioned admitted to having used marijuana at least once, while 2–7% admitted to the use of hallucinogens at one point in their lives. The author also found that, depending on the geographic area from which the sample was drawn, 0–15% of the high school students questioned admitted to the use of barbiturates, while 1–4% admitted to the recreational use of opiates at least once.

The data uncovered by Newcomb and Bentler (1989) was very similar to that reported by Mikkelsen (1985). Newcomb and Bentler reported that 92% of the high school seniors studied admitted to having used alcohol at least once, while 66% admitted to the use of alcohol in the preceding month. The authors found that 57% of high school seniors admitted to the use of an illicit drug at least once and more than one-third admitting to the use of an illicit drug other than marijuana. Surprisingly, the authors found that cocaine use among high school seniors seems to have fallen slightly. This is a welcome trend.

Because very little is known about adolescent drug use, it is difficult to identify the difference between experimental drug use, an early drug-use problem, a chronic drug-abuse problem, or drug addiction (Wheeler and Malmquist, 1987). Newcomb and Bentler (1989) reported that social variables such as low socioeconomic status, a lack of religious commitment, low self-esteem, and disturbed families all tend to influence adolescent drug-use patterns. The strongest influence on adolescent drug use, however, is the influence of peer groups (Newcomb and Bentler, 1989; Joshi and Scott, 1988).

Mikkelsen (1985) concluded that acute stressors such as a geographic move, a major psychological loss, an increase in family conflict, or increased pressure to perform in school were all predictors of the initial, usually transient, use of chemicals by adolescents. Teenagers vulnerable to chemical use because of genetic inheritance or psychosocial factors would be "at risk" for the development of a more chronic pattern of drug use.

Hoffmann, Belille, and Harrison (1987) reported on a research project that gathered data from more than 1000 adolescents in treatment for drug abuse. The authors found that *more than three-quarters* of their sample reported having developed tolerance to alcohol or other drugs, while one-third of their sample reported withdrawal symptoms from drugs or alcohol. This would suggest that, for many adolescents, drug use is more than a passing phase.

Not every adolescent who uses drugs is addicted. As Newcomb and Bentler (1989) pointed out, the occasional use of alcohol or marijuana at a party is not, automatically, abuse. Rather, if the individual (a) *is repeatedly* using chemicals, (b) *uses chemicals at an inappropriate time*, or (c) *is one whose chemical use results in legal, school, or social problems* that person might be said to have a drug abuse problem. This drug abuse problem may either be acute or chronic, depending on how often the individual engages in the drug use.

Zarek, Hawkins, and Rogers (1987) identified six criteria that act as indicators of adolescent drug abuse. These were: (a) the use of chemicals to get "smashed," (b) going to parties where drugs other than alcohol were in use, (c) refusing to attend parties where drugs were not present, (d) drinking liquor, as opposed to beer or wine, (e) using marijuana, and (f) being drunk at school. The authors concluded that the adolescent who has a drug abuse problem was likely to be "enrolled in school, but . . . experiencing behavior problems related to school, such as being sent to the principal, or skipping classes" (p. 485).

The key point to remember is that there is a difference between adolescent drug *use,* and *drug abuse.* Newcomb and Bentler (1989) pointed out that while the individual may have started to use drugs in response to social pressure, she or he will continue to use chemicals in response to internal emotional states. Joshi and Scott (1988) postulated that most adolescents initially use drugs out of curiosity or in response to peer pressure. However, the authors also expressed a belief that those adolescents who continued to use chemicals did so because of internal discomfort, such as depression.

Rogers, Harris, and Jarmuskewicz (1987) concluded that parental influence on subsequent drug-use behavior is the strongest during childhood, while peer influences play an increasingly important role in shaping the individual's drug-use pattern during adolescence. Pentz, Dwyer, MacKinnon, Flay, Handen, Wang, and Johnson (1989) pointed out that the early adolescent years are a time of special vulnerability for later drug abuse, as it is during this period of life that many adolescents begin to experiment with various "gateway" chemicals that open the door to later drug-abuse problems. The authors identified such "gateway" drugs as being tobacco, alcohol, and marijuana. As previously noted, Brunswick (1989) has advanced the possibility that inhalants also serve as a "gateway" drug.

There is virtually nothing known about childhood drug use, and a great deal to be learned about what constitutes "normal" and "abnormal" chemical use by adolescents. At this time, it is known that some adolescents become abusers of chemicals, and that some even become addicted to drugs. However, many adolescents pass through a period of experimental drug use without passing on to the phase of abuse or addiction. Mikkelsen (1985) reported that there were a "relatively small number of persons at each extreme" (p. 2) of the drug-use spectrum, suggesting that most of those who use chemicals during adolescence do not develop serious abuse problems. In spite of what might be said by the admissions officers of some treatment centers, the use of chemicals by adolescents does not *automatically* mean that there is a drug-abuse problem present.

Wheeler and Malmquist (1987) observed that adolescents, as a general rule, did not develop the "withdrawal symptoms, hepatic changes, or gross organic brain syndromes" (p. 438) that are the hallmark of drug addiction. However, when the individual's drug use *has* resulted in such physical changes, he or she is scarred for not just the rest of adolescence, but for life. Once a brain cell has died, it will never regrow. Once the liver is damaged, it is damaged for life.

The diagnosis of adolescent drug abuse, or addiction, is a complicated task, which requires an extensive data base in order to document drug use by the individual (Wheeler and Malmquist, 1987). At all times, the possibility that the individual has not developed a drug abuse problem, but that she or he is only going through a period of experimentation, should be considered by treatment professionals. While children and adolescents are often hidden victims of drug addiction, the treatment professional must steer a cautious path between underdiagnosis and overdiagnosis of chemical dependency among the young.

ADDICTION AND THE ELDERLY

The problem of alcoholism in the elderly has only recently been studied and presents an underrecognized challenge to mental health professionals (Ehlert, 1989; Wade, 1988). Research suggests that heavy drinking peaks in the 40–50 year age range, after which it declines until about age 70 (Abrams and Alexopoulos, 1987). It is estimated that problem drinking still might be found in 5–12% of men and 1–2% of women, in their sixties (Hurt, Finlayson, Morse, and Davis, 1988). A small number of the elderly become alcoholic at a later stage in life, without demonstrating earlier problem drinking. This phenomenon has been termed "late onset alcoholism" by Hurt, Finlayson, Morse, and Davis (1988).

It has been suggested (Abrams and Alexopoulos, 1987) that alcoholism is less likely to be detected in the elderly "in part because the impairments in social and occupational functioning attributable to alcoholism in younger people are not as obvious" (p. 1285). The authors point out that alcohol's effects on the individual's cognitive abilities mimic those changes associated with normal aging or dementia.

Ehlert (1989) agreed with this contention but pointed out that few health care providers attempt to identify older individuals who might be using alcohol while taking other medications. In spite of the fact that the elderly use 25% of all prescription and OTC medications, and that 7–10% of those over 55 years of age have an alcohol abuse problem, few health care providers search for alcohol use in the elderly (Ehlert, 1989). The result is, all too often, potentially deadly combinations of medications and alcohol in the elderly.

The consequences of social drinking are quite serious in the elderly. It is well known that alcoholism in the elderly results in psychiatric hospitalizations for one-third of older alcoholics. Surprisingly, however, social drinking has also been found to be associated with cognitive deterioration in the elderly (Abrams and Alexopoulos, 1987). This information would suggest that older persons should avoid the use of alcohol as much as possible.

Hurt et al. (1988), warned that elderly alcoholics were more likely to present medical complications as a result of their drinking than were younger adults and suggested a comprehensive medical evaluation for such patients. Ehlert (1989) agreed with this warning and observed that ". . . between 12 to 14 percent of older people hospitalized for *any* reason have a significant problem with alcohol. Alcoholics seem to use more health-care resources" (p. 10, italics added for emphasis).

Zimberg (1978) noted that there were three subgroups of older alcoholics. First, there were those individuals who had no drinking problem in young or middle adulthood, and thus demonstrated late-life alcoholism. Second were those individuals who had a history of intermittent problem drinking, but who had developed a more chronic alcohol problem in late adulthood. Third, there were those individuals whose alcohol problems started in young adulthood and continued into the later part of their lives.

Zimberg (1978) observed that the second and third groups of older alcoholics could be grouped together to form a classification of "early onset" (p. 240) alcoholism. This subgroup was thought to include about two-thirds of the older alcoholics. Those individuals who demonstrated alcohol problems only in the later phases of life were said to have "late onset" (p. 240) alcoholism and were thought to make up about one-third of the elderly alcoholic population.

Each subgroup was thought by Zimberg (1978) to present different needs to treatment centers, and each was thought to have a different prognosis. Zimberg (1978) postulated that early onset alcoholics were more likely to have developed medical complications to their alcohol use. Both early- and late-onset alcoholics were thought to be reacting to the factors of retirement, bereavement, loneliness, and physical illness found in the later stages of life. Group therapy approaches that included problem-solving and social-support components were thought to be useful in working with the older alcoholic.

It is obvious from the work of Abrams and Alexopoulos (1987), Wade (1988), and Zimberg (1978), that alcoholism in the elderly has been underestimated by mental health professionals. Zimberg (1978) reported that elderly widowers were more likely to be alcoholic, with a rate of 105 alcoholic widowers per 1000 population. He concluded that 10–15% of the elderly might be diagnosed as alcoholic.

Abrams and Alexopoulos (1987), who did not limit their research to alcohol alone, found that ". . . more than 20 percent of patients over 65 years old admitted to a psychiatric hospital in one year could be considered drug dependent" (p. 1286). Hurt et al. (1988) also found that the elderly have a significant chemical dependency problem, noting that 10% of the patients admitted to a chemical dependency treatment unit were over sixty-five years of age.

Drug misuse in the elderly was found to take several forms by Abrams and Alexopoulos (1987), including (a) intentional over use of a medication, (b) under use of a medication, (c) erratic use of a prescribed medication, or (d) the failure of the physician to obtain a *complete* drug history, including use of OTC medications. It was found that this intentional misuse of prescribed medications was the largest category of drug abuse in the elderly. The elderly were found to engage in the *underutilization* of pre-scribed medication, often because of financial limitations.

It was postulated that family and friends might feel shame, hurt, or guilt about a drug addiction problem in their grandparents or great-grandparents (Wade, 1988). For this reason, it was thought that family or friends might hesitate to report the addicted person's problem so that he or she might enter treatment. It has been noted (Wade, 1988) that only 15% of those elderly persons with a drug or alcohol problem are currently receiving help for that dependency, suggesting that addiction in the elderly is indeed underrecognized, underreported, and undertreated.

THE DUAL DIAGNOSIS CLIENT: ADDICTION AND MENTAL ILLNESS

There was a time, in the not-too-recent past, when the problem of drug abuse or dependency among those who were mentally ill was all but ignored. The problem of drug abuse/addiction in the mentally ill was thought to be rare, and was easily overlooked by health care professionals if only because they did not bother to look for the problem. If the client did abuse chemicals, or if the client was addicted to chemicals, this problem was rarely addressed by treatment professionals because the drug abuse/addiction was assumed to be secondary to the primary mental illness.

It has only been in the past decade, as health care professionals have come to understand more about the nature of mental illness, that it has been discovered that dual diagnosis clients were not as rare as once thought. Indeed, health care professionals have discovered that drug abuse/addiction is at least as much a problem for the mentally ill as for the general population. Since the acceptance of the problem of dual diagnosis clients, professionals have started to develop treatment methods that enable individuals to come to terms both with their addictions, and with their mental illness. In this subsection, we will briefly explore the problem of the dual diagnosis client, and discuss the treatment methods currently in use for this population.

The first step in working with a dual diagnosis client is to identify exactly what a "dual diagnosis" client is. Protracted chemical use may result in the development of a wide range of psychiatric syndromes, depending on the agents being used. The chronic cocaine user, for example, might experience a postcocaine depression of suicidal proportions, while the amphetamine addict might develop an amphetamine-related paranoia that is, at least for a time, indistinguishable from paranoid schizophrenia.

These are not primary psychiatric problems. Rather, the psychiatric disorders are secondary to the individual's chemical use, and on a diagnostic summary form are noted as being secondary to the individual's cocaine or amphetamine use. Dual diagnosis clients, those clients who both suffer from mental illness and who are addicted to chemicals, represent a special challenge to treatment professionals.

Both mental illness and drug abuse/addiction may be chronic disorders, each with an independent course, yet each able to influence the progression of the other (Carey, 1989). However, for the most part, mental health providers have not addressed the issue of drug abuse or addiction in the psychiatric population. Ananth, Vandewater, Kamal, Brodsky, Gamal, and Miller (1989) found that 75% of their sample of psychiatric patients could also be diagnosed as chemical abusers or addicts. Carey (1989) concluded that one-third to one-half of all psychiatric patients abused alcohol, chemicals, or both.

In a similar study, Kofoed, Kania, Walsh, and Atkinson (1986) reported that 21–39% of those who met the DSM-III diagnostic criteria for a substance abuse disorder also met the criteria for another psychiatric diagnosis. Brown et al. (1989), estimated that, in the younger mentally ill population, the ". . . substance abuse rate approaches or exceeds 50%" (p. 566). Substance abuse is now thought to be twice as common in the mentally ill as in the general population.

These clients are hidden victims of drug dependency. They generally do not benefit from traditional chemical dependency treatment (Kofoed and Keys, 1988), experience numerous brief periods of hospitalization for psychiatric problems (Carey, 1989), and are often not recognized by mental health professionals as chemical abusers (Peyser, 1989). Indeed, Ananth et al. (1989), reevaluated a sample of 75 psychiatric patients, each of whom had been seen and diagnosed by mental health professionals. The authors found that 54 of the 75 subjects should also have received a diagnosis of drug abuse or drug dependence in addition to their psychiatric diagnosis.

Ten of the 54 subjects found to use drugs were also either chemical abusers or addicted to alcohol, while two additional subjects were found to meet the diagnostic criteria for only alcohol abuse or dependence.

Rado (1988) suggested that the number of dual diagnosis clients is increasing, possibly because professionals are better trained and more likely to recognize the existence of a drug addiction in a psychiatric patient. However ". . . fewer and fewer clinics are accepting clients with this profile" (Rado, p. 5). Kofoed et al. (1986), reported that, unfortunately, dual diagnosis clients are often refused treatment at both psychiatric and chemical dependency treatment centers.

All too often, dual diagnosis patients are viewed as being psychiatric patients by chemical dependency professionals. At the same time, traditional psychiatric hospitals view such individuals as being chemical dependency patients. In either case, such clients are "hypervulnerable" (Brown et al., 1989, p. 567) to the effects of chemicals, while being unlikely to recognize that their substance abuse is a problem or accept abstinence as a viable treatment goal.

Because of a number of factors, the outlook for dual diagnosis clients has, traditionally, been thought to be quite poor. When working with a dual diagnosis client, the treatment philosophies of substance abuse counselors and mental health professionals often conflict. This may result in a significant degree of confusion and frustration for the client and treatment professionals.

Kofoed et al. (1986), noted that more severe levels of psychopathology have been associated with an unfavorable outcome for substance abusers, in part because ". . . coexisting thought or affective disorders may exacerbate denial of substance abuse" (p. 1209). Denial of substance abuse is a significant problem in the dual diagnosis client and contributes to the difficulty of working with such clients.

As McNeil (1967) pointed out, mental illness often brings with it a fear of the loss of control, and emotional storms. These emotional storms are often hidden from external view, but are violent enough to be termed by McNeil as "Quiet Furies." In many cases, psychiatric patients will abuse drugs in an attempt at self-medication, possibly because they mistrust prescribed medication. Self-administered drugs also provide an *illusion of control* (Brown, 1985), a strong incentive for using drugs in those who fear losing control to begin with.

The traditional approach to dual diagnosis clients has been to address the client's mental illness first, and after psychiatric stabilization has been achieved to begin to explore the client's chemical-use pattern (Rado, 1988). The decision whether to treat the psychiatric condition, or the drug dependency first is often quite arbitrary (Kofoed et al., 1986).

Kofoed and Keys (1988) suggest that the general psychiatric unit is unsuited to meet the needs of a dual diagnosis client. The authors suggested that psychiatric units might do best if treatment goals were limited to (a) detoxification from drugs of abuse, (b) psychiatric stabilization, and

(c) persuasion of the client to enter chemical dependency treatment. The clinician must be patient, often waiting years until conditions are right to persuade a dual diagnosis client to enter treatment.

Research suggests that it is impossible to achieve any degree of emotional stability until the client is drug free (Rado, 1988; Pursch, 1987). Thus, chemical detoxification is necessary as a first step to treatment of a dual diagnosis client. This requires psychiatric support from professionals who are knowledgeable in both the fields of psychiatry and chemical dependency (Pursch, 1987). Once detoxification has been achieved, the treatment team would be in a position to identify which problems were a result of the client's chemical use, which are manifestations of the client's psychiatric disorder, and in what order the problems need to be addressed.

Dual diagnosis clients may be treated on an outpatient (Kofoed et al., 1986) or inpatient (Pursch, 1987) basis, depending on the client's needs. The ideal program for a dual diagnosis client would have facilities for working with both the psychiatric and the addicted client. This would allow the dual diagnosis patient to be shifted from one program to another, as his or her needs change during treatment. Although Carey (1989) accepted that the dual diagnosis client might be seen on an outpatient basis, he recommended that the client be referred to an inpatient psychiatric treatment center if this became necessary.

In working with the dual diagnosis client, Kofoed and Keys (1988) concluded that peer-group therapy offered "a more acceptable source of support and confrontation than is usually available . . . on a general psychiatric ward" (p. 1209). Thus, the authors view group therapy as an important element in working with the dual diagnosis client, although they advocate that such groups be held in the psychiatric unit rather than in the substance abuse unit. Carey (1989) suggested that when confrontation is used with dual diagnosis clients this confrontation be less intense than that used with personality disordered individuals.

During group sessions, Kofoed and Keys (1988) strive to (a) persuade clients to accept the reality of their drug dependency, and (b) persuade clients to seek continued treatment for the drug dependency. Many of the same techniques used in general drug addiction treatment groups are useful in working with dual diagnosis clients, although the very nature of the client population offers unique challenges. For example, Kofoed and Keys warn that once the psychiatric condition is controlled the client's drug-related defenses again begin to operate. The client will often express a belief that, once their psychiatric symptoms are controlled, they are no longer in danger of being addicted to chemicals.

Dual diagnosis clients are both similar to, and vastly different from, the traditional addict. Although the process of denial is present in both forms of psychopathology, the added dimension of a psychiatric disorder will cause the client's denial of his or her drug addiction to express itself in different ways. In many cases, dual diagnosis clients will focus almost exclusively on their psychiatric disorder to avoid confronting their drug dependency. Once the psychiatric condition is controlled, such a client is likely to self-terminate (that is, drop out) from treatment.

This "floating" denial is best seen when the client tells the mental health professional that most of his or her problems are drug related, while claiming to the substance abuse counselor that most of his or her problems are caused by the mental illness. In a sense, it is not uncommon for the client to use one disorder as a shield against intervention for the other. Dropping out of treatment for such a client is the ultimate expression of denial.

Another form of denial, one that is frequently found in traditional clients, is evident when the client informs the drug rehabilitation specialist that she or he has discontinued all drug/alcohol use. In effect, the client enters into a period of trying to "tell the counselor what he or she wants to hear" in order to avoid confrontation. This is an evasion that is frequently used by all clients, including those who suffer from mental illness.

For this reason, a group of peers is most effective in working with the dual diagnosis client (Kofoed and Keys, 1988). Other group members who may have dropped out of treatment after their psychiatric disorder was controlled in the past can share their own experiences with the group. Rado (1988) noted that even occasional use of recreational chemicals may result in some degree of decompensation in terms of the individual's psychiatric status. Because the disease of addiction mirrors the psychiatric disorder in many cases, even limited drug use may exacerbate a psychiatric dysfunction, according to Rado.

The group provides an avenue through which clients may share their experiences with even limited recreational drug use, and discuss the need for the support of a twelve-step group (Rado, 1988; Kofoed and Keys, 1988). It was noted that, when the group is effective, dual diagnosis clients tend to achieve a lower rehospitalization rate (Kofoed and Keys, 1988).

Summary of the Dual Diagnosis Client

The dual diagnosis client presents a difficult challenge to the mental health and the chemical dependency professionals. Such clients often use an interchangeable system of denial, talking of their psychiatric problems with drug addiction counselors, while talking about their drug abuse or addiction with mental health professionals. This makes it difficult to work with dual diagnosis clients.

Traditional treatment methods have been found to require some modification when working with dual diagnosis clients: for example, the degree of confrontation useful in working with a personality disordered client is far too strong for working with a dual diagnosis client. However, gentle confrontation will often work with the mentally ill and drug dependent client.

UNSEEN VICTIMS OF "STREET" DRUG CHEMISTRY

Product reliability is hardly a strong component of clandestine, illegal, drug laboratories. During Prohibition, "bathtub gin" and "homebrew" might blind or even kill a person. In today's world, a simple mistake in the production of a drug or drug analog can produce lethal chemical combinations.

As often happened with alcohol during Prohibition, contaminated drugs are sold on the streets (Gallagher, 1986; Kirsch, 1986). Shafer (1985) explored the impact that many of these "mistakes," which were sold on the streets of California in the late 1970s under the guise of "new heroin," had on the user. These drugs, produced in clandestine laboratories, are known to have included chemical impurities capable of literally burning out parts of the brain.

Some addicts who used the drugs produced in these illegal laboratories developed a drug-induced Parkinson's disease, after using a drug sold as "synthetic heroin" (Kirsch, 1986). Many addicts, no one knows how many, died as a result of these mistakes in the manufacture of synthetic heroin.

There is no way to determine how many people have suffered, or died, because of impure street drugs. Parras, Patier, and Ezpeleta (1988) reported a case where a heroin addict was found to have developed lead poisoning as a result of lead-contaminated heroin. Allcott, Barnhart, and Mooney (1987) reported on two cases where users of methamphetamine developed lead poisoning as a result of impure street drugs. Many such cases, perhaps most, go unreported.

Lombard, Levin, and Winer (1989) reviewed a case where a cocaine abuser was found to have developed arsenic poisoning as a result of his cocaine use. When the individual was told of the cause of his nausea, vomiting, and diarrhea, he was reportedly quite unimpressed, and informed the physicians that it was "common knowledge" (p. 869) that cocaine might be mixed with compounds that contained arsenic. The authors warned that similar cases might be encountered by other physicians as the cocaine epidemic spread.

In a disturbing report, the *Minneapolis Tribune* (1989a) reported that a derivative of cocaine called *basuco* was being distributed in Colombia. This drug, a byproduct of the cocaine production process, produces an intense "high." However, because it is heavily contaminated with kerosene, sulphuric acid, and lead, even short-term use will bring about irreversible brain damage. One must ask whether this is the next chemical of abuse that will be exported to the United States, or if the use of basuco will remain endemic to South America.

SUMMARY

We all have, within our minds, a picture of what the "typical" addict looks like. For some, this is the picture of the "skid row" alcoholic, while for others the picture that is associated with "addiction" is that of a heroin addict, hidden in the ruins of an abandoned building, belt around the arm, ready to inject the drug. These images of addiction are correct, yet each image fails to accurately reflect the many hidden faces of addiction.

There is a grandmother, who is quietly drinking herself to death, or the mother who treats her unborn child with staggering amounts of cocaine, heroin, or alcohol. There is the working woman whose chemical addiction is hidden behind a veil of productivity, or who is an addict whose drug use is sanctioned by the unsuspecting physicians who are trying to help her cope with feelings of depression or anxiety. There are faces of addiction so well hidden that even today they are not recognized. As professionals, we must learn to look, and recognize, the hidden forms of addiction.

CHAPTER 16

Codependency and Enabling

The book *Alcoholics Anonymous* (1976) affirmed that alcoholism was a disease. Yet alcoholism is unlike other diseases in many ways. Alcoholism embraces not only the afflicted individual, but indirectly it also involves the people around the alcoholic. Indeed, concerned family and friends may actually *support* the very disease that they are fighting against through their *codependency* and *enabling*. In this chapter, we will briefly explore the concepts of codependency and enabling.

THE ENABLER

You do not have to be a family member to enable an addicted person. Indeed, in the booklet *The Family Enablers* (Johnson Institute, 1987), an enabler is defined as any person who "reacts to an alcoholic in such a way as to shield the alcoholic from experiencing the full impact of the harmful consequences of alcoholism" (p. 5). The enabler may be a well-meaning friend, a trusted advisor, a supervisor at work, or even a drug rehabilitation worker. *Any* person who *knowingly* acts in such a way as to protect the addicted person from the natural consequences of his or her behavior may be said to be an enabler.

To *enable* someone means to knowingly engage in certain behaviors. The enabler, by protecting the addicted person, prevents the individual from taking advantage of the many opportunities to discover first hand the cost of his or her adddiction. One father of a narcotics addict admitted, in a mixed group of family members and other addicts, that he had taken out personal loans more than once to pay off his daughter's drug debts. Another addict, who had been in recovery for some time, asked the father why. The father responded that, if he did not, his daughter "might leave us!". Several group members then suggested that the daughter might need to suffer some consequences on her own in order to "hit bottom" and come to terms with her addiction. The father was silent for a moment, then said "Oh, I couldn't do that! She's not ready to assume responsibility for herself, yet!".

It is difficult to understand the multitude of ways in which one person might enable an addict to continue his or her compulsive use of chemicals. A secretary may enable an alcoholic superior's continued drinking by providing an excuse as to why she or he missed an important staff meeting. Rather than say "She was drinking all morning, and I don't know where she is now," the secretary might explain that "There was an emergency at the downtown office, and she had to leave." In so doing, the secretary has prevented the superior from suffering the consequences of addiction. The secretary, in this hypothetical example, has enabled another person's continued use of chemicals.

Not uncommonly, the addicted person will treat the enablers as if they are being granted a favor for the privilege of living with, and taking responsibility for, the addicted person! When confronted by his or her supervisor for being late again, the addict might respond, "you are lucky that I work here in the first place!". Yet the supervisor, perhaps fearing legal or union action, takes no action other than to warn the addict not to let it happen again. The supervisor might be said to have enabled the addicted employee, though not a codependent of that person.

CODEPENDENCY

The issues of codependency and enabling are often intertwined within the same individual. One does *not* have to be codependent in order to enable an addict. Enabling involves knowingly protecting the addicted person from the consequences of his or her behavior. It does not require an ongoing relationship. A tourist who gives a street beggar a gift of money, knowing that the beggar is likely addicted and in need of drugs, might be said to have enabled the beggar. But the tourist is hardly in a meaningful relationship with the addicted person.

This is often a confusing point to the student of addiction. Codependency and enabling may be, and often are, found in the same person. However, one may also enable an addicted person without being codependent on that person. Enabling refers to *specific behaviors*, while codependency refers to *a relationship pattern*. Thus, one may enable addiction without being codependent.

The issues of codependency and enabling may be thought of as *overlapping* issues, which may or may not be found in the same individual. Figure 16-1 is a diagram of this relationship.

There is no standard definition of codependency (Beattie, 1989). Indeed, mental health professionals have yet to agree on such a basic issue as whether the word is hyphenated (*co-dependency*) (Beattie, 1989). However, addicted people's families and friends are rapidly becoming aware that they have been suffering as a result of

> . . . a relationship with a dysfunctional person. Sometimes, that person appeared in our childhoods, sometimes in our adult lives. Usually, we've had relationships with more than one dysfunctional person; this pattern began in childhood and repeated itself as we grew older (Beattie, 1989, p. 7).

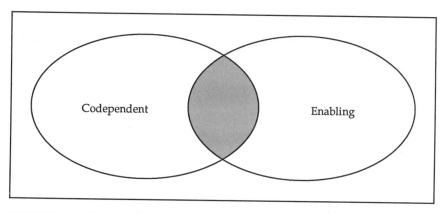

FIGURE 16-1. The overlapping relationships of codependency and enabling.

In an early paper on the subject, Beattie (1987) spoke of codependency as being a process where an individual's life had become unmanageable. The codependent's life has become unmanageable because she or he is involved in a committed relationship with an addict and is unable to "detach" from the addicted person. Because she or he cannot detach from the addicted person (or at least the addicted person's behavior), the codependent person comes to feel obsessed with controlling the addict's behavior. In an attempt to control the addicted person, the codependent will assume responsibility for the events not actually under his or her control.

May (1988) noted that codependency is

> . . . not simply a matter of other people trying to cope with the addicted person's behavior. They actually create their own interweaving webs of deception. They may even unconsciously develop new, more inventive mind tricks for the addicted person to use. Ironically, it is the most sympathetic, compassionate, loving persons in the addict's social circle that are most likely to fall into such collusion (p. 51).

A classic example of codependence might be found when the spouse attempts to use drugs with the addict in order to "show him or her how to control it." Codependents have been known to purchase drugs for the addict, or to include the purchase of drugs in the family budget, in an attempt to control the addict's drug use. One woman, herself codependent, even asked for marital counseling because her husband would not limit his cocaine use to the $100 a week that she had budgeted for his drug use!

Often, codependent and enabling behaviors are found in the same person. The wife who calls in to work to say that her husband is "sick" when he is actually hungover from the night before is both codependent and an enabler. Another example might be found in the husband who calls to tell the probation/parole officer that his wife cannot keep today's appointment because of illness, knowing full well that if the probation/parole officer were to ask for a urine sample for a drug screen, that his spouse would test positive and be sent to prison.

Several years ago, at a maximum security penitentiary for men somewhere in the Midwest, the elderly mother of an inmate asked a staff psychologist to "make sure that the man who shares my son's cell is a good influence" on her son, because "there are a lot of bad men in that prison, and I don't want him falling in with a bad crowd."

The woman in this case overlooked the grim reality that her son was not simply in prison for singing off key in choir practice, and that he had been to prison on several occasions for various crimes. Rather than let him live his life, and try to get on with hers, she continued to worry about how to "cure" him of his behavior problem. She continued to treat him as a child, was overly involved in his life, and was quite upset at the suggestion that it might be time to let her son learn to *suffer* (and perhaps learn from) *the consequences of his own behavior.*

This case demonstrates the classic symptoms of codependency: (a) the over-involvement with the dysfunctional family member, (b) the obsessive attempts on the part of the codependent person to control the dysfunctional family member's behavior, and (c) the tendency to make personal sacrifices in an attempt to "cure" the dysfunctional family member of his or her problem behavior.

Beattie (1989) identified several unspoken "rules" of codependency:

a. it's not O. K. for me to feel
b. it's not O. K. for me to have problems
c. it's not O. K. for me to have fun
d. I'm not lovable
e. I'm not good enough, and,
f. if people act bad or crazy, I'm responsible.

In an attempt to live up to these unspoken rules, codependency involves pain. The core of codependency, as viewed by Zerwekh and Michaels (1989) is ". . . related to low self-esteem" (p. 111) on the part of the codependent person. The authors concluded that

> Co-dependents frequently appear normal, which in our culture is associated with a healthy ego. Nevertheless, they also describe themselves as "dying on the inside," which is indicative of low self-worth or esteem (p. 111).

The codependent person is often—because of what Scarf (1980) termed "unfinished business" with his or her parents—unable to affirm the self. She or he does not feel capable of affirming self but turns to an external source of affirmation, the marital partner, for affirmation and approval. The codependent often comes to measure personal worth by how well he or she can take care of the addicted individual, or through the sacrifices that he or she makes (Miller, 1988). In this way, the codependent individual substitutes an external measure of personal worth for his or her inability to generate self-worth.

Drug rehabilitation workers are often surprised at the amount of suffering and pain that codependent family members experience.. There is a reward for such behavior! As Shapiro (1981) pointed out, there is a certain moral victory to be achieved through suffering. Suffering allows the codependent individual to accuse "the offender by pointing at his victim; it keeps alive in the mind's record an injustice committed, a score unsettled" (p. 115). Shapiro (1981) concluded that such suffering was, for some,

> . . . a necessity, a principled act of will, from which he cannot release himself without losing his self-respect and feeling more deeply and finally defeated, humiliated, and powerless (p. 115).

Thus, for some, the trials and suffering imposed on the codependent family member by the dysfunctional person become a defense against the admission of powerlessness or worthlessness. The codependent person, in many cases, comes to affirm personal worth by "carrying the cross" of another person's addiction or dysfunctional behavior.

It is almost as if the person believes that "As long as I suffer, I *am* somebody!". Rehabilitation workers are often left with the impression that the codependent person does not believe that she or he will have a life without the addict. Beattie (1989) observed that codependency is a *progressive disorder* that may include a tendency on the part of the individual to repeatedly become involved in different codependent relationships. The codependent may also "relapse" into old patterns of behavior, even after years of growth. The recovery process can be lifelong.

ADDICTION AND MARRIAGE

In the alcoholic marriage, there is often a "role reversal" (Ackerman, 1983) between the marital partners. The alcoholic will often assume a "sick dependency" (Phillips, 1979, p. 3) on other family members who are often codependent. As the other family members come to assume responsibilities formerly held by the addicted member of the family, the addict becomes less and less responsible for his or her family duties, and less involved in the family life.

Dulfano (1978) reviewed the role of the family in alcoholism, and concluded that once addiction to alcohol has developed, others in the individual's environment

> . . . may maintain his drinking behavior. As the alcoholic begins to build up a tolerance to alcohol, his functioning becomes impaired and his behavior changes, making him or her give up role tasks and concomitant responsibilities. The system around the alcoholic changes to accommodate the disability (p. 120).

It is for this reason that many professionals who work with chemical dependency view addiction as a family-centered disorder. Murray Bowen (1985), in his essay on the role of the family in the development of alcoholism, noted that ". . . every important family member plays a part in the dysfunction of the dysfunctional member" (p. 262). To understand addiction, Bowen believes that one must view the role of addiction in the family as a whole.

Bowen (1985) observed that, as a general rule, people tend to marry those who have achieved similar levels of "differentiation of self" (p. 263), a concept that was "roughly equivalent to the concept of emotional maturity" (p. 263). Bowen viewed each person as having to separate from one's parents, and to resolve the various emotional attachments to the parents that evolved during childhood. Inherent in Bowen's theory was the belief that, if individuals failed to resolve emotional attachments to their parents, they would seek to fuse with the marital partner to find emotional support that was once offered by the parents.

However, the partner may have found a different answer to life's problems. She or he may have turned to chemicals. The dance of codependency is now complete: on the one hand, there is the person who is addicted to chemicals, a person who seeks as little responsibility as possible in order to devote as much attention to drug use as possible. On the other hand, the codependent person seeks to fuse with the marital partner in order to find the emotional strength in the partner that is lacking in the self.

In many cases, the codependent person has been "trained" to be codependent through having been raised in a disturbed home environment. In such a situation, the individual will never have had the opportunity to differentiate from the family of origin. Such families are frequently so *un*differentiated that personal growth is virtually impossible. The individual is not allowed to have a life outside of the family, a situation that is called *enmeshment*.

The codependent person does not learn during childhood that she or he has the right to set limits within relationships, even in the marital relationship. In many cases, the codependent person will tolerate violations of personal boundaries in an attempt to win the approval and love of any person who offers even the remote promise of acceptance. In other cases, codependent people have had their boundaries violated so often they do not recognize appropriate limits to begin with, and do not even realize that their rights were ignored.

There is, between the addicted person and the codependent person, an interaction of pathologies. Addicts often attempt to foster the impression that they need somebody to take care of them because they are unable to face the demands of daily living alone. In so doing, addicts are apparently looking for somebody who will relieve them of some of the responsibilities of daily living, so that they might invest that energy into drug use.

If the codependent allows this to continue, other members of the family will quickly fall into the codependency trap, making it easier for the addict to continue to use drugs. In so doing, the family members enable the addict's sick behavior to continue, as they "feed into" the addict's dependency.

ADDICTION AND THE FAMILY

According to Bowen (1985) the treatment of addiction involves the identification and ultimately the modification of whatever dysfunctional family system allowed the development and maintenance of the addiction in the first place. In the alcoholic marriage, for example, it has long been known that alcoholism becomes a "secret partner" first of the marriage, and ultimately of the family. In time this "family secret" becomes the dominating force around which the family's rules and rituals are centered (Brown, 1985). The family comes to operate under two ironclad rules a) "There is no alcoholism in this family," and b) "Don't tell anyone" (Brown, 1985).

In a misguided effort to use these rules for guidance, the family struggles to cope with and adapt to the addict. Ackerman (1983) notes that "The key to surviving an alcoholic home is adaptation. . . ." (p.16), and the entire family struggles to adapt to the addicted person(s) in their lives. Often, family members come to use the same defense mechanisms so characteristic of addicts: denial, rationalization, and projection.

However, there is nobody to guide the family in its struggle to adapt, and the family often unknowingly comes to support the very addiction that it struggles against (Johnson Institute, 1987). Woititz (1983) and Ackerman (1983) both speak at length of the toll that alcoholism (and, by extension, other forms of drug addiction) take on the individual and ultimately the family.

Without professional intervention, the family is unlikely to learn to accept the insight that it might actually be far more healthy to distance themselves from the addict, to let the addict suffer the natural consequences of his or her behavior (Johnson Institute, 1987). Rather, the entire family assumes responsibility for the pathology of a single member, living their lives in an attempt to somehow "cure" the disturbed family member. In so doing, the addict is relieved of the responsibility for his or her addiction, or its cure. The family members have become codependent.

As the individual's drug use progresses, the addiction assumes a position of greater and greater importance in his or her life. Family commitments that interfere with drug use are dropped in favor of drug-centered activities. The son's long anticipated trip to the ball game is postponed because Dad is still too hungover from last night to stand the heat and noise of the city. The long-awaited camping trip is canceled at the last minute because Mom went on another drinking spree last night and is in no condition to go camping.

Surprisingly, as this addiction develops the family actually starts to unknowingly *accommodate* itself to the continued use of the drug. They do this, often against their better judgment, by becoming part of the addict's support system (Johnson Institute, 1987). The family learns to enable the alcoholic, and in so doing becomes codependent (Beattie, 1987).

As part of this process of family accommodation, the son keeps silent when the teacher asks for volunteer drivers for an upcoming school trip, knowing that Mom is unlikely to be sober enough to drive that day. The children stop bringing friends over to visit to avoid the embarrassment of having their alcoholic or otherwise addicted parent seen by their friends. The family struggles to accommodate itself to the addiction, and in the process become enablers.

The process of family accommodation to the addiction ultimately makes it easier for the addict to continue using chemicals. This is because the addict knows that she or he will not have to face co-workers, other PTA members, or their children's friends. The family "secret" is protected for another day.

Nor does the family simply stop at protecting the secret of the addict's dual life. Surprisingly, the family might actually resist positive change in the alcoholic's life. In addressing the interaction between the family and the specific addiction of alcoholism, Dulfano (1978) noted that as the family changes to accommodate the alcoholic's drinking, ". . . an environment that resists the removal of the alcoholism may have been created" (p. 120). Family members will come to accept their new roles with various degrees of satisfaction. The family, both individually and as a unit, will fight against giving up these new roles, and may actually work against the addict's recovery.

This process develops over time, and often it is not clearly seen until after the addiction has fully developed. The point to be kept in mind, however, is that addiction does not spring into being overnight. Rather, the addiction, be it to alcohol or any other drug, *evolves* over a period of time. Furthermore, the addict does not stand alone but has a family "support system" *that he or she has helped to mold and shape.* In turn, the family support system often functions to help the abuser become and *remain* an addict.

For example, there is the case of a man, now married for the third time, whose spouse not surprisingly was also an alcoholic. His two prior marriages were also to individuals who were addicted to chemicals. This person even went so far as to divorce one spouse who "saw the light," joined Narcotics Anonymous, and stopped using chemicals! In so doing, she stopped being part of his addiction support system, and he divorced her shortly after he became convinced that she really meant to stay sober.

CHILDREN OF ALCOHOLICS,
CHILDREN OF ADDICTION

As noted above, the alcoholic parent's behavior impacts on the entire family, creating a disturbed home environment. As Woititz (1983) observed, the alcoholic home is often an environment of physical, emotional, or sexual abuse. Until recently, these children were not seen as suffering from their parent's alcoholism. It is now understood that children raised by alcoholic parents often come to take on roles "similar to those taken on in other dysfunctional families" (Woititz, 1983, p. 7).

There is little information available about the effects of other forms of parental drug addiction on different members of the family constellation. What little is known about this subject addresses the issue of the impact of parental alcoholism on the family. There is, obviously, much to learn about how, for example, a mother's heroin addiction might impact on the emotional growth of her children.

It has been suggested that the impact of one person's alcoholism might reach beyond the children, to the *grandchildren* of the alcoholic (Beattie, 1989; Kohr, 1988). Codependent behaviors might be passed on from one generation to the next (Beattie, 1989), ensuring that the impact of parental addiction might thus extend two generations into the future.

Even if we limit our investigation to the immediate consequences of addiction, the impact of drug dependency is staggering. Robert Ackerman (1983) estimated that *more than 10% of the population of the United States* were raised in alcoholic homes. These children were often raised by dysfunctional rules within the home. They will then incorporate these rules into their personality, grow up to become adults, and carry the scars of their childhood with them. These are the rules: (a) there is no addiction in this family, and (b) don't you dare tell anybody about it.

Ackerman (1983) observed that there are several interrelated factors that influence the impact of parental alcoholism on the growing child. The first of these factors was the sex of the alcoholic parent. An alcoholic mother will obviously have a far different impact on the family than will an alcoholic father. Second, there is the length of time that the alcoholic parent has actively been addicted. An alcoholic parent who has used chemicals for "only" 3 years will have a far different impact on the family than an alcoholic parent who has used drugs for 17 years.

Third, the sex of the individual child plays a role in the impact that parental alcoholism has on the individual. A daughter will be affected differently by an alcoholic father than would a son (Ackerman, 1983).

Fourth, the specific family constellation will play a role in how parental alcoholism will impact on each individual child. For example, the third boy in a family of six children, with a recovering father who has a three-month relapse when the boy is nine years old will experience a far different family environment than would the oldest child in a family of six children whose father relapsed for three months when the child was nine years old. Both children would have a far different experience in life than would the third boy in a family of six children whose father was constantly drinking until his fourteenth year.

Even in the example of the oldest boy of a family of six children whose father was actively addicted for the first fourteen years of the child's life, it is possible for the child to protect himself from the full impact of his father's alcoholism. It has been found that, if the child is able to find a parental substitute (uncle, neighbor, real or imagined hero, and so on), it may be possible for the child to find a way to avoid the worst of his father's alcoholic parenting (Ackerman, 1983).

Werner (1989) studied "resilient" (p. 108D) children, those who were "at risk" because of social or biological trauma but went on to succeed in life. She found that these children seem "to be particularly adept at recruiting . . . surrogate parents when a biological parent was unavailable . . . or incapacitated (p. 108D). Werner's work provides partial support for Ackerman's (1983) conclusion that it is possible for the child to find a substitute parent and escape from the full consequences of parental alcoholism.

Research into the impact of parental alcoholism has revealed that children who were raised in a home where there was at least one alcoholic parent do indeed seem to suffer. The research team of Puig-Antich, Goets, Davies, Kaplan, Davies, Ostrow, Asnis, Towmey, Iyengar, and Ryan (1989) concluded that the "effects of living with an alcoholic parent may precipitate very early depression in children with loaded familial aggregation for affective disorders" (p. 413). Which is to say that the authors found an interrelationship between depressive disorders *and* alcoholism in certain families. When both conditions were present, the authors found that the children of these families were likely to suffer from a major depressive disorder.

Black (1987) suggested that children of alcoholic parents often do not trust their perceptions and have difficulty understanding feelings. Such children grow up to have trouble understanding interpersonal boundaries, may be impulsive, and experience a lack of trust in relationships. Webb (1989) pointed out that adolescents who are raised in the alcoholic home are often required to assume responsibilities far beyond their abilities or maturity. These adolescents will often "spend an inordinate amount of time worrying about the safety of the whole (family) system" (p. 47).

Often, these adolescents will stay awake while the alcoholic parent is out drinking, will check on the safety of sleeping siblings, and will develop elaborate fire-escape plans that might involve returning time and time again to the burning house to rescue siblings, pets, and valuables (Webb, 1989). In response to this distorted family environment, many adolescents will become very serious and organized in an attempt to maintain control. Others become addicted to the excitement and unpredictability of living with an alcoholic parent, and will possibly become involved in fire-setting behaviors (Webb, 1989). Either stance is thought to help the individual come to terms with the home environment by helping him or her gain control of the feelings of vulnerability experienced within the home.

It is Webb's position that adolescents raised in an alcoholic home spend so much time and energy meeting basic survival needs that they do not have the opportunity to establish a firm sense of personal identity. This is not to say that *every* child raised in an alcoholic home suffers psychological trauma, only that a greater percentage seem to experience long-lasting emotional injuries as a result of their home environment than do children raised in more normal homes.

Berkowitz and Perkins (1988) found that adult children of alcoholic parents are more critical of themselves, and depreciate themselves more, than do adult children of nonalcoholic parents. Collette (1988) spoke of how she blamed herself for her father's pain, and was close to the point of suicide until she became involved in an Adult Children of Alcoholics self-help group. Indeed, it was reported (Collette, 1988) that there were some 1100 known self-help groups for Adult Children of Alcoholics. This number is both a reflection of how many people have been hurt by another's alcoholism, and of the desire of these hidden victims of addiction to find peace.

SUMMARY

In recent years, mental health professionals have started to explore how parental addiction impacts on the developing child. It has been suggested that the effects of addiction within the marriage change the roles of the marital partners, and will also affect the children of that marriage. Preliminary research suggests that the impact of parental addiction might even reach past the children of the addict to influence the growth and development of the grandchildren.

Out of the early research have emerged the concepts of codependency and enabling. Codependency, a relationship pattern, reflects the family entering into an unspoken agreement with the addict to support continued drug use in return for some degree of peace. This "peace" is usually only on the surface, however, and under the seeming calm is an ocean of anger, confusion, and discontent. Both codependent and non-codependent people may enable the addict, through specific behaviors that are known to protect the addict from facing the consequences of his or her addiction.

CHAPTER 17

Assessment of Chemical Dependency

The chemical dependency assessment process attempts to answer several interrelated questions. First, the assessor should determine whether the client is or is not an abuser of chemicals. Second, the assessor seeks to determine whether the client is addicted to chemicals. Third, if there is evidence that the client is an abuser of chemicals, or is addicted to chemicals, the assessor attempts to provide an overview of the client's chemical-use pattern.

As Lewis, Dana, and Blevins (1988) pointed out,

> . . . merely walking into a substance abuse treatment facility does not, in and of itself, warrant a diagnosis of "chemical dependency" or "alcoholism." Rather, clinicians must carefully evaluate the client and only then make decisions concerning diagnosis and treatment (p. 75).

Thus, the first duty of the assessor should be to establish a firm basis for a diagnosis of chemical dependency. It is only after the diagnosis has been established, *if* it is established, that the need for treatment might be considered. Treatment centers that assume "they *must* have a problem with chemicals, or they wouldn't be here!" do not serve the client's interests, only their own. *The need for treatment must be established, and documented.*

Kerr (1988) noted that "Effective therapy depends on assessment; if the assessment is too narrow in scope, the therapy will probably be ineffective" (p. 35). The assessment process allows the therapist to identify the client's strengths, needs, and priorities in order to design a treatment plan that will be most beneficial to the client. If, as Kerr observed, the assessment fails to identify significant areas of need, the therapeutic intervention is unlikely to succeed.

The reverse is also true: if the assessment incorrectly identifies specific problems, which is to say if the assessment process reveals a need that is not there, therapy is also unlikely to benefit the client. Thus it is essential for the therapist to identify as many potential areas of strength, support, and need as is possible during the assessment process.

In Chapter 1 the concept of addiction as a continuum was introduced. The following chart was used to illustrate the continuum of drug use/

abuse, with the different points on the continuum ranging from total abstinence from chemicals to the stage of chronic addiction:

0	1	2	3	4
Total abstinence from use	Rare social use of drugs	Heavy social use/problem drug use	Early addiction to chemicals	Chronic addiction to drugs

FIGURE 17-1. The drug use continuum.

Quite simply, the assessment process involves a professional evaluation of where on the above continuum the individual being assessed might fall. The person, on evaluation, may present strong evidence of a drug dependency problem. However, it might also be determined that the client has not progressed past the stage of heavy social use of chemicals following a proper assessment. In some cases the assessment process will reveal that the client is a social user of chemicals. It all depends on the client and the specific information available to the assessor.

DEFINITION OF DRUG ABUSE AND DRUG DEPENDENCE

Kolb and Brodie (1982) identified the *abuse* of a chemical as being the "persistent or sporadic excessive drug use inconsistent with or unrelated to acceptable medical practice" (p. 644). In contrast to this, *dependence* on one or more chemicals is more complicated. Drug dependence is defined by Kolb and Brodie (1982) as

> . . . a state, psychic and sometimes also physical, resulting from the interaction between a living organism and a drug, characterized by behavioral and other responses that always include a compulsion to take the drug on a continuous or periodic basis in order to experience its psychic effects and sometimes to avoid the discomfort of its absence. Tolerance may or may not be present (p. 644).

Kamback (1978) is more concise, noting that the two elements necessary to define an addiction to chemicals are *dependence* on the chemical, and *tolerance* to the drug's effects. As the individual's body adapts to the continuous use of one or more chemicals, there is a declining effect from the initial dosage levels. In order to achieve the same effect once accomplished with a relatively low dose, larger and larger doses must be used. This is tolerance.

Dependence on a chemical is diagnosed by the presence of a characteristic *withdrawal syndrome* when the drug is discontinued. The body, as it adapts to the continued presence of the drug(s) being used, alters its normal biological activities. When the drug is discontinued, there is a period of time during which the body must again adapt, this time to the absence of the chemical. During this period of readaptation to the absence of the chemical, the individual will experience the characteristic withdrawal syndrome for that chemical.

Abel (1982), in addressing the difference between abuse of and dependence on a drug, identified four elements as being necessary to the diagnosis of addiction: (a) a compulsion to continue use of the drug, (b) the development of tolerance, (c) major withdrawal symptoms following withdrawal from the drug, and (d) adverse effects from drug use both for the individual and for society.

The diagnosis of chemical dependency is, unfortunately, retrospective. The diagnosis of drug addiction is made only after the disorder is fully developed. Even after the addict reaches this point, however, one does not always clearly see all four of the elements previously outlined. The existence of one symptom of addiction is often taken as evidence by health care professionals that the other symptoms also exist.

When a patient goes through major withdrawal symptoms from alcohol, benzodiazepines, barbiturates, or narcotics, one may safely assume that this person is also tolerant to the drug's effects. For tolerance is usually seen before the development of physical withdrawal symptoms from these chemicals. The withdrawal symptoms also imply the compulsive use of one or more drugs; the patient probably used the drug for a long period of time for physical dependency to develop. Further, the withdrawal process would suggest that the drug has brought about adverse effects upon the individual, if only in the form of the withdrawal process itself.

The exact nature of the withdrawal syndrome will reflect the specific drug(s) used, the length of time the individual used the drug(s), and whether the individual discontinued chemical use all at once or gradually. Tolerance and dependence must *both* be present in order to diagnose an addiction to one or more chemicals.

However, there is also a phenomenon known as *psychological dependence* on a chemical. This is a state wherein the individual will habitually use one or more drugs, usually in an attempt to deal with anxiety or stress. The term *habituation* has also been applied to this phenomenon (Kolb and Brodie, 1982). In such a case, there is *no* physical adaptation to the use of the drug, in the sense that the body does not incorporate the drug into its normal function. But there is a *psychological* adaptation, in the sense that the person comes to believe that they *need* the drug.

One might consider the individual whose only alcohol use is a "nightcap" every night just before going to bed, to "help me unwind." This individual has very likely developed a psychological dependence on the alcohol to help deal with the accumulated stress and frustration of daily living, and as such could be said to have become habituated to alcohol.

During the assessment process, it is the assessor's responsibility to determine if the client's chemical-use pattern might better be classified as "social use," "abuse," or "addiction" to one or more drugs. This process is quite complicated, however, and involves gathering information from a wide variety of sources. In so doing, the assessor must work with the data privacy laws.

THE ASSESSOR AND DATA PRIVACY

The client *always* has a right to privacy. Which is to say that the assessor does not automatically have access to personal information about the client. The client may refuse to answer a specific question, or refuse permission for another person to reveal specific information to the assessor. This is the client's right, and the assessor should respect the client's right to control access to personal information.

Both federal and state data privacy laws often apply when working with individuals who are thought to be addicted to drugs or alcohol. If the client agrees to the assessment, she or he is then willingly providing personal information during the assessment process. The client still retains permission to refuse to answer any question. If information is required from persons other than the client, *the professional should always obtain written permission* from the client authorizing the assessor to contact *specific* individuals in order to obtain information about the client's chemical use, or any other aspect of his or her life. This written permission is recorded on a *release-of-information authorization form*.

Occasionally, the client will refuse such permission. The client retains this right and can refuse to allow the assessor to speak with *any* other person. This refusal in itself might say a great deal about how open and honest the client has been with the assessor, especially if the evaluator has explained to the client exactly what information will be requested.

One possible solution, which some professionals advocate, is to have the client sit in on the collateral interview. One drawback to this solution is that the client's presence might inhibit the collateral information source from freely discussing his or her perception of the client. If this were to happen, a potentially valuable source of information about the client would be unavailable to the assessor. Thus it is rarely productive to have the client, or the client's representative, sit in on collateral interviews.

When the client is being referred for an evaluation by the court system, the court will often provide referral information about the client's previous legal history. The courts will often also include a detailed social history of the client, which was part of the presentence investigation. If asked, the evaluator should acknowledge having read this information, but should not discuss the contents of the referral information provided by the courts. Such discussions are to be avoided for two reasons.

First, the purpose of the clinical interview is to assess the client's *chemical use patterns*. A discussion of what information was provided by the court does nothing to further this evaluation. Second, the client, or his or her attorney, has access to this information through established channels. Thus, if the client wishes to review the information provided by the court, she or he may do so at another time through established legal channels.

Clients will occasionally ask to see the records provided by the court during the clinical interview. Frequently, these clients are checking to see what information has been provided by the courts in order to decide how much and what they should admit to during the interview period. This often reflects the philosophy of "let me know how much *you* know about me, so that I will know how 'honest' I should be."

The solution to this dilemma is the simple statement that the client may obtain a copy of the court record through the established legal channels. Those persistent clients who demand to see their court records on the grounds that "it is about me, anyway" are to be reminded that the purpose of this interview is to explore the client's drug- and alcohol-use patterns, not to review court records. However, under no circumstances should the chemical dependency/mental health professional let the client read his or her referral records. To do so would be a violation of the data privacy laws, since the referral information was released to the professional, *not* to the client.

When the final evaluation is written, the evaluator should identify the source of the information summarized in the final assessment. Collateral information sources should be advised that the client, or his or her attorney, has a right to request a copy of the final report before the interview. It is *extremely* rare for a client to request a copy of the final report, although technically the client does have the right to do so after the proper release-of-information authorization forms have been signed.

DIAGNOSTIC RULES

Two diagnostic rules should be followed as closely as possible in the evaluation and diagnosis of chemical dependency. Occasionally, it is not possible to adhere to each of these diagnostic rules; however, one should always attempt to carefully evaluate each case in light of these guidelines, even in special cases. Then, even if the rule is not followed, the professional making the diagnosis should identify why one guideline or another could not be met in a given situation to avoid missing important information.

Rule Number One: Gather Collateral Information

The nature of chemical dependency is deception. Because of this fact, and the importance of the diagnostic process, the individual attempting to make a diagnosis of addiction should *use as many sources of information as possible.* To illustrate the importance of collateral information, every chemical dependency professional has encountered cases where the individual being evaluated has claimed to drink "once a week . . . no more than a couple of beers after work." The spouse of the person being evaluated often reports, however, that the client was intoxicated "five to seven nights a week."

To minimize the danger of deception and to develop as comprehensive a history of the individual as possible, the chemical dependency professional should use as many different sources of information as possible. Slaby, Lieb, and Tancredi (1981) recommend that such collateral information sources include:

a. patient's families
b. friends of the patient
c. employer or coworkers
d. clergy members
e. local law enforcement authorities
f. primary care physician
g. psychotherapist (if any)

Obviously, the time restrictions imposed on the assessment process might prevent the use of some of these collateral resources. If the assessment must be completed by the end of the week, and the professional is unable to contact the client's mother, it may be necessary to write the final report without benefit of her input. In addition, the other people involved may simply refuse to provide any information whatsoever. It is the assessor's responsibility, however, to *attempt* to contact as many of these individuals as possible and include their views in the final evaluation report.

Rule Number Two: *Always* Assume Deception, Until Proven Otherwise

As noted earlier, the nature of addiction is deception. Alcoholics will frequently minimize the amount of alcohol they drink, while opiate addicts will exaggerate the amount of drugs that they use. Cocaine addicts may also exaggerate their drug use, although this is not consistent. Some cocaine addicts, rather than exaggerate their drug-use report, may initially deny or minimize their use of the drug.

When evaluating a person's drug use, one should always expect deception unless proven otherwise. On more than one occasion, professionals have encountered a person who claimed to be using a given amount of heroin or cocaine, only to later find out from friends of the client that the person has *never* used opiates or cocaine but is just attempting to impress the evaluator, the courts, or drug-using "friends."

Alcoholics have been known to admit to drinking "once or twice a week," until reminded that their medical problems were unlikely to have been caused by such moderate drinking levels. At this point, these individuals have sometimes admitted to more frequent drinking episodes. However, even when confronted with such evidence of serious, continual alcohol use, many alcoholics have been known to deny the reality of their alcoholism.

Clients have been known to admit to "one" arrest for driving under the influence of alcohol or possession of a controlled substance. Records provided by the court at the time of admission into treatment have often revealed in such cases that the person in question had been arrested in two or three different states for similar charges. When confronted, these clients might respond that they thought that the evaluator "only meant in *this* state!", or that "since that happened outside of this state, it doesn't apply." Thus to avoid the danger of deception the assessor *must use as many different sources of information as possible.*

THE EVALUATION FORMAT

Although ultimately each individual is unique, there is a general assessment format that may be used when confronted by either known or suspected chemical addiction. This assessment format is modified as necessary to account for the differences between individuals, and it provides a useful framework within which to evaluate the individual and his or her chemical-use pattern. This format will be used for this chapter.

Area One: Circumstances of Referral

The first step in the diagnostic process is to examine the circumstances under which the individual is seen. The case of a patient who is seen in a hospital alcohol detoxification (or "detox") unit for the first time is far different from the patient who has been in the detox unit ten times in the last three years. Thus, the first piece of data for the chemical dependency assessment is a review of the circumstances surrounding the individual's referral.

The manner in which the client responds to the question "what brings you here today?" can provide valuable information about how willing a participant the individual will be in the evaluation process. If the individual responds with words like "I don't know, they told me to come here. . . ." or "You should know, you've read the report. . . ." obviously is less than cooperative. The rare client who responds "I think I have a drug problem. . . ." is demonstrating some degree of cooperativeness with the assessor. In each case, the manner in which the client identifies the circumstances surrounding his or her referral for evaluation provides a valuable piece of information to the assessor.

Area Two: Drug and Alcohol Use Patterns

The next step is for the evaluator to explore the individual's drug- and alcohol-use patterns, *both past and present*. All too often, clients will claim to drink "only once a week," or to have had "nothing to drink in the last six months." Treatment center staff are not surprised to find that this drinking pattern has been the rule *only* since the person's last arrest for an alcohol-related offense.

From time to time, one will encounter a person who has proudly claimed not to have had a drink, or to have used chemicals, in perhaps the last 6–12 months, or even longer. This person may forget to report the fact that they were locked up in the county jail awaiting trial during that time, or were under strict supervision after being released from jail on bail, and had little or no access to chemicals. This is a far different situation from the client who reports that she or he has not had a drink or used chemicals in the last year, is not on probation or parole, and has no charges pending.

Thus, the evaluator should explore the client's living situation to determine if there were any environmental restrictions on the individual's drug use. Obviously, a person who is incarcerated, in treatment, or whose probation officer requires frequent, unannounced, supervised urine screens to detect drug or alcohol use, has an environmental restriction imposed on him or her. In such a case, a report of having "not used drugs in six months" may be the literal truth, but fall far short of the facts.

The individual's chemical-use pattern and *beliefs about his or her drug use* should then be compared with the circumstances surrounding referral: for example, there is the person who states the belief that she or he does not have a problem with chemicals. Earlier in the interview, she or he may have admitted to a recent arrest on the charge of possession of a controlled substance for the second time in four years. In this situation, the client has provided two important but quite discrepant pieces of information to the evaluator.

Several important areas should be explored at this point in the evaluation process. The evaluator needs to consider whether the client has ever been in a treatment program for chemical dependency, and whether the individual's drug or alcohol use has ever resulted in legal, family, financial, social, or medical problems. The assessor also needs to consider whether the client ever demonstrated any signs of either psychological dependency or physical addiction to drugs or alcohol.

To understand this point, one need only contrast the cases of two clients who were seen following their recent arrests for driving a motor vehicle while under the influence of chemicals. The first person claimed (and the collateral information agreed) that he only drank in moderation once every few weeks. Furthermore the background check conducted by the courts revealed that this client had no previous legal problems. After receiving a long awaited promotion, the client celebrated with some friends. The client was a rare drinker who had drunk heavily with friends to celebrate the promotion, and subsequently misjudged the amount of alcohol that had been consumed.

In contrast to this is the second client seen following his arrest for driving a motor vehicle under the influence of chemicals. This individual's collateral information sources seemed to suggest a more extensive chemical-use pattern to the evaluator than the individual admitted to during the interview (the interview process will be discussed in more detail). A background check that was conducted by the police at the time of the individual's arrest revealed several prior arrests for the same offense.

In the first case, one might argue that the client simply made a mistake. Admittedly, the person in question was driving under the influence of alcohol. However, in this case, he had *never* done so in the past, and does not fit the criteria necessary for a diagnosis of even heavy social drinking. The report to the court should outline the sources of data examined, and in this case provide a firm foundation for the conclusion that this individual made a mistake in driving after drinking.

In the second case, the individual's drunk driving arrest was the tip of a larger problem, which was outlined in the report to the court. The assessor detailed the sources of information that supported this conclusion, including information provided by family members, friends, the individual's physician, the individual himself, and the county sheriff's department. The final report concluded that the client had a significant addiction problem that required treatment in a formal chemical dependency treatment program.

Area Three: Legal History

Part of the assessment process should include an examination of the client's legal history. This information might be based on the individual's self-report, or on a review of the client's police record as provided by the court, the probation/parole officer, or other source. *It is important to identify the source of the information on which the report is based.* It is important to identify:

a. what charges have been brought against the client in the past by the local authorities, and their disposition;
b. what charges have been brought against the client in the past, by authorities in other localities, and their disposition; and
c. the nature of current charges (if any) against the individual.

There are many cases on record where the individual was finally convicted of a misdemeanor charge for possession of less than an ounce of marijuana. All too often, however, a review of the client's police record reveals that the individual was *arrested* for a felony drug-possession charge, and that the charges were reduced through plea bargaining agreements. In some states, it is possible for an arrest for the charge of driving a motor vehicle under the influence of alcohol (a felony in many states) to be reduced to a misdemeanor charge, such as public intoxication, by plea bargaining agreements.

The assessor needs to determine both the initial charge and the ultimate disposition of these charges. The assessor should specifically inquire as to whether the client has had charges brought against him or her in other states, or by federal authorities. Individuals may admit to *one* charge for possession of a controlled substance, only for the staff to later discover that this same client has had several arrests and convictions for the same charge in other states. Or the client may admit to having been *arrested* for possession charges in other states, but not mention that he or she had left the state before the charges were brought to trial.

Since the client was never *convicted* of the charges, she or he will not have to mention them during the assessment, or so the client might rationalize in such a case. The fact that the charges were never proven in court because he or she was a fugitive from justice (as well as the fact that interstate flight to avoid prosecution is a possible federal offense) may well be overlooked by the client.

Past military record. One important, and often overlooked, source of information is the client's *military history,* if any. Many clients with military history will report only on their civilian legal history, unless specifically asked about their military legal record. Clients who may have denied any drug or alcohol legal charges whatsoever may, upon inquiry, admit to having been reprimanded or brought before a superior officer on charges because of chemical use while in the military.

The assessor must specifically ask whether the individual has ever been in the service. If the client denies military service, it might be useful to ask *why* the client has never been in the service. Often this question will elicit a response to the effect that "I had a felony arrest record. . . .", or "I had a DWI [driving while under the influence of alcohol] on my record. . . .", which is valuable information to the assessor and opens new areas for investigation.

If the client has been in the military, was the client's discharge status "Honorable," a "General" discharge under honorable conditions, a "General" discharge under dishonorable conditions, or a "Dishonorable" discharge? Was the client ever brought up on charges while in the service? If so, what was the disposition of these charges? Was the client ever referred for drug treatment while in the service? Was the client ever denied a transfer or promotion because of drug or alcohol use? Finally, was the client ever transferred because of his or her drug or alcohol use?

The client's legal history should be verified, if possible, by contacting the court or probation/parole officer, especially if the client was referred for evaluation for an alcohol or drug-related offense. The legal history will often provide significant information about the client's life-style, and the extent to which his or her drug use has resulted in conflict with social rules and expectations.

Area Four: Educational/Vocational History

The next step in the assessment process is to determine the individual's educational and vocational history. This information, which might be based on the individual's self-report, school, records, or employment records, provides information on the client's level of function, and on whether chemical use has interfered with his or her education or vocation. As before, the evaluator should identify the source of this information.

For example, the client who says that she dropped out of school in the tenth grade "because I was into drugs" presents a different picture than does the client who completed a Bachelor of Science degree from a well known university. The individual who has had five jobs in the last two years might present a far different picture than the individual who has held a series of responsible positions, with regular promotions, with the same company for the last ten years. Thus, the assessor should attempt to determine the client's educational/vocational history, to determine the individual's educational level, potential, and the degree to which chemical use has started to interfere with his or her education or career.

Area Five: Developmental/Family History

The assessor can often uncover significant material through an examination of the client's developmental and family history. The client might reveal that his or her father was "a problem drinker" in response to the question "were either of your parents chemically dependent?", but hesitate to call that parent an alcoholic. How the client describes parental or sibling chemical use might reveal how the client thinks about his or her own chemical use.

For example, the client who says that his mother "had a problem with alcohol" might be far different from the client who says "My mother was an alcoholic." The client who hesitates to call a sibling alcoholic, but is comfortable with the term "a problem drinker" might be hinting that she is also uncomfortable with the term "alcoholic" as it applies to herself. But, she may also have accepted the rationalization that she was "a problem drinker," just like her brother or sister.

Information about either parental or sibling chemical use is important for another reason. As will be recalled from the chapter on alcohol, there is significant evidence suggesting a genetic predisposition toward alcoholism. By extension, one might expect future research to uncover a genetic link toward the other forms of drug addiction as well.

In addition to this, the reviewer will be able to explore the client's attitudes about parental alcohol/drug use in the home while he or she was growing up. Did the client view this chemical use as normal? Was the client angry or ashamed about his or her parents' chemical use? Does the client view chemical use as being a problem for the family?

It is important for the assessor to examine the possibility of either parental or sibling chemical use while the client was growing up or at the present time. Such information will offer insights into the client's possible genetic inheritance; whether she or he might be "at risk" to develop an addiction. Furthermore, an overview of the family environment provides clues about how the client views drug or alcohol use.

Family environments differ. The client whose parents were rare social drinkers would have been raised in a far different environment than the client whose parents were drug addicts. A client who reports that he never knew his mother because she was a heroin addict who put the children up for adoption when they were young might view drugs far differently than clients who report that they were raised to believe that hard work would see a person through troubled times, and whose parents never even drank.

Area Six: Psychiatric History

As was discussed in Chapter 1 of this book, chemical use will often result in either outpatient or inpatient psychiatric treatment. A natural part of the assessment process should be to discuss with the client whether she or he has ever been treated for psychiatric problems on either an inpatient or an outpatient basis. For example, clients have been known to admit to having been hospitalized for observation because they were hallucinating, had attempted suicide, were violent, or were depressed.

Upon admission to chemical dependency treatment, perhaps months or years later, clients reveal that they were using drugs at the time. Often, when asked, clients reveal that they failed to mention to the staff of the psychiatric hospital that they were using drugs. It might be that the client lied to the hospital staff, or the psychiatric admissions staff may simply not have asked the appropriate questions.

The assessor should always ask whether the client

a. has *ever* been hospitalized for psychiatric treatment,
b. has ever had outpatient psychiatric treatment, or
c. had revealed to the mental health professional the truth about his or her drug use.

If possible, the assessor should obtain a release-of-information form from the client and send for the discharge summary from the treatment center where the client was hospitalized. The possibility that drugs contributed to the psychiatric hospitalization or outpatient treatment should either be confirmed or ruled out if possible. This information will allow the assessor to determine if the client's drug use has—or has not—resulted in psychiatric problems serious enough to require professional help.

As noted in the chapter on the CNS stimulants, it is not uncommon for chronic use of amphetamines or cocaine to cause a drug-induced psychosis that is, at least in its early stages, very similar to paranoid schizophrenia. A client who reports having spent a short time in a psychiatric hospital for a "brief psychosis" may well have developed such a drug-related problem, even if it was not recognized as such by the hospital staff.

Area Seven: Medical History

Clients who are chemically dependent will often present a history of numerous hospitalizations for the treatment of accidents or injuries. These periods of hospitalization might be for drug-related injuries, such as one client who reported having been hospitalized many times after rival drug dealers had tried to kill him. He had accumulated an impressive assortment of knife wounds, gunshot wounds, and fractured bones from these "business transactions" that had "gone bad" over the years.

However, he had never been hospitalized for a drug overdose. An assessor who asks the question "Have you ever been hospitalized because of a drug overdose?" will miss out on the details of these hospitalizations, since the client viewed them as "business transactions," not a result of personal drug use. On a similar note, alcoholics who drive while under the influence of alcohol are often hospitalized following "accidents," which may or may not be alcohol-related.

The assessor should inquire about periods of hospitalization *for any reason*. Then the assessor should explore whether these were drug-related. A client who was hospitalized following an automobile accident may contract Hepatitis B (a viral liver infection that is transmitted through the blood) following a blood transfusion. If that accident was caused by the person's drinking, then indirectly this client may be said to have contracted Hepatitis B as a result of their drinking.

The client who admits to the use of intravenous drugs may be hospitalized for the treatment of an infection of the heart valves, known as endocarditis, and may have shared needles with other addicts. Or, he may have developed the infection only after being malnourished following a protracted period of drug use. It is up to the assessor to determine, if possible, whether chemical use was a causal agent in the client's hospitalization at any point. Such information will often help the assessor gain a better understanding of the client's chemical use and the consequences the client has had to face as a result of his or her chemical use.

Area Eight: Previous Treatment History

In working with a person who may be addicted to chemicals, it is helpful for the evaluator to determine whether the client has ever been in a treatment program for chemical dependency. This information, which may be based on the client's self-report, or on information provided by the court system, sheds light on the client's past and on the client's potential to benefit from treatment.

The person who has been hospitalized three times for a heart condition, who continues to deny having any heart problems, is denying the reality of his or her condition. The same is true for the client who says that she does not think she has a problem with chemicals, but who has been in drug treatment three times. She has not accepted the reality of her drug problem. The problem then becomes one of making a recommendation for the client in light of his or her previous treatment history and current status.

The assessor should pay attention to the discharge status from previous treatment programs and to the period of time after treatment the person maintained sobriety. Clients often claim to have been sober for three months, but upon close questioning may admit that they were in treatment for those three months, and that they started to use drugs shortly after they were discharged, if not before. Unfortunately, the situation of a client who reports using chemicals on the way home following treatment is well known to chemical dependency treatment professionals.

Clients who admit using chemicals throughout their treatment provide valuable information about their possible attitudes toward *this* treatment exposure, as well. Those clients would have prognoses different from clients who had maintained total sobriety for three years following their last treatment exposure, and then relapsed.

The evaluator should pay attention to the individual's past treatment history, the discharge status from these treatment programs, and to the total period of time that the individual was sober *after* finishing treatment. Specific questions should be asked about *when they entered treatment, how long they were there*, and *when they started to use chemicals following treatment*.

THE CLINICAL INTERVIEW

The clinical interview forms the cornerstone of the chemical dependency assessment. Client information should be an important source of data on the client's previous chemical use. But the client will either consciously or unconsciously distort the information that she or he provides. Thus, as noted above, other sources of data should be used to evaluate a person suspected of being addicted to chemicals.

The first part of the interview process is an introduction by the assessor. It is explained that the assessor will be asking questions about the client's possible chemical use patterns, and that *specific* responses are most helpful. It is explained that many of these questions may have been asked by others in the past, but that this information is important. The client is asked if she or he has any questions, after which the interview will begin.

The assessor should attempt to review the diagnostic criteria for chemical dependency outlined by the American Psychiatric Association's *Diagnostic and Statistical Manual of Mental Disorders* (3rd edition-revised), which is also known as the *DSM-III-R*. This manual provides a framework within which the diagnosis of chemical dependency might be made.

Many of the questions asked in the clinical interview are designed to explore the same piece of information from different perspectives: for example, at one point in the interview process the client might be asked "In the *average* week, how many nights would you say that you use drugs or alcohol?" At a later point in the interview, this same client might be asked "How much would you say, on the average, that you spend on drugs or alcohol in a week?"

The purpose of this redundancy is not to "trap" the client, but to provide different perspectives on the client's chemical-use pattern. The client who claims to use alcohol one or two nights a week might admit to spending fifty dollars a week on chemicals. The evaluator might then inquire how it is that the client said that they only drink once or twice weekly, but that this cost them fifty dollars a week. The client might then report that she or he drinks at a bar, and often buys drinks for friends. This information reveals more about the client's chemical-use pattern, helping the evaluator better understand the client.

OTHER SOURCES OF DATA: MEDICAL INFORMATION

The importance of information provided by medical professionals was discussed in the section on collateral information. However, medical tests and medical personnel can often shed further light on the client's chemical-use pattern at the time of the evaluation by either confirming or failing to confirm the client's claims to be using certain drugs.

Clients have been known to claim to be using a certain amount of heroin on a daily basis, while the physician working with the case discloses that the client's blood or urine tests failed to reveal *any* trace of narcotics whatsoever. (In more than one case, when confronted, the client admitted to having said this in the hopes of being put on methadone for a few days' "withdrawal.") The reverse is also true: clients have been known to deny the use of certain drugs, such as marijuana, only to have a supervised urine toxicology test detect marijuana in their urine.

Medical tests can often

    a. confirm the presence of certain chemicals in the client's blood or urine samples,

b. identify the *amount* of certain chemicals present in a person's blood sample, and

c. determine whether the drug levels in the blood or urine sample have increased (suggesting further drug use), remained the same (which also might suggest further drug use), or declined (suggesting no further drug use since the last test).

It is not uncommon for a client who was involved in an automobile accident to claim to have "only had two beers." A laboratory test conducted within an hour of the accident may reveal, however, that the client's blood alcohol level was far higher than what would be achieved from only two beers. This information would suggest some distortion on the client's part.

Clients who test negative for marijuana on one occasion may very well test positive for this same chemical only a few days later. Subsequent inquiry will often reveal that they used drugs sometime after the first test, thinking that they were "safe," and would not be tested for drugs again for a long time. Such drug use would be detected by *frequent* and *unannounced* urine tests, which are *closely supervised* to detect illicit drug use. Thus, medical test data is often a valuable source of objective information about a client's drug use.

A client's drowsiness may simply be a result of lack of sleep, or it may be due to recent drug or alcohol use. The laboratory test data often are valuable in making this determination or in the detection of continued drug use while the client is in treatment. The assessor should always attempt to use medical test information where possible to further establish a foundation for the diagnosis of chemical dependency.

PSYCHOLOGICAL TEST DATA

There are a number of psychological tests that may, either directly or indirectly, be of use in the diagnosis of chemical dependency. Many of the assessment tools available today are paper-and-pencil tests. These instruments are either filled out by the client (and as such are known as self-report instruments) or by the assessor as she or he asks questions of the person being evaluated. Self-report instruments are inexpensive and are usually inoffensive to the client (Stuart, 1980).

One of the most popular assessment instruments is the Michigan Alcoholism Screening Test (MAST). This test is composed of 24 questions that may be answered "yes" or "no," depending on whether the item applies to the respondent. Test items are weighted with a value of one, two, or in some cases, five points. A score of five points or more suggests alcoholism. The effectiveness of this test has been demonstrated in clinical literature (Miller, 1976), but this test addresses *only* alcoholism (Lewis, Dana, and Blevins, 1988) and thus is of limited value in cases where the person uses other chemicals.

There are other assessment tools available. In their recent work on the assessment of marijuana users, Roffman and George (1988) provided examples of a self-report instrument used in the evaluation of marijuana-use patterns. Washton, Stone, and Hendrickson (1988) discussed the use of a "Cocaine Abuse Assessment Profile" in their essay on the evaluation of cocaine users. These tests, while useful, are also of limited value in the assessment of polydrug users.

The MacAndrew Alcoholism Scale (also known as the "Mac" Scale) of the Minnesota Multiphasic Personality Inventory (MMPI) initially demonstrated some promise in the identification of alcoholics in psychiatric settings. Subsequent research has suggested that this scale might measure a general tendency toward addiction, rather than the specific behavior of alcoholism (Greene, 1980). Further, Otto, Lang, Megargee, and Rosenblatt (1989) have discovered that alcoholics may be able to "conceal their drinking problems even when the relatively subtle special alcohol scales of the MMPI are applied" (p. 7).

Unlike many of the other assessment tools, the MMPI offers the additional advantage of having three built-in "truth" scales. These scales offer insight into how truthful the individual taking the test may have been and are discussed in more detail by Greene (1980). A major disadvantage of the MMPI is that it is possible for the individual taking the test to "intentionally diminish . . . the level of pathology evident in overall MMPI profiles" (Otto, et al., 1989, p. 7). Furthermore, in spite of the "truth" scales built into the MMPI, individuals who are attempting to present themselves as being well adjusted may still accomplish their goal and reduce measured levels of distress.

A major disadvantage of paper-and-pencil tests is that they are best suited to situations where the client is unlikely to fake (the technical term is *positively dissimulate*) answers on the test in order to appear less disturbed (Anastasi, 1968). A common problem, well known to chemical dependency professionals, is that these instruments are subject to the same problems of denial, distortion, and outright misrepresentation often encountered in the clinical interview setting.

Clients have been known to initially deny the use of a chemical, say marijuana, only to subsequently test positive for THC on a urine toxicology test conducted at the time of admission. Clients have also been known to either overestimate the amount or frequency of their drug use, or to underestimate the amount or frequency of drug use. Such distortion might be unintentional, as in a case where the person simply forgets an episode of chemical use, or it might be quite intentional.

Roffman and George (1988) pointed out that another source of distortion in self-report inventories is that the client often does not know how potent the drug or drugs were. How did the drug or drugs interfere with the individual's ability to evaluate the drug's effects? A client might honestly believe that she or he was only mildly intoxicated, where an outside observer might express the belief that the client was quite intoxicated indeed.

One technique that may be useful in the detection of intentional dis-simulation is to review the test results with the client while the client's spouse or significant other is present. The assessor reviews the test item-by-item, stating the client's response. Often, the spouse or significant other will contradict the client's response to one or more test items, provid-ing valuable new data for the assessment process.

For example, on the MAST, clients often answer "no" to the question "Have you ever been involved in an alcohol-related accident." The client's wife, if present, may speak up at this point, mentioning "that time when you drove off the road into the ditch a couple of years ago." When the client points out that the police had ruled the cause of the accident as being ice on the road, the wife may respond "but you told me that you had been drinking earlier that night."

Another technique frequently used by this author is to administer the same test, or ask the same questions, twice during the assessment process: for example, the MAST may be administered during the initial interview and again at the follow-up interview a week or so later. Significant dis-crepancies are explored with the client in order to determine why there are so many differences between the two sets of test data.

Clients have been known to score 13 points on the initial administra-tion of the MAST, a score well above the cut-off score necessary to suggest alcoholism. At follow-up, a week later, the same client may score only 9 points on the same test, a score that, while lower, is still above the cut-off score necessary to suggest alcoholism. The difference between test scores would suggest some degree of deception on the client's part. When the test is later reviewed with the client's wife present, several other items may be found to apply to the client, suggesting a final score of perhaps 24 points.

Psychological test data can often provide valuable insights into the client's personality pattern, and his or her chemical use. Many such tests require a trained professional to administer and interpret. When used properly, however, psychological test data can add an important dimen-sion to the diagnostic process.

OUTCOME OF THE ASSESSMENT PROCESS

At the end of the assessment, the chemical dependency professional should be in a position to determine whether, in his or her opinion, the client is (a) addicted to one or more chemicals, (b) a serious abuser of one or more chemicals, or (c) does not seem to have a problem with chemicals. Based on this assessment, the professional should then be able to decide whether treatment is necessary and make some recommendations about the disposition of the client's case (see Figure 17-2).

Obviously, if the client is found to be addicted to one or more chemi-cals, a recommendation that she or he enter treatment would be appropri-ate. Such a recommendation would be for inpatient or outpatient treat-

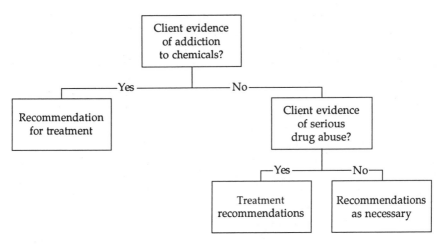

FIGURE 17-2. Flowchart of the assessment process.

ment, depending on the client's needs. If the client is found to be only an abuser of chemicals, the decision must be made whether to recommend chemical dependency treatment. Other recommendations might include participation in self-help groups such as Alcoholics Anonymous or Narcotics Anonymous, a referral to a mental health center for evaluation and treatment, and so on.

It is possible that the client will not be found to present a drug abuse/addiction problem, but still be in need of professional support. A referral for marital counseling might be made if there is evidence of a marital problem in a client who does not seem to be addicted to chemicals. The assessor may still make an appropriate referral, even if she or he has not found evidence of addiction.

SUMMARY

The assessment process should include information from a number of sources in order to provide the most comprehensive picture of the client's chemical-use pattern. Information from the client is collected during one or more clinical interviews, through which the assessor attempts to obtain accurate data on the individual's chemical use. Information should also be obtained from collateral sources whenever possible. Collateral information may be more revealing than that obtained from the client.

Information from medical personnel who would be in a position to evaluate the client's physical status can often prove valuable in understanding a client and the role that drugs have had in his or her life. Finally, psychological test data may reveal much about the client's personality profile and drug-use pattern. However, psychological test data is easily manipulated by a client who wishes to dissimulate.

The outcome of the assessment process should be a formal report in which the evidence supporting the conclusion that the client is or is not chemically dependent is outlined. Recommendations for further treatment may be made at this time, even if the client is found not to be addicted to chemicals.

CHAPTER 18

The Process of Intervention

Vernon Johnson (1980) noted that the alcholic, like all addicts, is "not in touch with reality" (p. 49). Alcholics are, however, "capable of accepting some useful portion of reality, *if that reality is presented in forms they can receive*" (p. 49, italics in original). The first step in treatment is the attempt to break through the individuals' system of denial, to get them to recognize and accept the fact that they are in need of help. This is done through the process known as *intervention.*

It is not easy to obtain a commitment from an addict to enter, *and remain in,* a treatment program. More than one addicted person has entered treatment and left shortly afterward, having satisfied the stipulation of parents, judges, or family that they "enter a treatment program." "After all," many seem to reason, "nobody said anything about my *staying* there, did they?"

Addicts will often openly admit "I am addicted to chemicals" not because of a desire to achieve or maintain sobriety, but because this admission offers an excuse to *continue* to use chemicals. Addicts enter into a circular pattern of logic, an elaborate rationalization by which the word "addicted" comes to mean "hopelessly addicted." Since they are "hopelessly addicted," at least in their own mind's eye, they give themselves permission to go on using chemicals.

This is a bizarre justification for chemical use that overlooks the fact that addiction is a treatable disease. The first part of the "treatment" is convincing the addicted person that she or he is indeed addicted, and that she or he needs help for the drug dependency that has come to dominate his or her life. This awareness, and the commitment to enter into treatment, is often achieved through the intervention process.

A DEFINITION OF INTERVENTION

It was once thought that for addicts to accept the need for help, they had to "hit bottom," to reach the point where they had to admit utter and total defeat. Vernon Johnson (1980, 1986), a pioneer in the intervention process, noted that it is *not* necessary for the addict to hit bottom. Rather, it was Johnson's hypothesis that addicts could learn to accept the reality of their addiction if this information was presented in language that they could understand.

Because of the physical and emotional damage that uncontrolled addiction could cause, Johnson advocated *early intervention* in cases of drug addiction. He identified intervention as being a

> . . . process by which the harmful, progressive and destructive effects of chemical dependency are interrupted and the chemically dependent person is helped to stop using mood-altering chemicals, and to develop new, healthier ways of coping with his or her needs and problems (p. 61).

Twerski (1983), who also advocated early intervention in cases of drug addiction, defined intervention as being

> . . . a collective, guided effort by the significant persons in the patient's environment to precipitate a crisis through confrontation, and thereby to remove the patient's defensive obstructions to recovery . . . (p. 1028)

Rothenberg (1988), who explored the legal ramifications of intervention, noted that the intervention process for alcoholism consisted of "talking to the alcoholic, confronting his or her denials, and breaking down defenses so as to secure agreement to seek treatment" (p. 22).

In this chapter, *intervention* shall be defined as an effort on the part of significant others in the addict's environment to break through the wall of denial, rationalization, and projection by which the addict seeks to protect his or her addiction. The purpose of this collective effort, which is usually supervised by a chemical dependency professional, is to secure an agreement to *immediately* seek treatment.

CHARACTERISTICS OF THE INTERVENTION PROCESS

There is no malice in the intervention process. This is not a session to allow people to vent pent-up frustration. The intervention process is seen as a "profound act of caring" (Johnson, 1986, p. 65) through which significant others in the addict's social circle break the rule of silence surrounding the addiction. Each person confronts the addict with specific evidence that she or he has lost control of his or her drug use, in language that the addict can understand.

The participants also express desire for the addict to seek professional help for his or her drug problem (Williams, 1989). In the process, each member affirms their concern for the addict, but will offer hard data showing how the addicted person is no longer in control of his or her life, in the hope of breaking through the addict's system of denial. The goal is that the addict might accept the need for help with their drug problem. This is the central theme around which an intervention session is planned.

Johnson (1986) noted that effective intervention sessions are *planned in advance.* In addition to this, intervention sessions are repeatedly *rehearsed* by the individual participants to ensure that the information presented is appropriate for an intervention session. Williams (1989) agreed that there is a need for a rehearsal session or sessions in the intervention process, and warned that participants should be informed that the goal of intervention

> . . . is not . . . that persons "admit" to being addicted, or that they have behaved in a manner that has caused others pain, or that they were wrong, or even that they were under the influence of a drug (including, of course, alcohol) in any given situation. Diagnosing chemical dependency is not part of an intervention. The goal is to elicit an agreement from the person to be evaluated for possible chemical dependency and to follow the resulting recommendations (p. 99).

THE MECHANICS OF INTERVENTION

The intervention process is, as previously noted, *planned* and should be rehearsed beforehand by the participants. The intervention process should involve *every* person in the addict's life who might possibly have something to add, including the addict's spouse, siblings, children, possibly friends, supervisor/employer, minister, co-workers, or others. Johnson (1986) suggested that the supervisor be included because the addict often will use his or her own perception of job performance as an excuse not to listen to the others in the intervention process. Each individual is advised to bring forward *specific incidents* where the addict's behavior, especially the chemical use, interfered with their lives in some manner.

Individually confronting an addicted person is difficult at best, and in most cases is an exercise in futility (Johnson, 1986). The addict will deny, rationalize, threaten, or simply try to avoid any confrontation that threatens his or her addiction. If the spouse, individually, questions whether the alcoholic was physically able to drive the car home last night, he or she might meet with the response "No, but Joe drove the car home for me, then walked home after he parked the car in the driveway."

However, if Joe is *also* present, he might then confront the alcoholic with the fact that he did *not* drive the car home last night, or any other night for that matter! The spouse is often surprised to hear this, as the excuse "Joe drove me home last night" might have been a common one. But quite likely nobody ever asked Joe whether he drove the family car home last night.

Before everybody was brought together for an intervention session, it was likely that nobody checked out the isolated lies, rationalizations, or episodes of denial. The addict's denial, projection, and rationalization will often crumble when confronted with all of the significant people in his or her environment. This is why a collective intervention session is most powerful in working with the addict.

Twerski (1983) observed that it is common for the person for whom the intervention session was called to make promises to change his or her behavior. Although these promises might be made in good faith, or might be made simply as a means of avoiding further confrontation, the fact remains that since the disease of addiction

> . . . responds to treatment and not to manipulation, it is unlikely that any of these promises will work, and the counselor must recommend treatment as the optimum course (Twerski, 1983, p. 1029).

Each participant in the intervention sessions should be prepared to detach from the addict if the addict refuses to acknowledge his or her addiction or refuses to enter treatment. This is *not* an attempt to manipulate the addict through empty threats. Rather, each person should be willing to follow through with a specific action to detach from the addict, should she or he refuse to enter treatment.

If the employer or supervisor has decided that the company can no longer tolerate the addict's behavior, she or he needs to clearly state that the addict's position will be terminated if he or she does not seek treatment. Then, if the addict refuses treatment, the employer/supervisor should follow through with this action.

Family members should also have thought about and discussed possible options through which they might begin to detach from the addict. This should be done prior to the start of the intervention session, and if the addicted person should refuse treatment (possibly by leaving the session before it ends) family members should follow through with their alternative plan. The options should be discussed with the other participants of the intervention process, and during the rehearsal each participant should practice telling the addicted person what that participant will do if the addict does not accept treatment.

There is, again, no malice in this. The participants are not engaging in threats to force the addicted person into treatment. Rather, each participant is exercising his or her right to choose how she or he will respond should the addict choose not to accept treatment. The addicted person is still able to exercise his or her freedom of choice, by either accepting the need for treatment or not. But now she or he will have a clear understanding of the consequences of not going into treatment.

FAMILY INTERVENTION

Family intervention is a specialized intervention process by which *every* concerned family member will, under the supervision of a trained professional, gather together and plan on a joint confrontation of the individual. The family intervention session, like all other forms of intervention, is carried out in order to break through the addict's denial and obtain a commitment from the addict to enter treatment. The focus is on the individual's drug-using behaviors and on the concern that the participants have for the addict.

Through this confontation, family members of the addicted person may begin to detach from the addict. For this reason, Meyer (1988) identified the intervention process as an "opportunity for healing" (p. 7). Twerski (1983) observed that the intervention session also allows family and significant others to deal with their feelings about the addict's chemical use, and their own mismanagement of the disease of addiction. The participants in the intervention session can express their love and concern for the addicted person, while at the same time rejecting the addict's drug-centered behaviors.

The family intervention process allows various members of the addict's social circle to come forward, compare notes, and express their concern for the individual's life-style. Sometimes, family members, friends, employers or anyone else involved in the intervention process will write down detailed lists of specific incidents. In order to avoid as much confusion as possible, information reviewed during the intervention session should be highly specific.

It is often helpful, during the stress of the moment, for the participants in the intervention process to have written notes. These notes should include information about the specific episodes of drug use, dates, and the addict's response to these episodes of drug use. Sometimes, family members will bring in a personal diary to use as a reference in the intervention session.

One advantage of this process is that it helps the participants focus on the specific information they wish to bring to the intervention session. During the rehearsal, the professional who coordinates the intervention session decides who will present his or her information and in what order. As much as possible, this planned sequence is followed during the intervention session itself. The participants do not threaten the addict. Rather, they present specific concerns and information that highlight the need for the addicted person to enter treatment. Johnson's (1980; 1986) work provides a good overview of the intervention process.

An Example of a Family Intervention Session

In one intervention session involving a patient by the name of "Jim," the parents, wife, two sisters, employer, and a chemical dependency counselor were present. During the early part of the session, Jim asserted that he never drank to the point of passing out. He also claimed that he always drank at home so that he wouldn't be out on the roads while intoxicated. For these reasons, he did not believe that his drinking was as bad as everybody said it was.

One of Jim's siblings, a sister by the name of "Sara," immediately pointed out how just three weeks ago Jim had run out of vodka early in the evening, after having four or five mixed drinks. Sara pointed out that Jim had driven to the liquor store to buy a new bottle or two.

Sara concluded that she was not calling Jim a liar, but that she *knew* he had driven a car after drinking on this occasion. She was concerned about the possibility that he would have an accident and still felt uncomfortable about this incident. She was afraid that he might do it again, and that the next time he might not be so lucky as to make it back home safely.

Jim's mother then spoke. She pointed out that she had found her son unconscious on the living room floor twice in the past month. She identified the exact dates that this had happened, and observed that she felt uncomfortable with his sleeping on the floor surrounded by empty beer bottles. So, Jim's mother picked up the empty bottles to keep them from being broken by accident and covered Jim with a blanket while he slept. But she also was concerned, and believed that her son was drinking more than he thought.

As Jim's mother finished, his other sister, "Gloria," began to present her information and concerns. She pointed out how she had to ask that Jim leave her house last week, which was news to the rest of the family. She took this step, she explained, because Jim was intoxicated, loud, and abusive toward his nephew. She pointed out that everybody who was present, including her son's friend, smelled the alcohol on Jim's breath, and was repulsed by his behavior. Gloria concluded by stating that Jim was no longer welcome in her home, unless he went through treatment.

At this point, the chemical dependency counselor spoke, pointing out to Jim that his behavior was not so very different from that of many thousands of other addicts. The counselor pointed out that this was about the point in the intervention session where the addict begins to make promises to cut back or totally eliminate the drug use, a prediction that caught Jim by surprise, because it was true. His protests and promises died in his throat, even before he opened his mouth.

Before he could think of something else to say, the counselor pointed out that Jim gave every sign of having a significant alcohol problem. The counselor listed the symptoms of alcohol addiction one by one, and pointed out how Jim's family had identified different symptoms of addiction in their presentations. "So now," the counselor concluded "we have reached a point where you must make a decision. Will you accept help for your alcohol problem?"

If Jim says "Yes," the family members will explain that they have contacted the admissions officer of two or three nearby treatment centers, which have agreed to hold a bed for him until after the intervention session. Jim will be given a choice of which treatment center to enter and will be told that travel arrangements have been taken care of. His luggage is packed in the car, waiting, and if he wishes, the family will escort him to treatment as a show of support.

If Jim says "No," the family members will confront him with the steps they are prepared to take to separate from his addiction. His sister may reinforce the injunction that Jim is no longer welcome in her home.

Jim may be told that, no matter what he may think, these steps are not being taken as punishment. Each person will inform him that, because of his drug addiction, they find it necessary to detach from Jim until such time as he chooses to get his life in order. Each person there will affirm his or her concern for Jim, but will also start the process of no longer protecting Jim from his addiction.

These decisions have all been made in advance of the intervention session. Which option the participants take rests, in large part, on Jim's response to the question: "Will you accept help for your alcohol problem?"

INTERVENTION AND OTHER FORMS OF CHEMICAL ADDICTION

Johnson (1986) addressed the issue of intervention when the person's drug of choice was not alcohol. The same techniques used in alcoholism also apply to cases where the individual's drug of choice is cocaine, benzodiazepines, marijuana, amphetamines, or virtually any other drug of abuse. Significant others will gather, discuss the problem, and review their data about the addict's behavior. Practice intervention sessions are held, and the problems are addressed during the practice sessions as they are uncovered.

Finally, when everything is ready, the formal intervention session is held with the addicted person. The addicted person might need to be tricked into attending the intervention session, but there is no malice in the attempt to help the addict see how serious his or her drug addiction has become. Rather, there is a calm, caring, review of the facts by person after person until the addict is unable to defend against the realization that she or he is addicted to chemicals and in need of professional help.

The goal of the intervention session is, again, to secure an agreement for the individual to immediately enter treatment. During the preintervention practice sessions, arrangements are made to find a time when the addicted person would be able to participate; for example, a family reunion.

Arrangements are made in advance for the individual's admission into treatment. This may be accomplished by a simple telephone call to the admissions officer of the treatment center. The caller may then explain the situation, and ask if they would be willing to accept the target person as a client. Usually, the treatment center staff will want to carry out their own chemical dependency evaluation to confirm that the person is an appropriate referral to treatment. But, most treatment centers should be more than willing to consider a referral from a family intervention project.

THE ETHICS OF INTERVENTION

As humane as the goal of intervention is, questions have been raised concerning the ethics of this practice. Rothenberg (1988), noted that there is some question as to whether it was necessary to validate the diagnosis of chemical dependency before an attempt at intervention is made. In other words, should there be an independent verification of the diagnosis of drug addiction before an attempt at intervention is carried out? If there is not, what are the legal sanctions that can be brought against a chemical dependency professional who, in good faith, supervised an attempt at intervention?

Furthermore, the question of whether chemical dependency professionals involved in an intervention project should tell the client that she or he was free to leave at any time has not been answered (Rothenberg, 1988). The possibility that current intervention methods were in violation of either state or federal law, in the sense that failing to inform the client that he or she is free to leave might be interpreted as a violation of the laws against kidnapping or unlawful detention, is also suggested.

Rothenberg's (1988) warning raises some interesting questions for the chemical dependency professional in both the moral and legal areas. In future years, the courts may rule that the professional is legally obligated to inform the client that she or he is free to leave the intervention session at any time. Furthermore, the courts may rule that the professional can make no move to hold the client either by physical force, or by threats, should he or she express a desire to leave.

On the other hand, the courts may rule that intervention is a legitimate treatment technique, when used by trained professionals. The legal precedent for this area has not yet been established. Obviously, legal counsel is necessary to guide the chemical dependency professional through this quagmire.

LEGAL INTERVENTION

Sometimes, the "intervention" comes in a much simpler form: through the courts. The individual may have been arrested for driving while under the influence of alcohol (DWI), for possession of chemicals, or for some other drug-related charge. The judge might offer an alternative to incarceration: *either* you successfully complete a drug treatment program, *or* you will be incarcerated.

The length of time the individual might spend in jail would depend on the nature of the charge brought against him or her. Either/or treatment situations are unique in that the individual is offered a choice. The addict might elect to spend time in jail in order to fulfill his or her obligation to the courts. This is a matter of choice. However, the individual might also elect to accept the treatment option. In so doing, she or he is not *ordered* into treatment. Rather, the individual has made a choice to enter treatment. The addict always has the choice of incarceration, if he or she does not believe that treatment is necessary or helpful.

Such "either/or" treatment admissions are easier to work with than voluntary admissions to treatment. The very fact that there is a legal hold on the person means that it is that much less likely that she or he will leave treatment when his or her denial system is confronted. Also, the very fact that he or she was admitted on an either/or basis is information that can be used to confront the individual about the nature of their addiction problem. After all, it is difficult for the person who has just been arrested for their second or third drug-related charge to deny that chemicals are a problem for them!

Collins and Alison (1983) found that, when the treatment programs of some 2200 addicts who were "legally induced to seek treatment" (p. 1145) were reviewed, those who chose treatment as an alternative to incarceration did as well in treatment as those who were there voluntarily. Furthermore, it was found that those who were in treatment at the court's invitation were more likely to stay in treatment longer than were those who had no restrictions placed on them. The authors concluded that

> . . . the use of legal threat to pressure individuals into drug treatment is a valid approach for dealing with drug abusers and their undesirable behaviors. Legal threat apparently helps keep these individuals constructively involved in treatment and does not adversely affect long-term treatment goals (p. 1148).

Matuschka (1985) stated that "Treatment which carried a coercive element has been shown to have a higher cure ratio than treatment without a coercive element" (p. 209). As Collins and Alison (1983) and Matuschka (1985) have concluded, those who accepted treatment as an alternative to incarceration seem to do better than individuals who enter treatment on a voluntary basis. Thus, legal intervention seems to be a viable alternative for some who, if left to their own devices, would not accept the need for treatment.

Treatment or Incarceration: When is Treatment Appropriate?

Frequently, the courts will offer the person convicted of a drug-related charge the opportunity to enter a drug treatment program rather than go to jail or prison. While many individuals have used this "last chance" to begin serious work on their recovery from drug addiction, in many cases the individual uses treatment to avoid jail or prison.

The opportunity to participate in a treatment program should not be substituted for incarceration in every case. Fingarette (1988) warned that

> Judges, legislators, and bureaucrats . . . can now with clear consciences get the intractable social problems posed by heavy drinkers off their agenda by compelling or persuading these unmanageable people to go elsewhere—that is, to get "treatment" (p. 66).

All too often, the individual is offered the opportunity to enter treatment without an examination of his or her motivation. One must question the individual's motivation in the case of the alleged drug "pusher" who was arrested with several pounds of a controlled substance and entered treatment prior to going to court. The motivation of the person arrested for the fifth time while driving under the influence of chemicals, who enters treatment on the advice of his or her attorney prior to going to court, must also be questioned.

Chemical dependency treatment professionals encounter time and time again the individual who, after being admitted to treatment, "suddenly remembered" having to go to court for a drug-related charge. This revelation, often comes within the week following admission. The treatment center staff then must allow the client to briefly leave treatment in order to go to court, knowing that they have been used by the addict against the courts.

Time and time again, chemical dependency professionals find themselves faced with narcotics addicts in need of detoxification, who report that they must go to court in two or three weeks. Discussion then reveals that the individuals' attorneys suggested that they enter into treatment in order to finish detoxification from opiates before going to court. Some addicts have openly boasted that they entered treatment in order to make a better impression on the judge and jury.

One must seriously question the benefit of using limited treatment resources on persons who might openly admit that they entered treatment in order to manipulate the courts. Another example of the way in which treatment is abused is found in the common situation where a person enters treatment in order to stop his or her use of chemicals, while openly admitting that she or he plans to continue to sell drugs to others.

One must ask, in these all too common situations, how seriously the individual is going to participate in the treatment program and how cost-effective treatment might be under these circumstances. Unfortunately, this is a question that the courts often do not ask. It is often easier for the overworked legal system to accept treatment as an option without an examination of whether such treatment is likely to be effective.

A physician who indiscriminately prescribed antibiotics for every patient who came into the office, without an examination to determine the individual's needs, would quickly be brought up on charges of incompetence. The decision to use one medication or another should not be taken lightly. Obviously, the physician must weigh the potential benefits of each approach to the patient's problems against the anticipated risk for each possible treatment method.

The same is true for chemical dependency treatment. While the option of treatment in place of incarceration should certainly be considered by the courts, it must be remembered at all times that the treatment program is not the answer to every problem. A most useful concept to help the professional identify when treatment is most appropriate is that *treatment should never stand between the individual and the natural consequences of his or her behavior.*

OTHER FORMS OF INTERVENTION

Another either/or situation comes about when the spouse or the addict's employer, sets down the law. *Either* you stop drinking (or drugging), *or* I will file for divorce, terminate your position here, or whatever. Often, the physician is the person who establishes the either/or situation by threatening to file commitment papers on the addict unless she or he enters treatment. One individual, in treatment shortly after his wife had filed for divorce, said simply "I didn't think that she meant it. . . . I guess she did!"

Adelman and Weiss (1989) found that "employees coerced into treatment by their employers had better treatment outcomes than employees who volunteered for treatment. . . ." for alcoholism (p. 515). The authors concluded that treatment programs using such "constructive coercion" (p. 515) may actually be more effective in working with alcohol addicts than programs that do not encourage the use of this method of intervention.

This is not to say that the intervention process will meet with success, or even that a court ordered treatment exposure will result in sobriety. As noted earlier, addicts reach a point where they will sacrifice just about everything in order to support their addiction. There are cases where the addicted person accepted the loss of job, family, and spouse as part of the price to be paid for his or her addiction.

The intervention process does, however, offer the opportunity for friends, family, and co-workers to make a united effort to confront the addicted individual with the reality of his or her addiction, *in terms that she or he is likely to understand* (Johnson, 1980).

The goals of this process, as noted previously, are (a) to help the individual gain an awareness of their true behavior, and (b) to gain a commitment from the individual to enter into treatment. Once the individual accepts the need for treatment, she or he is *immediately* referred to a treatment program. Often, family members have already arranged for transportation and admission into a specific treatment center and have luggage packed and waiting.

There are many different avenues by which the individual might come to enter treatment. In some states, it is possible for addicts to be committed to treatment against their will, if the courts have sufficient evidence to believe they are in imminent danger of harming themselves or others. "Harm to self" might include neglect, and many alcoholics who fell asleep in the snow while walking home has been found to be dangers to themselves and sent to treatment against their will.

The exact provisions of such a court-ordered commitment vary from state to state, and some states have no provision for such commitments. Obviously, chemical dependency professionals in each state must consult with an attorney to review the legal statutes that apply in that state. However, the reader should be aware that the laws of many states allow for the courts to intervene should a person's chemical use put his or her life, or the life of others, in danger.

Occasionally, the individual will enter treatment on a voluntary basis, though as Johnson (1986) observed, this is unusual. It is more common to learn that the addict would continue to use chemicals if she or he could do so without paying the consequences. For this reason, external pressure of some kind, be it family, legal, medical, or professional penalties, is often necessary to help the addicted person see the need to enter treatment.

CHAPTER 19

The Treatment of Chemical Dependency

In this chapter, the basic elements of treatment are explored. The specific components of treatment may vary from one program to another. For example, a treatment program that specializes in working with alcoholic businessmen would have little use for a methadone maintenance component. Yet, there are also many common elements to the treatment process.

It is the purpose of this chapter to review the common components of treatment so that the reader may become familiar with the basic features of chemical dependency programs and better understand how the treatment process works.

CHARACTERISTICS OF THE CHEMICAL DEPENDENCY PROFESSIONAL

Lewis, Dana, and Blevins (1988) noted that counseling addicted persons is difficult and demanding work. Individuals who work with chemical dependency or psychological issues of their own are discouraged from actively working with others until they have resolved their own problems. Counselors preoccupied with personal problems, including those of chemical addiction, would be unlikely to help the client.

Rogers (1951) identified personality characteristics of human service professionals, including the ability to be empathetic. This is to say the ability to understand the client's world, through the client's eyes. In a later work, Rogers (1961) identified other essential characteristics of the human services professional:

   a. warmth,
   b. dependability,
   c. consistency,
   d. the ability to care for and respect the client,
   e. the ability to be separate from the client (which is to say the ability to not try and "live through" a client),
   f. the ability to not be perceived as a threat to the client,

g. the ability to free oneself from the urge to judge or evaluate the client, and

h. the ability to see the client as a person capable of growth.

Adelman and Weiss (1989) discussed the personality attributes of successful treatment staff members at an alcoholism treatment center and concluded that those staff members who possessed good interpersonal skills were best equipped to help their clients. The authors reported that clients of alcoholism counselors with low interpersonal skills levels were twice as likely to relapse as were patients whose counselors had high interpersonal skill levels. Although Adelman and Weiss did not speak in the same terms that Rogers (1963) did, the implication is clear that the most effective counselor is one who is well adjusted and accepting of others.

One point that needs to be clarified is that *these characteristics do not mean that the chemical dependency professional should be permissive!!!* Human service professionals occasionally confuse permissiveness with interpersonal warmth. Just as it is possible to be too confrontative, a subject which will be discussed shortly, it is also possible to be too permissive. *Caring for clients does not mean protecting them from the consequences of their behavior.*

Clients, especially the addicted client, will often test the limits in order to determine whether the professional will be consistent with enforcement of the rules. The chemical dependency professional should be aware that "dependability" and "consistency" also apply to the enforcement of the rules of the program.

McCarthy and Borders (1985) explored the impact of limit-setting on further drug use in a group of patients in a methadone maintenance program. Patients were told that their urine would be tested to detect continued chemical abuse, and that if their urine tested positive for other drugs four times in the next year, they would be taken off of methadone maintenance and placed on a narcotic withdrawal program. It was found that patients in this structured program achieved significantly greater program compliance and were less likely to use drugs than were a control group of addicts who were not in such a structured program.

The Counselor and Treatment "Secrets"

Clients will sometimes ask for an individual conference with a staff member and then confess to a rules infraction. Often, this admission of guilt is made to a student or intern at the agency, rather than to a regular staff member. The confession might be an admission of having used chemicals while in treatment, or some other infraction of the rules. Then, after having made this admission, the client will ask that the staff member not bring this information to the group, other staff members, or the program director, for fear of being discharged from treatment.

Chemical dependency professionals who honor such requests enter into a partnership with the addict; a partnership that, because it was set up by the addict, will make the professional an "enabler." In some situations, to not report this rules violation will make the professional vulnerable to later extortion by the client, who would be able to report the professional to his or her superiors for not passing on the information to staff.

The proper response to this situation is to document the discussion, *immediately*, through proper channels. This might be a memo, an entry into the client's progress notes, or a discussion of the material revealed by the client with the professional's immediate supervisor. This is done without malice, in order to ensure both uniform enforcement of the rules for all clients and to protect the professional's reputation.

Confrontation and Other Treatment Techniques

Lewis, Dana, and Blevins (1988) warned that although many chemical dependency professionals might feel otherwise, confrontation is not the only technique necessary to work with addicted persons. Confrontation is often necessary and quite effective in breaking through the client's defenses so that she or he can begin to understand the reality of the addiction and the need for treatment (Twerski, 1983). To effectively work with an addicted person, the professional needs a firm foundation in *all* of the skills of counseling, of which confrontation is only one.

Effective intervention with an addicted person requires the application and modification of therapeutic counseling skills to a specialized sub-population: those who are chemically addicted. Confrontation is one skill that the professional must possess to work with this population, but the skills outlined by Rogers (1961) are also necessary. The chemical dependency professional should be well trained in the theory and practice of individual and group therapeutic counseling, as well as in the field of chemical dependency counseling, to be able to work in the field of addiction.

THE MINNESOTA MODEL OF CHEMICAL DEPENDENCY TREATMENT

The Minnesota Model of chemical dependency treatment is attributed to Dr. Dan Anderson. While in college, Dr. Anderson worked as an attendant at the State Hospital in Willmar, Minnesota (Larson, 1982). Following graduation, Anderson returned to the State Hospital in Willmar to work as a recreational therapist. He was assigned to work with the alcoholics who were in treatment at the hospital, the least desirable position at that time.

Anderson was influenced by the work of Mr. Ralph Rossen, who was later to become the Minnesota State Commissioner of Health. At the same

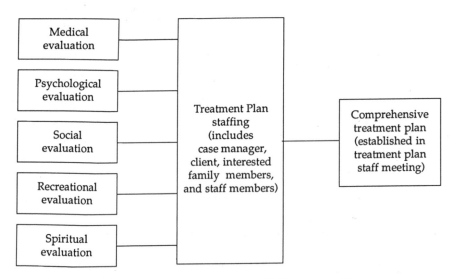

FIGURE 19-1. Flowchart of the Minnesota Model Treatment Plan.

time, the methods used by Alcoholics Anonymous, which had reached and spread across Minnesota by the late 1940s, were used by Anderson and a staff psychologist by the name of Dr. Jean Rossi as a means of understanding and working with the alcoholic. They were supported in this approach by the medical director of the Hospital, Dr. Nelson Bradley (Larson, 1982).

Each person contributed a different perspective on the individual's addiction. To this team was added the Rev. John Keller, who had been sent to Willmar State Hospital to learn about alcoholism in 1955. The staff then had

> . . . knowledge of medicine, psychology, A. A. and theology together under one roof to develop a new and innovative alcohol treatment program (Larson, 1982, p. 35).

This new treatment approach, since called the Minnesota Model of treatment, uses a *treatment team* comprised of chemical dependency counselors familiar with AA, psychologists, physicians, nurses, recreational therapists, and clergy. The first stage of the Minnesota Model treatment approach involves each member of the treatment team meeting with the client, to assess his or her needs from the professional's area of expertise. Each professional then makes recommendations for the client's *treatment plan* (see Figure 19-1).

In the second stage, these people meet *as a team* to discuss the areas that they feel should be the focus of treatment. The treatment-team meeting is chaired by the individual ultimately responsible for the execution of the treatment process. This is usually the chemical dependency counselor, who will function as the client's case manager. Each of the assessments, and the recommendations that come from these assessments, is reviewed and discussed by the treatment team. The team then selects those recommendations that, in their training and experience, they feel are most appropriate to help the client achieve and maintain sobriety.

The client, his or her parole/probation officer, and possibly interested family members also participate in the treatment-plan meeting. The client and family members are free to recommend additional areas of concern or to suggest specific goals they would like included in the treatment plan. The case manager will review the treatment goals identified as valuable to the client and discuss the rationale for these recommendations.

On the basis of this meeting, the case manager and client enter stage three of the treatment process. In this stage, the client and his or her case manager develop a formal *treatment plan*. The treatment plan that emerges as a result of this process is multimodal, and will offer a wide variety of potential treatment goals and recommendations. It will identify specific problem areas, behavioral objectives, methods by which one can measure progress toward these objectives, and a target date for each goal. The treatment plan will be discussed in more detail in the next section of this chapter.

The strength of the Minnesota Model of treatment lies in its redundancy and its multimember concept. The information provided by the client is reviewed by many different professionals, each of whom may on the basis of his or her training identify a potential treatment problem that others may have overlooked. This allows for the greatest possible evaluation of the client's needs, strengths, and priorities.

Another advantage of the Minnesota Model is that it allows for different professionals to work together in the rehabilitation of the client. The different professionals, with their training and experience, offer a wider range of services than any single chemical dependency counselor ever could. In addition to multidisciplinary intake evaluations, each professional on the treatment team can work with the client, *if that client presents special needs*.

Thus, the chemical dependency counselor does not need to be a jack-of-all-trades. Rather, if the client presents a need that one staff member cannot fulfill, a referral to another member of the team for specialized treatment may be made. This feature has helped make the Minnesota Model one of the dominant treatment program models in the field of chemical dependency rehabilitation, although few people are aware of its roots.

THE TREATMENT PLAN

The treatment plan, as noted by Lewis, Dana, and Blevins (1988), is "the foundation for success" (p. 118) of the treatment process. It is a highly specific form, which in some states might be viewed as a legal document.

Different treatment centers tend to use different formats, depending on the specific licensure requirements in that state. However, all treatment plans are composed of several different sections.

First, there is a brief summary of the problem(s) that brought the client into treatment. In the second section, there is a brief summary of the client's physical and emotional state of health. The third section contains the individual's own input into the treatment process. The fourth section is the heart of the treatment plan. This is where the specific goals of treatment are reviewed. The fifth section, the discharge criteria, lists the steps that must be accomplished in order to discharge the client from treatment. The sixth section is a brief summary of those steps that will be part of the client's *aftercare* program.

The heart of the treatment plan, as noted above, is where the specific treatment goals are outlined. This section of the treatment plan is often identified as the *Treatment Goals*. Such treatment goals should include (a) a *problem statement*, or brief statement of the problem, (b) *long-term goals*, (c) *short-term objectives*, (d) *measurement criteria*, and (e) a *target date*.

The problem statement is a short statement, usually a sentence or two in length, which identifies a *specific problem* that will be addressed in treatment. The *long-term goal* is the ultimate objective, and as such is a general statement of a hoped-for outcome. The long-term goal statement is usually also only one or two sentences in length.

Following the long-term goal is a *short-term objective*. The objective is *a very specific behavior, which can be measured*. The objective statement is usually one to three sentences long and identifies the measurement criteria by which both the client and staff will be able to assess whether progress toward this objective is being made. Finally, there is the *target date*, which is usually a simple sentence identifying a specific date by which this goal will be achieved.

An example of a treatment goal for a 24-year-old male polydrug addict (cocaine, alcohol, marijuana, and occasionally benzodiazepines) who has used chemicals daily for the last 27 months might appear as follows:

PROBLEM: Client has used chemicals daily for at least the past two years and has been unable to abstain from drug use on his own.

LONG-TERM GOAL: That the client achieve, and maintain, sobriety.

SHORT-TERM OBJECTIVE: That the client not use mood-altering chemicals while in treatment.

METHOD OF MEASUREMENT: Random supervised urine toxicology screens to detect possible drug use.

TARGET DATE: Scheduled discharge date.

The typical treatment plan identifies perhaps five or six different problem areas. Each of these goals might be modified as the treatment program progresses, and each provides a yardstick of the client's progress.

Obviously, if the client is not making progress on *any* of the goals, it is time to question whether the client is serious about treatment. The goals become the heart of the treatment program.

Aftercare

The *aftercare* program involves those elements of treatment that will be carried out after the individual has been discharged from treatment. If, for example, the person entered into individual psychotherapy to address an issue uncovered in treatment, it is entirely likely that this therapy will continue long after the individual is discharged from the typical 28–35-day inpatient rehabilitation program. Individual therapy on a once-per-week basis with a psychotherapist would then become a part of the aftercare program.

Participation in Alcoholics Anonymous, or Narcotics Anonymous, following discharge from treatment should also be identified as part of an aftercare program. A medical problem that requires ongoing medical supervision and support should be a part of the aftercare program, as well as aftercare placement in a transitional living facility such as a halfway house. If the individual presents any special needs, these should also be included as specialized elements of the aftercare program.

The aftercare program is designed and carried out on the assumption that treatment does not end with the individual's discharge from a formal treatment program. Rather, treatment is the first part of a recovery program that (it is to be hoped) continues for the rest of the individual's life. The aftercare component of the treatment plan addresses those issues that should be addressed following the individual's discharge from the rehabilitation program.

Relapse

Even with the strongest legal or family pressure, there is no guarantee that the individual will actually accept treatment, or remain in treatment once she or he has started the program. Baekeland and Lundwall (1975) found that a significant percentage of those admitted to inpatient and outpatient chemical dependency treatment programs failed to complete treatment. Entry into a treatment program is no guarantee that the person will actually complete the program, or that he or she will benefit from treatment.

Even following the best of treatment it is possible for a person to "relapse," and return to the use of chemicals. Indeed, the nature of drug addiction leads one to expect the individual to relapse from time to time. Svanum and McAdoo (1989) concluded that in the first four years following treatment, approximately 90% of those persons treated will relapse. The authors stated that "Few treated persons show a stable pattern of failure, and fewer still show a long-term pattern of stable recovery. Most alternate between more or less favorable treatment outcomes" (p. 222). This does not mean that treatments are doomed to failure, rather it is a grim reality of addiction: the disease of addiction is one that can be *arrested*, but can never be *cured*.

Relapse Prevention

In recent years, an awareness has developed that it is possible to block relapse, through a concept termed *relapse prevention*. As health care professionals have gained a greater understanding of the forces that undermine recovery, treatment programs have started to help the individual anticipate and deal with these problems.

Cummings, Gordon, and Marlatt (1980) discussed a drug relapse as evolving out of a series of "mini-decisions" (p. 297) that, individually, do not appear to bring the individual closer to chemical use. However, both individually and collectively these mini-decisions "begin a chain of behaviors which may set the stage for a relapse to occur" (p. 297). Examples of such mini-decisions might be the recovering addict's continuation of a friendship with an active addict, or the recovering addict going to the local bar "just to play pool."

The authors point out that these seemingly innocent mini-decisions increase the chance that the recovering addict will encounter a situation where she or he is likely to relapse. Addicts have been known to "see if I could just walk down the same street, and not feel the urge to use anymore," or have only "stopped off to pay him some money that I owed him, and I found drugs all over the place!", as if the drug-using behavior of this friend were a revelation.

At such times, newly recovering addicts are at a decision point; they must reaffirm their commitment to sobriety or start back on the path to the active use of chemicals. Individuals with adequate sober coping skills will reaffirm their commitment to sobriety. However, individuals with inadequate sobriety-based coping skills might relapse. At best, they would find the experience frightening, which may make them question whether they are *ever* going to be capable of self-sustained sobriety.

Often, such a mini-decision is the individual's choice to stop going to AA or NA. The initial decision might be to cut back from five meetings a week to four meetings a week. The next decision might be to cut back from four meetings to perhaps only one or two. Eventually, the decision might be to go to meetings only every other week, then once a month, until the individual no longer has any contact with their sober support system.

It is virtually guaranteed that every recovering addict will encounter at least one high-risk situation. Cummings, Gordon, and Marlatt (1980) found that these high-risk situations could be grouped together by categories, with the largest category being situations that brought about *negative emotional states* in the individual. Another category of high-risk situations involved *social pressure*, while a third category of such high-risk situations involved *negative physical states*.

This last category, negative physical states, actually accounted for only a small percentage of relapses, but in the recovering drug addict sample (as opposed to the recovering alcoholic), this factor was reported to be a more significant cause of relapse. The authors interpreted this trend as evidence that the different forms of addiction might have different patterns of relapse stressors, although this theory has not been tested.

Cummings, Gordon, and Marlatt (1980) also found that alcoholics and gamblers tended to place themselves in high-risk situations in order to *test personal control* over their addiction. Finally, *positive emotional states* were an infrequently reported cause of relapse for drug or alcohol addicts.

Lewis, Dana, and Blevins (1988) identified the first step in relapse prevention as being the *identification of the high-risk situation* for each individual. Self-monitoring and direct observation by treatment center staff are just two methods by which high-risk situations could be identified. The patient history might also underscore high-risk situations of particular significance for that individual, and treatment staff should pay particular attention to the client's self-report to identify possible high-risk factors.

Once the high-risk factors have been identified, *specific coping responses* for each high-risk situation must be devised by the treatment center staff. Lewis, Dana, and Blevins (1988) also suggested that a reminder card be carried in the addict's wallet or purse, in case of a relapse, so that the individual will have written instructions on the steps to take to limit the relapse.

The concept of relapse prevention has offered some insight into the forces that might precipitate a relapse. The theoretical models of relapse and its prevention seem to offer some promise in the treatment of chemical dependency, and in the next few years research should disclose whether current models of relapse prevention are useful in the treatment of addiction or if there is a need for further research in this area.

A Word on Controlled Drinking

The concept of helping the alcoholic to return to "social" or "controlled" drinking has been a controversial one for many years (Helzer, Robins, Taylor, Carey, Miller, Combs-Orme, and Farmer, 1985). Unfortunately, ever since the first preliminary reports that it *might* be possible to train a percentage of alcoholics to return to a state of "controlled" drinking, many alcoholics have seized on the concept as a justification for their continued drinking.

Unfortunately, research (Helzer et al., 1985; Schuckit, 1984) has suggested that less than 2% of those individuals with a drinking problem might return to a state of social drinking again. *Every* alcoholic, however, would like to believe that they are in the 1–2% who might return to "controlled" or "social" drinking. Schuckit (1984) questioned if these individuals who could return to social drinking were actually alcoholic. Indeed, one must question whether it is possible to teach the actual alcoholic to drink only on a social basis.

In either case, given the fact that *only 1–2%* of the alcoholics who have been tested to date have been able to achieve a return to social drinking patterns, one must argue against the experiment of attempting to discover if any given alcoholic is in the lucky 1–2%. The alcoholic who believes that he or she can learn social drinking behaviors once again, *and maintain* a pattern of social drinking for life, is taking a bet where the odds are at best 49 to 1, if not 99 to 1, against them.

There are very few of us who would be willing to chance an operation where the odds were 50 to 1 against us. Few would be willing to consent to a surgical procedure where the person only had a 1- or 2-% chance of recovery. Yet many alcoholics have voiced the secret wish that they could win this bet, and land in what more than one alcoholic has called "the lucky two percent."

Optional Elements of a Chemical Dependency Treatment Program

In addition to the treatment plan, the various assessments conducted at the time of admission, the development of an aftercare plan, and relapse prevention, other elements of treatment might be included in a specific program, depending on the needs of the population served. Below is a brief exploration of some important subcomponents of treatment.

Pharmacological Approaches to Alcoholism Treatment

Perhaps the most common pharmacological treatment method is the use of the drug Antabuse (also known as disulfiram). Antabuse has shown promise in the treatment of alcoholics. However, Antabuse has serious dangers, and cannot be used with patients who have serious medical disorders (Schuckit, 1984). For those patients who *can* use Antabuse, it often provides the time for a "second thought" desperately needed by the alcoholic who is tempted to drink.

In brief, Antabuse does *not* decrease the alcoholic's desire to drink. However, it does interfere with the metabolism of alcohol, causing a number of unpleasant side effects when the individual mixes alcohol with Antabuse. The interaction between Antabuse and alcohol will bring about facial flushing, heart palpitations and a rapid heart rate, difficulty in breathing, nausea, vomiting, and possibly a serious drop in blood pressure (Schuckit, 1984). The strength of these side effects depends on how much alcohol has been ingested, and how long ago the last dose of Antabuse was ingested. The patient is warned about these effects when the medication is prescribed.

Treatment professionals have often been asked by a codependent spouse about the possibility of obtaining Antabuse. Inquiry usually reveals that the spouse wants some Antabuse in order to place it in the alcoholic's coffee, to "teach him (or her) a lesson" the next time she or he drinks. Antabuse should *never* be given to anyone without their knowledge and consent.

Some treatment centers advocate a learning process where the patient takes Antabuse for a short period of time (usually a few days) after which they are allowed to drink a small amount of alcohol under controlled conditions. This is done so that the alcoholic might experience the negative consequences of mixing alcohol and Antabuse. In such a demonstration, the treatment staff has access to emergency medical support to help the client recover from the experiment.

The interaction between Antabuse and alcohol is *potentially serious and may require emergency hospitalization for observation and treatment.* By allowing alcoholics to experience the negative consequences of Antabuse and alcohol under controlled conditions, it is hoped that they will not attempt to drink a large amount of alcohol on their own, outside of the treatment center.

Another serious drawback of Antabuse is that it takes about 30 minutes for the drug to react to alcohol (Schuckit, 1984), and thus is of little value as an aversive conditioning program. Aversive conditioning programs use *immediate* consequences paired to undesired behavior. In such behavior modification programs, the person learns to associate the undesired behavior with a negative response, and gradually discontinues the undesired behavior. The 30-minute delay between the ingestion of alcohol and the Antabuse/alcohol reaction is far too long for it to be an *immediate* consequence, making it difficult for the person to associate the alcohol with the delayed discomfort caused by the subsequent chemical interaction.

A third problem with Antabuse is that its full effects last only about 24–48 hours. The individual needs to take the drug every day, or perhaps every other day, for optimal effectiveness. The Antabuse will gradually be eliminated from the body by the liver. Thus, it is up to the individual to take the medication according to the schedule established by his or her physician to ensure that there is an adequate supply of the drug in the body at all times.

Finally, Antabuse reacts to the alcohol found in many over-the-counter cough syrups, as well as in aftershaves, or in any of a wide range of other products. The individual on Antabuse should be warned to avoid such products. Most treatment centers or physicians utilizing Antabuse have lists of such products and foods, and will provide a copy to patients on Antabuse.

In spite of these disadvantages, research has demonstrated that those alcoholism treatment programs that use Antabuse as a part of the overall treatment program have a lower relapse rate than programs that do not (Adelman and Weiss, 1989). What Antabuse does, once an individual has taken the daily dose, is provide the individual with the knowledge that she or he will be unable to drink for that day, at least not without becoming very sick.

Admittedly, some alcoholics will drink in spite of the Antabuse in their system, and many alcoholics believe that they know how to neutralize the drug while it is in their body. For the majority of those who choose Antabuse, the drug provides an extra bit of support during a weak moment.

There are other medications, such as Flagyl (or metronidazole), which also cause discomfort when mixed with alcohol. Graedon (1980) reported that, when mixed with alcohol, Flagyl would cause nausea, vomiting, flushing, and headache. One physician, when faced with a patient who was allergic to Antabuse, elected to use Flagyl as a short-term substitute, although this is not currently a recommended use of this medication by the Food and Drug Administration.

In this case, however, the physician was able to provide pharmacological support for an alcoholic who needed some external constraint during the initial period of sobriety, when the individual felt most at risk of relapsing. This is not to say that Flagyl should be routinely administered to alcoholics who require pharmacological support. There is evidence to suggest that Flagyl has a significant potential for causing cancer (Graedon, 1980). The patient who uses Flagyl should do so only when the benefits clearly outweigh the risks presented by this medication.

Narcotic Blockers

Recently, a new drug by the name of Trexan (naltrexone hydrochloride), was introduced. Trexan blocks the euphoric effects of injected opiates. The theory behind the use of Trexan is that, if the person does not experience any feelings of euphoria from opiates while on Trexan, she or he is less likely to use opiates again.

This medication *should be used only after the person is* **completely** *detoxified from opiates*, in order to avoid bringing about an undesired withdrawal syndrome in an opiate addict. Callahan (1980) noted that few addicts attempt to use narcotics even once while on narcotic antagonist blocking agents. However, when the medication is discontinued, the opiate addict will begin to reexperience a craving for narcotics. Thus, there is no extinction of the craving for the drug.

To date, there is no research that demonstrates an *unequivocal* benefit from this medication, according to the *1987 Physician's Desk Reference* (PDR). It does seem to offer pharmacological support during the initial period after detoxification, when an addict is most vulnerable to relapse. However, until research can demonstrate the unequivocal usefulness of this medication, it is suggested that clinicians keep an open mind about the usefulness of narcotic antagonist blockers.

Detoxification From Drugs

Many chemical dependency programs offer detoxification services, either as part of their regular treatment program, or as a separate component of treatment. Such detoxification programs should meet the standards of state licensing boards, and detoxification should be carried out under the supervision of a physician who has training and experience in this area.

As was noted in the chapters on alcohol and CNS depressants, withdrawal from these chemicals can often result in life-threatening seizures. While detoxification from *some* drugs is possible on an outpatient basis, detoxification from many of the chemicals of abuse is so dangerous that it should *only* be attempted on an inpatient basis. Miller, Frances, and Holmen (1988) advocated that each patient in withdrawal be evaluated by a trained physician to determine whether inpatient or outpatient detoxification were necessary.

Outpatient detoxification requires daily follow-up by the detoxification staff to monitor the patient's progress and compliance with treatment (Miller, Frances, and Holmen, 1988). Inpatient detoxification programs should have adequate facilities for the medical support of clients, including on-duty medical personnel (nurses and physicians), as well as appropriate medications (anticonvulsants) and equipment to administer them. Patients on medication for withdrawal should be closely monitored by staff to detect signs of drug overdose or seizures (Miller, Frances, and Holmen).

Narcotic Withdrawal

Programs that specialize in the treatment of narcotic addiction often offer controlled withdrawal from opiates. Occasionally, a hospital will offer narcotic withdrawal programs even if that hospital does not attempt to provide long-term treatment for narcotic addicts. The detoxification component in each center is very much the same.

Methadone is the drug of choice for narcotic withdrawal (Mirin and Weiss, 1983). Methadone is a synthetic narcotic, first developed by German chemists in World War II. The drug is taken orally and was developed as a substitute for morphine, which the Germans were unable to obtain because of the war. Mirin and Weiss (1983) observed that methadone has the additional advantage of a duration of action of between 24 and 36 hours. The authors noted that daily dosage levels of 10–40 mg per day of methadone are usually sufficient to prevent withdrawal symptoms in narcotic addicts.

Mirin and Weiss (1983) advocated a methadone dosage schedule of 10 mg per hour for the first day, until withdrawal symptoms are brought under control. The total amount of methadone administered forms the basis for the withdrawal dosage. On the morning of day two of withdrawal, the addict receives this dosage as a single dose. Starting on the third day, the dose is reduced by 5 mg. On each successive day the dosage is reduced by this amount (5 mg/day) until the patient is completely detoxified from opiates (Mirin and Weiss, 1983).

The usual detoxification program lasts 3–21 days (Mirin and Weiss, 1983). Baekeland and Lundwall (1975) reported that opiate detoxification programs suffer from a significant dropout rate. Mirin and Weiss (1983) noted that as the daily dosage levels drop to the 15–20 mg per day range, the individual will experience a return of withdrawal symptoms. Indeed, a timely reminder from the authors is that opiate addicts going through withdrawal should be reminded that they should *not* expect a symptom-free withdrawal.

Other programs, however, operate on the philosophy that methadone withdrawal is inappropriate. Some narcotic addicts have reported that methadone withdrawal is, in their opinion, worse than withdrawal from their drug of choice. As was noted in the chapter on narcotics, withdrawal from opiates is not life-threatening, and many addicts have reported that it is no worse than having a bad cold or the flu.

Some programs offer pharmacological support during the withdrawal phase—such as benzodiazepines to help the person relax and sleep—but do not use narcotics. Indeed, Charney, Heninger, and Kleber (1986) outlined a treatment program in which two different drugs, an anti-hypertensive, Catapres (clonidine hydrochloride), and an opiate antagonist, Narcan (naloxone), were used to bring about a 4–5 day opiate withdrawal.

Catapres was used to control the drug craving, while the antagonist blocked the drug receptor sites in the brain and counteracted the effects of the narcotics. The authors found that over 90% of their sample were completely withdrawn from narcotics at the end of five days, without significant distress. Charney, Heninger, and Kleber (1986) went on to suggest this drug program as part of a narcotic addiction treatment program.

Methadone Maintenance Programs

Mirin and Weiss (1983) identified the theory behind methadone maintenance as reflecting a belief that some narcotics addicts might be unable to totally abstain from narcotics use. Dole (1988), one of the founders of methadone maintenance, advanced a theory that the chronic use of opiates might bring about permanent changes in brain function at the cellular level. When the narcotics are removed from the system, these changes in neurological function bring about a craving for narcotics that may last for months or even years.

The goal of methadone maintenance is to provide medically supervised doses of methadone to eliminate the drug craving in the "otherwise intractable" (Dole, 1989, p. 1980) addict. Orally administered methadone has also been found to block the euphoric effects of injected narcotics. Methadone maintenance allows the addict to function without the need for further illegal drug use. The usual dosage level is 40–120 mg of methadone each day.

The initial results of methadone maintenance were quite promising (Calahan, 1980), although subsequent research has uncovered a number of weaknesses in the concept of methadone maintenance. While the person may not crave narcotics, and may even be unable to experience the euphoria of injected narcotics while on methadone, he or she is not prevented from using cocaine, alcohol, marijuana, benzodiazepines, and so on.

Indeed, Calahan (1980) noted that methadone maintenance clinics quickly became centers of drug dealing, as the clinic became the focal point of the addicts' life. Mirin and Weiss (1983) reported that *at least* 20% of addicts in a methadone maintenance program could be expected to abuse other chemicals besides narcotics. Even Dole (1989) acknowledged that methadone is "highly specific for the treatment of opiate addiction" (p. 1880), and that there is no similar pharmacological therapy for nonopiate addictions.

As Baekeland and Lundwall (1975) noted, methadone maintenance programs suffer from a significant dropout rate in spite of the advantages supposedly offered by this treatment approach. Dole (1988) observed that methadone maintenance was "corrective, but not curative" (p. 3025) for a suspected neurological dysfunction that brings about the compulsive use of narcotics. Further, when the neurological function disrupted by chronic use of narcotics

> . . . has been normalized, the ex-addict, supported by counseling and social services, can begin the long process of social rehabilitation (Dole, 1988, p. 3025).

Even after maintenance therapy has been initiated, there remains a need for the individual to participate in a formal rehabilitation program. Calahan (1980) noted that many methadone maintenance clinics have become little more than "warehouses in which methadone could be doled out to a great number of people each day" (p. 148). Methadone maintenance is not, as advocated by Dole and Nyswander, a complete treatment modality in itself, but may be a part of a larger rehabilitation program for the narcotics addict.

The methadone maintenance program concept assumes that the addicted person is not just using the program as a guaranteed source of narcotics to avoid withdrawal. Careful screening of clients, and strict contingency contracting (in which addicts are informed in advance that they will be withdrawn from the program if their urine shows traces of drugs other than methadone, and are then withdrawn if this does occur) have been found useful in helping clients use methadone maintenance as it was intended (Calahan, 1980).

Blood/Urine Toxicology Screens

Many, perhaps most, treatment programs have arrangements for the testing of blood samples and/or urine samples to detect illicit drug use. The treatment program should use *frequent, unannounced, random* drug toxicology screens on *all* clients, not just on those suspected of using chemicals while in treatment.

Such toxicology screening offers an additional measure of support during the initial period of sobriety and discourages chemical use while the individual is in treatment. Each client knows that illicit drug use will likely be detected rather quickly and the individual is thus less likely to use chemicals while in treatment. The toxicology sample would also be one measure of program compliance by the client.

Blood samples offer the advantage of being drawn *directly* from the client. This is often an advantage, especially with an unconscious, or uncooperative client. It is difficult for the client to substitute somebody else's blood sample for his or her own in order to hide illicit drug use, a common problem with urine toxicology testing. However, blood samples require that a skilled professional (nurse, or laboratory technician) draw the blood under proper sterile conditions.

It is easier to run a urine sample through a toxicology screen to detect illicit drug use than a blood sample. Urine samples are more easily obtained than is a blood sample, and the collection of a urine sample does not require a needle. It is also easier for the client to "fake" a urine sample, either by substituting another person's urine for his or her own, or by other means.

One favorite trick is for the client to have a "clean" (that is, drug-free) urine sample on hand, possibly hidden in a balloon or small bottle. When asked for a urine sample, the client may empty the container into the sample bottle, safe in the knowledge that the urine to be tested is clean. Another trick is for the client to "accidentally" dip the bottle into the water in the toilet, diluting their urine so much that it is unlikely that the laboratory could detect any *urine,* never mind possible chemical use!

Thus, *extremely close supervision of clients,* **both male and female,** *must be the rule when using urine samples for detection of illicit drug use.* This means that the person supervising the collection of the urine sample *must actually see the urine enter the bottle,* not just stand outside the bathroom while the client is inside. Clients have been known to hide clean urine samples in the toilet area beforehand in order to substitute the clean urine sample for their own later that day.

If the staff person suspects that the client has substituted another person's urine for his or her own, there are several techniques that may be used to counter this. First, *urine is within 1–2 degrees of the core body temperature,* and by immediately taking the temperature of the urine sample, one can determine if it is cooler than normal human body temperature. The client whose urine sample is 70 degrees is likely to have substituted somebody else's urine sample for his or her own, and should be confronted with this fact.

Another technique is for a staff person to wait until the client is about to enter the lavatory, then tell him or her that they have been selected for another urine sample. It is unlikely that the client will carry around a bottle of urine all the time on the off chance that she or he will be asked for a urine sample. This procedure is likely to force the client to give a sample of his or her own urine, especially if care is taken to ensure that the client does not "accidentally" drop the bottle into the water.

Still another technique is for the counselor to announce, at the beginning of a group session, that the client has two hours in which to provide a supervised urine sample for toxicology screen. The client will then be unable to leave the group to pick up a urine sample stored in his or her room without staff being aware that she or he has left the group. The client should have access to water, coffee, or soda to stimulate the production of urine, which can be collected for toxicology testing.

Depending on the method used, laboratories can detect the drugs, or metabolites produced by the body as the liver breaks down the drugs, for various periods of time. The chemical dependency professional should request a written summary from the laboratory concerning

a. the *methods* by which the laboratory attempts to detect illicit chemical use,
b. the *accuracy* of these methods,
c. *the specific chemicals that can be detected* by that laboratory, and
d. *the period of time following chemical use in which the urine test may reveal such drug use.*

A second use of urine toxicology testing is to check medication compliance. In other words, urine toxicology screening can be used to help determine whether the client is taking the medications that have been prescribed. Obviously, a person being detoxified from narcotics through methadone withdrawal should have methadone in his or her urine. If he or she does not, the staff should consider the possibility that this person has substituted another's urine sample, and examine why the client should wish to do so.

Family and Marital Therapy

There are many treatment programs that include a family or marital therapy component. Kaufman (1985), in addressing the role of alcoholism in the family, observed that within the family unit

> . . . the use of alcohol is *purposeful, adaptive, homeostatic,* and *meaningful.* The problem of alcoholism is not just the consequences of drinking per se, but, more importantly, the *system functions* which drinking fills in the psychodynamics of the family system (p. 381, italics in original).

Williams (1989) observed that the addict's defense system, and those of the family, tend to be inter-reinforcing. The family members come to develop defense mechanisms that reinforce those of the addicted person. Within such a family-systems approach, it becomes necessary to modify the role the drug-use behavior fills in the family. The family system as a whole needs to be modified, a process often best carried out during the intervention session. Otherwise, the family *as a unit* will resist any change in the alcoholic's behavior.

There are many theoretical models of family therapy, and this is rapidly becoming a specialized area of expertise (Bowen, 1985). It is beyond the scope of this chapter to provide a comprehensive overview of the fields of marital and family therapy. The chemical dependency professional should be aware that these are specialized areas of training, as family and marital counseling are quite complicated. It is sufficient at this point to identify family and marriage therapy as a component of many treatment programs, so that the chemical dependency professional might be aware of the role of this element of treatment in the program as a whole.

Group Therapy Approaches

Yalom (1975) noted that the therapy group offered a number of advantages over individual therapy. First, therapy groups allowed one professional to work with a number of different individuals at once. Second, in the therapy group, group members would be able to learn from each other and offer each other feedback. Third, because of the nature of the therapy group, each individual would find within the group members a reflection of his or her family of origin, allowing him or her to work through problems from earlier stages of growth.

These advantages are used in chemical dependency treatment programs where therapy groups are frequently the primary treatment approach. While individual sessions might be used for special problems too sensitive to discuss in a group therapy situation, the client is usually encouraged to bring his or her concerns to group, which may meet every other day, daily, or more often than once a day, depending on the pace of the program.

The skills necessary for effective group leadership are quite complex and are beyond the scope of this text. However, the reader should be aware that groups are often the mainstay of inpatient and outpatient treatment programs.

Assertiveness Training

Lewis, Dana, and Blevins (1988) identified special assertiveness training groups as being useful in building self-esteem and self-confidence in interpersonal relationships. Individuals who are addicted to chemicals often lack the ability to assert themselves, and could benefit from training in this interpersonal skill. Many programs offer an assertiveness training component to clients who are thought to be in need of remedial training.

Alcoholics Anonymous/Narcotics Anonymous

Although Alcoholics Anonymous and Narcotics Anonymous are discussed in some detail in chapter 22, brief mention of AA and NA should be made at this time. Participation in a self-help group such as AA should be a component of both inpatient and outpatient treatment. Many community AA or NA groups have extended an invitation to local treatment programs to allow their clients to participate in scheduled meetings. If the treatment program is large enough, an on-site AA or NA meeting may be scheduled, which is limited to clients in treatment.

There are a number of advantages to AA or NA involvement for clients in treatment. Both AA and NA are potentially chemical-free support groups for new members. As such, both AA and NA offer opportunities for members to model drug-free interpersonal interactions for clients in treatment. Each group also offers the opportunity for the new member to develop a drug-free support system to use in times of crisis following treatment. Members in the AA or NA group may, in speaking of their own problems, offer the newcomer insight into his or her own problems, and suggest possible solutions based on their own experience. Thus, the treatment program should have some provision for self-help group participation.

SUMMARY

This chapter reviewed the Minnesota Model of treatment, which is one of the primary treatment models found in this country. The concept of a *comprehensive treatment plan* that serves as the heart of the treatment process was also discussed. Various pharmacological supports for persons who are in the early stages of sobriety, and for those going through detoxification from chemicals, were explored.

In this chapter, the concept of relapse prevention was discussed, as was the role of assertiveness training, and the role of marital and family therapy as a component of a larger treatment program. The use of blood and urine samples for toxicology screening to detect medication compliance, and illicit drug use, was also reviewed.

CHAPTER 20

Outpatient Treatment
of Chemical Dependency

Outpatient treatment programs for addiction come in a variety of shapes and sizes. For the individual who might have been arrested for the first time while driving under the influence of chemicals, there is the "DWI school." The DWI school is an outpatient psycho-educational approach for first time offenders, who are assumed to have made a mistake by driving under the influence of chemicals, but who do not seem to be addicted to drugs. The whole thrust of the DWI school is to help the individual understand the dangers inherent in driving while under the influence of chemicals, in the hope that she or he might learn from this mistake.

Many community mental health centers offer outpatient chemical dependency treatment. There are numerous private clinics, or therapists in private practice, who also provide outpatient treatment for addiction (Zimberg, 1978). The mental health center or private clinic might use individual or group therapy as part of the treatment approach, and outpatient treatment programs usually will offer marital and family counseling as part of the rehabilitation effort.

Although outpatient treatment programs may have borrowed many concepts from AA and may use AA literature, they are not to be confused with AA itself. In a sense, AA could be classified as an outpatient treatment program for drug addiction. However, for the purpose of this chapter, AA will not be considered as such, since it does not meet the strict definition of outpatient treatment.

OUTPATIENT TREATMENT: A WORKING DEFINITION

Outpatient chemical dependency treatment may best be defined as a formal treatment program that (a) involves one or more professionals trained to work with individuals who are addicted to chemicals, (b) is designed specifically to work with the addicted person to help him or her achieve and maintain sobriety, (c) will utilize family, marital, individual, and/or group therapy to help the addicted person come to terms with his or her problems, and (d) does so on an outpatient basis.

Outpatient treatment programs use many of the components of treatment discussed in Chapter 12. Such programs generally use individual and group therapy formats, and possibly marital and family therapy, in working with the addicted person. Most such programs follow a twelve-step philosophy similar to AA's or NA's, and the individual is expected to attend regular self-help group meetings as part of the treatment format.

The individual's treatment program is usually coordinated by a certified chemical dependency counselor (sometimes called an *addictions* counselor). A formal treatment program is established, review sessions are scheduled on a regular basis, and the client's progress toward the goals established in the treatment programs is monitored by staff.

The general approach of individual and group therapy is the confrontation of the addict's system of denial, combined with counseling designed to help the client learn how to face the problems of daily living *without* the use of chemicals. This is accomplished, in part, through psychoeducational lectures in which the individual is presented with factual information about the disease of chemical addiction and its treatment.

Referrals to vocational counseling centers or community mental health centers for individual, family, or marital counseling, are made as necessary. Some programs provide a weekly or monthly "family night," where family members are encouraged to participate. Other programs feature a "family group" orientation, where couples participate together on a day-to-day basis as part of the program. In such a format, the spouse of the addicted person will sit in on the group sessions and participate as an equal with the addicts in the group therapy.

Whatever the general approach, the goal of any outpatient treatment program is to enhance the highest level of functioning, while providing support for the alcoholic. Some programs require that the detoxification phase of treatment, when the individual is withdrawn from chemicals, is carried out either at a detoxification center or in a general hospital. However, the individual is expected to have stopped all chemical use before starting any treatment program.

Abstinence from alcohol as well as from other drug use is expected. Many treatment programs will require the use of Antabuse, or will carry out random urine tests to detect alcohol or drug use by the patient. One advantage of using random urine samples for toxicology screening is that this also allows the staff to determine if there is evidence of Antabuse in the urine sample. Such information will reveal whether the individual is taking the Antabuse as prescribed.

The goal of outpatient treatment is to allow the individual the opportunity to live at home, continue to work, and to continue family activities while participating in a rehabilitation program designed to help the client achieve and maintain sobriety. This approach is helpful for some, although research suggests a high dropout rate for outpatient treatment programs (Baekeland and Lundwall, 1975).

The most attractive feature of outpatient treatment is that the client is able to live outside of the treatment facility. In many cases, the client is expected to carry out a daily routine, which may include regular work or homemaking activities. However, the client is also expected to participate in treatment and take part in a formal chemical dependency treatment program. Such treatment participation may be through an *outpatient day treatment* program, where treatment activities are scheduled during normal working hours, or through an *outpatient evening treatment* program.

INPATIENT OR OUTPATIENT TREATMENT?

In recent years, questions have been raised as to whether inpatient treatment of chemical dependency is inherently better than outpatient treatment programs. Outpatient treatment programs offer several advantages over inpatient programs. It is usually less expensive to participate in an outpatient treatment program than to enter an inpatient treatment program.

Outpatient treatment programs are also usually more flexible, in terms of scheduling, than are inpatient treatment programs. A person may arrange to participate in outpatient treatment after work hours. In spite of these advantages, many professionals still question whether outpatient treatment is better for the client than inpatient drug addiction treatment.

Whether to place an individual in an inpatient or outpatient treatment program is a decision that rests on many factors. First of all, there is the available funding for treatment (Nace, 1987; Bonstedt, Ulrich, Dolinar, and Johnson, 1984). A sad, rarely discussed fact is that the restrictions on funding will play a role in deciding which treatment options are available for the individual. The person whose insurance will only pay for outpatient chemical dependency treatment will have certain financial restrictions placed on his or her treatment options.

Nace (1987) identified several other criteria by which one could select a successful candidate for outpatient alcoholism treatment. These criteria were

a. The client's *motivation* for treatment,
b. The client's *ability to discontinue* the use of alcohol,
c. The client's social support system,
d. The client's employment situation,
e. The client's medical condition,
f. The client's psychiatric status, and
g. The client's past treatment history.

Although Nace (1987) addressed only the issue of alcoholism, these criteria also serve as excellent criteria by which the suitability of outpatient treatment for other forms of drug addiction might be evaluated.

Outpatient rehabilitation is best suited to those clients who have not had an extensive prior treatment history (Nace, 1987). The individual's motivation for treatment, and the need for inpatient detoxification from chemicals, should be considered in the decision whether to recommend inpatient or outpatient treatment. Another factor that should be considered is the patient's overall medical condition.

Finally, the individual's psychiatric status and availability of social support should be evaluated when considering outpatient treatment (Nace, 1987). Obviously, a deeply depressed individual who is recovering from an extended period of cocaine use might benefit more from the greater support offered by an inpatient treatment program, at least during the initial recovery period when the depression is most severe.

Miller and Foy (1981) identified three factors that they thought should be considered by treatment professionals in working with the addicted person to set up goals to be accomplished in treatment. These factors were (a) the client's physical condition, (b) the client's social support system, and (c) the client's expectations for treatment. The authors postulated that these factors were most important in working with an addicted person to establish a viable treatment plan with appropriate goals. These are also factors that should be evaluated when considering inpatient as opposed to outpatient treatment for an individual client.

Bonstedt et al. (1984), challenged the need for inpatient treatment in more chronic cases of alcoholism. The authors noted that "aggressive outpatient treatment" (p. 1039) is more cost-effective than inpatient treatment for alcoholism, in most cases. The authors went on to point out that ". . . the majority of alcoholics do not have to be hospitalized each time they present for treatment . . ." (p. 1039). The issue of whether a prior history of chemical dependency treatment automatically excludes outpatient treatment is disputed by different professionals.

As noted by Klar (1987), the final criterion for whether to suggest an inpatient or an outpatient treatment program is, *given the client's resources and needs, what is the least restrictive treatment alternative?* The treatment referral criteria advanced by Miller and Foy (1981) or Nace (1987) are useful guides to the selection of the least restrictive alternative that will meet the client's needs.

Treatment options should be selected on the basis of meeting the client's needs, not on what resources happen to be easily available. One should be suspicious of a detoxification center associated with the only inpatient treatment program in the county, which coincidentally referred 90% of those admitted to detox for inpatient treatment. An essential question is whether these referrals are meeting the client's needs or those of the treatment program.

Newcomb and Bentler (1989) recognized that the treatment of chemical dependency has become a multimillion dollar industry, where, on occasion, the client's needs are placed after those of the treatment center. The authors, who discussed adolescent drug use, warned that:

> . . . there is growing concern that for various reasons, not the least of which is the profit motive, treatment programs are purposefully blurring

the distinction between use and abuse (any use equals abuse) and preying on the national drug hysteria to scare parents into putting their teenager in treatment with as little provocation as having a beer or smoking a joint (p. 246).

When evaluating the client's needs, it is necessary for the treatment professional to determine (a) does the client need treatment for drug addiction, and (b) if so, what are the least restrictive alternatives for this client? This is a point that is often overlooked when the client is evaluated, but is essential for adequate and appropriate care.

ADVANTAGES OF OUTPATIENT TREATMENT

In addition to the obvious cost advantage inherent in outpatient treatment, outpatient chemical dependency treatment programs avoid the need to remove the patient from his or her environment. Unlike inpatient treatment programs, there is no community reorientation period needed after outpatient treatment (Bonstedt, et al., 1984).

Nace (1987) recommended a treatment program that would last one year. This in itself is an advantage over inpatient treatment programs, which tend to be shorter in duration. A treatment program one year in duration would offer long-term follow-up for the crucial first year of sobriety, a time when the individual is likely to relapse. The patient who knew that he or she would be subjected to random urine toxicology screening as part of a year-long outpatient program may be less likely to use drugs.

Lewis, Dana, and Blevins (1988) noted that outpatient treatment programs are more flexible than inpatient treatment programs. Lewis, Dana, and Blevins (1988) believe that the outpatient treatment option offers the counselor a longer period of time to help the client achieve the goals outlined in the treatment plan. The client also has an extended period of time in which to practice and perfect new behaviors that will support sobriety.

Finally, outpatient treatment programs offer the client the opportunity to practice sobriety while still living in the community. This is a significant advantage over traditional inpatient treatment programs, where the client is removed from his or her home community for the duration of treatment.

OUTPATIENT TREATMENT AND SELF-HELP GROUPS

Outpatient chemical dependency treatment programs generally use a twelve-step philosophy. Some programs include AA meetings in their schedule, although it is more common for the program to require client attendance of either AA or NA meetings in the community. Attendance may be verified by having two or more program participants attend the same meeting, or by having a member of AA sign an attendance verification form for the patient.

Zimberg (1978) advanced the position that individuals in outpatient treatment for addiction should also enter AA. Zimberg believed that AA attendance allowed the patient to see that others have faced their addiction to alcohol and have recovered.

While the addict is in treatment, family members are encouraged to attend either Al-Anon or Alateen meetings, while the client attends AA. This is to introduce family members to the potential support available through Al-Anon or Alateen while the client is still in treatment. Resistance on the part of family members to participation in such self-help groups is explored during family night or family group meetings. This is done to help members of the client's immediate family use community support systems as they learn how to support the client's sobriety.

DRAWBACKS OF THE OUTPATIENT TREATMENT APPROACH

Although statistical research has found no significant difference in the percentage of outpatient treatment program "graduates" who remain sober, as opposed to those who complete inpatient treatment programs for drug addiction, this is not to say that outpatient treatment is as effective as inpatient treatment. Rather, inpatient treatment programs tend to deal more effectively with a different class of client than do outpatient treatment programs, making comparisons between these different forms of treatment difficult.

Outpatient treatment programs have difficulty with clients who require detoxification from chemicals, although outpatient detoxification is possible for some forms of drug addiction. Outpatient treatment programs also do not offer the same degree of structure and support found in an effective inpatient drug addiction program, and are of limited value for some patients who require a great deal of support during the early stages of sobriety.

SUMMARY

There is significant evidence that, at least for some addicted individuals, outpatient treatment is an option that should be considered by treatment professionals. For those with the proper social support, and for whom there is no coexisting psychiatric illness or need for inpatient hospitalization, outpatient therapy for drug addiction may offer the individual the chance to participate in treatment while still living at home. This avoids the need for a reorientation period following treatment, as is often seen in patients who have been hospitalized in an inpatient rehabilitation facility.

Outpatient treatment also allows for long-term therapeutic support, which is often not available from shorter term inpatient programs. Within an outpatient drug addiction program, random urine toxicology screening may be used to check on medication compliance and to identify those individuals who have engaged in illicit drug use.

Research evidence suggests that, for many patients, outpatient drug addiction treatment is as effective as inpatient chemical dependency programs. There is a significant dropout rate from outpatient treatment programs; however, and there remains much to be learned about making outpatient addiction treatment more effective.

CHAPTER 21

Inpatient Treatment of Chemical Dependency

The inpatient treatment program might best be defined as a residential treatment facility where the client lives while he or she participates in treatment. Such programs usually deal with the hard-core, the seriously ill, or the "difficult" patient. These are individuals for whom outpatient treatment has either not been successful, or for whom outpatient treatment has been ruled out due to the severity of the person's chemical use.

In response to the challenge presented by the client, residential treatment programs have evolved in order to provide the greatest degree of support and help. Inpatient treatment also is "the most restrictive, structured, and protective of treatment settings" (Klar, 1987, p. 340). It combines the greatest potential for positive change with high financial cost, and the possibility of branding the patient for life (Klar). The decision to use inpatient treatment should not be made lightly.

Often the inpatient treatment program provides detoxification services as part of the treatment program, and there is rapid access to medical support services for the seriously ill patient. Such programs are usually found in a hospital setting. Other forms of inpatient treatment might not provide the same degree of medical support, and might be found in *therapeutic communities* or in a *halfway house* setting, as well as in nonhospital based inpatient rehabilitation programs.

VARIETIES OF INPATIENT TREATMENT

Detoxification Programs

These programs are popular in some parts of the country, and involve detoxification services for the addicted person. This may be carried out as part of a hospital-based service or at a regional "crisis center." The main emphasis of such detoxification programs is medically supervised detoxification from chemicals. These centers have, for the most part, replaced the "drunk tank" once so common in county jails.

The detoxification center provides the individual with a place where detoxification might be carried out under the supervision of trained medical staff. As noted in Chapter 3, alcohol withdrawal carries some risk. Withdrawal from barbiturates or similar agents (see Chapter 4) also carries some risk. While withdrawal from other drugs, such as cocaine and the narcotics, does not normally involve a risk to human life, there is a significant risk of relapse during the initial period of detoxification from most of the drugs of abuse.

Miller and Hester (1986) warned that detoxification is not, in itself, a treatment for chemical dependency. Detoxification does not bring about a major change in drug-use behavior in most individuals. Rather, detoxification is a prelude to the treatment process. While detoxification from chemicals is often carried out on an inpatient basis, Miller and Hester (1986) concluded that only a minority of alcoholics actually required inpatient detoxification. Other patients, perhaps a majority, could safely be detoxified from alcohol in a community setting, according to the authors. This would result in a significant savings over inpatient detoxification, with approximately the same results as inpatient detoxification, according to Miller and Hester (1986).

Therapeutic Communities

The therapeutic community (TC) is a residential treatment program that "employs vigorous and forceful confrontation of addicts' attitudes and behavior, although the intensity of the confrontation varies considerably in different programs" (Klein & Miller, 1986, p. 1083). These programs usually require a commitment of one to three years (Klein & Miller, 1986), although some programs have a minimal commitment of only six months. Bassin (1970) reported that Daytop Village, an early TC for narcotics addicts, required a stay of one-and-a-half to two years.

Lewis, Dana, and Blevins (1988) noted that the TC has "become most prevalent as an intervention for drug abusers, particularly those addicted to opiates" (p. 33). The characteristics of TCs include social and physical isolation, structure, a system of rewards and punishments, an emphasis on self-examination and the confession of past wrong doing, and an expectation that the client work. The TC serves as an extended family for the individual. Indeed, according to Lewis, Dana, and Blevins (1988), the original members of Synanon (an early therapeutic community) were expected to remain there on a permanent basis.

There is a great deal of controversy surrounding TCs. Some (Ausabel, 1983) caution that the TC might not be a positive step for the individual because many programs use methods such as ego stripping and unquestioned submission to the rules of the program. However, others

(Yablonsky, 1967) note that the TC has been effective in some cases where traditional treatment methods have been of limited value.

Lewis, Dana, and Blevins (1988) pointed out that the social isolation inherent in the TC prevents the client from going out into the community to try new social skills. The harsh confrontation and high relapse rates often found in the TC have also drawn criticism (Lewis, Dana, and Blevins, 1988). Baekeland and Lundwall (1975) reported that drug-free treatment programs (which would include TCs) suffer the highest dropout rates found in drug treatment centers, including a dropout rate of 88.2% in the first 14 weeks at one drug-free treatment center.

Bassin (1970) reported that one early TC, Daytop Village, suffered a significant dropout rate. Eight percent of those admitted dropped out in the first 30 days, while another 17% left within 90 days of admission. Some 25% of those admitted to Daytop Village left treatment in the first three months, according to Bassin (1970). This is hardly a hallmark of a successful treatment program. Thus, the issue of whether the TC is an effective treatment modality has yet to be settled.

Hospital-Based Inpatient Treatment

Traditional inpatient drug rehabilitation is often carried out either in a center that specializes in chemical dependency treatment or in a traditional hospital setting as part of a specialized drug treatment unit. Many of these programs use the Minnesota Model, which was explored in detail in Chapter 14. There is no standard treatment program under the Minnesota Model, but there is a great deal of flexibility to meet the various needs of different individuals. Residential treatment programs usually have a strong emphasis on a twelve-step philosophy, and use individual and group therapy extensively.

Inpatient rehabilitation programs, especially those in a hospital setting, will often include a detoxification component. Adelman and Weiss (1989) reported that medically supervised withdrawal from alcohol dependency results in higher patient retention rates, improving the patient's chances of achieving and maintaining sobriety. Whether part of a hospital, inpatient treatment programs use a variety of treatment methods and draw on the varied skills of the different members of the treatment team to best help the client.

The client's length of stay in treatment depends on several factors. These will include the motivation of the client, whether the client has community resources that she or he might call on to help stay sober, and a range of other variables that the treatment team considers when working with any given individual.

THE NEED FOR INPATIENT TREATMENT: IS THERE A LEGITIMATE DEMAND FOR SUCH SERVICES?

Miller and Hester (1986), in speaking of alcoholism treatment programs, noted that ". . .the relative merits of residential treatment are less than clear" (p. 794). Indeed, the authors concluded after a review of some 16 research studies that there was no significant difference between inpatient and outpatient alcoholism rehabilitation programs on various measures of patient improvement.

Further, when the authors explored only the *length* of inpatient treatment, they found no statistically significant improvement for longer duration treatment programs as compared with shorter duration inpatient alcohol rehabilitation programs. The authors did admit that their data suggested that inpatient treatment was possibly more advantageous for the longer term addict, while outpatient treatment was more effective for short-term addicts. However, aftercare programs were found to play a more significant role in posttreatment success or failure than the specific form of treatment used.

In response to the work of Miller and Hester (1986), Adelman and Weiss (1989) reported that research has found that 77% of those alcoholics treated for their alcoholism eventually required some form of inpatient treatment. The authors found that treatment programs in "medically oriented facilities" (p. 516) had lower dropout rates than did treatment programs in nonmedical centers. The authors also concluded that patients discharged after short inpatient treatment programs tended to relapse more frequently than did those who remained in treatment longer.

However, Miller and Foy's (1981) work identified three factors that the professional should address when establishing treatment goals for the client. These factors also provide a framework within which to consider the client's need for inpatient treatment, as opposed to outpatient drug rehabilitation services. Miller and Foy (1981) identified these factors as being (a) the client's physical status, (b) the client's social support system, and (c) the client's expectations for treatment. Each of these factors will be considered in more detail in the following subsections.

The Client's Physical Status

The physical status of the client includes the psychiatric status, as well as the physical health status. Included in this category is the length of time that the individual has been addicted to chemicals, his or her history of past treatment exposures, and more traditional measures of physical health.

Clients who are suffering from any of a wide range of psychiatric disorders, or who might be thinking about suicide, will require inpatient treatment. Obviously, for the client whose addiction has resulted in serious medical complications such as alcoholic hepatitis, or any of a wide range of infections (including AIDS), inpatient treatment should be the treatment method of choice.

Those with a long history of drug addiction seem to benefit more from inpatient treatment rather than outpatient treatment. Evidence suggests that outpatient treatment works best for those with little prior treatment experience. The client with multiple past treatment exposures might benefit more from an inpatient rehabilitation program. Obviously, clients who are addicted to one or more chemicals may require close medical supervision during withdrawal.

Finally, those clients whose health status requires close medical supervision would require inpatient treatment, at least during the detoxification period preceding treatment itself. Such patients include those with potentially life-threatening disorders, possibly acquired as a result of their chemical use. Such a determination should be made by the client's physician; however, when in doubt, inpatient treatment should be considered the treatment option of choice.

The Client's Social Support System

The social support system available to the client will play a significant role in the client's recovery. The client who has a supportive family and a stable circle of friends might do well in an outpatient drug rehabilitation program. However, if the client does not have a stable social support system, or if the client's social system is drug-using, inpatient treatment as a means of helping the client break away from this peer group might be the most viable option.

The client's spouse or significant other should be considered when this evaluation is made. Obviously, a client whose spouse either actively uses chemicals or has a desire to keep the client actively addicted to chemicals because she or he is easier to control, is unlikely to provide a stable home environment within which the patient might regain a sense of stability in his or her life. This individual might be more likely to benefit from inpatient treatment than would a client whose spouse and children are caring and supportive, and have joined Al-Anon.

If withdrawal within the home is being attempted, treatment staff need to assesss whether the client's immediate family is likely to report known or suspected drug use during the withdrawal or treatment phase of rehabilitation. Obviously, the client whose spouse and/or children make excuses or support the client's continued chemical use by not reporting suspected new episodes of drug use to treatment staff might not benefit from outpatient detoxification. For such clients, inpatient treatment might be a better option.

The Client's Expectations for Treatment

This is perhaps the most important factor in the client's recovery from drug addiction. Just as the client's expectations for the drug's effects play a significant role in the way the pharmacological action of the drug is interpreted, so the client's expectations for treatment seem to influence the client's treatment progress.

Treatment is unlikely to have a lasting impact on the individual who views it as a period of confinement imposed upon him or her by the courts, parents, or employer. Unless she or he experiences a spiritual awakening, treatment is unlikely to benefit the individual. If the addicted person views treatment as an intermission between periods of drug use, then that is all that treatment will likely remain.

But for the client who views treatment as being of value in the struggle against chemical addiction, the client who acknowledges his or her spiritual need, treatment is likely to be of value in the rehabilitation process. Another word for the client's expectations is the client's *motivation* for treatment.

EVALUATION OF THE NEED FOR INPATIENT TREATMENT

The decision whether to use inpatient or outpatient treatment for a client is perhaps one of the most important decisions that a treatment professional will make (Washton, Stone, and Hendrickson, 1988), and is often a difficult one. Nace (1987) outlined several criteria that, in his opinion, mandated inpatient hospitalization for the treatment of alcoholism. These criteria could be grouped into three categories, as follows:

a. A serious medical problem, including: seizures, physical injuries, serious infections, heart problems, significant vomiting or dehydration, serious metabolic diseases, or a history of serious medication reactions.
b. A serious psychiatric/behavioral problem, such as: confusion, fluctuations in the level of consciousness, coma, depression, thoughts or ideas of suicide, uncontrolled psychiatric disorder such as bipolar affective disorder, or schizophrenia, and behavioral problems such as aggressive acting out.
c. An inability to abstain from chemical use during outpatient treatment.

In their essay on when inpatient treatment for drug abuse might be necessary, Washton, Stone, and Hendrickson (1988) identified several criteria by which the need for inpatient treatment might be evaluated. Some of the factors to be evaluated are the same as those identified by Nace

(1987). The criteria identified by Washton, Stone, and Hendrickson (1988) were: (a) the concurrent dependence on different chemicals, (b) serious medical or psychiatric illness, (c) poor motivation for treatment, (d) heavy involvement in dealing drugs, (e) a past history of failure in outpatient treatment, (f) severe psychosocial problems, and (g) a proven inability of the client to discontinue further drug use while in outpatient treatment. These criteria serve as a good guide to when it is necessary to hospitalize a client for inpatient treatment.

THE ADVANTAGES OF INPATIENT TREATMENT

Although there is a strong case for outpatient treatment programs, there are certain advantages to inpatient treatment programs. These advantages make the inpatient treatment the method of choice in some cases, especially more advanced cases of addiction.

Inpatient rehabilitation programs offer *more comprehensive treatment programming* than is possible in an outpatient treatment setting (Klar, 1987). This is an advantage in more advanced cases of drug dependency because addicts often center their lives around chemicals for such a long period of time that they will be unable to use a less restrictive treatment approach.

Inpatient treatment programs offer the advantage of almost total control over the client's environment. For clients who have lived at least the most recent portion of their lives in a drug-centered life-style, the concept of a drug-free way of life is often quite foreign. Inpatient treatment programs offer the advantage of a structured environment where individual and group therapy sessions, meals, recreational opportunities, self-help group meetings, and spiritual counseling are all part of the schedule.

Often, clients will report that they have not been eating on a regular basis prior to entering treatment. An inpatient rehabilitation setting allows staff to monitor and treat dietary disorders that may have been caused by the individual's addicted life-style. Supplementary vitamins, or dietary supplements, have often been valuable in such cases, and inpatient treatment allows staff to closely monitor the client's recovery from the physical effects of his or her addiction.

Many clients attend their first AA meeting while in an inpatient setting. In some cases, clients affirm that they would never have attended the AA or NA meeting if they had not been required to do so by treatment staff. Adelman and Weiss (1989) concluded that participation in AA was an essential component of an effective inpatient treatment program.

Another advantage of inpatient treatment is that it can provide *around-the-clock support during the earliest stages of sobriety*. It is not unusual to find a client awake at 2 o'clock in the morning, talking about personal problems with a staff member. Nor is it uncommon to find a client awake at 3 o'clock in the morning, pacing through the earliest stages of withdrawal. When these clients are asked what they would do if they were not in treatment, the most common answer is, "I would go out and score [buy, or obtain] some drugs!"

But, because they are in treatment, clients are able to draw on the support services of the staff to help them through the discomfort of withdrawal. This support might be in the form of a sympathetic ear to listen when the client needs somebody to talk to, or the administration of previously prescribed medications to help the client through the discomfort of withdrawal. Staff members might offer suggestions to help the client through the trials of withdrawal, such as suggesting that he or she walk around the ward or have something to eat. The presence of staff members ensures that someone will always "be there" for the client.

Inpatient treatment programs offer the additional advantage of *close supervision of the clients*. This is an advantage for several reasons. Often, addicted clients live alone, or lack close interpersonal support. In such cases, a medical emergency might go undetected for hours or days. In an inpatient treatment setting, medical emergencies may be quickly detected, and the appropriate action taken by staff to help the client.

The close supervision by staff members also helps to discourage further drug use. Clients, especially those with long-standing drug problems, are often tempted to "help out" with the detoxification process by taking a few additional drugs or drinks during withdrawal. Narcotic addicts have been known to inject drugs that they brought into treatment with them, while alcoholics have been known to take drinks from bottles thoughtfully packed away in the hidden corners of suitcases.

Some inpatient treatment centers search the client's belongings upon admission, while other treatment programs use the "honor system" in which other clients will confront the individual using chemicals in treatment. Most inpatient treatment centers use urine toxicology screenings to detect illicit-drug use during treatment. The close supervision inherent in an inpatient treatment setting provides the opportunity for staff members to request a urine sample *immediately*, should staff members suspect drug use by clients.

As Nace (1987) noted, inpatient treatment is of value in cases where outpatient treatment has become a "revolving door" (p. 130). Inpatient settings are also of value in cases where the individual has experienced repeated crisis situations while in outpatient treatment, has had several aborted attempts to use outpatient treatment, or has been unable to establish an effective therapeutic alliance in a less restrictive setting. Cases where the individual must be treated for multiple problems (physical and psychiatric) while being treated for drug addiction also benefit from inpatient treatment, according to Nace.

Although there are those who will argue that the inpatient treatment program sounds very similar to a concentration camp experience, one must recall that the dysfunction caused by drug addiction often requires drastic forms of intervention. Just as drastic forms of intervention are often necessary in the practice of medicine, such as the case where surgery is necessary when medical treatment of an ulcer has failed, inpatient treatment may also be necessary in more advanced cases of addiction to chemicals.

PARTIAL HOSPITALIZATION OPTIONS

In recent years, several new treatment formats, which combine elements of inpatient and outpatient rehabilitation programs, have been explored. Each of these rehabilitation formats offers advantages and disadvantages, yet each should be considered a viable treatment option for clients who present themselves for treatment. Depending on the client's needs, some of the new treatment formats might prove to be quite beneficial.

Two by Four Programs

One proposed solution to the treatment dilemma of whether to use inpatient or outpatient treatment is the so called "two by four" program. This program format borrows from both inpatient and outpatient treatment programs, to establish a two-phase rehabilitation system that seems to have some promise.

The individual is first hospitalized for a short period of time, usually two weeks, in order to achieve total detoxification from chemicals. Depending on the individual's needs, the initial period of hospitalization might be shorter or longer than the two-week time span. The goal is to help the client reach as quickly as possible the point where it is possible for him or her to participate in outpatient treatment.

If, as will occasionally happen, the client is unable to function in the less restrictive outpatient rehabilitation program, she or he may be returned to the inpatient treatment format. Later, when additional progress has been made, the client may again return to an outpatient setting to complete his or her treatment program.

Day Hospitalization

The day hospitalization format is also known as partial day hospitalization. As Lewis, Dana, and Blevins (1988) observed, this type of rehabilitation program combines elements of inpatient treatment with the opportunities for growth possible by having the client live at home. After detoxification has been achieved, the client is allowed to spend the evening hours at home and comes to the treatment center during normal working hours to participate in the rehabilitation program.

Although Klar (1987) explored the advantages and disadvantages of partial day hospitalization programs for psychiatric patients, his insights into the advantages of day hospitalization for chemical dependency treatment are equally valid. Klar noted that since the patient will

> . . . live at home, the acute partial hospital program is akin to a full-time job, and is consequently less disruptive to social and family roles and is less stigmatizing. Partial hospitalization is a less regressive treatment modality than inpatient care, asks more of the patient, and actively attempts to mobilize the patient's adaptive skills and support network in the treatment (p. 338).

An essential element of day hospitalization is that the client have a supportive, stable, family. Obviously, if the client's spouse (or other family members) also has a chemical abuse problem, day hospitalization may not be a viable treatment option. If the client's spouse is severely codependent, and continues to enable the client's continued chemical use, day hospitalization should not be the treatment of choice.

However, for the client with a stable home environment, day hospitalization offers the opportunity to combine the intensive programming possible through inpatient treatment programs with the opportunities for growth possible by having the client spend the evening hours at home. Such a program is of value for clients who need to rebuild family relationships after a protracted period of chemical use.

Halfway Houses

The halfway house concept emerged in the 1950s, in response to the need for an intermediate step between the inpatient treatment format and independent living (Miller and Hester, 1980). For those clients who lack a stable social support system, the period of time following treatment is often most difficult. The client, even if strongly motivated to remain sober, must struggle against the urge to return to chemical use without the social support necessary to aid in this struggle. The halfway house provides a transitional living facility for such a client during the period of time immediately following treatment.

Miller and Hester (1980) identified several common characteristics of halfway houses, including (a) small patient population (usually less than 25 individuals), (b) a brief patient stay (less than a few months), (c) emphasis on AA or similar twelve-step philosophy, (d) minimal rules, and (e) small number of professional staff members.

As noted above, most halfway houses use a twelve-step philosophy. Many hold in-house self-help group meetings such as AA, while other halfway houses require a specified number of community self-help group meetings a week. Each individual is expected to find work within a specified period of time (usually two to three weeks) or is assigned a job within the halfway house.

The degree of structure found in the traditional halfway house setting is somewhere between the structure found in an inpatient treatment program setting and a traditional household. This provides the client with enough support to function during the transitional period between treatment and self-sufficiency, yet at the same time provides the client with the ability to make choices about his or her life. As Miller and Hester (1980) pointed out, halfway houses usually have fewer rules than an inpatient treatment center. Halfway house participation is usually time-limited, usually three to six months, after which the client is ready to assume his or her responsibilities again.

Surprisingly, there is little evidence to support the halfway house concept, according to Miller and Hester (1980). The authors reported that research had failed to uncover significantly greater improvement from patients admitted to halfway houses following treatment than from patients who refused admission to a halfway house following inpatient treatment.

Adelman and Weiss (1989) challenged this conclusion, however, observing that research has found an inverse relationship between length of stay and rehospitalization in the first six months following treatment. In other words, those patients who elected to enter a halfway house following inpatient treatment were less likely to be hospitalized for relapse than those who did not. Finney, Moos, and Chan (1975) examined the relationship between length of stay in a halfway house setting following treatment and treatment outcome. The authors concluded that, for some subgroups of patients, length of stay was correlated with successful treatment outcomes.

SUMMARY

Inpatient treatment is often viewed as a drastic step. Yet, for a minority of those addicted to chemicals, such a drastic step is necessary if the client is ever to regain control of his or her life. The inpatient rehabilitation program offers many advantages over less restrictive treatment options, including a depth of support services unavailable in outpatient treatment. For many of those in the advanced stages of addiction, inpatient treatment offers the only realistic hope of recovery.

In recent years, questions have been raised concerning the need for inpatient treatment programs or halfway house placement following treatment (Miller and Hester, 1980). It has been suggested that inpatient treatment does not offer any advantage over outpatient treatment, or that a longer stay was any more effective than short-term treatment (Miller and Hester). However, Adelman and Weiss (1989) concluded that length of stay was inversely related to the probability of relapse following treatment. Furthermore, it was concluded by Adelman and Weiss that halfway house placement was appropriate for some clients following inpatient treatment.

CHAPTER 22

Alcoholics Anonymous and Narcotics Anonymous

THE TWELVE STEPS OF ALCOHOLICS ANONYMOUS

STEP ONE: We admitted that we were powerless over alcohol—that our lives had become unmanageable.

STEP TWO: Came to believe that a Power greater than ourselves could restore us to sanity.

STEP THREE: Made a decision to turn our will and our lives over to the care of God *as we understood Him.*

STEP FOUR: Made a searching and fearless moral inventory of ourselves.

STEP FIVE: Admitted to God, to ourselves, and to another human being the exact nature of our wrongs.

STEP SIX: Were entirely ready to have God remove all these defects of character.

STEP SEVEN: Humbly asked Him to remove our shortcomings.

STEP EIGHT: Made a list of all persons we had harmed, and became willing to make amends to them all.

STEP NINE: Made direct amends to such people wherever possible, except when to do so would injure them or others.

STEP TEN: Continued to take personal inventory and when we were wrong, promptly admitted it.

STEP ELEVEN: Sought through prayer and meditation to improve our conscious contact with God *as we understood Him,* praying only for knowledge of His will for us, and the power to carry that out.

STEP TWELVE: Having had a spiritual awakening as the result of these steps, we tried to carry this message to alcoholics, and to practice these principles in all our affairs.

The diverse forces that were to blend together to form Alcoholics Anonymous (AA) include the American temperance movement of the late

The Twelve Steps are reprinted by permission of Alcoholics Anonymous World Services, Inc. *Note:* The opinions stated in this chapter are those of the author, and not those of Alcoholics Anonymous or Narcotics Anonymous.

1800s (Peele, 1984); a nondenominational religious group known as the Oxford Group, which was popular in the 1930s (Nace, 1987); and the psychoanalysis of an American alcoholic by Carl Jung in the year 1931 (Edmeades, 1985). Over the years, both of the cofounders of AA were hospitalized, mistakes were made, questions were asked, and the early pioneers of AA embarked on a struggle for sobriety that transcended individual members.

Historically, AA was thought to have been founded on June 10, 1935, the day that an alcoholic physician had his last drink (Nace, 1987). Earlier, following a meeting between a stockbroker, William Griffith Wilson, and the surgeon, Dr. Robert Holbrook Smith, the foundation to AA was set down. William Wilson was struggling to protect his new-found sobriety while on a business trip in a strange city. After making several telephone calls in an effort to find support in his struggle, Wilson was asked to talk to Dr. Smith, who was drinking at the time that Wilson called.

Rather than looking out for his own needs, Wilson chose a different approach. He carried a message of sobriety to another alcoholic. The self-help philosophy of AA was born at that moment. In the half-century since then, it has grown to a fellowship of 50,000 "clubs" or AA groups, which includes chapters in 114 countries, with a total membership estimated at more than 1 million people (Edmeades, 1985; *Alcoholics Anonymous*, 1976).

During its early years, AA struggled to find a program that would enable its members to achieve and maintain sobriety. Within three years of its founding, three different AA groups were in existence, but even with three groups ". . . it was hard to find twoscore of sure recoveries . . . ." (*Twelve Steps and Twelve Traditions*, 1981, p. 17). Nace (1987) reported that, by the fourth year following its inception, there were about 100 members in the isolated AA groups.

In spite of this, the early members wrote of their struggle to achieve sobriety and published the first edition of the book *Alcoholics Anonymous* in 1939. The organization took its name from the title of the book *Alcoholics Anonymous* (*Twelve Steps and Twelve Traditions*, 1981), which has since come to be known as the "Big Book" of AA.

ELEMENTS OF AA

Peele (1984) noted that many of the features of AA are "peculiarly American" (p. 1338), including public confession, contrition, and salvation through spirituality. The *Twelve Steps and Twelve Traditions* (1981) noted that AA freely borrowed from the fields of medicine and religion to establish a program that worked.

The book *Al-Anon's Twelve Steps and Twelve Traditions*, which has borrowed the Twelve Steps of AA for use with families, divides the Twelve Steps into three groups. The first three steps are viewed as necessary for the acceptance of one's limitations. Through these first three steps, the individual is able to come to accept that his or her own resources are not sufficient to solve life's problems, especially the problems inherent in living with an addicted person. In the AA twelve-step program, these steps serve to help the individual accept that his or her resources are insufficient for dealing with the problems of life, especially one's addiction.

Steps four through nine are a series of change-oriented activities. These steps are designed to help the individual identify, confront, and ultimately overcome character shortcomings that were so much a part of the individual's addicted life-style. Through these steps, one may work through the guilt associated with past behaviors and learn to recognize the limits of personal responsibility. These steps allow the person to learn the tools of nondrug-centered living, something that at first is often alien to both the addict and his or her family.

Finally, steps ten through twelve challenge the individual to continue to build on the foundation established in steps four through nine. The individual is asked to continue to search out personal shortcomings and to confront them. The person is also challenged to continue the spiritual growth initiated during the earlier steps and to carry the message of hope to others.

Alibrandi (1978) viewed the components of the AA program that made it so effective in a different way. AA was viewed by Alibrandi as a form of "folk psychotherapy," which offered a program for change that involved five different phases. Alibrandi identified the first stage as starting on the first day of membership in AA, and lasting for one week. During this phase, the individual's goal is simply to stay away from the first drink or chemical use.

The second phase of recovery starts at the end of the first week and lasts until the end of the second month of AA membership. Major steps during this part of the recovery process include acceptance of the disease concept of addiction, and "letting go and letting God." During this phase, the individual struggles to replace old drug-centered behavioral habits with new, sobriety-oriented habits.

The third stage of recovery spans the interval from the second through the sixth months of sobriety, according to Alibrandi (1978). During this stage, the individual is to use the Twelve Steps as a guide, and to try and let go of old ideas. Guilt feelings about past chemical use are to be replaced with gratitude for sobriety, wherever possible, and the member is to stand available for service to other addicts.

The fourth stage begins at around the sixth month, and lasts until the first year of sobriety. During the fourth stage, the addict is encouraged to take a searching and fearless moral inventory of "self," and to share this with another person. At the same time, if the individual is still "shaky," he or she is encouraged to work with another addict. Emphasis during this phase of recovery is on acceptance of responsibility and the resolution of the anger and resentments upon which addiction is so often established.

Finally, after the first year of sobriety the recovery process has reached what Brown (1985) termed "ongoing sobriety." Alibrandi (1978) identified the goal during this phase of recovery as being the maintenance of a "spiritual condition." The person is warned not to dwell on the shortcomings of others, to suspend judgment of self and others, and to beware of the false pride that could bring one back to chemical use.

Alcoholics Anonymous appears to offer its members a program for living that includes a series of twelve successive steps towards lifelong behavioral change. The Twelve Steps might be viewed as a series of successive approximations toward the goal of sobriety. While the steps are not required for AA membership, the steps are a proven method of behavioral change that offers the addict a chance to rebuild his or her life. There are many who believe that these steps were instrumental in saving their lives.

AA AND RELIGION

Alcoholics Anonymous makes a distinction between spirituality and religion (Berenson, 1988). AA identifies with no single religious group or religious doctrine (*Twelve Steps and Twelve Traditions*, 1981). AA is a spiritual recovery program, but it does not endorse a specific religious doctrine or belief.

Jensen (1987) noted that Step Three "doesn't demand an immediate conversion experience . . . but . . . does call for a decision" (p. 22). This decision is for the addict to make a conscious decision to turn his or her will over to God. In addressing the issue of religion, Jensen (1987) noted that "Step Three simply assumes that there is a God to understand and that we each have a God of our own understanding" (p. 23).

In this manner, AA sidesteps the question of religion, while still addressing the spiritual disease that it views as existing within addiction. In turning one's will over to another, the addict comes to accept that his or her own will is not enough to maintain sobriety. Thus, AA offers a spiritual program that ties the individual's will to that of a higher power, without offering a specific religious dogma that might offend members.

ONE "A" IS FOR ANONYMOUS

Anonymity is central to the AA and the NA programs (*Understanding Anonymity*, 1981) This is one major reason most meetings are "closed." During a "closed" meeting, which is limited only to members, members will talk about "personal problems or interpretations of the Twelve Steps or the Twelve Traditions" (Lewis, Dana, and Blevins, 1988, p. 151). In an open meeting, which is open to any interested person, one or two volunteers will speak, and visitors are encouraged to ask questions about AA and how it works.

Anonymity is a central concept of AA. This is both to protect the identities of members, and to ensure that no identified spokesperson emerges who "speaks" for AA (*Understanding Anonymity*, 1981). Through this policy, the members of AA strive for humility, each knowing that she or he is equal to the other members. The concept of anonymity is so important that it is said to serve "as the spiritual foundation of the Fellowship" (*Understanding Anonymity*, 1981, p. 5) of AA.

The concept of equality of the members underlies the AA tradition that no "directors" are nominated or voted on. Rather, "service boards" or special committees are created from the membership, as needed. These boards always remain responsible to the group *as a whole*, and must answer to the entire AA or NA group. As is noted in Tradition Two of AA ". . . our leaders are but trusted servants; they do not govern" (*Twelve Steps and Twelve Traditions*, 1981, p. 10).

AA AND OUTSIDE ORGANIZATIONS

The AA group is both self-supporting and not-for-profit. Each individual group is autonomous and must support itself only through the contributions of the members. Outside donations are discouraged in order to avoid the problem of having to decide how to deal with these gifts. Outside commitments are also discouraged for AA groups. As is stated in the text *Twelve Steps and Twelve Traditions* (1981), AA groups will not

> . . . endorse, finance, or lend the A. A. name to any related facility or outside enterprise, lest problems of money, property and prestige divert us from our primary purpose (p. 11).

The relationships between different autonomous AA groups, and between AA groups and other organizations, are governed by the Twelve Traditions of AA. The Traditions are a set of guidelines or a framework within which different groups may interact, and through which AA as a whole may work together. They will not be reviewed in this chapter; however, interested readers might wish to read *The Twelve Steps and Twelve Traditions* (1981) to learn more about the Traditions.

THE PRIMARY PURPOSE OF AA

This "primary purpose" of AA is twofold. First, the members of AA strive to "carry the message to the addict who still suffers" (*The Group*, 1976, p. 1). Second, AA seeks to provide for its members a program for living without chemicals. This is done not by preaching at the alcoholic or drug addict. Rather, it is accomplished by presenting to the addict a simple, truthful, realistic picture of the disease of addiction.

To accomplish this, it is necessary to confront the addict with the facts of his or her addiction in plain language, language that she or he can understand. The manner in which this confrontation is carried out is somewhat different from the usual methods of confrontation. In AA, speakers share their own life stories, a public confession of sorts where each individual tells of the lies, the distortions, the self-deceptions, and the denial that supported their own chemical use. In so doing, the speaker hopes to break through the defensiveness of the addict by showing that others have walked the same road and found a way to sobriety.

The *Twelve Steps and Twelve Traditions* (1981) of AA noted that

> Even the newest of newcomers finds undreamed rewards as he tries to help his brother alcoholic, the one who is even blinder than he. . . . And then he discovers that by the divine paradox of this kind of giving he has found his own reward, whether his brother has yet received anything or not (p. 109).

In this, one finds a therapeutic paradox (not the only one!) in AA. For the speaker seeks first of all to help himself or herself through the public admission of his or her powerlessness over chemicals. Through the public admission of weakness, the speaker seeks to gain strength. It is almost as if, by owning the reality of his or her addiction, the speaker says "This is what *my* life was like, and by having shared it with you, I am reminded again of the reason why I will not return to drugs, again."

Through this process, the speaker uses the methods first pioneered by Bill Wilson in his first meeting with Bob Smith. In that meeting, Bill Wilson spoke at length of his own addiction to alcohol, of the pain and suffering that he had caused others, and how he had suffered in the service of his addiction. He did not preach, but simply shared with Dr. Smith the history of his own alcoholism. Bill Wilson concluded with the statement: "So thanks a lot for hearing me out. I know now that I'm not going to take a drink, and I'm grateful to you" (Kurtz, 1979, p. 29).

Earlier, it was noted that the methods of AA present a paradox, in that it is by helping others that the speaker comes to receive help for his or her addiction. The speaker, in sharing, receives help for his or her drug problem. At the same time, he or she confronts the defenses of the new member by saying, in effect, "I am a mirror of yourself, and just as you cannot look into a mirror without seeing your own image, you cannot look at me without seeing yourself." In this way, the speaker seeks to carry the message to others.

As previously mentioned, AA is a spiritual program that is at the same time not religious. In place of the disease of the spirit upon which addiction rests, AA offers a program for living. Lewis, Dana, and Blevins (1988) pointed out that the Twelve Steps are usually introduced with the words: "Here are the steps we took, which are suggested as a program for recovery" (p. 149).

One is not *required* to follow the Twelve Steps to participate in AA. Jensen (1987) observed that ". . . *the program* does not issue orders; it merely *suggests* Twelve Steps to recovery" (p. 15, italics in original). Thus, the individual is offered a choice between the way of life that preceded AA, or acceptance of a program that others have used to achieve and maintain their sobriety.

The Twelve Steps offer the promise and the tools necessary for daily sobriety. But it is up to the individual to pick up the tool and put it to use. The member of AA is not encouraged to look for the "cause" of their addiction. Rather, the individual's addiction is accepted as a given fact. "It is not so much *how* you came to this place, as what you are going to do now that you are here," as one member said to a newcomer.

Neither is the member admonished for being unable to live without chemicals. Chemical addiction is assumed in membership: "If chemicals were not a problem for you, you would not be here!" In place of the chemical-centered life-style, the new member is offered a step-by-step program for living that allows him or her to achieve, and maintain, sobriety.

To take advantage of this program, the member need only accept *the program*. Admittedly, in doing so the individual is asked to accept yet another therapeutic paradox, known as Step One. For Step One of the AA step program asks that the addict first of all accept that she or he is powerless over chemicals. She or he is asked to do so not on the superficial level necessary to speak the words "I am powerless over chemicals," but on the deepest level of his or her being.

Many an addict has found that conformity, at least to the point of saying the phrase "I am addicted to chemicals," was enough to help them escape from the consequences of their addiction. It is easy to say the words, if one does not believe them to be true. To accept *the program* the member must confront, on the deepest level of his or her soul, that he or she is *addicted* and is *totally powerless* over chemicals.

William Springborn (1987) noted that when he confronts the rationalization that chemicals alone are the person's bane, that the person is a helpless victim of the disease of addiction, he will

> . . . stress the idea that it is we ourselves, not the pills or alcohol, who cause most of our problems. Chemicals will not bring destruction upon a person until that person learns how to justify continual use and abuse of those chemicals (p. 8).

When addicts accept the painful, bitter, frightening reality that their lives are no longer their own, but are spent in the service of their addiction, and when they come to understand that *nothing* they do will allow them to control their chemical use, the addict "hits bottom." It is at this point that the addict is able to turn to another person, and say, "My way does not work for me. I need help." At this moment in time, the person takes the First Step (the ultimate admission of powerlessness), and becomes receptive to learning a solution to addiction.

OF AA AND RECOVERY

Alcoholics Anonymous does not speak of a "cure" for the disease of alcoholism. The members of AA do not speak of themselves as having "recovered." For while it is believed by the members of AA that addiction is a disease whose progress may be arrested, it is acknowledged that alcoholism can never be cured. Thus, persons may speak of themselves as *recovering*, but never as having *recovered*.

Alcoholics Anonymous does not speak of an ultimate "cure" because a recovering addict is only a moment away from the next "slip." The 25-year veteran may, in a weak moment, relapse. No matter what a person's motivation for sobriety, she or he can only strive to be sober for today. If "today" is too long a period to think about, the addict is encouraged to think about remaining sober for the next hour, or the next minute, or just the next second.

Jensen (1987) explored this point, and noted that

> We may not have freely chosen to go to AA or perhaps treatment. We may have been pressured by an employer, a spouse, or other family members, a medical doctor, or even a court. We may not have a sincere desire to quit drinking or using and are proceeding with *the program* only because it appears to be better than the consequences of not complying (p. 24, italics in original).

But once the addict accepts *the program*, he or she finds a way of living that provides support 24 hours a day for the rest of his or her life. In accepting *the program*, the addicted person may discover a second chance that she or he thought was forever lost.

SPONSORSHIP

To help each person on the spiritual odyssey that can result in their sobriety, new members of AA are encouraged to find a "sponsor." This is a person who has worked his or her way through the twelve-step program, and who has achieved a basic understanding of their own addiction. The sponsor acts as a spiritual (but not a religious) guide, offering confrontation, insight, and support, in equal amounts, to the new member.

Alibrandi (1978) noted that it is the duty of the sponsor to take an interest in the newcomer's progress, but *not to take responsibility for it*. The responsibility for recovery is placed on the individual. It is a way of saying "I can be concerned for you, but I am not responsible for you." In today's terminology, the sponsor is a living example of "tough love."

The sponsor should not try to control the newcomer's life, and ideally should recognize his or her limitations. Many of the same characteristics of the healthy human services professional identified by Rogers (1961) apply to the AA sponsor as well. The sponsor, acting as an extension of AA, is a tool. It is up to the newcomer to grasp and use this tool to achieve sobriety. There are no guarantees, and the sponsor often struggles with many of the same issues that face the newcomer. The newcomer must assume the responsibility for reaching out and using the tools that are offered.

Sponsorship is, in essence, an expression of the second mission of AA, which is to "carry the message" to other addicts, who are still actively using chemicals. This is a reflection of Step Twelve, and one will often hear the sponsor speak of having participated in a twelfth-step visit, or of having been involved in twelfth-step work. The sponsor is, in a sense, a guide, friend, peer-counselor, fellow traveler, conscience, and devil's advocate all rolled into one.

AA AND PSYCHOLOGICAL THEORY

Alibrandi (1978) observed that the AA step program is different from other therapeutic programs in which the addict may have been involved, in the sense that the steps are "reports of action taken rather than rules not to be broken" (p. 166). Each step then is a public (or private) demonstration of action taken in the struggle to achieve and maintain sobriety, rather than a rule that might be broken.

Brown (1985) speaks of the AA steps as serving another purpose, as well. The Twelve Steps serve to keep the recovering addict focused on his or her addiction. Just as the alcohol was an "axis" around which the individual centered his or her life while drinking, through the Twelve Steps the addict continues to center his or her life around alcohol in a different way: without chemicals.

During the period of active chemical use the individual learned to center his or her life around drugs (Brown, 1985). In order to avoid the danger of being deceived, the individual needs to learn a new way to openly relate to his or her addiction. The addict must learn to do so in such a way that allows him or her to achieve and maintain, sobriety. The Twelve Steps accomplish this by providing a structured program by which the individual might continue to relate to his or her addiction, while still being able to draw on the group for support and strength.

WHAT MAKES AA EFFECTIVE?

Charles Bufe (1988) offered three reasons why he thought AA was effective "at least for some people" (p. 55). First, Bufe hypothesized that AA was a social outlet for its members. "Loneliness," Bufe observed, "is a terrible problem in our society, and people will flock to almost *anything* that relieves it—even AA meetings" (p. 55, italics in original). This hypothesis, however, has not been tested.

Second, Bufe (1988) suggested that AA allows its members to recognize that their problems are not unique. Alibrandi (1978) reached a similar conclusion in his research into the elements of AA that made this program effective. Nace (1987) noted that through AA participation the individual member is able to restore identity and self-esteem through the unconditional acceptance of its members. Each member of AA has walked the same roads and experienced the same trials. Through this, each member of AA is able to discover a relatedness to others.

Third, as Bufe (1988) observed, AA can offer a proven path to follow that can "look awfully attractive when your world has turned upside down and you no longer have your best friend—alcohol—to lean on" (p. 55). While there is some truth in this, one must wonder if, as Bufe concluded, "These things, especially the first two, are all that is really needed" (p. 55). This view, while perhaps accurate, would also appear to be rather limited. For AA seems to offer more than just a way to deal with loneliness, or a way of relating to others.

Herman (1988) observed that AA's Twelve Step program offers at least one more feature to the recovering addict: predictability. Consistency was one of the characteristics identified by Rogers (1961) as being of value in the helping relationship, and one must wonder if the predictability of AA is not one of the curative forces of this self-help group. However, research into this area is lacking, and this remains only a hypothesis.

Berenson (1988) noted that the AA program was "designed so that a person can stop drinking by either education, therapeutic change, or transformation" (p. 71). As part of the therapeutic transformation inherent in AA participation, Berenson also speculated that people would ". . . bond to the group and use it as a social support and a refuge to explore and release their suppressed and repressed feelings" (p. 71).

Alcoholics Anonymous meetings, as noted by Nace (1987) "are generally characterized by warmth, openness, honesty, and humor" (p. 242). Yet as Ogborne and Glaser (1985) noted, there has been surprisingly little research into the subject of what factors make AA so effective for so many different people.

OUTCOME STUDIES: THE EFFECTIVENESS OF AA

In spite of the fact that AA is viewed by many treatment professionals as being the single most important component of a person's recovery program, it is not without its critics (Ogborne and Glaser, 1985). Lewis, Dana, and Blevins (1988) warn that AA "should be used only as a supportive adjunct to treatment" (p. 151). Questions have even been raised as to whether AA is necessary for every addict's recovery. However, even its critics seem to accept the fact that AA might be helpful at least to some, but not necessarily all, of those who have a problem with chemicals (Ogborne and Glaser, 1985).

In spite of its potential, at least half of the newcomers to AA relapse during the first year (Alibrandi, 1978). This would suggest that the remainder do *not* relapse during the first year of AA membership. Nace (1987) reported that one study of AA members found that 70% of those who stay sober for one year will remain sober at the end of their second year, while 90% of those who were sober at the end of their second year were still sober at the end of their third year of AA participation.

Ogborne and Glaser (1985) reviewed the limited number of research studies that attempted to measure the effectiveness of AA and concluded that AA "is not effective for *all* kinds of persons with alcohol problems" (p. 188). Rather, it was concluded that AA was most effective with a subset of problem drinkers who were more likely to be socially stable white males, over 40 years of age, who were physically dependent on alcohol, prone to guilt, and the firstborn or only child. The evidence supporting the discriminatory power of these characteristics was found to be quite weak, and Ogborne and Glaser noted that these characteristics "should not be taken too seriously" (p. 185–86).

It was the hope of Ogborne and Glaser (1985) that these findings would serve as a stimulus for further research. Obviously, there are also many members of AA who do not demonstrate the same characteristics of a successful member outlined by Ogborne and Glaser. For example, in 1983, AA estimated that one-third of its membership was composed of women. Because of this, and because the discriminatory power of their statistical model of a successful AA member was quite weak, the authors called for further research into the question of what makes AA effective.

In an earlier paper, Glaser and Ogborne (1982) noted that AA certainly does not seem to be effective with those who are coerced into attending AA meetings by the courts. As the authors noted, such people are extremely difficult to work with, and to date no method of intervention has been shown to be effective in working with them. Thus, the authors do not view this as an adequate measure of the effectiveness of AA. Glaser and Ogborne postulated that the issue of whether AA is effective is far too complex to be measured by a single research study and called for a series of well-controlled research studies to identify all of the variables that might influence the outcome of AA participation.

The question of the effectiveness of AA has yet to be settled. One might suspect that the very nature of the question "Is AA effective?" makes it unanswerable. Would the chronic alcoholic who, as a result of participation in AA, stopped continual drinking but then entered into a pattern of binge drinking with month-long periods of sobriety be measured as a successful outcome? Would the chronic alcoholic who entered AA, stopped drinking, but died six weeks later as a result of the effects of many years of chronic alcohol use be measured as an unsuccessful outcome?

The thrust of Ogborne and Glaser's (1982, 1985) work is that the simplistic question "Is AA effective?" is unlikely to generate a meaningful answer.

Rather, one must ask "What are the factors that make/do not make AA effective for this subgroup of people?" in order to better understand the strengths and abilities of AA.

NARCOTICS ANONYMOUS

In 1953, another self-help group patterned after AA was founded, a group that called itself "Narcotics Anonymous" (NA). Although this group honors its debt to AA, the members of NA feel that

> We follow the same path with only a single exception. Our identification as addicts is all-inclusive in respect to any mood-changing, mind-altering substance. "Alcoholism" is too limited a term for us; our problem is not a specific substance, it is a disease called "addiction" (*Narcotics Anonymous*, 1982, p. x).

To the members of NA it is not the specific chemical that is the problem, but the common disease of addiction. Narcotics Anonymous emerged as a self-help group to help those whose only "common denominator is that we failed to come to terms with our addiction" (*Narcotics Anonymous*, 1982, p. x).

The major difference between AA and NA seems to be one of emphasis. Alcoholics Anonymous addresses only alcoholism, while NA addresses addiction to chemicals in addition to alcohol. The growth of NA has been phenomenal, with a *600%* increase in the number of NA groups in the period from 1983 to 1988 (Coleman, 1989). Currently, there are in excess of 14,000 NA meetings in the United States each week (Coleman).

The two programs are not affiliated, although there is an element of cooperation between AA and NA (Jordan, M., *Personal Communication*, 27 February, 1989). Each follows essentially the same twelve-step program, which offers the addict a day-by-day program for recovery. This is understandable, since NA is essentially an outgrowth of AA. The language of AA speaks alcoholism, while NA speaks of "addiction," or "chemicals." Each offers the same program, with minor variations, to help the addicted person struggle to achieve sobriety.

The most important point is this: which group works best for the individual? Some people feel quite comfortable going to AA for their addiction to alcohol. Other people feel that NA offers them what they need to deal with their addictions. In the final analysis, the name of the group does not matter so much as the fact that it offers the recovering person the support and understanding that she or he needs to remain sober for today.

AL-ANON AND ALATEEN

The book *Al-Anon's Twelve Steps and Twelve Traditions* provides a short history of Al-Anon in its introduction. According to this history, while their husbands were at the early AA meetings, the wives would often meet to wait for their husbands. As they waited, they would often talk over their problems. At some point, the decision was made to try and apply to their own lives the same Twelve Steps that their husbands had found so helpful, and Al-Anon was born.

In the beginning, each isolated group made whatever changes it felt necessary in the Twelve Steps. But by 1948 the wife of one of the co-founders of AA became involved in the growing organization, and in time a uniform family support program emerged. This program, known as the Al-Anon Family Group, borrowed and modified the AA Twelve Steps and Twelve Traditions to make them applicable to the needs of families of alcoholics.

By 1957, in response to the recognition that teenagers presented special needs and concerns, Al-Anon in turn gave birth to a modified Al-Anon group for teens known as "Alateen." Alateen members follow the same Twelve Steps outlined in the Al-Anon program. The goal of the Alateen program is to provide the opportunity for teenagers to come together to share their experiences, discuss current problems, learn how to cope more effectively with their various concerns, and to provide encouragement to each other (*Facts about Alateen*, 1969).

Through Alateen, teenagers learn that alcoholism is a disease and are helped to detach emotionally from the alcoholic's behavior, while still loving that individual. The goal of Alateen is also to help the participant learn that she or he did not "cause" the alcoholic to drink, and to see that she or he can build a rewarding life in spite of the alcoholic's continued drinking (*Facts about Alateen*, 1969).

SUMMARY

The self-help group Alcoholics Anonymous has emerged as one of the predominant forces in the field of drug abuse treatment. Drawing on the experience and knowledge of its members, AA has developed a program for living that is spiritual without being religious, confrontive without using confrontation in the traditional sense of the word, relies on no outside support, and which many of its members believe is effective in helping them stay sober on a daily basis.

The program for living established by AA is based on those factors that early members believed were important to their own sobriety. This program for living is known as the Twelve Steps. The Twelve Steps are suggested as a guide to new members. Emphasis is placed on the equality of all members, and there is no board of directors within the AA group.

Questions have emerged as to whether AA is effective. Researchers agree that it seems to be effective for some people, but not for all of those who join. The question of how to measure the effectiveness of AA is quite complex. A series of well-designed research projects to identify the multitude of variables involved in making AA effective for some people is required.

In spite of these unanswered questions AA has served as a model for many other self-help groups, including Narcotics Anonymous. Narcotics Anonymous holds that the alcohol focus of AA is too narrow for persons who have become addicted to other chemicals, either alone or in combination with alcohol. Narcotics Anonymous expounds the belief that addiction is a common disease that may express itself through many forms of drug dependency. Narcotics Anonymous has established a program that is based on the Twelve Steps, and draws heavily from its parent, AA. But NA seeks to reach out to those whose addiction involves chemicals other than alcohol, and thus avoids the strict alcohol focus of AA.

Other self-help groups that have emerged as a result of the AA experience include Al-Anon and Alateen. Al-Anon emerged from informal encounters between the spouses of early AA members and strives to provide an avenue for helping the families of those who are addicted to alcohol. Alateen emerged from Al-Anon, in response to the recognition that adolescents have special needs. Both groups strive to help the member learn how to be supportive of, without being dependent on, the alcoholic and to learn how to detach from the alcoholic and his or her behavior.

CHAPTER 23

Drugs and Sexuality

Students are often surprised to learn that sexual arousal is a multiphasic process that involves the neurological, vascular, muscular, and hormonal systems of the human body (Kaplan, 1974). Not surprisingly, many of the drugs of abuse have their greatest impact on these same body systems, a fact that often results in the drug abuser or addict experiencing some form of sexual dysfunction. In this chapter, the interaction between the drugs of abuse and the sexual dysfunctions will be explored.

PROBLEMS IN THE ASSESSMENT
OF THE EFFECTS OF DRUGS ON SEXUAL AROUSAL

There are several problems associated with the assessment of how chemicals impact on the sexual arousal process. First, there are the specific chemical(s) present in the individual's body. Second, there is the specific amount of each chemical in the body. Third, there is the specific amount of each chemical already in the bloodstream, and the specific amount of each chemical that will potentially reach the blood. Fourth, there are the potential interactions between the chemicals present in the individual's body.

These are difficult variables to assess, and as Kaplan (1974) observed, the same drug may have different effects on the sexual arousal process as a result of input from still other factors. These additional factors include the individual's physical health (including the state of health of the individual's nervous system, and prescription and nonprescription medications being used by the individual), and the individual's emotional health (which includes the individual's expectations for the drug or drugs being used).

Gold (1988) postulated that there are three elements to normal sexual function: (a) desire, (b) performance, and (c) satisfaction. Unfortunately, the various drugs of abuse may impact on each of these elements of normal sexual function. To understand the impact of a chemical or chemicals on the individual's sexual arousal, one must understand how chemicals of abuse disrupt the desire process, interfere with sexual performance, and in many cases block sexual satisfaction.

THE IMPACT OF DRUG
EXPECTATIONS ON SEXUAL AROUSAL

Brown, Goldman, Inn, and Anderson (1980) explored the expectations that people have for alcohol and found that there were six different areas where people had preconceptions about alcohol's effects. The authors reported that subjects expected positive effects from alcohol use on life experiences, that alcohol use would enhance both social and physical pleasure, and that it would enhance sexual performances. The authors also found that their subjects thought that moderate alcohol use would increase social aggressiveness, increase assertiveness, and reduce tension.

Kaplan (1974) noted that while research evidence suggests that LSD is either nonstimulating, or possibly even a drug that depresses sexual desire, the individual's expectations for the drug still may play a role in how the drug's effects are interpreted by the individual. Thus, in a highly erotic situation with a desired partner, an individual who is under the influence of LSD *might* report an "unusually intense sexual encounter" (Kaplan, 1974, p. 87), in spite of the drug's known physiological effects.

Drug expectations, many of which are learned through social interactions, help to shape the individual's subjective interpretation of a drug's effects. The phenomenon of individual expectations has been found to have a powerful impact on the human body, including the sexual arousal process (Kaplan, 1979). When certain drugs are used at low dosage levels, the individual is likely to interpret the effects of the drug based on his or her expectations.

CHEMICALS AND INTIMACY DYSFUNCTION

Intimacy might be thought of as an element of sexual desire or emotional health. The person who is emotionally secure will desire both sexual and nonsexual intimacy without feeling anxious, ashamed, or insecure. Unfortunately, many people do not feel comfortable with the desire for sexual intimacy as a normal human function. Often, these people will come to believe that one must drink, or be under the influence of chemicals, in order to be sexual.

Masters and Johnson (1966) reported that it is a common belief that alcohol increases sexual desire. Farkasfalvy (1979) noted that, for women, ". . . the belief that drunkenness and sexual acting out go hand in hand" (p. 1), in spite of the fact that research fails to suggest such a relationship. In such a case, the alcohol seems to be used as an excuse for normal sexual desires to be expressed, and possibly acted upon.

Covington (1987) defined alcoholism as an intimacy disorder, stating that alcoholism was "a love affair with alcohol" (p. 21). It was Covington's belief that the shame, guilt, and pain associated with a history of physical, sexual, or emotional abuse set the stage for chemical use as a way of dealing with the anxiety the individual would experience when offered the opportunity for intimacy. The history of abuse would inhibit the development of trust, which Covington (1987) viewed as allowing for "surrender, which is part of the sexual experience" (p. 21).

Coleman (1982) suggested that, for many, chemical dependency itself may have resulted from a lack of adequate intimacy skills. In such a case, the person might initially have turned to drugs as a way of dealing with the painful lack of intimacy skills. By substituting chemicals for the desired intimacy skills, the individual is ultimately faced with an even more painful awareness of continued isolation.

This sets the stage for a cycle of continued drug use. However, chemical use may in itself bring about sexual dysfunction (Gold, 1988), the discovery of which may cause the individual to avoid further opportunities for intimacy. This results in a renewed sense of loneliness and shame, which may then be self-medicated through further drug or alcohol use.

Often the newly recovering alcoholic must learn how to be sexual without the use of chemicals (Covington, 1987; Phillips, 1979), a process that might be difficult for some. Covington noted that the media often bombards women with the message that, in order to be sensual, sexual, and attractive, she must use alcohol. These are messages that make it difficult for the recovering female addict to separate her sexuality from continued chemical use.

Miller and Foy (1981) observed that marital counseling is often a necessary component of chemical dependency treatment programs. Such marital counseling programs help as addicts struggle to develop the intimacy skills that often have been lacking throughout the history of their relationships.

THE IMPACT OF SPECIFIC CHEMICALS ON SEXUAL PERFORMANCE

An *aphrodisiac* is a substance that will enhance sexual pleasure and/or performance. Kolodny (1985) noted that, while empirical research consistently demonstrates that chemical use is likely to interfere with sexual performance rather than enhance it, there continues to be a persistent belief that one drug or another will function as an aphrodisiac. First one drug will be rumored to be the long-awaited aphrodisiac, followed by clinical research that ultimately disproves the rumors. Then another drug will be touted as an aphrodisiac, only to have these rumors disproved in turn.

Alcohol

Alcohol has long been thought to be an effective aphrodisiac. In recent years, however, Shakespeare's observation that alcohol "provokes the desire but . . . takes away the performance" (*Macbeth*, act 2, scene 3) has been found to be quite accurate. Gold (1987) noted that even at blood alcohol levels below that of legal intoxication, male college students experienced a significant decrease in the erectile response while viewing erotic films.

Under certain conditions, however, alcohol may actually enhance sexual excitement through the disinhibition effect. Kaplan (1974) noted that low doses of alcohol depress the action of that portion of the brain involved in anxiety and fear responses. This allows alcohol to lower the individual's anxiety level, making it easier for him or her to engage in sexual activities.

But, in moderate to high doses, or in cases of chronic use, alcohol disrupts sexual desire, performance, and satisfaction (Gold, 1988). Blood tests taken before, during, and after the use of alcohol have revealed that serum testosterone levels decrease as blood alcohol levels increase (Gold, 1987). The chronic use of alcohol will result in abnormally low serum testosterone levels, a condition that results in decreased sexual desire. If significant liver or testicular damage has occurred, this condition may be permanent (Gold, 1988).

Moderate to high doses of alcohol, or chronic use of alcohol, may also inhibit sexual arousal through a disruption of the spinal cord nerves necessary in the erection process for males (Gold, 1988). Women who drink will experience lowered levels of vaginal vasocongestion at higher levels of intoxication, which will inhibit sexual desire and possibly performance. This information might explain why Gold (1987) found that 55% of women who drank reported a decrease in sexual pleasure (Gold, 1987).

In their study of human sexuality, Masters and Johnson (1966) concluded that the excessive use of alcohol was the most frequently encountered cause of impotence in middle-aged men. The authors noted that in many cases the men will develop a fear of further sexual performance problems after their first bout of alcohol-induced impotence. This fear may then motivate the male to avoid further sexual activity with his partner in order to escape from further anticipated failure. This will, in turn, establish the groundwork for sexual adjustment problems within the relationship (Masters and Johnson, 1966).

According to Masters, Johnson, and Kolodny (1986), research has revealed that alcohol may decrease the intensity and pleasure of orgasm in the male, while at even moderate levels of intoxication alcohol makes it more difficult for the woman to achieve orgasm. Masters and Johnson (1966) concluded that, for chronic alcoholics, the sexual desire will "simply disappear" (p. 268).

Narcotics

The narcotic family of drugs impair sexual desire, performance, and satisfaction (Gold, 1988). Obviously, in that the narcotics are used in the control of severe pain, few people who are receiving narcotics for medical reasons will be so motivated as to engage in sexual activity while under the influence of this family of drugs.

Males who abuse or are addicted to the narcotics will experience decreased erection and orgasm (Gold, 1988). Chronic use of narcotics will also reduce sexual desire (Masters, Johnson, and Kolodny, 1986) and inhibit the individual's ability to achieve orgasm (Kaplan, 1979). The need to resort to prostitution as a way of supporting their habit also decreases sexual desire for many women (Masters, Johnson, and Kolodny, 1986).

Kolodny (1985) reported that research has found both a lowered testosterone level, and lowered libido, in male narcotics addicts. Research has also found lowered libido in the majority of female narcotic addicts studied (Kolodny, 1985). The lowered libido level will usually resolve itself in the first three months of abstinence (Kolodny, 1985).

Masters, Johnson, and Kolodny (1986) postulated that two reasons for the decreased sexual desire found in chronic narcotic addicts were the malnutrition and history of infections inherent in the life-style of the addict. Illness and malnutrition are factors known to reduce sexual desire and performance, and it is thus not surprising that narcotic addicts might experience sexual problems as a result of their addiction.

Kolodny (1985) observed that the male narcotic addict, like the male alcoholic, may have discovered to his dismay that his drug of choice has interfered with his ability to achieve or maintain an erection. This individual may, like the male alcoholic, withdraw from further sexual activities in order to avoid further injuries to his self-concept through later periods of drug-related impotence (Kolodny, 1985).

Masters, Johnson, and Kolodny (1986) noted that it is often difficult to determine whether the sexual dysfunction or the opiate addiction came first, because for some individuals addiction could be a response to sexual dysfunction. The authors concluded that a significant number of narcotic addicts do experience disorders of desire, performance and satisfaction that either precede or result from their addiction. Kaplan and Moodie (1982) reported that the primary drug addiction must be addressed first when working with an addicted person with a sexual dysfunction.

Amphetamines and Cocaine

Kolodny (1985) warned that there was little reliable research data on the effects of the CNS stimulants on sexual performance or satisfaction. However, the amphetamines and cocaine have at various times been touted as aphrodisiacs (Kolodny, 1985).

Both the team of Masters, Johnson, and Kolodny (1986), and Kaplan (1979), concluded that the CNS stimulants may increase sexual responsiveness when used at low doses, a factor that may have contributed to their reputation as aphrodisiacs. Gold (1988) reported that the drug-naive male (a male with little or no drug use experience) *might* experience a sustained erection and delay in orgasm at low dosage levels of amphetamines or cocaine.

Kolodny (1985) advanced the theory that, since these drugs produce physiological changes in the body similar to those seen in states of sexual excitement (increased blood pressure, increased heart rate, and an increase in blood flow to the genitals), as well as a feeling of well-being, these drugs may have been thought of as aphrodisiacs. However, at high dosage levels or when used for extended periods of time the CNS stimulants have a negative impact on sexual performance and satisfaction.

Kaplan (1979) noted that the amphetamines and cocaine may inhibit orgasm, especially in women. Kolodny (1985) agreed with this conclusion, noting that about one-third of the women who frequently use cocaine freebase will have problems achieving orgasm.

Gold (1988) concluded that moderate to high dosage levels of the amphetamines may result in impotence and difficulty achieving orgasm in the male. In an earlier paper, Gold (1987) reported that 14 of 39 males (36 %) on cocaine experienced some difficulty achieving or maintaining an erection. In this same paper, it was reported that some men who use cocaine might experience *priapism,* a serious vascular disorder during erection that may require surgical intervention.

Masters, Johnson, and Kolodny (1986) observed that one practice is for the woman (or her partner) to rub a little cocaine powder on to the clitoris prior to intercourse. This is done on the theory that the cocaine will increase the woman's sexual arousal and responsiveness. Surprisingly, cocaine is often placed on the tip of the penis for the opposite reason: to reduce responsiveness so that the male may engage in intercourse for a longer period of time.

As was discussed in Chapter 4, cocaine is a local anesthetic, and it is difficult to understand how the use of a local anesthetic on the clitoris might increase sexual arousal and responsiveness. Both the team of Masters, Johnson, and Kolodny (1986) and Gold (1987) concluded that the individual's expectations for cocaine might influence how the combination of cocaine plus the sexual encounter were interpreted.

The amphetamines and cocaine are drugs with significant potential for harm and injury, as discussed in Chapter 4. The practice of placing cocaine powder on the tip of the penis immediately prior to intercourse is quite dangerous. This is done to prolong the male's ability to engage in intercourse, since the nerves at the tip of the penis are quite sensitive under normal conditions. The cocaine's local anesthetic effects help to lower the male's responsiveness, allowing him to engage in intercourse for a longer period of time.

Unfortunately, some of the contaminants of street cocaine are quite irritating to tissues of the body. Local irritation may establish the necessary break in skin integrity necessary for an infection to develop. On occasion, these infections have allowed the development of gangrene at the site of the infection, which will require the amputation of the infected organ. Further, cocaine serves as a vasoconstrictor. This action, when combined with the constriction of blood vessels in the penis to achieve erection, may cause damage to the very blood vessels necessary for erection in the male. This may result in long-term erectile problems in the male.

Marijuana

Marijuana's *reported* sexual effects on the user are somewhat different from its known physiological properties. Masters, Johnson, and Kolodny (1986) reported that research has demonstrated that marijuana either has no impact on tactile perception, or that it actually lessens touch perception. Yet, they observed that over 80% of 1000 subjects examined claimed that the use of marijuana prior to intercourse led to an increased awareness of being touched all over their bodies by their partner.

As was discussed in Chapter 5, marijuana alters the individual's perceptions through an unknown mechanism. It has been postulated that this effect is due to the individual's *subjective perception* of marijuana's effects on the sexual experience, more than any significant change in the individual's awareness (Masters, Johnson, and Kolodny, 1986). The authors supported their argument with the observation that when one partner is under the effects of marijuana but the other partner is not, the sexual encounter is unlikely to be reported as being quite so pleasurable. Kaplan (1974) advanced an alternative theory, suggesting that marijuana's disinhibiting effects helped the individual to release sexual feelings normally inhibited by the cortex of the brain.

Masters, Johnson, and Kolodny (1986) also noted that research has found 20% of the men who use marijuana on a daily basis will experience erectile problems. No corresponding problem has been found for women who use marijuana on a daily basis, according to Masters, Johnson, and Kolodny (1986). Kolodny (1985) reported that some women who used marijuana reported vaginal dryness during intercourse, which contributed to painful intercourse. However, Kolodny (1985) agrees that marijuana users seem to report enhanced sexual awareness when both participants are under the influence of this drug.

Marijuana has also been found to lower the testosterone levels of regular users, which is one factor associated in a loss of sexual desire (Kaplan, 1979). Evidence also suggests that the regular use of marijuana will disrupt normal sperm production in men (Kolodny, 1985). These changes seem to reverse over time, after the individual discontinues further use of the drug.

Hallucinogenics

There are a number of hallucinogens that have been viewed as being aphrodisiacs at one time or another. Masters, Johnson, and Kolodny (1986) noted that there has been little research on the effects of these drugs on sexual functioning, and suggested that because these drugs affect perception the individual might be distracted by mental imagery during sexual activities.

Kolodny (1985) concluded that there is little research on the effects of the hallucinogenics on sexual performance, but did note that professionals have encountered sexual performance problems in individuals who were using hallucinogenics. Kaplan (1979) reported that LSD had little measurable impact on sexual performance, although it was noted that the individual might report altered sexual perceptions as a result of LSD use.

CNS Depressants

The effects of CNS depressants such as the barbiturates and the benzodiazepines on sexuality have not been studied in detail. Gold (1988) noted that alcohol, the barbiturates, and the benzodiazepines decreased the strength of spinal reflexes necessary in the erection and orgasm responses. Women who use CNS depressants might experience decreased vaginal secretions before and during intercourse (Gold).

Kolodny (1985) estimated that more than 50% of those addicted to barbiturates experience some form of sexual dysfunction. Masters, Johnson, and Kolodny (1986) concluded that while some people might find the antianxiety effects of some CNS depressants helpful in achieving a state of sexual excitement, these medications could cause erectile dysfunctions in the male, loss of sexual desire, and difficulty achieving orgasm. Kaplan (1979) warned that when used at high dosage levels, the CNS depressants could cause impotence in males.

Other Drugs

Lingeman (1974) noted that *amyl nitrite,* a prescription drug in most states that is used to relieve the pain of angina pectoris, is also favored by some as a stimulant during orgasm. Amyl nitrite and similar agents, are quick acting, taking effect in less than 30 seconds in some cases. These drugs will cause the blood vessels leading to the heart to dilate for a brief period of time, usually less than five minutes.

In some circles, amyl nitrite is used to prolong the moment of orgasm (Masters, Johnson, and Kolodny, 1986), although at a cost of such possible side effects as nausea, vomiting, headaches, and a loss of consciousness. This practice is common among homosexual men (Masters, Johnson, and Kolodny, 1986).

SUMMARY

Human sexuality, as a field of study, has received little attention from addiction specialists (Gold, 1987). This is surprising, since each class of commonly abused drugs has been found to present a wide range of effects on sexual desire, performance, and sexual satisfaction. Further, there is evidence to suggest that, for some, initial drug use was a response to a lack of adequate intimacy skills.

The final determination of a given drug's effects on any individual is based on the individual's state of health, the individual's drug-use history, and what expectations (if any) the individual might have for the drug. Little research has been conducted into the effects of many drugs of abuse on sexual desire, performance, or satisfaction. However, the limited research that is available strongly suggests that each class of drugs currently being abused offers the potential to detract from the individual's ability to enter into, or enjoy, normal sexual relations.

Alcohol Abuse Situation Sample Assessment

HISTORY AND IDENTIFYING INFORMATION

Mr. John D—— is a 35-year-old married white male, from ——— County, Missouri. He is employed as an electrical engineer for the ——— Company, where he has worked for the last three years. Prior to this, Mr. D—— was in the United States Navy, where he served for four years. He was discharged under Honorable conditions, and reported that he only had "a few" minor rules infractions. He was never brought before a Courts Martial, according to Mr. D——.

CIRCUMSTANCES OF REFERRAL

Mr. D—— was seen after having been arrested for the charge of driving while under the influence of alcohol. Mr. D—— reported that he had been drinking with co-workers to celebrate a promotion at work. His measured blood alcohol level (BAL) was .150, well above the legal limit necessary for a charge of driving while under the influence. Mr. D—— reported that he had "seven or eight" mixed drinks in approximately a two-hour time span. By his report, he was arrested within a quarter hour of the time that he left the bar.

After his initial court appearance, Mr. D—— was referred to this evaluator by the court to determine whether Mr. D—— has a chemical dependency problem.

DRUG AND ALCOHOL USE HISTORY

Mr. D—— reports that he first began to drink at the age of fifteen, when he and a friend would steal beer from his father's supply in the basement. He would drink an occasional beer after that, and first became intoxicated when he was seventeen, by Mr. D——'s report.

When he was eighteen, Mr. D—— enlisted in the United States Navy, and after basic training he was stationed in the San Diego area. Mr. D—— reported that he was first exposed to chemicals while he was stationed in San Diego, and that he tried both marijuana and cocaine while on weekend liberty. Mr. D—— reported

1

that he did not like the effects of cocaine, and that he only used this chemical once or twice. He did like the effects of marijuana, and reported that he would smoke one or two marijuana cigarettes obtained from friends perhaps once a month.

During this portion of his life, Mr. D—— reports that he would drink about twice a weekend, when on liberty. The amount that he would drink ranged from "one or two beers" to twelve or eighteen beers. Mr. D—— reported that he first had an alcohol-related blackout while he was in the Navy, and reported that he "should" have been arrested for driving on base while under the influence of alcohol on several occasions, but was never stopped by the Shore Patrol.

Following his Honorable discharge from the Navy at the age of 22, Mr. D—— enrolled in college. His chemical use declined to the weekend use of alcohol, usually in moderation, but Mr. D—— reported that he did drink to the point of an alcohol-related blackout "once or twice" in the four years that he was in college. There was no other chemical use following his discharge from the Navy, and Mr. D—— reports that he has not used other chemicals since the age of 20 or 21.

Upon graduation, at the age of 26, Mr. D—— began to work for the —— Company, where he is now employed. He met his wife shortly after he began work for the —— Company, and they were married after a courtship of one year. Mr. D——'s wife, Pat, does not use chemicals other than an "occasional" social drink. Exploration of this revealed that Mrs. D—— will drink a glass of wine with a meal about twice a month. She denied other chemical use.

Mrs. D—— reported that her husband does not usually drink more than one or two beers, and that he will drink only on weekends. She reported that the night when he was arrested was "unusual" for him, in the sense that he is not a drinker. His employer was not contacted, and court records failed to reveal any other arrest records for Mr. D——.

Mr. D—— admitted to several alcohol-related blackouts, but none since he was in college. He denied seizures, DT's or alcohol-related tremor. There was no evidence of ulcers, gastritis, or cardiac problems noted. His last physical was "normal" according to information provided by his personal physician. There were no abnormal blood chemistry findings, nor did his physician find any evidence suggesting alcoholism. Mr. D—— denied having ever been hospitalized for an alcohol-related injury, and there was no evidence suggesting that he has been involved in fights.

On the Michigan Alcoholism Screening Test, Mr. D——'s score of four (4) points would not suggest alcoholism. This information was reviewed in the presence of his wife, who did not suggest that there was any misrepresentation on his test scores. On this administration of the MMPI, there was no evidence of psychopathology noted. Mr. D——'s MacAndrew Alcoholism Scale score fell in the normal range, failing to suggest an addictive disorder at this time.

PSYCHIATRIC HISTORY

Mr. D—— denied psychiatric treatment of any kind. He did admit to having seen a marriage counselor "once" shortly after he married, but reported that overall he and his wife are happy together. Apparently, they had a question about a marital communications issue that took place after three or four years of marriage, and was cleared up after one visit.

SUMMARY AND CONCLUSIONS

At this point in time, there is little evidence to suggest an ongoing alcohol problem. Mr. D—— would seem to be a well-adjusted young man who drank to the point of excess after having been offered a long-desired promotion at work. This would seem to be an unusual occurrence for Mr. D——, who usually limits his drinking to one or two beers on the weekends. There was no evidence of alcohol-related injuries, accidents, or legal problems noted.

RECOMMENDATIONS

Recommend light sentence, possibly a fine, limited probation, with no restrictions on license. It is also recommended that Mr. D—— attend "DWI School" for eight weeks, to learn more about the effects of alcohol on driving.

Sample Assessment: Chemical Dependency Situation

HISTORY AND IDENTIFYING FEATURES

Mr. Michael S—— is a 35-year-old divorced white male who is self-employed. He has been a resident of —— County, Kansas, for the last three months. Prior to this, he apparently was living in —— County, New York, according to information provided by Mr. S——. On the night of June 6th of this year, Mr. S—— was arrested for the charge of possession of a controlled substance. In specific, Mr. S—— was found to be in possession of two grams of cocaine, according to police records. This is his first arrest for a drug-related charge in Kansas, although he has been arrested on two other occasions for similar charges. A copy of his police record is attached to this report.

CIRCUMSTANCES OF REFERRAL

Mr. S—— was referred to the undersigned for a chemical dependency evaluation, which will be part of his presentence investigation (PSI) for the charge of felony possession of a controlled substance, and the charge of sale of a controlled substance.

DRUG AND ALCOHOL USE HISTORY

Mr. S—— reported that he began to use alcohol when he was 13 years of age, and that by the age of 14 he was drinking on a regular basis. Exploration revealed that, just prior to his 15th birthday, Mr. S—— was drinking on "weekends," with friends. He reported that he first became intoxicated on his 15th birthday, but projected responsibility for this on to his friends, who by his report "kept on pouring more and more into the glass until I was drunk."

By the age of 16, Mr. S—— was using alcohol "four or five nights a week," and was also using marijuana and hallucinogenics perhaps two or three times a week. He projected responsibility for his expanded chemical use on to his environment, noting that "everybody was selling the stuff, you couldn't walk down the street without people stopping you to ask if you wanted to buy some."

1

Also, by the age of 16, Mr. S—— was supporting his chemical use through burglaries, which he committed with his friends. He was never caught, but volunteered this information informing the undersigned that since the statute of limitations has expired, he does not have to fear being charged for these crimes.

By the age of 21, Mr. S—— was using cocaine "once or twice a week." He was arrested for the first time, when he was about 22, for possession of cocaine. This was when he was living in the state of ———. After being tried in court, he was convicted of felony possession of cocaine, and placed on probation for five years. When asked if he used chemicals while he was on probation, Mr. S—— responded that "I don't have to answer that."

Mr. S—— reported that he first entered treatment for chemical dependency when he was 27 years of age. At that time, he was found to be addicted to a number of drugs, including alcohol, cocaine, and "downers." Although in treatment for two months at the chemical dependency unit of ——— Hospital, Mr. S—— reported that "I left as addicted as when I arrived," and reported with some degree of apparent pride that he had found a way to use chemicals even while in treatment. His chemical use apparently was the reason for his ultimate discharge from this program. While Mr. S—— was somewhat vague about the reasons he was discharged, he did report that "they did not like how I was doing" while he was in treatment.

Since that time, Mr. S—— has been using cocaine, alcohol, various drugs obtained from a series of physicians, and opiates. Mr. S—— was quite vague as to how he would support his chemical use, but noted that "there are ways of getting money, if you really want some."

In the last year, Mr. S—— reported that he has been using cocaine "four or five times a week," although on occasion he did admit to having used cocaine "for a whole week straight." He has been sharing needles with other cocaine users from time to time, but reported that "I am careful." In spite of this, however, he was diagnosed as having Hepatitis B in the last year, according to Mr. S——. He also reported that he has overdosed on cocaine "once or twice," but that he treated this overdose himself with benzodiazepines and alcohol.

In addition to the possible cocaine overdoses noted above, Mr. S—— admitted to having experienced chest pain while using cocaine on at least two occasions, and has used alcohol or tranquilizers to combat the side effects of cocaine on a regular basis. He has admitted to frequently using tranquilizers or alcohol to help him sleep after using cocaine for extended periods of time. He also admits to having spent money on drugs that was meant

2

for other expenses (loan payments, and so on), and by his report has had at least one automobile repossessed for failure to make payments on the loan.

Mr. S—— has been unemployed for at least the last two years, but is rather vague as to how he supports himself. He apparently was engaged in selling cocaine at the time of his arrest, this being one of the charges brought against him by the police.

Mr. S—— has not seen a physician for several years. During this interview, however, it was noted that he had scars strongly suggestive of intravenous needle use on both arms. When asked about these marks, he referred to them as "tracks," a street term for drug needle scars. This would suggest long-term intravenous drug use on Mr. S——'s part. He denied the intravenous use of opiates, but did admit to using oral narcotics from time to time, if they were available.

On this administration of the Michigan Alcoholism Screening Test (MAST), Mr. S—— achieved a score of 17 points, a score that is strongly suggestive of alcoholism. He reported that the longest period that he has been able to go without using chemicals in the last five years was only "hours." His profile on this administration of the Minnesota Multiphasic Personality Inventory (MMPI) was suggestive of a very impulsive, immature individual, who is likely to have a chemical dependency problem.

PSYCHIATRIC HISTORY

Mr. S—— reported that he has been hospitalized for psychiatric reasons only "once." This hospitalization took place several years ago, while Mr. S—— was living in ——. Apparently, he was hospitalized for observation following a suicide attempt in which he slit his wrists with a razor blade. Mr. S—— was unable to recall whether he had been using cocaine prior to this suicide attempt, but thought that it was "quite possible" that he had experienced a cocaine-induced depression.

SUMMARY AND CONCLUSIONS

Overall, it is quite apparent that Mr. S—— has a long-standing chemical dependency problem. In spite of his evasiveness and denial, there was strong evidence of significant chemical dependency problems. Mr. S—— seems to support his drug and alcohol use through criminal activity, although he is rather vague about this. He has been convicted of drug-related charges in the state of ——, and was on probation following this conviction. One might suspect that Mr. S——'s motivation for treatment is quite low at this time, as he has expressed the belief that his attorney will "make a deal for me" where he will not have to spend time in prison.

3

RECOMMENDATIONS

1] Given the fact that Mr. S—— has contracted Hepatitis B from infected needles, it is strongly recommended that he have a blood test for AIDS immediately, to determine whether he has been exposed to the AIDS virus.

2] It is the opinion of this reviewer that Mr. S——'s motivation for treatment is low at this time. If he is referred to treatment, it is recommended that this be made part of his sentencing agreement with the court. If he is incarcerated, chemical dependency treatment might be made part of his treatment plan in prison.

3] Referral to a therapeutic community should be considered for Mr. S——, for long-term residential treatment.

Signed /s/

4

Acquired Immunodeficiency Syndrome (AIDS)

Addicts who inject drugs and fail to use proper sterile technique run the risk of either local or systemic infections (Wetli, 1987). Some of the infections commonly found include peripheral cellulitis, skin abscesses, viral hepatitis, infection of the heart valves (a condition known as endocarditis), pneumonia, lung abscesses, tetanus, and malaria (Wetli, 1987). If the individual shares a needle with another addict, she or he also runs the risk of contracting AIDS.

Actually, AIDS is the end stage of a viral infection thought to be caused by a virus known as human immunodeficiency virus (or HIV). This virus may rapidly change its outer shell, a trait that may help it escape the body's immune system (Patlak, 1989). As many as 200 strains of this virus have been identified, each with subtle genetic variations (Patlak, 1989).

Over time, this virus infection brings about the immune system dysfunction known as the acquired immunodeficiency syndrome, or AIDS (Redfield and Burk, 1988). In the first weeks following infection, the infected person may not even have developed antibodies against the invading virus. But he or she is capable of passing the virus on to others through blood or sexual contact. Langone (1989) estimated that 1.4 million Americans, and 10 million people worldwide, have already contracted the virus.

During the next stage of the infection, the infected individual will have developed antibodies in a struggle against the virus. This person, when tested, will be "antibody positive." The virus will attack various components of the immune system, especially the antibodies. As the infection progresses, the body's immune system will be impaired, but still functional at a reduced level of efficiency. This is the stage known as "AIDS Related Complex," or ARC, and the body's impaired immune system will be easily detected through blood tests.

In the final phase of the infection, the body's weakened immune system is no longer able to fight off infection by organisms once easily controlled. The individual will develop one of a range of opportunistic infections that is the hallmark of AIDS. As time progresses, these infections are no longer controlled by antibiotics, and death will follow from these opportunistic infections. In a technical sense, the destruction of the body's immune system is only one stage, in this case the final stage, of the infection caused by HIV.

HIV is a fragile virus, which is not easily transmitted from one person to another (Langone, 1989). There is no evidence to date that it is possible to catch the virus through saliva, tears, or toilet seats. The virus must be passed directly from one individual to another, in either blood or semen. The modes of transmission are limited to certain forms of intimate sexual contact with an infected person, direct contamination of blood with infected fluids, the passage of the virus from the mother to the fetus, or transmission through the mother's milk to the suckling baby (Redfield and Burk, 1988).

Addicts who share drug paraphernalia are "at risk" for becoming infected with HIV (Redfield and Burk, 1988). The *Morbidity and Mortality Weekly Report* (Massachusetts Medical Society, 1987) noted that *in some communities, more than 65% of opiate addicts tested had been exposed to the AIDS virus*. The virus that ultimately brings about the destruction of the individual's immunological system is passed through an exchange of blood, or blood products, such as is found either in the syringe, or the contaminated needles.

But the virus is also found in the semen of infected men, and persons involved in sexual relationships with addicts, those who engage in promiscuous sexual activity, or male homosexuals are also "at risk." This is because of the high probability that these persons are infected, and thus able to pass the infection on to their partners.

At one point it was thought that perhaps only about one-third of those who tested positive for the virus would develop AIDS within five years (Patlik, 1988). Recent research, however, suggests that "nearly all those infected will develop the disease within a mean period of 7.8 years" (Patlik, 1988, p. 26). No vaccine to prevent the infection, or cure for AIDS once the infection has been transmitted, is available at this time (Gallo and Montagnier, 1988).

It should be noted that the AIDS incidence rates for intravenous drug users are increasing more rapidly than for homosexual males. Indeed, Heyward and Curran (1988) reported that AIDS was currently the leading cause of death for illegal intravenous drug users. Furthermore, intravenous drug users are the primary source of transmission of the virus to the heterosexual population, and to children, at this time (Langone, 1989; Valdiserri, Hartl, and Chambliss, 1988).

Because of the long latency period between the initial transmission of the virus, and the development of AIDS, the number of AIDS cases will continue to increase for several years after the infection pattern has either stabilized, or actually started to decline (Heyward and Curran, 1988). Preliminary evidence would suggest that this stabilization has started to emerge in the homosexual male population, as well as with transfusion recipients and people with hemophilia (Langone, 1989; Heyward and Curran, 1988).

Addicts continue to share contaminated needles, syringes, or both, simply because they do not want to wait until a clean needle or syringe is available. Although rinsing the needle and syringe with bleach will often destroy the AIDS virus, many addicts simply do not engage in this practice because it takes too much time. Other addicts have been known to wait in line to use another person's needle and syringe, in spite of the fact that they had a new needle and syringe at home.

There are those who continue to engage in high-risk behavior, although it is not known how representative this group is of national trends. It is important for the chemical dependency professional to have a working knowledge of AIDS in order to help their clients understand, and come to terms with, this problem.

References

ABEL, E. L. (1982). *Drugs and behavior: A primer in neuropsychopharmacology.* Malabar, FL: Robert E. Krieger Publishing Co.

ABRAMS, R. C., & ALEXOPOULOS, G. (1987). Substance abuse in the elderly: Alcohol and prescription drugs. *Hospital & Community Psychiatry, 38,* 1285–1288.

ACKERMAN, R. J. (1983). *Children of alcoholics: A guidebook for educators, therapists, and parents.* Holmes Beach, FL: Learning Publications, Inc.

ADAMS, J. K. (1988). Setting free chemical dependency. *Alcoholism & Addiction, 8* (4), 20–21.

ADELMAN, S. A., & WEISS, R. D. (1989). What is therapeutic about inpatient alcoholism treatment? *Hospital & Community Psychiatry, 40* (5), 515–519.

Al-Anon's Twelve Steps & Twelve Traditions. (1985). New York: Al-Anon Family Group Headquarters, Inc.

Alcoholics Anonymous. (1976). New York: Alcoholics Anonymous World Services, Inc.

ALIBRANDI, L. A. (1978). The folk psychotherapy of Alcoholics Anonymous. In *Practical approaches to alcoholism psychotherapy.* (Zimberg, S., Wallace, J., & Blume, S., eds.). New York: Plenum Press.

ALLCOTT, J. V., BARNHART, R. A., & MOONEY, L. A. (1987). Acute lead poisoning in two users of illicit methamphetamine. *Journal of the American Medical Association, 258,* 510–511.

American Druggist. (1989). The top 200 drugs. *199* (2), 38–48.

AMERICAN PSYCHIATRIC ASSOCIATION. (1987). *Diagnostic and statistical manual of mental disorders.* (3rd ed., revised). Washington, DC: American Psychiatric Association.

AMERICAN PSYCHIATRIC ASSOCIATION. (1985). Research on mental illness and addictive disorders: Progress and prospects. *American Journal of Psychiatry, 142,* Supplement A.

ANANTH, J., VANDEWATER, S., KAMAL, M., BRODSKY, A., GAMAL, R., & MILLER, M. (1989). Missed diagnosis of substance abuse in psychiatric patients. *Hospital & Community Psychiatry, 40,* 297–299.

ANASTASI, A. (1968). *Psychological testing* (3rd ed.). New York: Macmillan Publishing Co., Inc.

ANGEVINE, J. B., & COTMAN, C. W. (1981). *Principles of neuroanatomy.* New York: Oxford University Press.

ANSEVICS, N. L., & DOWEIKO, H. E. (1983). A conceptual framework for intervention with the antisocial personality. *Psychotherapy in Private Practice, 1* (3), 43–52.

ARONOFF, G. M., WAGNER, J. M., & SPANGLER, A. S. (1986). Chemical interventions for pain. *Journal of Consulting and Clinical Psychology, 54,* 769–775, 1986.

ATKINSON, H. (1986). Cocaine: Could you get hooked? *New Woman, 42,* 62–64, 66–67.

AUSABEL, D. P. (1983). Methadone maintenance treatment: The other side of the coin. *International Journal of the Addictions, 18,* 851–862.

BACORN, C. N. (1987). Treating the alcohol-abusing marriage. Workshop presented at the Annual Meeting of the American Psychological Association: New York.

BAEKELAND, F., & LUNDWALL, L. (1975). Dropping out of treatment: A critical review. *Psychological Bulletin, 82,* 738–783.

BALES, J. (1988). Legalized drugs: Idea flawed, debate healthy. *APA Monitor, 19* (8), 22.

BARNES, D. (1988). New data intensify the agony over Ecstasy. *Science, 139,* 864–866.

BASSIN, A. (1970). Daytop village. In *Readings in social psychology today.* Del Mar, CA: CRM Books.

BAUMAN, J. L. (1988). Acute heroin withdrawal. *Hospital Therapy, 37,* 60–66.

BEAN-BAYOG, M. (1988). Alcohol and drug abuse: Alcoholism as a cause of psychopathology. *Hospital & Community Psychiatry, 39,* 352–354.

BEASLEY, J. D. (1987). *Wrong diagnosis, wrong treatment: The plight of the alcoholic in America.* New York: Creative Infomatics, Inc.

BEATTIE, M. (1987). *Codependent no more.* New York: Harper & Row.

BEATTIE, M. (1989). *Beyond codependency.* New York: Harper & Row.

BERENSON, D. (1988). *Alcoholics Anonymous:* From surrender to transformation. *Utne Reader, 30,* 70–71.

BERG, R., FRANZEN, M. M., & WEDDING, D. (1987). *Screening for brain impairment: A manual for mental health practice.* New York: Springer Publishing Co.

BERGER, P. A., & DUNN, M. J. (1982). Substance induced and substance use disorders. In *Treatment of mental disorders* (Griest, J. H., Jefferson, J. W., & Spitzer, R. L., eds.). New York: Oxford University Press.

BERKOWITZ, A., & PERKINS, H. W. (1988). Personality characteristics of children of alcoholics. *Journal of Consulting and Clinical Psychology, 56,* 206–209.

BERTONE, R. J., GOMEZ, M., JACQUES, M. A., & MATTIKO, M. J. (1988). Comprehensive nicotine treatment. *Alcoholism & Addiction, 9* (2), 14–17.

BLACK, C. (1987). How different is recovery for a COA? *Alcoholism & Addiction, 8* (6), insert.

BLACK, C. (1981). *It will never happen to me.* Denver: M. A. C. Printing and Publications.

BLISS, R. E., GARVEY, A. J., HEINOLD, J. W., & HITCHCOCK, J. L. (1989). The influence of situation and coping on relapse crisis outcomes after smoking cessation. *Journal of Consulting and Clinical Psychology, 57,* 443–449.

BLOODWORTH, R. C. (1987). Major problems associated with marijuana abuse. *Psychiatric Medicine, 3* (3), 173–184.

BLUM, K. (1988). The disease process in alcoholism. *Alcoholism & Addiction, 8* (5), 5–8.

BLUM, K., & TRACHTENBERG, M. C. (1988). Neurochemistry and alcohol craving. *California Society for the Treatment of Alcoholism and Other Drug Dependencies News, 13* (2), 1–7.

BLUME, S. (1985). Women and alcohol. In *Alcoholism and substance abuse: Strategies for clinical intervention.* (Bratter, T. E., & Forrest, G. G., eds. New York: The Free Press.

BONSTEDT, T., ULRICH, D. A., DOLINAR, L. J., & JOHNSON, J. J. (1984). When and where should we hospitalize alcoholics? *Hospital & Community Psychiatry, 35,* 1038–1040.

BOWEN, M. (1985). *Family therapy in clinical practice.* Northvale, NJ: Jason Aronson.

BRADSHAW, J. (1988). Compulsivity: The black plague of our day. *Lear's Magazine, 42,* 89–90.

BRECHER, E. M. (1972). *Licit and illicit drugs.* Boston: Little, Brown & Co.

BRENT, D. A., KUPFER, D. J., BROMET, E. J., & DEW, M. A. (1988). The assessment and treatment of patients at risk for suicide. In *American Psychiatric Association Annual Review* (Vol. 7). (Frances, A. J., & Hales, R. E., eds.). Washington, DC: American Psychiatric Association Press, Inc.

BRESLIN, J. (1988). Crack. *Playboy, 35* (12), 109–110, 210, 212–213, 215.

BRIGGS, G. G., FREEMAN, R. K., & YAFFE, S. J. (1986). *Drugs in pregnancy and lactation* (2nd ed.). Baltimore: Williams and Wilkins.

BROPHY, J. J. (1985). Psychiatric disorders. In *Current medical diagnosis and treatment.* (Krupp, M. A., Chatton, M. J., & Werdegar, D., eds.). Los Altos, CA: Lange Medical Publications.

BROWN, R. T., & BRADEN, N. J. (1987) Hallucinogens. *Pediatric Clinics of North America, 34* (2), 341–347.

BROWN, S. (1985). *Treating the alcoholic: A developmental model of recovery.* New York: John Wiley & Sons, Inc.

BROWN, S. A., GOLDMAN, M. S., INN, A., & ANDERSON, L. R. (1980). Expectations of reinforcement from alcohol: Their domain and relation to drinking patterns. *Journal of Consulting and Clinical Psychology, 48,* 419–426.

BROWN, S. A., CREAMER, V. A., & STETSON, B. A. (1987). Adolescent alcohol expectancies in relation to personal and parental drinking patterns. *Journal of Abnormal Psychology, 96,* 117–121.

BROWN, S. J. (1987). Morphine: the benefits are worth the risks. *RN, 50* (3), 20–26.

BROWN, V. B., RIDGELY, M. S., PEPPER, B., LEVINE, I. S., & RYGLEWICZ, H. (1989). The dual crisis: Mental illness and substance abuse. *American Psychologist, 44,* 565–569.

BRUNSWICK, M. (1989). More kids turning to inhalant abuse. *Minneapolis Tribune. VII* (356), 1A, 6A.

BUBER, M. (1970). *I and thou.* New York: Charles Scribner's Sons.

BUFE, C. (1988). A. A.: Guilt and god for the gullible. *Utne Reader, 30,* 54–55.

BURDEN, L. L. & ROGERS, J. C. (1988). Endocarditis: When bacteria invade the heart. *RN, 51* (12), 38–43.

BUTCHER, J. N., (1988). Introduction to the special series. *Journal of Consulting and Clinical Psychology, 56,* 171.

BYCK, R. (1987). Cocaine use and research: Three histories. In *Cocaine: Clinical and Behavioral Aspects* (Fisher, S., Rashkin, A., & Unlenhuth, E. H., eds.). New York: Oxford University Press.

BYRNE, C. (1989). Pregnancy and crack: Trying to heal horror. *Minneapolis Star Tribune, VIII* (89), 1, 4A.

CAHALAN, D. (1978). Implications of American drinking practices and attitudes for prevention and treatment of alcoholism. In *Behavioral approaches to alcoholism.* (Marlatt, G. A., & Nathan, P. E., eds.). New Brunswick, NJ: Rutgers Center of Alcohol Studies.

CALAHAN, E. J. (1980). Alternative strategies in the treatment of narcotic addiction: A review. In *The addictive behaviors* (Miller, W. R., ed.). New York: Pergamon Press.

CAMERON, N. (1963). *Personality development and psychopathology: A dynamic approach.* Boston: Houghton-Mifflin Co.

CAREY, K. B. (1989). Emerging treatment guidelines for mentally ill chemical abusers. *Hospital and Community Psychiatry, 40,* 341–342, 349.

CHARNEY, D. S., HENINGER, G. R., & KLEBER, H. D. (1986). The combined use of clonidine and naltrexone as a rapid, safe, and effective treatment of abrupt withdrawal from methadone. *American Journal of Psychiatry, 143,* 831–837.

CHASNOFF, I. J., & SCHNOLL, S. H. (1987). Consequences of cocaine and other drug use in pregnancy. In *Cocaine: A clinician's handbook* (Washton, A. M., & Gold, M. S., eds.). New York: The Guilford Press.

CHASNOFF, I. J. (1988). Drug use in pregnancy: Parameters of risk. *The Pediatric Clinics of North America, 35* (6), 1403–1412.

CLIMKO, R. P., ROEHRICH, H., SWEENEY, D. R., & AL-RAZI, J. (1987). Ecstasy: A review of MDMA and MDA. *International Journal of Psychiatry in Medicine, 16* (4), 359–372.

CLONINGER, C. R., GOHMAN, M., & SIGVARDSSON, S. (1981). Inheritance of alcohol abuse: Cross fostering analysis of adopted men. *Archives of General Psychiatry, 38,* 861–868.

COHEN, L. S. (1989). Psychotropic drug use in pregnancy. *Hospital & Community Psychiatry, 40* (6), 566–567.

COHEN, N. L., & MARCOS, L. R. (1989). The bad-mad dilemma for public psychiatry. *Hospital and Community Psychiatry, 40,* 677.

COHEN, S. (1977). Inhalant abuse: an overview of the problem. In *Review of Inhalants: Euphoria to Dysfunction* (Sharp, C. W., & Brehm, M. L., eds.). Washington, DC: U.S. Government Printing Office.

COHEN, S. (1984). Cocaine: Acute medical and psychiatric complications. *Psychiatric Annuals. 14,* 747–749.

COLEMAN, E. (1982). Family intimacy and chemical abuse: The connection. *Journal of Psychoactive Drugs, 14,* 153–158.

COLEMAN, E. (1982). How chemical dependency harms marital and sexual relationships. *Medical Aspects of Human Sexuality, 16* (10), 42n–42x.

COLEMAN, J. C., BUTCHER, J. N., & CARSON, R. C. (1984). *Abnormal psychology and modern life* (7th ed.). Glenview, IL: Scott, Foresman & Co.

COLEMAN, P. (1989). Letter to the editor. *Journal of the American Medical Association. 261* (13), 1879–1880.

COLLETTE, L. (1988). Step by step: A skeptic's encounter. *Utne Reader, 30,* 69–76.

COLLINS, J. J., & ALISON, M. (1983). Legal coercion and retention in drug abuse treatment. *Hospital & Community Psychiatry, 34,* 1145–1150.

COLQUITT, M., FIELDING, L. P., & CRONAN, J. F. (1987). Drunk drivers and medical and social injury. *The New England Journal of Medicine, 317,* 1262–1266.

CONNELLY, J. C. (1980). Alcoholism as indirect self-destructive behavior. In *The many faces of suicide.* (Farberow, N. L., ed.). New York: McGraw-Hill.

COVINGTON, S. S. (1987). Alcohol and female sexuality. *Alcoholism & Addiction, 7* (5), 21.

CRITCHLOW, B. (1986). The powers of John Barleycorn: Beliefs about the effects of alcohol on social behavior. *American Psychologist, 41,* 751–764.

CROWLEY, T. J. (1988). Substance abuse treatment and policy: Contributions of behavioral pharmacology. Paper presented at the 1988 meeting of the American Psychological Association: Atlanta, GA.

CUMMINGS, C., GORDON, J. R., & MARLATT, G. A. (1980). Relapse: Prevention and prediction. In *The addictive behaviors,* (Miller, W. R., ed.). New York: Pergamon Press.

DAVIS, J. M., & BRESNAHAN, D. B. (1987). Psychopharmacology in clinical psychiatry. In *American Psychiatric Association Annual Review* (Vol. 6). Washington, DC: American Psychiatric Association Press, Inc.

DEANGELIS, T. (1989). Behavior is included in report on smoking. *APA Monitor, 20* (3), 1, 4.

DECKER, S., FINS, J., & FRANCES, R. (1987). Cocaine and chest pain. *Hospital & Community Psychiatry, 38,* 464–466.

DEFRANCO, C., TARBOX, A. R., & MCLAUGHLIN, E. J. (1985). Cognitive deficits as a function of years of alcohol abuse. *American Journal of Drug and Alcohol Abuse, 11* (3 & 4), 279–293.

DIETCH, J. (1983). The nature and extent of benzodiazepine abuse: An overview of recent literature. *Hospital & Community Psychiatry, 34,* 1139–1144.

DOGHRAMJI, K. (1989). Sleep disorders: a selective update. *Hospital & Community Psychiatry, 40,* 29–40.

DOLE, V. P. (1988). Implications of methadone maintenance for theories of narcotic addiction. *Journal of the American Medical Association, 260,* 3025–3029.

DOLE, V. P. (1989). Letter to the editor. *Journal of the American Medical Association, 261* (13), 1880.

DONOVAN, D. M. (1988). Assessment of addictive behaviors: Implications of an emerging biopsychosocial model. In *Assessment of addictive behaviors.* (Donovan, D. M., & Mariatt, G. A., eds.). New York: Guilford.

DOWEIKO, H. (1979). Identifying the street names of drugs. *Journal of Emergency Nursing, 5* (6), 44–47.

DREGER, R. M. (1986). Does anyone really believe that alcoholism is a disease? *American Psychologist, 37,* 322.

DULFANO, C. (1978). Family therapy of alcoholism. In *Practical approaches to alcoholism psychotherapy* (Zimberg, S., Wallace, J., & Blume, S., eds.). New York: Plenum Press.

DuPONT, R. L. (1987). Cocaine in the workplace: The ticking time bomb. In *Cocaine: A clinician's handbook* (Washton, A. M., & Gold, M. S., eds.). New York: The Guilford Press.

EDMEADES, B. (1987). Alcoholics Anonymous celebrates its 50th year. In *Drugs, society and behavior* (Rucker, W. B., & Rucker, M. E. eds.). Guilford, CT: Dashkin Publishing Group, Inc.

EDWARDS, D. G. (1982). *Existential psychotherapy: The process of caring.* New York: The Gardner Press, Inc.

EHLERT, B. (1989). Alcoholism among the elderly. *Minneapolis Star Tribune Sunday Magazine, VII* (363), 6–14.

EISENHAUER, L. A., & GERALD, M. C. (1984). *The nurse's 1984–85 guide to drug therapy: Drug profiles for patient care.* Englewood Cliffs, NJ: Prentice-Hall.

EISON, A. S., & TEMPLE, D. L. (1987). Buspirone: Review of its pharmacology and current perspectives on its mechanism of action. *The American Journal of Medicine, 80* (Supplement 3B), 1–9.

ERIKSON, E. H. (1963). *Childhood and society.* New York: W. W. Norton & Co.

ESTROFF, T. W. (1987). Medical and biological consequences of cocaine abuse. In *Cocaine: A clinician's handbook* (Washton, A. M., & Gold, M. S., eds.). New York: The Guilford Press.

FABIAN, M. S., & PARSONS, O. A. (1983). Differential improvement of cognitive functions in recovering alcoholic women. *Journal of Abnormal Psychology, 92,* 87–95.

Facts about Alateen. (1969). New York: Al-Anon Family Group Headquarters.

FARKASFALVY, B. (1979). Alcohol and sexuality: The alcoholic woman—practicing and recovering. *CAFC News, 2* (3), 5–6.

FEIGHNER, J. P. (1987). Impact of anxiety therapy on patients' quality of life. *The American Journal of Medicine, 82* (Supplement A), 14–19.

FINGARETTE, H. (1988). Alcoholism: The mythical disease. *Utne Reader, 30,* 64–69.

FINNEY, J. W., MOOS, R. H., & CHAN, D. A. (1975). Length of stay and program component effects in the treatment of alcoholism. *Journal of Studies on Alcohol, 36,* 88–108.

FISS, H. (1979). Current dream research: A psychobiological perspective. In *Handbook of Dreams* (Wolman, B. B., ed.). New York: Van Nostrand Reinhold Co.

FLOWER, R. J., MONCADA, S., & VANE, J. R. (1985). Analgesic-antipyretics and anti-inflammatory agents: Drugs employed in the treatment of gout. In *The Pharmacological Basis of Therapeutics* (7th ed.). (Gilman, A. G., Goodman, L. S., Rall, T. W. & Murad, F., eds.). New York: MacMillan.

FORREST, G. G. (1985). Psychodynamically oriented treatment of alcoholism and substance abuse. In *Alcoholism and substance abuse: Strategies for clinical intervention.* (Bratter, T. E., & Forrest, G. G., eds.). New York: The Free Press.

FOSSUM, M. A., & MASON, M. J. (1986). *Facing shame: Families in recovery.* New York: W. W. Norton & Co.

FOULKES, D. (1979). Children's dreams. In *Handbook of dreams* (Wolman, B. B., ed.). New York: Van Nostrand Reinhold Co.

FRANKL, V. E. (1978). *The unheard cry for meaning.* New York: Touchstone Books.

FRANKLIN, J. (1987). *Molecules of the mind.* New York: Dell Publishing Co.

FREDERICK, C. J. (1980). Drug abuse as indirect self-destructive behavior. In *The Many Faces of Suicide.* (Farberow, N. L., ed.). New York: McGraw-Hill.

FRIEDMAN, D. (1987). Toxic effects of marijuana. *Alcoholism & Addiction, 7* (6), 47.

FRIEL, J. P. (1974). (Ed.). *Dorland's Illustrated Medical Dictionary* (25th ed.). Philadelphia: W. B. Saunders.

FROMM, E. (1956). *The art of loving.* New York: Harper & Row.

FROMM, E. (1968). *The revolution of hope.* New York: Harper & Row.

GALANTER, M. (1986). Treating substance abusers: Why therapists fail. *Hospital & Community Psychiatry, 37,* 769.

GALLAGHER, W. (1986). The looming menace of designer drugs. *Designer, 7* (8), 24–35.

GALLO, R. C., & MONTAGNIER, L. (1988). Aids in 1988. *Scientific American,* 259 (4), 41–48.

GAWIN, F. H., ALLEN, D., & HUMBLESTONE, B. (1989). Outpatient treatment of "Crack" cocaine smoking with flupenthixol deconate: A preliminary report. *Archives of General Psychiatry, 46,* 122–126.

GAWIN, F. H. & ELLINWOOD, E. H. (1988). Cocaine and other stimulants: Actions, abuse, and treatment. *New England Journal of Medicine, 318,* 1173–1182.

GAWIN, F. H., & KLEBER, H. D. (1986). Abstinence symptomology and psychiatric diagnosis in cocaine abusers. *Archives of General Psychiatry,* 43, 107–113.

GAWIN, F. H., KLEBER, H. D., BYCK, R., ROUNSAVILLE, B. J., KOSTEN, T. R., JATLOW, P. I. & MORGAN, C. (1989). Desipramine facilitation of initial cocaine abstinence. *Archives of General Psychiatry, 46,* 117–121.

GAZZANIGA, M. S. (1988). *Mind matters.* Boston: Houghton-Mifflin.

GELENBERG, A. J. (1983). Anxiety. In *The practitioner's guide to psychoactive drugs* (2nd ed.). (Bassuk, E. L., Schoonover, S. C., & Galenberg, A. J., eds.). New York: Plenum Medical Book Co.

GIACONA, N. S., DAHL, S. L., & HARE, B. D. (1987). The role of nonsteroidal antiinflammatory drugs and non-narcotics in analgesia. *Hospital Formulary, 22,* 723–733.

GLASER, F. B., & OGBORNE, A. C. (1982). Does A. A. really work? *British Journal of the Addictions, 77,* 88–92.

GLASSMAN, A. H., STETNER, F., WALSH, T., RAIZMAN, P. S., FLEISS, J. L., COOPER, T. B., & COVEY, L. S. (1988). Heavy smokers, smoking cessation and clonidine. *Journal of the American Medical Association, 259,* 2863–2866.

GOLD, M. S., & VEREBEY, K. (1984). The psychopharmacology of cocaine. *Psychiatric Annuals, 14,* 714–723.

GOLD, M. S. (1987). Sexual dysfunction challenges today's addictions clinicians. *Alcoholism & Addiction, 7* (6), 11.

GOLD, M. S. (1988). Alcohol, drugs, and sexual dysfunction. *Alcoholism & Addiction, 9* (2), 13.

GOLD, S., & SHERRY, L. (1984). Hyperactivity, learning disabilities, and alcohol. *Journal of Learning Disabilities, 17* (1), 3–6.

GONZALES, L. (1985). Cocaine: A special report. *Playboy, 30* (3), 13–14, 148, 194–202.

GOODWIN, F. K. (1989). From the alcohol, drug abuse, and mental health administration. *Journal of the American Medical Association, 261,* 3517.

GOTTLIEB, A. M., KILLEN, J. D., MARLATT, G. A., & TAYLOR, C. B. (1987). Psychological and pharmacological influences in cigarette smoking withdrawal: Effects of nicotine gum and expectancy on smoking withdrawal symptoms and relapse. *Journal of Clinical and Consulting Psychology, 55,* 606–608.

GOVONI, L. E., & HAYES, J. E. (1985). *Drugs and Nursing Implications* (5th ed.). Norwalk, CT: Appleton-Century-Crofts.

GRAEDON, J. (1980). *The people's pharmacy*—2. New York: Avon Books.

GRAHAM, B. (1988). The abuse of alcohol: Disease or disgrace? *Alcoholism & Addiction, 8* (4), 14–15.

GRANT, I. (1987). Alcohol and the brain: Neuropsychological correlates. *Journal of Clinical and Consulting Psychology, 55,* 310–324.

GREENBLATT, D. J., & SHADER, R. I. (1975). Treatment of the alcohol withdrawal syndrome. In *Manual of psychiatric therapeutics.* (Shader, R. I., ed.). Boston: Little Brown.

GREENE, R. L. (1980). *The MMPI: An interpretive manual.* New York: Grune & Stratton.

GRIFFIN, M. L., WEISS, R. D., MIRIN, S. M., & LANG, U. (1989). A comparison of male and female cocaine abusers. *Archives of General Psychiatry, 46*, 122–126.

GRINSPOON, L., & BAKALAR, J. B. (1985). Drug dependence: Nonnarcotic agents. In *Comprehensive textbook of psychiatry/IV*. Baltimore: Williams & Wilkins.

HAMMER, S., & HAZELTON, L. (1984). Cocaine and the chemical brain. *Science Digest, 92* (10), 58–62, 100–103.

HAND, R. P. (1989). Taking another look at triazolam—is this drug safe? *Focus on Pharmacology: Theory and Practice, 11* (6), 1–3.

The Harvard Medical School Mental Health Letter. (1988). Sleeping pills and anti-anxiety drugs. 5 (6), 1–4.

HARVEY, S. C. (1985). Hypnotics and sedatives. In *The pharmacological basis of therapeutics* (7th ed.). (Gilman, A. G., Goodman, L. S., Rall, T. W., & Murad, F., eds.). New York: MacMillan Publishing Co.

HAYNER, G. N., & MCKINNEY, H. (1986). MDMA: The dark side of Ecstasy. *Journal of Psychoactive Drugs, 18* (4), 341–347.

HELZER, J. E. (1987). Epidemiology of alcoholism. *Journal of Consulting and Clinical Psychology, 55* (3), 284–292.

HELZER, J. E., ROBINS, L. N., TAYLOR, J. R., CAREY, K., MILLER, R. H., COMBS-ORME, T., & FARMER, A. (1985). The extent of long-term moderate drinking among alcoholics discharged from medical and psychiatric treatment facilities. *The New England Journal of Medicine, 312*, 1678–1682.

HENNINGFIELD, J. E., & NEMETH-COSLETT, R. (1988). Nicotine dependence. *Chest, 93* (2), 37s–55s.

HERMAN, E. (1988). The twelve step program: Cure or cover? *Utne Reader, 30*, 52–53.

HEYWARD, W. L., & CURRAN, J. W. (1988). The epidemiology of AIDS in the U.S. *Scientific American, 259* (4), 72–81.

HINSIE, L. E., & CAMPBELL, R. J. (1970). *Psychiatric dictionary* (4th ed.). London: Oxford University Press.

HIRSCHFIELD, R. M. A., & DAVIDSON, L. (1988). Risk factors for suicide. In *Review of psychiatry*, (Vol. 7) (Frances, A. J., & Hales, R. E., eds.). Washington, DC: American Psychiatric Association Press, Inc.

HOARD, P. S. (1988). Premenstrual syndrome can trigger relapse. *Alcoholism & Addiction, 8* (6), 41–42.

HOBSON, J. A. (1989). Dream theory: A new view of the brain-mind. *The Harvard Medical School Mental Health Letter, 5* (8), 3–5.

HOFFMANN, H., LOPER, R. G., & KAMMEIER, M. L. (1974). Identifying future alcoholics with MMPI alcohol scales. *Quarterly Journal of Studies on Alcohol, 35*, 490–498.

HOFFMANN, N. G., BELILLE, C. A., & HARRISON, P. A. (1987). Adequate resources for a complex population? *Alcoholism & Addiction, 7* (5), 17.

HONIGFELD, G., & HOWARD, A. (1978). *Psychiatric drugs: A desk reference* (2nd ed.). New York: Academic Press, Inc.

HORNEY, K. (1964). *The neurotic personality of our time.* New York: W. W. Norton & Co.

HORNEY, K. (1950). *Neurosis and human growth.* New York: W. W. Norton & Co.

HUGHES, J. R., GUST, S. W., & PECHACEK, T. F. (1987). Prevalence of tobacco dependence and withdrawal. *American Journal of Psychiatry, 144,* 205–208.

HURT, R. D., FINLAYSON, R. E., MORSE, R. M., & DAVIS, L. J. (1988). Alcoholism in elderly persons: Medical aspects and prognosis of 216 inpatients. *Mayo Clinic Proceedings, 63,* 753–760.

HYMAN, S. E. (1984). *Manual of psychiatric emergencies.* Boston: Little Brown & Co.

JAFFE, J. H. (1985a). Drug addiction and drug abuse. In *The pharmacological basis of therapeutics* (7th ed.). (Gilman, A. G., Goodman, L. S., Rall, T. W., & Murad, F., eds.). New York: Macmillan Publishing Co.

JAFFE, J. H. (1985b). Opioid dependence. In *Comprehensive textbook of psychiatry/IV.* Baltimore: Williams & Wilkins.

JAFFE, J. H. (1986). Opioids. In *American Psychiatric Association Annual Review* (Vol. 5). Washington, DC: American Psychiatric Association.

JAFFE, J. H., & MARTIN, W. R. (1985). Opioid analgesics and antagonists. In *The pharmacological basis of therapeutics* (7th ed.). (Gilman, A. G., Goodman, L. S., Rall, T. W., & Murad, F., eds.). New York: Macmillan Publishing Co.

JELLINEK, E. M. (1960). *The disease concept of alcoholism.* New Haven, CT: College and University Press.

JENIKE, M. A. (1987). Drug abuse. In *Scientific american medicine* (Rubenstein, E., & Federman, D. D., eds.). New York: Scientific American Press, Inc.

JENSEN, J. G. (1987). Step Two: A promise of hope. In *The Twelve Steps of Alcoholics Anonymous.* New York: Harper & Row.

JENSEN, J. G. (1987). Step Three: Turning it over. In *The Twelve Steps of Alcoholics Anonymous.* New York: Harper & Row.

JOHNSON INSTITUTE. (1987). *The family enablers.* Minneapolis, MN: The Johnson Institute.

JOHNSON, V. E. (1980). *I'll quit tomorrow.* San Francisco: Harper & Row.

JOHNSON, V. E. (1986). *Intervention.* Minneapolis, MN: Johnson Institute Books.

JONES, R. T. (1987). Psychopharmacology of cocaine. In *Cocaine: A clinician's handbook* (Washton, A. G., & Gold, M. S., eds.). New York: The Guilford Press.

JOSHI, N. P., & SCOTT, M. (1988). Drug use, depression, and adolescents. *The Pediatric Clinics of North America, 35* (6), 1349–1364.

JUERGENS, S. M., & MORSE, R. M. (1988). Alprazolam dependence in seven patients. *American Journal of Psychiatry, 145,* 625–627.

JULIEN, R. M. (1981). *A primer of drug action.* New York: W. H. Freeman & Co.

KANDEL, D. B., & RAVEIS, V. H. (1989). Cessation of illicit drug use in young adulthood. *Archives of General Psychiatry, 46,* 109–116.

KAMBACK, M. C. (1978). Animal models of addictive behavior. In *Basic psychopathology, Vol III.* (Balis, G. U., ed.). Boston: Butterworth Publishers, Inc.

KAPLAN, H. S. (1974). *The new sex therapy.* New York: Brunner/Mazel.

KAPLAN, H. S. (1979). *Disorders of sexual desire.* New York: Brunner/Mazel.

KAPLAN, H. S., & MOODIE, J. L. (1982). Psychosexual dysfunctions. In *Treatment of mental disorders.* (Greise, J. H., Jefferson, J. W., & Spitzer, R. L., eds.). New York: Oxford University Press.

KAUFFMAN, J. F., SHAFFER, H., & BURGLAS, M. E. (1985). The biological basics: Drugs and their effects. In *Alcoholism and substance abuse: Strategies for clinical intervention* (Bratter, T. E., & Forrest, G. G., eds.). New York: The Free Press.

KAUFMAN, E. (1985). Family therapy in the treatment of alcoholism. In *Alcoholism and substance abuse: Strategies for clinical intervention* (Bratter, T. E., & Forrest, G. G., eds.). New York: The Free Press.

KERR, M. S. (1988). Chronic anxiety and defining a self. *The Atlantic Monthly, 262* (3), 35–45.

KHANTZIAN, E. J. (1986). A contemporary psychodynamic approach to drug abuse treatment. *American Journal of Drug and Alcohol Abuse, 12* (3), 213–222.

KHANTZIAN, E. J. (1985). The self-medication hypothesis of addictive disorders: Focus on heroin and cocaine dependence. *American Journal of Psychiatry, 142,* 1259–1264.

KIRN, T. F. (1989). Studies of adolescents indicate just how complex the situation is for this age group. *Journal of the American Medical Association, 261,* 3362.

KIRSCH, M. M. (1986). *Designer drugs.* Minneapolis, MN: CompCare Publications.

KISSIN, B. (1985). Alcohol abuse and alcohol-related illness. In *Cecil textbook of medicine* (17th ed.). (Wyngaarden, J. B., & Smith, L. H., eds.). Philadelphia: W. B. Saunders.

KLAG, M. J., & WHELTON, P. K. (1987). Risk of stroke in male cigarette smokers. *The New England Journal of Medicine, 316,* 628.

KLAR, H. (1987). The setting for psychiatric treatment. In *American Psychiatric Association Annual Review* (Vol. 6). (Frances, A. J., & Hales, R. E., eds.). Washington, DC: American Psychiatric Association Press, Inc.

KLASS, P. (1989). Vital signs. *Discover, 10* (1), 12–14.

KLEIN, J. M., & MILLER, S. I. (1986). Three approaches to the treatment of drug addiction. *Hospital & Community Psychiatry, 37,* 1083–1085.

KOFOED, L., KANIA, J., WALSH, T., & ATKINSON, R. M. (1986). Outpatient treatment of patients with substance abuse and coexisting psychiatric disorders. *American Journal of Psychiatry, 143,* 867–872.

KOFOED, L., & KEYS, A. (1988). Using group therapy to persuade dual-diagnosis patients to seek substance abuse treatment. *Hospital & Community Psychiatry, 39,* 1209–1211.

KOHR, J. (1988). Grandchildren of alcoholics. *Alcoholism & Addiction, 9* (1), 44.

KOLB, L. C., & BRODIE, H. K. H. (1982). *Modern clinical psychiatry* (10th ed.). Philadelphia: W. B. Saunders Co.

KOLODNY, R. C. (1985). The clinical management of sexual problems in substance abusers. In *Alcoholism and substance abuse: Strategies for clinical intervention* (Bratter, T. E., & Forrest, G. G., eds.). New York: The Free Press.

KORNETSKY, C., & BAIN, G. (1987). Neuronal bases for hedonic effects of cocaine and opiates. In *Cocaine: Clinical and biobehavioral aspects.* (Fisher, S., Raskin, A., & Uhlenhuth, E. H., eds.). New York: Oxford.

KOZLOWSKI, L. T., WILKINSON, A., SKINNER, W., KENT, W., FRANKLIN, T., & POPE, M. (1989). Comparing tobacco cigarette dependence with other drug dependencies. *Journal of the American Medical Association, 261,* 898–901.

KUNITZ, S. J., & LEVY, J. E. (1974). Changing ideas of alcohol use among Navaho Indians. *Quarterly Journal of Studies on Alcohol, 46,* 953–960.

KURTZ, E. (1979). *Not God: A history of Alcoholics Anonymous.* Center City, MN: Hazelden.

LADER, M. (1987). Assessing the potential for buspirone dependence or abuse and effects of its withdrawal. *The American Journal of Medicine, 82* (Supplement 5A), 20–26.

LAMAR, J. V. (1987). The drug war bogs down. *Time, 130* (21), 28.

LAMAR, J. V., RILEY, M., SMGHABADI, R. (1986). Crack: A cheap and deadly cocaine is spreading menace. *Time, 128,* 16–18.

LANGONE, J. (1989). Hot to block a killer's path. *Time, 133* (5), 60–62.

LARSON, K. K. (1982). Birthplace of "The Minnesota Model". *Alcoholism, 3* (2), 34–35.

LEIGH, G. (1985). Psychosocial factors in the etiology of substance abuse. In *Alcoholism and substance abuse: Strategies for clinical intervention.* (Bratter, T. E., & Forrest, G. G., eds.). New York: The Free Press.

LEVENSON, R. W., OYAMA, O. N., & MEEK, P. S. (1987). Greater reinforcement from alcohol for those at risk: Parental risk, personality risk, and sex. *Journal of Abnormal Psychology, 96,* 242–253.

LEWIS, J. A., DANA, R. Q., & BLEVINS, G. A. (1988). *Substance abuse counseling.* Pacific Grove, CA: Brooks/Cole.

LICHTENSTEIN, E., & BROWN, R. A. (1980). Smoking cessation methods: Review and recommendations. In *Addictive behaviors.* (Miller, W. R., ed.). New York: Pergamon Press.

LINGEMAN, R. R. (1974). *Drugs from A to Z: A dictionary.* New York: McGraw Hill.

LINNOILA, M., DEJONG, J., & VIRKKUNEN, M. (1989). Family history of alcoholism in violent offenders and impulsive fire setters. *Archives of General Psychiatry, 46,* 613–616.

LOMBARD, J., LEVIN, I. H., & WINER, W. J. (1989). Arsenic intoxication in a cocaine abuser. *The New England Journal of Medicine, 320,* 869.

LORANGER, A. W., & TULIX, E. H. (1985). Family history of alcoholism in borderline personality disorder. *Archives of General Psychiatry, 42,* 153–157.

MACDONALD, D. I. (1988). Cardiovascular consequences of combining cocaine and marijuana. *Journal of the American Medical Association, 260,* 459.

MADDUX, J. F., DESMOND, D. P., & COSTELLO, R. (1987). Depression in opioid users varies with substance use status. *American Journal of Drug & Alcohol Abuse, 13* (4), 375–378.

MARANTO, G. (1985). Coke: The random killer. *Discover, 12* (3), 16–21.

MARTIN, E. W. (1971). *Hazards of medication.* Philadelphia: J. B. Lippincott Co.

MASTERS, W. H., & JOHNSON, V. E. (1966). *Human sexual response.* Boston: Little, Brown & Co.

MASTERS, W. H., JOHNSON, V. E., & KOLODNY, R. C. (1986). *Sex and human loving.* Boston: Little, Brown & Co.

MATUSCHKA, E. (1985). Treatment, outcomes and clinical evaluation. In *Alcoholism and substance abuse: Strategies for clinical intervention.* (Bratter, T. E., & Forrest, G. G., eds.). New York: The Free Press.

MATUSCHKA, P. R. (1985). The psychopharmacology of addiction. In *Alcoholism and substance abuse: Strategies for clinical intervention.* (Bratter, T. E., & Forrest, G. G., eds.). New York: The Free Press.

MAY, G. G. (1988). *Addiction and grace.* New York: Harper & Row.

MAY, R. (1975). *The courage to create.* New York: W. W. Norton & Co.

MCCARTHY, J. J., & BORDERS, O. T. (1985). Limit setting on drug abuse in methadone maintenance patients. *American Journal of Psychiatry, 142,* 1419–1423.

MCHUGH, M. J. (1987). The abuse of volatile substances. *The Pediatric Clinics of North America, 34* (2), 333–340.

MCNEIL, E. B. (1967). *The quiet Furies.* Englewood Cliffs, NJ: Prentice-Hall.

MEDICAL ECONOMICS COMPANY. (1987). *1987 Physician's Desk Reference* (41st ed.). Oradell, NJ: Author.

MEDICAL ECONOMICS COMPANY. (1989). *1989 Physician's Desk Reference* (43rd ed.). Oradell, NJ: Author.

MERTON, T. (1961). *New seeds of contemplation.* New York: New Directions Publishing.

MERTON, T. (1978). *No man is an island.* New York: New Directions Publishing.

MEYER, R. (1988). Intervention: Opportunity for healing. *Alcoholism & Addiction, 9* (1), 7.

MEYER, R. E. (1989). Who can say no to illicit drug use? *Archives of General Psychiatry, 46,* 189–190.

MIKKELSEN, E. (1985). Substance abuse in adolescents and children. In *Psychiatry.* (Michels, R., Cavenar, J. O., Brodie, H. K. H., Cooper, A.

M., Guze, S. B., Judd, S. B., Klerman, G., & Solnit, A. J., eds.). New York: Basic Books.

MILLER, A. (1988). *The enabler.* Claremont, CA: Hunter House.

MILLER, F. T., & TANENBAUM, J. H. (1989). Drug abuse in schizophrenia. *Hospital and Community Psychiatry, 40,* 847–849.

MILLER, G. W. JR. (1985). The cocaine habit. *American Family Physician, 3,* 173–176.

MILLER, P. M., & FOY, D. W. (1981). Substance abuse. In *Handbook of clinical behavior therapy* (Turner, S. M., Calhoun, K. S., & Adams, H. E. eds.). New York: John Wiley & Sons.

MILLER, S. I., FRANCES, R. J., & HOLMEN, D. J. (1988). Use of psychotropic drugs in alcoholism treatment: A summary. *Hospital & Community Psychiatry, 39,* 1251–1252.

MILLER, W. R. (1980). The addictive behaviors. In *The addictive behaviors* (Miller, W. R., ed.). New York: Pergamon Press.

MILLER, W. R. (1976). Alcoholism scales and objective measures. *Psychological Bulletin, 83,* 649–674.

MILLER, W. R., & HESTER, R. K. (1986). Inpatient alcoholism treatment. *American Psychologist, 41* (7), 794–806.

MILLER, W. R., & HESTER, R. K. (1980). Treating the problem drinker: Modern approaches. In *The addictive behaviors* (Miller, W. R., ed.). New York: Pergamon Press.

MILLMAN, R. B. (1978). Drug and alcohol abuse. In *Handbook of treatment of mental disorders in childhood and adolescence* (Wolman, B. B., Egan, J., & Ross, A. O., eds.). Englewood Cliffs, NJ: Prentice-Hall, Inc.

MILLON, T. (1981). *Disorders of personality.* New York: John Wiley.

Minneapolis Tribune. (1989a). Toxic drug widespread in Colombia. *VII* (286), 15a, 17a.

Minneapolis Tribune. (1989b). Study finds 'casual' use of drugs down 37% since '85. *VIII* (119). 1, 7a.

MIRIN, S. M., & WEISS, R. D. (1983). Substance abuse. In *The practitioner's guide to psychoactive drugs* (2nd ed.). (Bassuk, E. L., Schoonover, S. C., & Galenberg, A. J., eds.). New York: Plenum Medical Book Co.

MITCHELL, J. R. (1988). Acetaminophen toxicity. *The New England Journal of Medicine, 319,* (1601–1602).

MONTGOMERY, G. (1989). The infant brain. *Discover, 10* (8), 30, 32.

MOREY, L. C., SKINNER, H. A., & BLASHFIELD, R. K. (1984). A typology of alcohol abusers: Correlates and implications. *Journal of Abnormal Psychology, 93,* 408–417.

MORTON, W. A., & SANTOS, A. (1989). New indications for benzodiazepines in the treatment of major psychiatric disorders. *Hospital Formulary, 24,* 274–278.

NACE, E. P. (1987). *The treatment of alcoholism.* New York: Brunner/Mazel.

NAHAS, G. G. (1986). Cannabis: Toxicological properties and epidemiological aspects. *The Medical Journal of Australia, 145,* 82–87.

Narcotics Anonymous. (1982). Van Nuys, CA: Narcotics Anonymous World Service Office, Inc.

NATHAN, P. E. (1980). Etiology and process in the addictive behaviors. In *The addictive behaviors* (Miller, W. R., ed.). New York: Pergamon Press.

NATHAN, P. E. (1988). The addictive personality *is* the behavior of the addict. *Journal of Consulting and Clinical Psychology, 56,* 183–188.

NELSON, D. J. (1989). Group helps smokers break addictive cycle. *Minneapolis Star Tribune, VIII* (53), 8 Ex.

NEWCOMB, M. D., & BENTLER, P. M. (1989). Substance use and abuse among children and teenagers. *American Psychologist, 44,* 242–248.

NEWELL, T., & COSGROVE, J. (1988). Recovery of neuropsychological functions during reduction of PCP use. Paper presented at the 1988 annual meeting of the American Psychological Association, Atlanta, GA.

NEWTON, R. E., MARUNYCZ, J. D., ALDERDICE, M. C., & NAPOLIELLO, M. J. (1986). Review of the side effects of buspirone. *The American Journal of Medicine, 80* (Supplement 3B).

OGBORNE, A. C., & GLASER, F. B. (1985). Evaluating Alcoholics Anonymous. In *Alcoholism and substance abuse: Strategies for clinical intervention.* (Bratter, T. E., & Forrest, G. G., eds.). New York: The Free Press.

O'MALLEY, P. M., JOHNSTON, L. D., & BACHMAN, J. G. (1985). Cocaine use among American adolescents and young adults. In *Cocaine use in America.* (Kozel, N. J., & Adams, E. H. eds.). Rockville, MD: National Institute on Drug Abuse.

OLIWENSTEIN, L. (1988). The perils of pot. *Discover, 9*(6), 18.

OTTO, R. K., LANG, A. R., MEGARGEE, E. I., & ROSENBLATT, A. I. (1989). Ability of alcoholics to escape detection by the MMPI. *Critical Items, 4* (2), 2, 7–8.

PAPE, P. A. (1988). EAP's and chemically dependent women. *Alcoholism & Addiction, 8* (6), 43–44.

PARRAS, F., PATIER, J. L., & EZPELETA, C. (1988). Lead contaminated heroin as a source of inorganic lead intoxication. *The Staff, 316,* 755.

PATIAK, M. (1988). The treatment dilemma. *Discover, 9* (10), 26–27.

PATIAK, M. (1989). The fickle virus. *Discover, 10* (2), 24–25.

PECK, M. S. (1978). *The road less traveled.* New York: Simon & Schuster.

PEELE, S. (1984). The cultural context of psychological approaches to alcoholism. *American Psychologist, 39,* 1337–1351.

PEELE, S. (1988). On the diseasing of America. *Utne Reader, 30,* 67.

PELUSO, E., & PELUSO, L. S. (1988). *Women and drugs.* Minneapolis: CompCare Publishers.

PENNA, M. W., & LADDIS, A. (1980). Chronic brain syndromes. In *Clinical psychopathology.* (Balis, G. U., ed.). Boston: Butterworth Publishers, Inc.

PENTZ, M. A., DWYER, J. H., MacKINNON, D. P., FLAY, B. R., HANDEN, W. B., WANG, E. Y. I., JOHNSON, A. (1989). A multicommunity trial for primary prevention of adolescent drug abuse. *Journal of the American Medical Association, 261* (2), 3259–3266.

PEROUTKA, S. J. (1989). 'Ecstasy': A human neurotoxin? *Archives of General Psychiatry, 46,* 191.

PERRIN, P., & COLEMAN, W. (1988). Is addiction actually a misguided move to wholeness? *Utne Reader, 30,* 58–59.

PERRY, J. C., & COOPER, S. H. (1989). An empirical study of defense mechanisms. *Archives of General Psychiatry, 46,* 444–452.

PEYSER, H. S. (1989). Alcohol and drug abuse: Underrecognized and untreated. *Hospital & Community Psychiatry, 40* (3), 221.

PHELPS, J. K., & NOURSE, A. E. (1986). *The hidden addiction.* Boston: Little, Brown & Co.

PHILLIPS, D. A. (1979). The alcoholic man—too much/too little. *CAFC News, 2* (2), 5–8.

PLASKY, P., MARCUS, L., & SALZMAN, C. (1988). Effects of psychotropic drugs on memory: Part 2. *Hospital & Community Psychiatry, 39,* 501–502.

Playboy. (1988). Forum Newsfront, *35* (4), 51.

POST, R. M., WEISS, S. R. B., PERT, A., & UHDE, T. W. (1987). Chronic cocaine administration: Sensitization and kindling effects. In *Cocaine: Clinical and behavioral aspects* (Fisher, S., Rashkin, A., & Unlenhuth, E. H., eds.). New York: Oxford University Press.

POTTER, W. Z., RUDORFER, M. V., & GOODWIN, F. K. (1987). Biological findings in bipolar disorders. In *American Psychiatric Association Annual Review (Vol. 6).* Washington, DC: American Psychiatric Association Press, Inc.

POWELL, B. J., READ, M. R., PENICK, E. C., MILLER, N. S., & BINGHAM, S. F. (1987). Primary and secondary depression in alcoholic men: An important distinction. *Journal of Clinical Psychiatry, 48,* 98–101.

PRICE, L. H., RICAURTE, G. A., KRYSTAL, J. H., & HENINGER, G. R. (1989). Neuroendocrine and mood responses to intravenous L-tryptophan in 3, 4-Methylenedioxymeth-amphetamine (MDMA) users. *Archives of General Psychiatry, 46,* 20–22.

PUIG-ANTICH, J., GOETS, D., DAVIES, M., KAPLAN, T., DAVIES, S., OSTROW, L., ASNIS, L., TOWMEY, J., IYENGAR, S., & RYAN, N. D. (1989). A controlled family history of pre-pubertal major depressive disorder. *Archives of General Psychiatry, 46,* 406–418.

PURSCH, J. A. (1987). Mental illness and addiction. *Alcoholism & Addiction, 7* (6), 42.

RACHLIN, H. (1970). *Introduction to modern behaviorism.* New York: W. H. Freeman & Co.

RADO, T. (1988). The client with a dual diagnosis—A personal perspective. *The Alcohol Quarterly, 1* (1), 5–7.

RAY, O. S. (1983). *Drugs, society and human behavior* (3rd ed.). St. Louis, MO: C. V. Mosby.

REDFIELD, R. R., & BURK, D. S. (1988). HIV infection: The clinical picture. *Scientific American, 259* (4), 90–98.

REISER, M. F. (1984). *Mind, brain, body.* New York: Basic Books, Inc.

REISS, B. S., & MELICK, M. E. (1984). *Pharmacological aspects of nursing care.* Albany, NY: Delmar Publishers, Inc.

REULER, J. B., GIRARD, D. E., & COONEY, T. G. (1985). Wernicke's encephalopathy. *New England Journal of Medicine, 316,* 1035–1039.

RICKELS, K., SCHWEIZER, E., & LUCKI, I. (1987). Benzodiazepine side effects. In *American Psychiatric Association Annual Review* (Vol. 6). (Hales, R. E., & Frances, A. J., eds.). Washington, DC: American Psychiatric Association Press, Inc.

RICKELS, K., SCHWEIZER, E., CSANALOSI, I., CASE, W. G., & CHUNG, H. (1988). Long-term treatment of anxiety and risk of withdrawal. *Archives of General Psychiatry, 45,* 444–450.

RICKELS, L. K., GIESECKE, M. A., & GELLER, A. (1987). Differential effects of the anxiolytic drugs, diazepam and buspirone on memory function. *British Journal of Clinical Pharmacology, 23,* 207–211.

ROBERTSON, J. C. (1988). Preventing relapse and transfer of addiction. *EAP Digest, 8* (6), 50–56.

ROFFMAN, R. A., & GEORGE, W. H. (1988). Cannabis abuse. In *Assessment of addictive behaviors* (Donovan, D. M., & Marlatt, G. A., eds.). New York: Guilford.

ROGERS, C. R. (1951). *Client centered therapy.* Boston: Houghton-Mifflin Co.

ROGERS, C. R. (1961). *On becoming a person.* Boston: Houghton-Mifflin Co.

ROGERS, P. D., HARRIS, J., & JARMUSKEWICZ, J. (1987). Alcohol and adolescence. *The Pediatric Clinics of North America, 34* (2), 289–303.

ROHSENOW, D. J., & BACHOROWSKI, J. (1984). Effects of alcohol and expectancies on verbal aggression in men and women. *Journal of Abnormal Psychology, 93, 418–432.*

ROME, H. P. (1984). Psychobotanica revisited. *Psychiatric Annuals, 14,* 711–712.

ROSE, K. J., (1988). *The body in time.* New York: John Wiley & Sons, Inc.

ROTHENBERG, L. (1988). The ethics of intervention. *Alcoholism & Addiction, 9* (1), 22–24.

ROY, A., DeJONG, J., & LINNOILA, M. (1989). Extraversion in pathological gamblers. *Archives of General Psychiatry, 46,* 679–681.

RUSTIN, T. (1988). Treating nicotine addiction. *Alcoholism & Addiction, 9* (2), 18–19.

SACKS, O. (1970). *The man who mistook his wife for a hat.* New York: Harper & Row.

SALZMAN, C., & HOFFMAN, S. A. (1983). Clinical interaction between psychotropic and other drugs. *Hospital & Community Psychiatry, 34,* 897–902.

SBRIGLIO, R., & MILLMAN, R. B. (1987). Emergency treatment of acute cocaine reactions. In *Cocaine: A clinician's handbook.* (Washton, A. M., & Gold, M. S., eds.). New York: The Guilford Press.

SCARF, M. (1980). *Unfinished business.* New York: Ballantine Books.

SCHUCKIT, M. A. (1983). Alcoholic patients with secondary depression. *American Journal of Psychiatry, 140,* 711–714.

SCHUCKIT, M. A. (1984). *Drug and alcohol abuse: A clinical guide to diagnosis and treatment* (2nd ed.). New York: Plenum Press.

SCHUCKIT, M. A. (1986). Primary men alcoholics with histories of suicide attempts. *Journal of Studies on Alcohol, 47,* 78–81.

SCHUCKIT, M. A. (1987). Biological vulnerability to alcoholism. *Journal of Consulting and Clinical Psychology, 55,* 301–309.

SCHUCKIT, M. A., ZISOOK, S., & MORTOLA, J. (1985). Clinical implications of DSM-III diagnoses of alcohol abuse and alcohol dependence. *American Journal of Psychiatry, 142,* 1403–1408.

SCHWARTZ, R. H. (1987). Marijuana: an overview. *The Pediatric Clinics of North America, 34* (2), 305–317.

SCOTT, N. (1987). Dealing with nicotine addiction. *Alcoholism & Addiction, 7* (6), 24.

SEGAL, R., & SISSON, B. V. (1985). Medical complications associated with alcohol use and the assessment of risk of physical damage. In *Alcoholism and substance abuse: Strategies for clinical intervention.* (Bratter, T. E., & Forrest, G. G., eds.). New York: The Free Press.

SEYMORE, R. A., & RAWLINS, M. D. (1982). The efficacy and pharmacokinetics of aspirin in post-operative dental pain. *British Journal of Clinical Pharmacology, 13,* 807–810.

SHAPIRO, D. (1981). *Autonomy and rigid character.* New York: Basic Books.

SHAFER, J. (1985). Designer drugs. *Science '85, 12* (3), 60–67.

SHARP, C. W., & BEHM, M. L. (1977). Review of inhalants: Euphoria to dysfunction. NIDA Research Monograph 15. Washington, DC: U.S. Government Printing Office.

SHERIDAN, E., PATTERSON, H. R., & GUSTAFSON, E. A. (1982). *Falconer's the drug, the nurse, the patient* (7th ed.). Philadelphia: W. B. Saunders.

SHEVRIN, H., & SHECTMAN, F. (1982). The diagnostic process in psychiatric evaluations. In *Diagnostic understanding and treatment planning.* (Shectman, F., & Smith, W. H., eds.). New York: John Wiley & Sons.

SIEGEL, B. S. (1986). *Love, medicine and miracles.* New York: Harper & Row.

SIEGEL, B. S. (1989). *Peace, love and healing.* New York: Harper & Row.

SIEGEL, L. (1989). Want to take the risks? It should be your choice. *Playboy, 36,* (1), 59.

SIEGEL, R. K. (1984). Cocaine smoking disorders: Diagnosis and treatment. *Psychiatric Annuals, 14,* 728–732.

SIEGEL, R. L. (1986). Jungle revelers: When beasts take drugs to race or relax, things get zooey. In *Drugs, Society and Behavior 87/88.* (Rucker, W. B., & Rucker, M. E., eds.). Guilford, CT: Dushkin Publishing Group, Inc.

SIMPSON, D. D., CRANDALL, R. L., SAVAGE, J., & PAVA-KRUEGER, E. (1981). Leisure of opiate addicts at posttreatment follow-up. *Journal of Counseling Psychology, 28,* 36–29.

SKYELBRED, P. (1984). The effects of acetylsalicylic acid on swelling, pain, and other events after surgery. *British Journal of Clinical Pharmacology, 17,* 379–384.

SLABY, A. E., LIEB, J., & TANCREDI, L. R. (1981). *Handbook of psychiatric emergencies* (2nd ed.). Garden City, NY: Medical Examination Publishing Co., Inc.

SPRINGBORN, W. (1987). Step one: The foundation of recovery. In *The Twelve Steps of Alcoholics Anonymous.* New York: Harper & Row.

STANTON, M. D., TODD, T. C., HEARD, D. B., KIRSCHNER, S., KLEIMAN, J. I., MOWATT, D. T., RILEY, P., SCOTT, S. M., & VAN DEUSEN, J. M. (1978). Heroin addiction as a family phenomenon: A new conceptual model. *American Journal of Drug and Alcohol Abuse, 5,* 125–130.

STEINER, L., HENSON, C. D., COLLIVER, J. A., & MACLEAN, D. G. (1988). Prevalence of a history of sexual abuse among female psychiatric patients in a state hospital system. *Hospital & Community Psychiatry, 39* (3), 300–308.

STEVENS, V. J., & HOLLIS, J. F. (1989). Preventing smoking relapse, using an individually tailored skills-training technique. *Journal of Consulting and Clinical Psychology, 57,* 420–424.

STUART, R. B. (1980). *Helping couples change.* New York: The Guilford Press.

SULLIVAN, H. S. (1953). *The interpersonal theory of psychiatry.* New York: W. W. Norton & Co.

SUSSMAN, N. (1988). Diagnosis and drug treatment of anxiety in the elderly. *Geriatric Medicine Today, 7* (10), 1–8.

SVANUM, S., & MCADOO, W. G. (1989). Predicting rapid relapse following treatment for chemical dependence: A matched-subjects design. *Journal of Consulting and Clinical Psychology, 34,* 1027–1030.

SWAIM, R. C., OETTING, R. W., EDWARDS, R. W., & BEAUVAIS, F. (1989). Links from emotional distress to adolescent drug use: A path model. *Journal of Consulting and Clinical Psychology, 57,* 227–231.

SWANSON, L., & BIAGGIO, M. K. (1985). Therapeutic perspectives on father-daughter incest. *American Journal of Psychiatry, 142,* 667–674.

SWINSON, R. P. (1980). Sex differences in the inheritance of alcoholism. In *Alcohol and drug problems in women* (Kalant, O. J. ed.). New York: Plenum Press.

SZASZ, T. S. (1972). Bad habits are not diseases: a refutation of the claim that alcoholism is a disease. *Lancet, 2,* 83–84.

SZASZ, T. S. (1988). A plea for the cessation of the longest war of the twentieth century—The war on drugs. *The Humanistic Psychologist, 16* (2), 314–322.

TANNER, I. J. (1973). *Loneliness: The fear of love.* New York: Harper & Row.

TARTER, R. E. (1988). Are there inherited behavioral traits that predispose to substance abuse? *Journal of Consulting and Clinical Psychology, 56,* 189–197.

TATE, C. (1989). In the 1800's, antismoking was a burning issue. *Smithsonian, 20* (4), 107–117.

The group. (1976). Van Nuys, CA: Narcotics Anonymous World Service Office, Inc.

The triangle of self-obsession. New York: Narcotics Anonymous World Service Office, Inc.

TRACHTENBERG, M. C., & BLUM, K. (1987). Alcohol and opioid peptides: Neuropharmacological rationale for physical craving of alcohol. *American Journal of Drug and Alcohol Abuse, 13* (3), 365–372.

Twelve steps and twelve traditions. (1981). New York: Alcoholics Anonymous World Services, Inc.

TWERSKI, A. J. (1983). Early intervention in alcoholism: Confrontational techniques. *Hospital & Community Psychiatry, 34,* 1027–1030.

Understanding anonymity. (1981). New York: Alcoholics Anonymous World Services, Inc.

UNITED STATES PHARMACOPEIAL CONVENTION, INC. (1981). *The physician's and pharmacist's guide to four medicines.* New York: Ballantine Books.

UNITED STATES PHARMACOPEIAL CONVENTION, INC. (1983). *1983 drug information for the health care provider.* Rockville, MD: USPC Board of Trustees.

UPJOHN COMPANY. (1989). Anxiety center. *Science Digest, 2* (1), 69–70.

VAILLANT, G. E. (1983). *The natural history of alcoholism.* Cambridge, MA: Harvard University Press.

VALDISERRI, E. V., HARTL, A., & CHAMBLISS, C. A. (1988). Practices reported by incarcerated drug abusers to reduce the risk of AIDS. *Hospital & Community Psychiatry, 39* (9), 966–972.

WADE, R. (1988). Prescription drugs entwined with alcoholism. *Alcoholism & Addiction, 8* (3), 52.

WALKER, C. E., BONNER, B. L., AND KAUFMAN, K. I. (1988). *The physically and sexually abused child.* New York: Pergamon Press.

WASHTON, A. M. (1988). Cocaine: A catalyst for change. *EAP Digest, 8* (6), 30–31.

WASHTON, A. M., STONE, N. S., & HENDRICKSON, E. C. (1988). Cocaine abuse. In *Assessment of addictive behaviors.* (Donovan, D. M., & Marlatt, G. A., eds.). New York: The Guilford Press.

WEBB, S. T. (1989). Some developmental issues of adolescent children of alcoholics. *Adolescent Counselor, 1* (6), 47–48, 67.

WEIL, A. (1986). *The natural mind.* Boston: Houghton-Mifflin Co.

WEINER, N. (1985). Norepinephrine, epinephrine, and the sympathomimetic amines. In *The pharmacological basis of therapeutics* (Gilman, A. G., Goodman, L. S., Rall, T. W., & Murad, F., eds.). New York: Macmillan.

WEISMAN, A. P. (1986). As reporters grow dependent on their regular drug-crisis fix. In *Drugs, society and behavior* (Rucker, W. B., & Rucker, M. E. eds.). Guilford, CT: Dashkin Publishing Group, Inc.

WEISS, R. D., MIRIN, S. M., GRIFFIN, M. L., & MICHAEL, J. L. (1988). Psychopathology in cocaine users: changing trends. *Journal of Nervous and Mental Disease, 176,* 719–725.

WERNER, E. E. (1989). Children of the garden island. *Scientific American, 260* (4), 106–111.

WESTERMEYER, J. (1987). The psychiatrist and solvent-inhalent abuse: Recognition, assessment and treatment. *American Journal of Psychiatry, 144*, 903–907.

WETLI, C. V. (1987). Fatal reactions to cocaine. In *Cocaine: A clinician's handbook.* (Washton, A. M., & Gold, M. S., eds.). New York: The Guilford Press.

WHEELER, K., & MALMQUIST, J. (1987). Treatment approaches in adolescent chemcial dependency. *The Pediatric Clinics of North America, 34,* (2), 437–447.

WHITE, P. T. (1989) Coca. *National Geographic, 175* (1), 3–47.

WILBUR, R. (1986). A drug to fight cocaine. *Science '86, 7* (2), 42–46.

WILLENBRING, M. L. (1986). Measurement of depression in alcoholics. *Journal of Studies on Alcohol, 47,* 367–372.

WILLIAMS, E. (1989). Strategies for intervention. *The Nursing Clinics of North America, 24* (1), 95–107.

WILLOUGHBY, A. (1984). *The alcohol troubled person: Known and unknown.* Chicago: Nelson-Hall.

WOITITZ, J. G. (1983). *Adult children of alcoholics.* Pompano Beach, FL: Health Communications, Inc.

WOODS, J. H., KATZ, J. L., & WINGER, G. (1988). Use and abuse of benzodiazepines. *Journal of the American Medical Association, 260* (23), 3476–3480.

WOODS, J. H., WINGER, G. D., & FRANCE, C. P. (1987). Reinforcing and discriminative stimulus effects of cocaine: Analysis of pharmacological mechanisms. In *Cocaine: Clinical and behavioral aspects* (Fisher, S., Raskin, A. & Unlenhuth, E. H., eds.). New York: Oxford University Press.

WRAY, S. R., & MURTHY, N. V. A. (1987). Review of the effects of cannabis on mental and physiological functions. *West Indian Medical Journal, 36* (4), 197–201.

WURMSER, L. (1978). Addictive disorders: Drug dependence. In *Clinical psychopathology* (Balis, G. U., ed.). Boston: Butterworth Publishers, Inc.

YABLONSKY, L. (1967). *Synanon: The tunnel back.* Baltimore: Penguin Books.

YALOM, I. D. (1975). *The theory and practice of group psychotherapy* (2nd ed.). New York: Basic Books.

YOUCHA, G. A. (1978). *A dangerous pleasure.* New York: Hawthorn Books.

ZAREK, D., HAWKINS, D., & ROGERS, P. D. (1987). Risk factors for adolescent substance abuse. *The Pediatric Clinics of North America, 34* (2), 481–493.

ZERWEKH, J., & MICHAELS, B. (1989). Co-dependency. *The Nursing Clinics of North America, 24* (1), 109–120.

ZIMBERG, S. (1978a). Psychiatric office treatment in alcoholism. In *Practical approaches to alcoholism psychotherapy.* (Zimberg, S., Wallace, J., & Blume, S. B., eds.). New York: Plenum Press.

ZIMBERG, S. (1978b). Psychosocial treatment of elderly alcoholics. In *Practical approaches to alcoholism psychotherapy.* (Zimberg, S., Wallace, J., & Blume, S. B., eds.). New York: Plenum Press.

ZUCKER, D. K., & BRANCHEY, L. (1985). Variables associated with alcoholic blackouts in men. *American Journal of Drug and Alcohol Abuse, 11* (3 & 4), 295–302.

ZUCKER, R. A., & GOMBERG, E. S. L. (1986). Etiology of alcoholism reconsidered: The case for a biopsychosocial process. *American Psychologist, 41,* 783–793.

Index

AA (*see* Alcoholics Anonymous)

Accomodation, of family to alcoholism, 204

Acetaldehyde, as byproduct of tobacco use, 137

Acetaminophen:
  and clotting of blood, 115
  and liver damage, 116
  normal dosage levels, 116
  overdose of, 119
  pregnancy and, 120
  role in inhibition of prostaglandins, 115
  use by chronic alcoholics, 116

Acetylsalicylic Acid (*see also* Aspirin), 113

ACOA (*see* Adult Children of Alcoholics)

Addiction:
  and adolescents, 184–188
  alcoholism, 8
  cocaine, 8, 65
  defined, 10–11
  diagnosis of, 210–212
  and the elderly, 188–190
  elements of, 166–167
  as a form of insanity, 166
  as imposter, 1
  marijuana, 9
  narcotics, 8, 95, 97–99
  percentage of population addicted, 3
  as a process, 12–13
  as a spiritual disease, 163
  tobacco, 137

Adolescents, drug abuse and, 8, 184–188

Adult Children of Alcoholics, 207

Aerosols (*see* Inhalants)

Aftercare, defined, 247

AIDS, 313–315
  acquired from mother, 183
  amphetamine use and, 75
  from intravenous cocaine use, 64

Al-Anon, 292–293

Alateen, 293

Alcohol:
  and amphetamine abuse, 75
  as analgesic, 21
  as antianxiety agent, 38
  as aphrodisiac, 297
  as central feature in alcoholic's life, 165–166
  and decrease in sexual desire, 298
  effects on sleep, 22
  history, 15
  pharmacology of, 18–19
  potentiation of CNS depressants, 19
  production of, 16–17
  pseudo-stimulant effect of, 19

Alcoholics Anonymous, 164, 165, 259
  as adjunct to treatment, 4
  history, 281–282
  as a form of folk psychotherapy, 283
  and organized religion, 284
  primary purpose of, 285–286
  outcome studies, 289–292

Alcoholics Anonymous ("Big Book"), 167, 180, 282

Alpha alcoholic, 145–146

Alprazolam (*see also* Xanax), 44–45

Amnesia (*see also* Blackout, Memory loss), as result of benzodiazepine use, 48

Amotivational syndrome, 84